CRUCIBLE

MILLER CENTER STUDIES ON THE PRESIDENCY

Marc J. Selverstone, Editor

The First Year Project

CRUCIBLE

The President's First Year

EDITED BY MICHAEL NELSON,
JEFFREY L. CHIDESTER, AND
STEFANIE GEORGAKIS ABBOTT

UNIVERSITY OF VIRGINIA PRESS
Charlottesville and London

University of Virginia Press
© 2018 by the Rector and Visitors of the University of Virginia, Miller Center
All rights reserved

Printed in the United States of America on acid-free paper

First published 2018

ISBN 978-0-8139-4096-0 (cloth)
ISBN 978-0-8139-4097-7 (ebook)

9 8 7 6 5 4 3 2 1

Library of Congress Cataloging-in-Publication Data is available for this title.

CONTENTS

V ★ RACE AND IMMIGRATION

VI ★ MANAGING THE EXECUTIVE

VII ✭   PRESIDENTIAL COMMUNICATIONS

FOREWORD

ANN COMPTON

Seeking inspiration in the challenging first year of his presidency, Donald J. Trump requested that a new portrait be hung on the Oval Office wall. It looks down, literally, over the president's left shoulder as he works. It is a gilt-framed profile of the populist Andrew Jackson, whose own first year in the White House, 1829, set a tone for a presidency often described as fiery and strident.

Unlike his predecessors, Trump had never served one day in government before becoming president. Neither had many of his chosen cabinet secretaries or senior West Wing advisors. But there was a new source of guidance never before available to a president—a rich trove of essays, by scholars and practitioners, commissioned by the Miller Center at the University of Virginia. Drawing on its own wealth of archives, presidential oral histories, and secret White House tapes, the Miller Center has published pragmatic, constructive, nonpartisan roadmaps connecting history to policy and impact.

The transition from campaigning to governing is difficult for any president, no matter how large or small the mandate from the voters. President Trump, who became the second Republican in recent elections to lose the popular vote but win in the Electoral College, seems to be clinging to much of his campaign style in running the government. He holds boisterous rallies, keeps many of his policy proposals vague, and, most notably, continues to speak unfiltered to the world through his own Twitter account, exacerbating his war with the mainstream media covering his administration. Although the president scored an important early victory with the confirmation of Neil Gorsuch to the U.S. Supreme Court, he underwent a slow-motion process of filling key political appointments in the executive branch and dealing with Congress. The president's own Republican Party controlled both chambers, but factions were deeply divided over his landmark promises, such as repealing and replacing the Affordable Care Act and significant tax reform. Trump confronted all of these obstacles as dark clouds of investigations gathered over possible Russian influence on America's election process.

The Miller Center–commissioned essays that make up *Crucible: The President's First Year* trace through history parallels that offer constructive ideas on how to govern, such as collaborating with factions on Capitol Hill, as Ronald Reagan did in passing deep tax and spending cuts in his first year, despite Democrats' control of purse strings in the House of Representatives. A newcomer to Washington can use advice about how to work most effectively with the government's hundreds of thousands of career employees who keep agencies and departments functioning while the president's new policies are unfurling. First years are vulnerable times for national security—witness John F. Kennedy's Bay of Pigs calamity and the September 11 terrorist attacks. *Crucible* offers valuable lessons tied closely to experience.

As an ABC News correspondent assigned to the White House on December 2, 1974, weeks after the Watergate scandal brought down the Nixon presidency, I had the privilege of covering the first years of the next seven American presidents through the end of the Cold War, economic crises, and the rise of global terrorism. I have found that presidents often come to be defined not by their campaign promises kept or broken but by sudden crises rolling unbidden into a president's path.

A few examples:

▶ April 1975: the fall of Saigon, the troubled end of the Vietnam War, and the new president's decision to grant amnesty to draft resisters.
▶ November 1989: the collapse of the Berlin Wall and the president's rush to nurture fledgling democracies in central and eastern Europe.
▶ September 11, 2001: I was allowed to remain on Air Force One when the president was unable to return to Washington but vowed to respond to the stunning attacks on the World Trade Center towers and Pentagon, ushering in what he called the "Global War on Terror."
▶ 2008–9: the election year financial collapse and resulting Great Recession.

I also covered the growing dysfunction in Washington, which has encouraged new presidents to attempt to govern by executive order, with legal authority but without the political strength, consensus, and permanence that come with legislation passed by Congress. I have witnessed the pall of scandal and investigation in which administrations find themselves drowning in distractions. There is sound advice on all these pitfalls from the Miller Center's expert scholars and experienced practitioners.

Americans seem inclined to believe the current era is the most troubling, worrisome time of all. But Abraham Lincoln's was certainly the worst first year, as the threads of the Union unraveled and southern states seceded. Thomas Jefferson established a landmark moment in history—the first peaceful transfer of power from one elected political party to another. The Miller Center First Year Project teaches us that America's more than two centuries offer rich lessons in how a vibrant democracy and its elected leaders have coped with challenges and learned from their experiences.

Captured in this unique volume are priceless lessons for the ages: for presidents, for men and women in public service aspiring to contribute, for citizens and businesses, for the media and interest groups, all of whom have a real and important stake in the success of every American president.

PREFACE

WILLIAM ANTHOLIS

You've got to give it all you can that first year. Doesn't matter what kind of majority you come in with. You've got just one year when they treat you right, and before they start worrying about themselves. . . . So, you've got one year. —LYNDON B. JOHNSON, January 1965

A president's first year in office is the culmination of our great national democratic moment, when the peaceful transfer of power takes place and the new chief executive transitions from campaigning to governing. It is a time of peril and challenges, of promise and opportunity.

Presidents can set priorities and begin to enact great achievements during the first year—whether attempting to renew America's promise at home or make historic breakthroughs on the world stage. All newly elected presidents rightly claim some sort of electoral mandate, which they use to confirm a cabinet and advance a legislative agenda, but the salad days of a presidency are almost always fleeting.

The president's first year is so crucial, in fact, that the Miller Center at the University of Virginia has made it a cornerstone project. The word "cornerstone" is a loaded one at the university because it was two hundred years ago—October 6, 1817—when three presidents came together to lay the cornerstone for the new institution. Thomas Jefferson, James Madison, and James Monroe (the sitting president at the time) shared a belief that the nation needed to be guided by educated citizens.

The Miller Center has carried that spirit forward in the First Year Project. Steered by a bipartisan advisory council composed of leading figures from previous administrations, as well as national business, media, and philanthropic leaders with an interest in advancing research on the presidency, the First Year Project has examined on both a strategic and granular level the history and structure of presidential first years.

Led by our scholars, we set out to work with the nation's leading historians, political scientists, policy analysts, and practitioners to assess the challenges and opportunities facing the first-year president. In 2016, we brought our findings directly to the Republican and Democratic presidential nominees, their transition teams, opinion leaders, and the public at large—and then, after the election, to President Donald Trump's transition team and administration.

What were the fruits of our research? At its most basic level, a president's first-year challenges resemble those attending any new job. The new president is still finding his way around his new (home) office, unpacking the boxes, and trying to hire his staff.

That said, nothing fully prepares a new president of the United States for the enormity of the undertaking.

John F. Kennedy famously said after his own first year, "The problems are more difficult than I had imagined them to be. The responsibilities are greater than I imagined them to be. And there are greater limitations on our ability to bring about a favorable result than I had imagined."

Echoing Kennedy, Trump acknowledged on his ninety-ninth day in office: "This is more work than in my previous life. I thought it would be easier."

Like other political leaders, an American president has to plan an agenda for governing the nation. Doing so has become more complex, thanks not just to our complicated federal constitutional system but also to the political polarization that has made Washington appear ungovernable to many.

Perhaps the greatest limitation on any president is his or her constitutional partner sixteen blocks east on Pennsylvania Avenue. Congress—even when controlled by the new president's party—works on its own timetable for both legislation and the vetting and confirmation of senior executive officials and federal judges.

Congressional attention quickly turns to the looming midterm elections. Presidents thus have a short-term window of opportunity for legislative success—often operating with a half-staffed government—and must pursue it while considering their long-term objectives. President Lyndon Johnson, a former Senate majority leader, knew this well. His assessment, quoted at the top of this preface, framed this project for us.

And then there are the national security challenges that almost invariably arise during the first year. Unlike any other political leader in the world, the president of the United States sits atop both a massive national security establishment (including 1.5 million men and women in uniform) and a global system of integrated economies and alliances. At the core of that system are the world's leading market democracies, which have struggled to keep pace with sweeping strategic, technological, economic, and cultural changes.

Regardless of who is president, the first year is a time when the world takes its measure of the new American leader—and often seeks to take advantage when it sees vulnerability.

As I write this preface, on Trump's one hundredth day in office, the new president has expressed his own frustration: "It's a very rough system. It's an archaic system. . . . It's really a bad thing for the country." Woodrow Wilson felt the same way, as have many others.

Some presidents have mastered the system; others have failed. But until we have a different system, new presidents need trusted roadmaps and an awareness that time is of the essence. Our First Year undertaking has been a humble attempt to help guide new presidents in this democratic journey. This book, with forty-one essays commissioned by the project, includes some of its finest fruits.

Crucible is a product of the First Year Project at the Miller Center. Without the work done by Howard Witt, the Miller Center's managing editor; Tony Lucadamo, the lead policy analyst; as well as the Miller Center's entire web team, the First Year Project would not have been a success. The editors would like to thank Ann Compton for contributing the foreword to this volume.

We also thank the following people for their hard work in soliciting, editing, and managing the various online First Year volumes: Douglas Blackmon (senior fellow in presidential studies, Miller Center), W. Bernard Carlson (professor of science, technology, and society and professor of history at the University of Virginia), Nicole Hemmer (assistant professor of presidential studies, Miller Center), William Hitchcock (professor of history at the University of Virginia and Randolph P. Compton Professor at the Miller Center), David Leblang (professor of politics and J. Wilson Newman Professor of Governance, Miller Center), Melvyn Leffler (Edward Stettinius Professor of History at the University of Virginia), Cristina Lopez-Gottardi Chao (assistant professor, Miller Center), Guian McKee (associate professor of public policy, Miller Center), Sidney Milkis (White Burkett Miller Professor of Politics, Miller Center), Barbara Perry (White Burkett Miller Center Professor of Ethics and Institutions and director of presidential studies, Miller Center), Raymond Scheppach (professor of public policy at the University of Virginia), and Larry Sabato (director of the University of Virginia's Center for Politics). Thank you as well to Stuart deButts, a research assistant at the Miller Center, who helped us immensely in the editing process.

At the University of Virginia Press, we thank Dick Holway, Bonnie Gill, Ellen Satrom, Morgan Myers, Margaret Hogan, Anne Hegeman, and Cecilia Sorochin.

Finally, without the enthusiastic support of the Miller Center's First Year Advisory Council members, this project would not have been possible. Their thoughtful guidance helped the vision that animates this book become a reality.

CRUCIBLE

INTRODUCTION

STEFANIE GEORGAKIS ABBOTT
AND JEFFREY L. CHIDESTER

The first year is a uniquely important time in the life of a presidency. Fresh off an election victory, the new president is offered a rare window of opportunity to craft a vision for the nation, free from the day-to-day burdens that will accumulate later in the term. Most presidents claim some sort of electoral mandate, and Congress and the media typically afford the new president a "honeymoon" period in which to staff the administration, establish decision-making processes, and set priorities. Over the course of the next three or seven years, such blue-sky thinking gradually will become engulfed by the realities of occupying the most powerful office in the world. But all that lies ahead. On Day One, a new president inherits maximum opportunity and minimal burden.

Presidents often use the first year to promote signature legislative priorities. Lyndon B. Johnson spent both of his first years—the twelve months following the assassination of John F. Kennedy and the year following his own inauguration in January 1965—passing a broad package of domestic legislation known collectively as the Great Society. Ronald Reagan achieved the cornerstones of Reaganomics, including tax cuts and increases in defense spending, midway through his first year. Even in the midst of responding to the September 11 terror attacks, George W. Bush secured passage of the No Child Left Behind education reform bill weeks before his one-year anniversary in office. The Affordable Care Act was passed in the early part of Barack Obama's second year, but he spent much of his first-year political capital pushing it through Congress.

In many ways, then, presidents are at the height of their power in the first year. At the same time, they are at the lowest point of their experience. They are still figuring out how to take the reins of a government with more than 4 million civilian employees and uniformed service members around the world. They are staffing several thousand positions across the executive branch, many with people who are in their first tours of government duty. Meanwhile, allies and adversaries are taking the measure of their new counterparts, the latter often testing the new leadership in its first year. It is a time of peril as well as promise.

Throughout history, new commanders in chief have stumbled on the world stage when confronted with their first challenge. Kennedy approved the ill-fated

Bay of Pigs incursion into Cuba. George H. W. Bush's first foray into Panama in the fall of 1989 was marred by setbacks, leading critics to deride the new president. Bill Clinton's intervention in Somalia in October 1993 left eighteen American soldiers dead and the new president badly bruised in his first international action. Yet these same presidents went on to lead the Cuban Missile Crisis negotiations, the end of the Cold War, and the Bosnian peacekeeping intervention, respectively, indicating that the damage was short-lived. No matter how good a president's team looks on paper, new administrations often take time to hit their stride.

No amount of time or planning can prepare a new administration for the exogenous shocks that occur in every first year. Since Reagan's first term, presidential first years have witnessed an assassination attempt, the collapse of communism in Eastern Europe, two separate attacks on the World Trade Center, and the biggest financial crisis since the Great Depression. In an earlier time, John Adams was greeted when he took office in 1797 by the XYZ Affair. In May 1801, the pasha of Tripoli declared war on the United States, leading Adams's successor, Thomas Jefferson, into armed conflict barely two months into his presidency.

To expect the unexpected is axiomatic in the first year, and each new president faces his or her own set of challenges and opportunities. Nonetheless, there is a long list of questions that every first-year president must address: How does one build a national security team? What does one do about the first budget due on Capitol Hill just weeks into the new presidency? How does one deal with promises made during the campaign? What is the proper division of labor between cabinet departments and White House staff?

In addressing these questions, history is instructive. In October 2015, the Miller Center at the University of Virginia launched First Year: POTUS 2017—a three-year project aimed at providing a historical framework to guide future presidents and their teams in the first year. The project has explored some of the core governance questions facing a new president, including how to approach the first year, how to navigate a broken political system, and how to thrive in a changing media environment. It also has examined challenges and opportunities in certain policy areas, including national security, race, immigration, opportunity and mobility, and fiscal policy.

Within each of these topic areas—posted as "volumes" on the firstyear2017.org website—we asked leading thinkers from the academy and policy community to provide guidance for incoming administrations, drawing from their experiences in office, the latest academic research, and often both. The authors are as diverse as the subjects they cover: progressives and conservatives, idealists and realists, Boomers and Millennials, scholars from various disciplines and practitioners from numerous agencies. Although history has much to offer any new administration, the applications are not always immediately apparent. The First Year Project offers a unique combination: it pairs historical evidence with contemporary policy analyses and identifies the points of intersection. Individually, the essays offer important perspectives to incoming government officials. Collectively, they provide a comprehensive blueprint to guide each new administration during its crucible year.

Part I of *Crucible: The President's First Year* begins by examining the rise of Donald Trump in 2016 and reflecting on his first six months in office in 2017. Yale University's Stephen Skowronek encourages each new president to ask a critical question before entering the first year: what time is it? According to Skowronek, the various elements of American government run on either "secular time," during which the president's main job is "finding solutions that work," or "political time," which occurs between "periodic resets of the nation's ideological trajectory."

Michael Nelson of Rhodes College and the Miller Center provides an early review of the first year of the Trump presidency. The history of the Trump administration will be fully written in the years to come, but Nelson makes some early observations in light of the insights offered throughout this volume.

Part II begins by presenting an overarching view of the first year as a distinct period in one's presidency, worthy of focused examination. The essays center on a fundamental question: Why does the first year matter? Why not focus, as many— journalists, pundits, and most presidential candidates—do, on the first one hundred days? Or the entire first term? This part casts the first year as a useful frame for all incoming chief executives. New administrations are often eager to hit the ground running, delivering on campaign promises and taking advantage of the traditional post-inauguration honeymoon. Yet, when the adrenaline of the first hundred days wears off, more complex policy proposals often come to the fore and greater political capital must be expended. More than one hundred days is needed for a president to build a team and seriously tackle larger policy challenges.

University of Virginia presidential scholar Sidney M. Milkis sees the first year of contemporary presidents as the fulfillment of a trend that began with the Progressive-Era administrations of Theodore Roosevelt and Woodrow Wilson. It was during this time that the White House, not the parties or Congress, became the center of domestic and foreign policymaking—a trend that expanded dramatically during the New Deal and continues to the present day. Milkis argues that the next president should practice restraint in his first year by empowering a strong cabinet and cultivating relationships in Congress.

H. W. Brands of the University of Texas at Austin argues that the first year initially is shaped by how the president enters the White House, whether by succeeding to the office, surviving a close election, or winning a landslide. Nonetheless, all new presidents must appoint a cabinet and White House staff, build a domestic policy agenda, and establish their leadership as commander in chief. Using history as a guide, Brands offers guidance on these three critical tasks.

Michael Nelson suggests ten lessons for the first year from those who actually served in recent administrations. Using the vast collection of interviews from the Miller Center's Presidential Oral History Project, Nelson organizes his advice into lessons for the transition and for taking office. These lessons, drawn from the insights of senior officials in the Carter, Reagan, Bush, and Clinton administrations, include building relations on Capitol Hill, staffing the administration wisely, and advancing a policy agenda.

Barbara A. Perry of the Miller Center examines court vacancies in presidential first years. As Perry notes, Trump took office in an unusual position: no other new president since Harry S. Truman has had the opportunity to choose a Supreme Court nominee in his first year.

Northwestern University's Daniel J. Galvin discusses the structural constraints faced by the president, which put campaign promises and ambitious agendas to the test during the first year. As Galvin notes, presidents often find that their ability to enact lasting change is constrained by institutional realities.

Robert F. Bruner, dean emeritus of the University of Virginia's Darden School of Business, examines the inevitable first-year crisis. Bruner's essay focuses on domestic financial crises, describing eight that happened during various presidents' first years. "One can either harness the power of the nation's economy, or be run over by it," Bruner concludes. The historically informed new president masters four principal levers of influence: priorities, personnel, processes, and politics.

In the concluding essay of Part II, Peter Wehner, who served as director of the Office of Strategic Initiatives under George W. Bush, draws on his experiences in the White House to chart how the new president can maximize the chances for successful leadership. His "Dear Mr. or Madam President" memo covers a range of topics, from using political capital to selecting advisors to engaging with both Congress and the public.

The eight essays in Part III focus on the new president's role as commander in chief. The historical evidence is that the first year is the most dangerous in a president's tenure in the foreign-policy domain. Previous first years offer instructive lessons to help minimize these dangers.

Marc Selverstone of the Miller Center offers the Bay of Pigs episode as a case study in first-year course correction. The Kennedy administration used the botched invasion to examine and implement changes in the management of national security policy. A review conducted after the invasion by retired general Maxwell Taylor led the administration to make a series of important structural and personnel changes, as well as to create a more formal procedure for handling national security during the remainder of the Kennedy presidency.

Johns Hopkins University professor Hal Brands examines the lessons of the Reagan administration for national security policymaking. He credits Reagan for bringing into office a set of core strategic ideas that helped orient his policies and his subordinates. Brands also notes three first-year deficiencies that future presidents would be wise to avoid: failing to select advisors who are compatible with the president's management style, disempowering the national security advisor, and refused to change poor advisors or unsuccessful strategies.

Jeffrey A. Engel of Southern Methodist University credits the first year of Reagan's successor, George H. W. Bush, with a "Hippocratic" strategy of first doing no harm. The first year of the Bush presidency was a time of remarkable change on the world stage—the fall of communism in Eastern Europe, the Tiananmen Square crackdown in China, and attempted coups in Panama and the Philippines. In each of these ambiguous situations, the Bush administration demonstrated that less can be more.

University of Texas at Austin historian Jeremi Suri argues that although Bill Clinton hoped to focus almost exclusively on domestic policy in his first year, global events required his immediate attention. Like Kennedy, Clinton eschewed organized planning in favor of improvisation as he dealt with challenges in Haiti, Somalia, North Korea, Eastern Europe, and the former Soviet Union. In the end, the Clinton years demonstrated the importance of consistent presidential focus on personnel, goals, and strategies.

Melvyn P. Leffler of the University of Virginia assesses the personnel challenges that plagued the first year of the George W. Bush presidency. Although Bush's national security team was impressive on paper, the principals did not agree on a policy vision or trust one another, leading to fragmentation and disorder. Bush became more engaged after the September 11 attacks, but any new president, Leffler argues, would do well at the outset to establish clear lines of authority, effective processes, defined goals and priorities, and a strong national security advisor.

Two essays by former senior policymakers Michèle A. Flournoy, undersecretary of defense for policy under Barack Obama, and Philip Zelikow, who served under George H. W. Bush and George W. Bush, offer remarkably consistent advice to the new president. Both authors emphasize the importance of choosing a good staff; of setting clear goals, priorities, and plans to achieve them; and of focusing early on the budgetary aspects of national security policy.

Part III concludes with an essay by Harvard University professor Jeffry Frieden, who argues that because the threat of financial crisis is the greatest danger facing the global economy, new presidents should work to minimize this danger by harmonizing financial regulation and macroeconomic policies among the world's major economies.

Part IV concerns domestic affairs, with essays on a range of policies, including health care, fiscal reform, infrastructure, and rebuilding the American Dream. University of Virginia professor Peter Norton uses the Interstate Highway System to illustrate that the predicate for a fourth-year legislative achievement may sometimes be a first-year legislative push. Dwight D. Eisenhower's deliberate approach to articulating a strategy, building coalitions, and selling the proposal to Congress ultimately led to his greatest domestic achievement.

Guian McKee, a Miller Center scholar, offers a case study on how Lyndon Johnson succeeded in passing Medicare and Medicaid legislation during what some consider the most successful first year in history. Johnson's patience, agility, and ability to negotiate with allies and adversaries alike offer useful lessons for any new president.

Next, a series of essays examines the use of first-year action to advance the needs of the working and middle classes. Michael Nelson begins with another look into the Miller Center's Presidential Oral History archives for insights from the Carter, Reagan, Bush, and Clinton presidencies. Nelson highlights key moments in the politics of opportunity and mobility, including Jimmy Carter's food stamp policy, Reagan and the AIDS epidemic, George H. W. Bush and the Americans with Disabilities Act, and Clinton's health care reform effort.

How policymakers can build a more secure future for those not yet in the workforce is the subject of University of Washington historian Margaret O'Mara's essay. She makes the case for investing in the next-generation economy so that more Americans can enjoy the fruits of innovation. O'Mara uses examples from throughout the twentieth century to call for greater investment in people and ideas, an internationalist approach defined by more open borders, and a commitment to income security.

Turning to infrastructure, an area with seemingly bipartisan potential, Albright College historian Mason B. Williams reaches into the 1930s to support a call for substantial investment to modernize America's cities as a way to expand both economic growth and social justice.

The University of Virginia's Willis Jenkins reframes the political question of how humans interact with the natural environment. Humans have fundamentally altered "nature," and political considerations must now be directed toward questions of *how* and not *if* we will alter evolutionary systems.

Part IV concludes with paired memos from Democrat William A. Galston, who served as deputy domestic policy advisor under Bill Clinton, and Republican Peter Wehner, each of whom offers suggestions for how the new president can build an opportunity agenda. Wehner and Galston identify several areas of consensus between the two parties, including tax reform and workforce training.

Part V examines a broad theme that has animated several recent presidential elections: race, immigration, and American identity. In the first essay, University of Oregon political scientist Daniel Tichenor offers Lyndon Johnson's 1965 immigration reforms as a case study in coalition building and compromise.

The next three essays explore challenges awaiting new presidents in the area of race relations. Orlando Patterson, a professor of sociology at Harvard University, identifies matters that should be addressed in the first year, including mass incarceration, police training and culture, and residential and school segregation. Georgetown sociologist Michael Eric Dyson urges the president to use the bully pulpit both to confront America's legacy of racism and to seek a common way forward. Finally, the Miller Center's Douglas A. Blackmon examines how a president's rhetoric can influence racial dialogue. Historically, presidents have limited power to enact policies to tackle discrimination. However, Blackmon urges, the president does have the ability to employ moral persuasion and should do so on matters related to race, gender, and other similar concerns.

Part VI examines how presidents can effectively manage the executive branch, particularly in an era of partisan dysfunction. As bitterly contested as some recent presidential elections have been, University of Virginia historian Alan Taylor reminds us that it has always been thus. The election of 1800 brought about the first transfer of presidential power from one party to another, but for a time Jefferson faced the specter of civil war from a Federalist Party that did not want to surrender authority to its bitter foe. Taylor urges the new president to pursue a moderate course and engage fully Congress and the public.

Next, Gary W. Gallagher of the University of Virginia examines the first year of Abraham Lincoln's presidency—what many consider to be the worst first year experienced by any president in history. Although Lincoln's first year was unlike any other, it illustrates that in times of heightened division, presidents must try to build bridges to political opponents, including bringing some into the administration.

Brookings Institution scholar Elaine C. Kamarck's essay shifts the focus from the politics of the presidency to the management of the executive branch. As the head of Clinton's "Reinventing Government" initiative, Kamarck urges new presidents to concentrate on understanding the capacities and knowledge of the federal government. By giving attention to the "managerial presidency," the president increases the likelihood that good governance and good politics go hand in hand.

Andrew Rudalevige from Bowdoin College cautions against the excessive use of executive action. Acting unilaterally, although tempting, especially in a fractured political climate, endangers a president's policy legacy and does not guarantee lasting results. Instead, for both political and policy reasons, any new president would be wise to work toward bipartisan solutions.

Patrick O'Brien urges new presidents to concentrate on two powers that are often ineffectively used: "the appointment power and the agenda-setting power." Doing so can be especially helpful, O'Brien argues, in seeking to improve the economy.

In the essay written by McKinsey and Company's Carolyn Dewar, Tom Dohrmann, Andrew Erdmann, Ryan Harper, and Kunal Modi, the group analyzes a set of CEO transitions and offers twelve management lessons that could apply to an incoming presidential administration. These lessons include the importance of establishing an overarching vision and a limited set of priorities, building an effective team, and constructing a model that can be sustained throughout the presidency, not just during the early phase.

Bruce Katz of the Brookings Institution presents a pessimistic view of what can be accomplished by the federal government and encourages the next president to empower cities and metropolitan areas to be the source of innovation. He argues that the partisan dysfunction that has plagued Washington in recent decades has sparked a range of ambitious, bottom-up solutions. The next president can seize this energy by giving cities greater flexibility in designing federal investments.

Finally, the five essays of Part VII assess how the president can seize the bully pulpit in the first year, particularly in an age of new media. Rutgers professor David Greenberg debunks the hype surrounding the "First One Hundred Days" and cautions new administrations to ignore this arbitrary benchmark in favor of longer-term goals. Successful first years have less to do with communication techniques and more to do with good policy, Greenberg argues. Develop a short list of substantial policy proposals, including a major economic plan, and good headlines and positive social media posts will follow.

According to Clinton speechwriter Jeff Shesol, "The diminishing draw of the bully pulpit is a reality of the contemporary presidency." In his essay, Shesol urges new presidents to forgo high rhetoric in place of a more authentic, conversational style; to revamp the traditional State of the Union address; and to fully empower the speechwriting staff.

Mary Kate Cary, who served as a speechwriter under George H. W. Bush, examines so-called micro-moments—the many times throughout the day when people check their smartphones for a quick hit of information, creating excellent opportunities for the administration to deliver content tailored to each new platform or device.

Susan J. Douglas of the University of Michigan offers a blueprint for navigating the increasingly fragmented and ubiquitous media environment by balancing the perils of heightened scrutiny with the benefits of more direct connectivity with the American people. Like Franklin D. Roosevelt, Kennedy, and Reagan, presidents must understand the media environment within which they operate and harness the tools at their disposal.

Finally, Obama White House Communications Director Anita Dunn urges her successors to evolve with the changing media environment. As the pace of technological change quickens, the White House must be an early adopter of new technology and seek to bring content directly to the public. The traditional bully pulpit no longer exists. The ability to govern effectively depends on the ability to communicate effectively in this new environment.

Successful American presidents have come from the left and the right, from the decisive and the patient, from the educated and the self-made, from the exceptionalist and the internationalist, from the creator of destiny and the beneficiary of good fortune. Important lessons can be drawn from both the best and the worst presidencies in American history, as well as from all those in between. Although the election of 2016 and the presidency of Donald Trump have been seen as unusual, there is historical precedent for many "unprecedented presidencies." No common thread runs through the list of forty-five presidents, no playbook provides the right answers to all the challenges future presidents will face. What we do have is more than 225 years of presidential history to inspire, deter, and ultimately enlighten each new administration.

I ★ DONALD TRUMP'S FIRST YEAR

WHAT TIME IS IT?

Tracking Trump in Secular and Political Time

STEPHEN SKOWRONEK

The oath each new president takes on inauguration day marks the start of an implacable four-year countdown. But the calendar is only one measure of time for the nation's political leader. In the course of a presidential campaign, competing candidates offer the nation different answers to the question, "what time is it?" Capturing the moment is critical to their leadership prospects in office, but getting it right is seldom straightforward.

It is hard for modern presidents to tell time because the organization of American government and politics is increasingly complex, and its various aspects run on different clocks. One clock keeps "secular time." It marks the inexorable thickening of the institutional universe of political action, the widening array of stakeholders in government policy, and the press of ever-more-complicated problems for government to solve. Secular time casts the president as a hands-on manager of the government's sprawling commitments, as the master orchestrator of expected services and competing demands, as the responsible steward of a policy state. In secular time, performance is about finding solutions that work.

Another clock keeps "political time." Political time measures the years that unfold between periodic resets of the nation's ideological trajectory. It tells of the state of the political movements contesting national power, of the expectations of the mobilized polity. Those thinking in political time see the president as an agent of change poised to break through the knot of interests and institutions that block concerted action on the agenda the candidate was chosen to champion. They anticipate a populist intervention, a purge of the entrenched, a thoroughgoing reconstruction of governmental operations. Performance in political time is about reconfiguring government to conform to a particular political ideal or reform principle.

Nothing in recent years has so tested the political skills of incumbents as striking a workable balance between these two competing frameworks for presidential action. Consider Ronald Reagan, the last president to successfully reset political time. The "revolution" of 1980 thrust a conservative insurgency into control of the national agenda, and Reagan's first budget followed up with a programmatic breakthrough that locked in movement priorities. Implementation, however, proved a management nightmare, as fabricated budget projections and a collision of priorities with policy at the Federal Reserve sent the nation into an economic tailspin. It was just the opposite for Reagan's successor, George H. W. Bush. Although an affiliate of the "Reagan Revolution," Bush chose to elevate responsible management over movement priorities. But when he orchestrated an ecumenical budget compromise designed to address the nation's economic problems through a balanced scheme of tax increases and spending cuts, he drew the wrath of the conservative insurgency, sending his presidency into a political tailspin.

What time is it now? Since Reagan reset the political clock nearly four decades ago, we have had two iterations of affiliated leadership. Like his father, George W. Bush had to wrestle with the dilemmas of upholding conservative orthodoxy while trying to respond to the relentless press of new demands for responsible management and problem solving. He avoided his father's misstep on taxes with cuts that appealed to his political base, but other initiatives—on education, prescription drug benefits, and emergency responses to the financial crisis—confounded the expectations of movement conservatives and stiffened their confrontational stance.

We have also had two iterations of opposition leadership. Neither was able to dislodge the conservative project and reconstruct American government and politics, but both Bill Clinton and Barack Obama exploited vulnerabilities in conservative orthodoxy and exposed its difficulties in coming up with responsive new solutions to the problems of the day. Clinton disavowed orthodoxies on the right and the left alike. He goaded both sides with a policy strategy of "triangulation" and achieved great popularity with the political attractions of his "Third Way." Obama was more aggressive. He wanted to "change the trajectory" of national affairs and do for progressives what Reagan had done for conservatives, but he promised to do it in an ecumenical way, one that acknowledged the full range of interests in national action. His signature initiative, the Affordable Care Act, pulled his followers in the progressive movement kicking and screaming behind a measure that reached out to all the stakeholders in the health care industry. But again, implementation proved a management nightmare, and the movement mobilization was all on the opposition side.

The political sequence as it has unfolded since 1980 fits well-known historical patterns. Think for example of the rise and fall of Jacksonian Democracy between 1828 and 1860 or the rise and fall of New Deal liberalism between 1932 and 1980, each of which followed a similar rotation of alternating victories, first for the party that carried forward the newly installed political orthodoxy of the day, then for the party at odds with it. Affiliated leaders marked political time with increasingly awkward adjustments to received governing formulas; opposition preemptors marked it with increasingly candid but still unresolved challenges. The current sequence has the added complication of widening disparities between the demands of political and secular time. By historical standards, the Reagan Revolution was relatively shallow, the president increasingly deferential after that first budget to demands for responsible problem-solving and interest management.

The Trump administration must navigate these cross currents, testing their relative strength. But there is mistaking how it is telling time. No incumbent since Ronald Reagan has so forcefully avowed his intention to reset the political clock and reconstruct American government and politics. Although he ran as a Republican, Donald Trump crafted a sui generis political brand. He trounced a field of more orthodox candidates in the party's primaries, and even after winning the nomination, he barely mentioned Reagan's name. Asserting his distance from both parties, Trump renounced the political system in its entirety, declaring it "rigged," "corrupt," a "mess," and a "disaster." He promised a "great disruption" and a redemptive drive to "make America great again." His aggressive populism and strident nationalism recalled the rise of Andrew Jackson, prompting many conservatives to declare him risky and dangerous.

If reconstructive moments could be created by presidential proclamation there would be a lot more of them. Trump deftly capitalized on the political frustrations that mount as old orders linger and grow more confused, but following through is another matter altogether. Since the Reagan Revolution, the incorporation of new groups into the managerial calculus has proceeded apace and the interdependence of interests has become even more pronounced in judgments of performance. Trump lost the popular vote in 2016 by a substantial margin to a candidate who had countered his promise to transform the state with promises to make it work. Hillary Clinton was all about leadership in secular time—programs vetted by experts, experience in solving problems, managerial prowess. Although many predicted she would win the 2016 race, it is worth noting that such an outcome would have come as a conspicuous wrinkle in political time. Never has an opposition leader like Bill Clinton and Barack Obama (both of whom fell short of a fundamental reordering) been able to pass power to a handpicked successor. And yet, Al Gore and Hillary Clinton each outpolled the Electoral College victor, largely on boasts of competence and continuity. Secular time has not yet overtaken political time in presidential politics, but the competition between these two frames for action is getting stiffer, and the former harder to discount.

The prospects for reconstruction are further clouded by Trump's relationship to his own ostensible allies. The Trump victory threatened to displace the conservative/progressive cleavage that has defined American politics since the Reagan Revolution, and although Republicans took control of all branches of the federal government, the president's agenda cuts against many of the core commitments of his fellow partisans in Congress. On a strict reading of political time, this looks less like a reconstructive moment than a late, shaky, conflicted reinstallment of the conservative regime, and if history is any guide, the prospects for leadership in those circumstances are especially daunting.

President Trump would be well advised to consider carefully the plight of presidents similarly situated in earlier political sequences. The closest exemplar historically is Jimmy Carter, a third-round affiliate of the liberal, New Deal order. Reaching back farther, Franklin Pierce, the third-round affiliate of the Jacksonian regime, is also illuminating. In each instance, a long-dominant party had grown so fractious and ideologically strained that it could not coalesce around any one of its recognized national leaders. In both cases, the party chose an outlier, reaching for a candidate on the distant fringes of power and hoping to control him once victory was assured. Pierce won the presidency on a pledge to take no further action with regard to slavery, the very issue that was tearing his party and the nation apart. Carter won in a campaign in which he cast a wary eye over his party's liberal agenda. There were, he advised, "no easy answers" to the questions facing the nation. Trump's boast upon accepting his party's nomination, "I alone can fix it," was eerily reminiscent of Carter's campaign slogan, "Why Not the Best?" as each candidate substituted his own unique skill and personal acumen for his party's collective resolve, emphasizing independence from orthodoxy and distance from party commitments.

In all three of these cases, the mobilized elements of the coalition the president brought back to power were pressing more extreme and controversial demands on government, demands that threatened the new incumbent's standing as a responsible steward of national affairs. Pierce and Carter opted for different ways out of this shared dilemma, but on assuming office, both threw the old order into an existential crisis. Pierce broke his pledge on slavery, reached out to his party's stalwarts, and pushed through the controversial Kansas-Nebraska Act, which repealed the Missouri Compromise and let new states decide for themselves whether to allow slavery. That choice crushed his presidency under a political revolution. It provided the opposition with proof that the old order was bankrupt of responsible solutions to the problems of the day, and it ultimately led Pierce's own party to drop him as a political liability. Carter, on the other hand, stiffened his resistance to his party's orthodoxy, even to the point of reversing the Democrats' traditional formula for economic management and elevating the fight against inflation over a commitment to full employment. Charges of betrayal from liberals within his ranks fueled a dump-Carter movement, leaving him politically weakened in the face of an emboldened conservative insurgency.

For Trump this dilemma appears particularly acute. If he shifts too far toward his congressional party, he risks losing much of his appeal as an independent movement leader. But Republicans in Congress are far more secure in office than their president; the pressure to release the pent-up demands of the party caucus and seize the opportunities presented by unified party control will be intense. The choices at hand all appear explosive. On the one hand, presidential resistance to congressional Republicans threatens a conservative implosion; on the other, presidential indulgence of an all-fronts assault on the policy state tempts a political counterrevolution. For all the talk of a decisive reconstruction, Trump appears to be courting a politically disastrous disjunction of the sort experienced by Pierce and Carter.

The difference between Pierce and Carter is instructive. Pierce chose to stand with his party's stalwarts and quickly found himself marginalized and discarded by them as damaged goods; Carter resisted his party's stalwarts, took his stand as a steady manager of national affairs, and defeated their challenge to his renomination. Carter deployed the expanded institutional resources of the modern presidency to project a national political persona that was steady and responsible, indifferent to the ideological alternatives contending for the passions of the electorate. He used the president's enhanced position in secular time to elevate the managerial ideal. It was a gamble he ultimately lost, but it was also a bet on the future. For a president desperate to escape the dismal cycles of political time, the opportunities opened by secular time beam brightly.

At this writing, it appears unlikely that Trump will adopt either the Pierce or Carter strategy. Rather than capitulate to his party's leaders in Congress or take his stand for responsible management, the president appears determined to press ahead with his own vision of a new order. In the circumstances at hand, that will be a telltale test of the political capacities of the modern presidency to transform American government by its own lights and remake parties at will. The odds of success would appear slim, and the results may, paradoxically, demonstrate the opposite of what the president has chosen to seek. The question that hangs in the balance is whether the best bet for modern presidents is to govern in secular time.

DONALD TRUMP'S FIRST YEAR

Decreasing Influence without Increasing Effectiveness

MICHAEL NELSON

Donald Trump won an astonishing victory in the 2016 presidential election. At each turn of the electoral calendar, from June 16, 2015, when Trump announced he was running, until well into the evening of Election Day—November 8, 2016—political analysts of every stripe were confident that he would not be the forty-fifth president of the United States. His candidacy would not last long enough even to contest the Iowa caucuses and New Hampshire primary, they—we—all said. The Huffington Post, for example, refused for months to "report on Trump's campaign as part of [our] political coverage. Instead we will cover his campaign as part of our entertainment section."[1] Election eve forecasts placed his chances of victory against Democratic nominee Hillary Clinton at 1 percent (the Princeton Election Consortium), 2 percent (HuffPost), even 0 percent (the celebrated Democratic political strategist David Plouffe).[2]

The presidential election was not the only one whose outcome surprised the experts. Most forecast that the results of the Senate elections, in which the Republicans were forced to defend more than twice as many seats as the Democrats, would turn over control of that chamber from the Republican to the Democratic Party. Wrong again. The Democrats gained just two seats, not the five they needed to secure a majority. Predictions for the House elections generally were that the Democrats would add about fifteen to twenty seats, bringing them within striking distance of a majority. That didn't happen either. They gained a paltry seven seats, leaving the Republicans in charge of a united party government: the presidency and both houses of Congress.

Although surprising in its result, the 2016 election was less remarkable in its magnitude. It was not, as Trump claimed, "a massive landslide victory, as you know, in the Electoral College," much less "the biggest Electoral College win since Ronald Reagan."[3] From 1788 to 2012, forty-five of fifty-seven presidential elections were decided by a larger electoral vote majority than Trump's 306–232 victory over Hillary Clinton (304–227 after seven "faithless electors" voted for different candidates than the ones to whom they were pledged).[4] In the seven elections after Reagan, the winning candidate outdid Trump in the Electoral College five times. In only four elections in two and a quarter centuries did the winner fail to secure more votes from the people than his opponent. Yet Trump ran a record 2.9 million behind Clinton in the national popular vote, and his postelection claim that "between three and five million illegal votes [for Clinton] caused me to lose the popular vote" was completely unsubstantiated by evidence.[5]

Similarly, although the election gave Trump a united party government the Republican majority in both congressional chambers was perilously thin. In the House of Representatives, Republicans outnumbered Democrats by 241 to 194, and in the Senate by 52 to 48. In the face of cohesive Democratic opposition, this meant that any legislative proposal that alienated just a small group of Republican members was unlikely to be enacted. This was especially the case in the filibuster-prone Senate, where it takes sixty votes to pass most legislation. To enact even those measures that required only a simple majority, all but two Republican members would need to vote together.

An additional complication for President Trump arose from the nature of the election campaign waged by candidate Trump, which was marked by name-calling and extravagant promises. He branded leading Democratic contenders Sanders and Clinton as "Crazy Bernie" and "Crooked Hillary," respectively, and led chants of "Lock her up!" at campaign rallies. He challenged President Barack Obama's bona fides as a natural-born citizen and, when Obama produced proof that he was born in Hawaii, suggested that the "birth certificate is a fraud."[6] Most astonishing, in a video-recorded 2005 conversation with *Access Hollywood* host Billy Bush that became public one month before the election, Trump bragged that when he saw beautiful women, "I just start kissing them. . . . And when you're a star they let you do it. You can do anything. Grab 'em by the pussy."[7]

Nor did Trump spare Republican rivals Ted Cruz and Marco Rubio, whom he dubbed "Lyin' Ted" and "Little Marco." He dismissed Republican senator John McCain, an authentic hero of the Vietnam War who endured unending torture as a prisoner of war rather than be released before his fellow captives, as "not a war hero. . . . I like people who weren't captured."[8] Neither McCain nor any of the other four living Republican nominees for president regarded Trump as fit to hold the office; nor did any of the leading conservative publications.[9] Multiple party leaders called on him to withdraw from the election after the *Access Hollywood* recording was released. The result was that Trump became president with almost no support from his party's elected leaders that was rooted in anything other than short-term political expedience, chiefly their fear of alienating his followers.

Trump's campaign promises stretched far beyond realism. Concerning the economy, he pledged to create twenty-five million jobs in ten years and to eliminate the $19 trillion national debt two years sooner than that, historically unprecedented targets that somehow would be reached while raising defense spending and "sav[ing] Medicare, Medicaid, and Social Security without cuts."[10] Within thirty days of taking office, Trump promised, he would have "a plan for soundly and quickly defeating ISIS."[11] He would not only "build a great, great wall on our southern border" but also "have Mexico pay for that wall."[12] Of the "at least 11 million people that came in this country illegally," he said, "They will go out."[13] "We're going to win so much," Trump declared, "you're going to be so sick and tired of winning, you're going to come to me and go, 'Please, please, we can't win any more.'"[14]

The president is the nation's chief of government—its political leader as the head of the winning party and thus an inherently divisive figure—but also its chief of state, the living symbol of national unity. By virtue of the latter role, newly elected presidents normally enjoy a surge of public approval that represents the vote of confidence granted to anyone who ascends to the office. This is the basis of the traditional "honeymoon" period, which usually lasts well into the president's first year and can readily be converted into a governing asset in the form of increased influence in Congress.[15] To be sure, in the contemporary era of polarized partisan politics, in which many Democratic and Republican voters regard each other not as friendly rivals but as enemies,[16] presidential honeymoons have grown shorter and less idyllic. But Trump's brutalistic campaign assured that he would have no honeymoon at all. His 46 percent level of support on Election Day began declining almost immediately. Public protests broke out the day after the election and even larger ones, involving more than three million women in dozens of cities and towns, occurred one day after Trump's inauguration. An organized campaign was waged to persuade electors to vote for candidates other than Trump or Clinton in order to deny Trump a majority of electoral votes and throw the election into the House.[17]

That said, the same freewheeling style that alienated Democrats during the election solidified Trump's support among many Republican voters, who regarded his rhetorical excesses as evidence of authenticity, undiluted by the normal social constraints that Trump dismissed as "political correctness." Supporters cheered when he said that Mexican immigrants were "bringing drugs, they're bringing crime[,] they're rapists,"[18] as they did when he called for a "total and complete shutdown of Muslims entering the United States."[19] They nodded approvingly when Trump claimed that former Republican president George W. Bush "lied" about weapons of mass destruction as a pretext for waging war against Iraq.[20] In the global war on terror, Trump declared, "Torture works. . . . Water boarding is fine, but it's not nearly tough enough."[21] "We're going to be saying 'Merry Christmas' at every store," he offered. "You can leave 'Happy Holidays' at the corner."[22]

Trump's voters also valued his experience as a businessman rather than a politician. Historically, nearly everyone elected or even nominated by a major political party for president has been a current or former senator, governor, vice president, general, or cabinet member. In the quarter century after World War II, senators and vice presidents (most of whom had been senators) dominated presidential elections because Cold War–era voters valued their experience dealing with national security affairs. Then, in the aftermath of the Vietnam War and the Watergate scandal, the electorate turned to state governors, who were untainted by the incompetence and corruption now associated with a Washington-based political career: Jimmy Carter in 1976, Ronald Reagan in 1980, Bill Clinton in 1992, and George W. Bush in 2000.

The ascendant Tea Party movement that helped the Republican Party win control of the House in 2010 and the Senate in 2014, however, was not just anti-Washington but anti-government in all its forms. As someone who had never held public office, Trump appealed to voters as a complete outsider who promised to clean up "the mess in Washington" or, in his more vivid phrase, to "drain the swamp."[23] "The problem with politicians," he told a rally: "[they're] all talk and no action. It's true, All talk, and it's all bullshit."[24] Trump's wealth became part of his allure. Other candidates were "controlled by those people," he averred, referring to wealthy individuals and interest groups. "I'm not controlled. . . . I'm using my own money. I'm not using the lobbyists. I'm not using the donors. I don't care. I'm really rich."[25] Remarkably, on Election Day 20 percent of voters who said Trump lacks "the temperament to serve effectively as president" voted for him anyway, along with 18 percent of those who said he is not "qualified to be president."[26]

Taken together, these aspects of the 2016 election were enough to get Trump elected but augured poorly for his first year as president. Not once has the economy gained twenty-five million jobs in ten years. Nor has the national debt ever shrunk at a rate anywhere close to $2.5 trillion per year over two four-year terms. As William Safire has written, presidents who promise rain will be held responsible for the droughts that inevitably come.[27] Further, surprising as Trump's victory was, it was modest in magnitude. His party's other leaders felt no sense of personal loyalty to him, and the opposition party was determined to see him fail. He earned none of the good will from people who voted against him that traditionally sets the stage for a first-year honeymoon. On top of that, as Stephen Skowronek points out in the previous essay, Trump took office at the same late stage of "political time" as did Franklin Pierce at the tail end of the Jacksonian era and Jimmy Carter in the waning years of New Deal liberalism. Like these two hapless predecessors, Trump faced the challenge of holding together a crumbling majority coalition. In his case the coalition included blue-collar Republicans motivated by conservative social views but opposed to free trade and to reductions in (some) entitlement programs, as well as white-collar Republicans who were little concerned about social issues but cared deeply about these conservative economic policies. Most important, perhaps, Trump had been elected mostly by harshly attacking the opposition, not by offering a positive program for governing.

CYCLES OF INFLUENCE AND EFFECTIVENESS

As Paul Light has argued, almost every president has suffered a "cycle of decreasing influence" during his tenure in office.[28] When expectations raised during the campaign cannot all be met, some because they are excessive and others because they are contradictory, people become disappointed. As a former Gerald Ford aide lamented, "Each [presidential] decision is bound to hurt somebody. . . . He will satisfy one group but anger three others."[29] Consequently, presidents experience what Paul Brace and Barbara Hinckley have called a "decay curve," a decline in public approval of the president's performance that normally begins about halfway through the first year and lasts well into the third year, "independently of anything the president does" and "irrespective of the economy . . . or outside events."[30] According to Light, one implication of the "race against time" that marks the cycle of decreasing influence is that "the first year offers the greatest opportunity."[31] "I know this honeymoon won't last," said Lyndon Johnson. "Every day I lose a little more political capital."[32] "When an administration really makes great successes," observed veteran Republican senator Roy Blunt a half-century later, "it's usually in that first year—and more importantly, in that first seven months of that first year."[33]

Fortunately for new presidents, starting right after the election they typically benefit from the simultaneous "cycle of increasing effectiveness" that comes with experience in office. New chief executives learn on the job. As Light observes, "The presidential information base should expand; the president's personal expertise should increase. As the president and the staff become more familiar with the working of the office, there will be a learning effect. They will identify useful sources of information; they will produce effective strategies."[34]

As with Trump's election, so with his early presidency: the historical rules generally did not apply. To be sure, during the nearly nine months between his election and the midpoint of his first year in office, Trump's influence in most matters of politics and governance decreased. But it did so at a pace that accelerated from the very beginning. After six months Congress had not passed a single piece of major legislation. Of the ten items in the "Contract with the American Voter" that constituted Trump's "100-Day action plan to Make American Great Again," nine had not even been introduced.[35] His job approval rating was 39 percent, the lowest of any newly elected president in the history of opinion polling, and his disapproval rating was 55 percent, the highest. The average net approval rating—that is, the percent approving minus the percent disapproving—for the nine elected presidents from Dwight Eisenhower to Barack Obama was +36 percent at the six-month mark. Trump's was -16 percent.[36]

Beyond that, not much in the way of increasing effectiveness occurred. Instead, Trump learned little about how to be president from the experience of being president. Once in office, "I will be more effective and more disciplined," he promised during the campaign.[37] "At the right time I will be so presidential that you'll call me and you'll say, 'Donald, you have to stop that'" because "you will be so bored."[38] As of August 2017, no one had called President Trump out of boredom to tell him he was being too presidential. Trump himself decided that although, "with the exception of the late, great Abraham Lincoln, I can be more presidential than any president who has ever held this office, . . . that's not going to get it done. . . . Sadly we have to move a little faster than that."[39]

The remainder of this chapter explains why Trump's early months as president were so ineffective, not just in general terms but also, with few exceptions, in particular aspects of presidential leadership: the formation of Trump's administration; his reliance on unilateral executive action; his relations with the courts, Congress, and state and local governments; his domestic and foreign policies; his approach to presidential communications; and the early discussions—unprecedented for a newly elected president—of how to remove him from office before his four-year term expired.

FORMING THE ADMINISTRATION

Presidents need to accomplish multiple tasks in the aftermath of their election, but none is more important than forming the administration. The dozen or so people whom the president places in key positions on the White House staff and the hundreds who are nominated to fill vital policy making positions in the departments and agencies either will serve the newly installed chief executive ably and faithfully or will fail to do so, with grievous consequences for his influence and effectiveness.

Trump was fortunate to take office when he did. Crises, foreign or domestic, have not been unusual occurrences during presidents' first years, but at least during the nine months after Trump's election, none occurred. Although the world had its share of problems, they were ongoing, not new or urgent. The stock market boomed, rising about 15 percent between November 2016 and August 2017, partly for reasons that had nothing to do with Trump and partly because investors expected that a united Republican government's economic policies would foster a favorable business climate. The economy grew at about the same sluggish but steady 2 percent annual rate that it had since the 2008 financial crisis receded. Inflation and interest rates remained modest, and in May unemployment shrank to 4.3 percent, the lowest rate in sixteen years.

Because he had never served in government, Trump knew very few people who were prepared by virtue of knowledge and experience to occupy the most important positions in his administration. Nor, as a business man who had run his own relatively small private company for several decades, had he ever had to answer to shareholders or a board of directors. Instead, Trump had grown used during decades as a real estate developer to acting on his own, surrounded by a handful of loyal subordinates and family members. Nothing in his professional career or presidential campaign—also small and ad hoc—made him think that he needed to do things any differently as president. Although Trump appointed Governor Chris Christie of New Jersey to lead an intensive transition planning process that would generate a list of able candidates for each appointed position, he fired Christie right after the election because he thought that the governor was trying to slip too many of his own people into the administration.[40] Trump also tossed out all of the research Christie's team had done concerning policy and administration. As a result, the new president took office knowing little about what the executive branch does or who could run it on his behalf.

One consequence of Trump's lack of preparation was that, not having any ideas of his own about how the White House should be organized, he accepted the "institutional presidency" as he inherited it from his recent predecessors: a chief of staff with two deputies, a national security advisor and staff, a National Economic Council director and staff, a communications director and press secretary, a White House counsel, and so on.[41] Vice President Mike Pence had been the sort of running mate whom any Republican presidential nominee might have chosen; he was experienced as a leader in the House of Representatives and as governor of Indiana and enjoyed support from both social and economic conservatives. Once in office, Trump assigned Pence all of the perquisites and responsibilities that vice presidents had been accumulating since the 1970s: a West Wing office, a professional staff, ready access to the president, and a wide ranging role as senior advisor on virtually every issue. Pence also became Trump's most effective liaison to Republicans on Capitol Hill, repairing the previously testy relationship between the president and Speaker of the House Paul Ryan and working to shepherd nominations and other measures through the congressional process.[42]

A second, less fortunate consequence of Trump's lack of relevant experience was that he filled most White House positions by drawing from the small circle of people with whom he had become acquainted during the late stages of his election campaign. These included Republican National Committee chair Reince Priebus as chief of staff, foreign policy adviser Michael Flynn as national security adviser, campaign spokesman Sean Spicer as press secretary, campaign strategist Steve Bannon as chief political strategist, and election lawyer Donald McGahn as counsel. Not knowing these individuals very well, Trump also brought in his daughter Ivanka Trump and her husband Jared Kushner as free-floating advisers. Kushner was charged with tasks as various as infusing business practices into government and "produc[ing] peace in the Middle East," while Ivanka pursued causes that captured her interest, such as persuading her father to propose paid family leave and support a World Bank initiative to help woman entrepreneurs.[43] An axiom of staffing for presidents who lack experience in the federal government is to stock the White House with people who have that experience and then rely on their judgment. Trump took a different approach. The result was that a president who had never spent a day in office was surrounded by advisers who had never spent a day in office.

An additional consequence of Trump's unfamiliarity with both staffing in general and his own staff (Ivanka and Kushner aside) in particular was that he placed aides in unusual relations to each other. Bannon was granted a seat on the principals committee of the National Security Council (NSC), for example, while Priebus was denied real authority to perform the chief's role of managing the flow of information between the president and the staff. Spicer was undermined by Trump's barely concealed scorn for how he handled the press. Lines of responsibility were notoriously unclear in the Trump White House. Factions formed based on ideological differences and personal rivalries. Staff members leaked disparaging comments about each other to the press corps—leaked, that is, until within days of becoming communications director in late July, Anthony Scaramucci unleashed an obscenity-laced public tirade at Priebus and Bannon in the *New Yorker,* saying that within the White House "me and the president" are the only "two fish that don't stink."[44] Priebus was shown the door the following day; within the week, Scaramucci was out as well. Talented prospective appointees, turned off by the turmoil, declined to join the staff. A general air of chaos prevailed. Within six months of Trump's taking office, the White House saw the firing or resignation of his first national security advisor, chief of staff, deputy chief of staff, communications director, press secretary, and other aides. Some, especially Priebus, were so widely rumored to be on the chopping block that they were rendered ineffective even while still nominally on the job.

Trump was equally unfamiliar with the talent pool from which presidents usually draw cabinet members and their high-ranking subordinates: the secretaries, deputy secretaries, undersecretaries, and assistant secretaries who do the real work of governing in the executive branch. Without them, the change-resistant (especially so to Republican changes) permanent civil service, few of whose members voted for Trump, would be free to keep doing things as they had under his Democratic predecessor.[45] In filling the most important executive positions Trump was drawn to people who had succeeded in domains he respected—business (Exxon chief executive Rex Tillerson as secretary of state, investor Steven Mnuchin as secretary of the Treasury) and the military (General James Mattis as secretary of defense, General John F. Kelly as secretary of homeland security and, six months later, as Priebus's replacement as White House chief of staff)—as well as to the small set of Republican politicians who had supported him in the election, notably Senator Jeff Sessions as attorney general. Most of Trump's other cabinet appointees were members of Congress or political figures whose names Trump got from Pence.[46] Early tensions arose between the president and Tillerson and, especially, between Trump and Sessions, who Trump decried as "VERY weak" and "disappoint[ing]," declaring that he wished he had "picked someone else." Outside of his immediate family, loyalty for Trump was something he demanded but did not give.

Urged on by grassroots Democrats who were against everything Trump was for, Democratic senators assumed an unprecedentedly adversarial stance in the confirmation process. Democratic National Committee chair Thomas Perez set the tone by urging his party to hit Trump "between the eyes with a two-by-four."[47] All but five Democratic senators voted against the relatively uncontroversial Tillerson, the most opposition any nominee for secretary of state had ever received. All but one voted against Sessions, whom most Democrats knew as a friend and fellow senator. Because Senate Democrats had abolished the filibuster for all but Supreme Court appointments in 2013, when they controlled the chamber, Trump was able to form his cabinet with only Republican votes. But Democratic delaying tactics meant that the confirmation process for cabinet members took much longer than in the past, an average twenty-five days each compared with two days for Obama's nominees, one day for Clinton's, and zero days for Bush's.[48]

Trump's main problem in forming an administration, however, was not the Democrats but rather his own slowness in filling most of the hundreds of sub-cabinet positions that department heads rely on to help lead their organizations. As late as the end of July, Trump had failed to nominate candidates for 379 of 566—more than two-thirds—of key positions in the executive branch, hampered by a selection process that valued loyalty above competence and gave a half dozen quarreling White House aides veto power over possible nominees. Only 49 of his 187 actual nominees—just 26 percent—had been confirmed by the Senate, compared with 201 at the midpoint of Obama's first year and 185 in Bush's.[49] Ten of fifteen cabinet departments lacked a deputy secretary (second in the departmental chain of command), and 163 of 169 undersecretary and assistant secretary positions remained unfilled. As with the staff, numerous potential candidates for departmental leadership positions, turned off by the perceived chaos within the Trump White House and by Trump's humiliating treatment of Sessions, refused to be considered. Instead, Trump assigned junior White House staff members to each department to monitor the secretaries' behavior.[50]

Many of Trump's early innovations were soon abandoned. After Flynn was forced to resign as national security adviser less than a month into the term for lying to Pence about his post-election discussions with the Russian ambassador, his successor, General H. R. McMaster, insisted that Bannon be removed from the NSC's principals committee.[51] Cabinet members ignored the junior staffers sent to their departments; when one of them told Secretary of Transportation Elaine Chao that he needed to sign off on her decisions, she asked, "What's your name again?"[52] Eventually they were withdrawn. Trump was slow to understand that his disinclination to fill many executive jobs ("I look at some of these jobs and . . . I say, 'What do all these people do?'") was only making his cabinet members and agency heads more dependent on the permanent civil service, which felt no loyalty to him.[53]

In developing domestic and foreign policies in his first year, Trump was frequently surprised to learn that impressions he had formed outside government were misplaced. "Nobody knew that health care could be so complicated," he said, a turnabout from his claim during the campaign that "nobody knows more about health care than Donald Trump."[54] Mattis quickly convinced Trump to defer to the general's view that torture is ineffective.[55] The Chinese were "not currency manipulators," as Trump often had charged, and they lacked the power to dictate policy to North Korea, another assumption abandoned. "After listening [to Chinese president Xi Jinping] for ten minutes," Trump said, "I realized that it's not so easy."[56] As a candidate for president, Trump dismissed NATO as "obsolete." Soon after taking office, he said it was "no longer obsolete."[57] During the campaign Trump promised, "My Number One priority is to dismantle the disastrous nuclear deal with Iran."[58] Twice during his first six months as president his administration certified that Iran was fulfilling its promise not to build nuclear weapons. Trump also confessed, "This is more work than in my previous life. I thought it would be easier."[59]

EXECUTIVE ACTION

In the modern era presidents—especially those whose party controls Congress— usually have turned to unilateral executive actions as the primary means of pursuing their goals only after their efforts to secure legislation have failed. Trump would have done well to adhere to this pattern. His main bastion of institutional support in Washington when he took office was the Republican Congress. During his first year, most congressional Republicans were reluctant to oppose the president and thereby invite primary challenges from ambitious contenders who shared their Republican constituents' early enthusiasm for Trump. Among Republican voters he retained a job approval rating above 80 percent even as his overall rating slid below 40 percent.[60] The executive branch was initially less reliable. Trump's White House staff was inexperienced and divided. Except for cabinet members, the top layers of the executive departments and agencies were mostly unoccupied. This left both staff and cabinet dependent on career civil servants, who in most cases (Immigration and Customs Enforcement and to some extent the Pentagon excepted) were unsympathetic to the new president's agenda.[61]

Yet instead of turning to Congress with his major first-year initiatives—the equivalent in the world of publicly traded corporations of securing approval from a board of directors—Trump's very different business experience prompted him to issue a flurry of executive orders and take other unilateral actions from the beginning of his term.

The appeal of executive actions is that they lie within the president's own authority. With cameras present, Trump was able to sign a series of orders, proclamations, and memorandums without having to wait for Congress to pass laws and send them to his desk. In some cases, the orders were effective. For example, Trump signed one to redirect $100 million from existing federal job-training funds to new apprenticeship programs.[62] Meanwhile, his EPA administrator, Scott Pruitt, who as attorney general of Oklahoma had come to know the agency well by frequently filing lawsuits against it, sought to obstruct dozens of regulations that the president's business supporters disliked.

Executive actions entail certain disadvantages as well, which is why presidents usually turn to them as a last rather than a first resort. For one thing, each can be undone by another action by a subsequent president. Starting with Reagan in 1981, for example, every change of party in the White House has witnessed the immediate issuance of an executive order that either forbids (Reagan and his Republican successors, including Trump) or allows (Clinton and his Democratic successors) giving foreign aid to nongovernmental agencies that offer women abortion counseling or referrals. For another, such actions often are of limited effectiveness. An order cannot repeal a regulation that already has undergone the Administrative Procedures Act's lengthy "notice and comment" process. All the order can do is launch a new, equally lengthy notice and comment process aimed at undoing the regulation, and even then the new process must result in what the Supreme Court has called "a reasoned basis" to explain why the old regulation was wrong and the new one is right.[63] Trump took aim at Obama's 2015 anti-coal Clean Power Plan, for example, but to undo it will entail a years-long process and an almost certain series of legal challenges—with no guarantee of success. As for Pruitt, when he moved to suspend a regulation that restricts methane emissions from new oil and gas wells, a federal appeals court voided his decision as "unreasonable," "arbitrary," and "capricious" and said that he would have to launch the required notice and comment process to have any chance of prevailing.[64]

Trump's first executive order, issued on the day of his inauguration to relevant executive agencies telling them to do whatever they could, "to the maximum extent permitted by law," to rein in the Affordable Care Act (ACA), better known as Obamacare, was only partially effective for yet another reason. It had no specific content, which meant its consequences were wildly uneven from agency to agency. (It did lead the IRS to stop enforcing the penalty for not having health insurance.) The same was true of his order that every department and agency must create a task force to identify existing regulations that should be revised or repealed.

Trump's most controversial executive order was his least successful in one way but perhaps his most successful in another. One week after taking office, Trump issued an order to ban entry to the United States to visitors, even those with a visa, from seven predominantly Muslim nations for 90 days and to ban all refugees from entering the country for 120 days. Devised entirely within the White House, with no advice from the agencies that would have to interpret and enforce it, the order created chaos at airports around the world as officers tried to make sense of what it required. Federal courts undid the original order as well as a revised one, ruling that both of them violated the First Amendment's establishment clause by discriminating against people on the basis of religion. The judges cited statements Trump made as a candidate as evidence of the orders' intent, including his oft-repeated call to bar all Muslims from entering the country. Trump's executive order "speaks with vague words of national security, but in context drips with religious intolerance, animus and discrimination," the Fourth Circuit Court of Appeals ruled.[65]

In late June, the Supreme Court allowed a restricted version of Trump's order to take effect pending a full review of the lower federal courts' decisions in the fall. The real effect of the order was not its legal standing, however, but rather the message it sent to Muslims and Latin Americans who were thinking of coming into the country: in a word, don't even try. Arrests of undocumented immigrants already within the United States rose sharply during the president's first year even as arrests at the nation's southern border—a useful index of how many people are trying to cross into the United States illegally—declined dramatically.[66] The number of visas the state department issued to residents of the countries named in Trump's executive order fell by 55 percent from the previous year.[67]

THE COURTS

Conflict with the courts is atypical of presidents' first years but unsurprising in Trump's case. After several lower federal courts ruled against his travel ban, Trump attacked a "so-called judge" on a district court and lambasted an appeals court hearing as "disgraceful."[68] During the campaign Trump had said that the Indiana-born federal judge who ruled against him in a lawsuit was biased by his "Mexican heritage."[69] Far from denying that he would apply a "litmus test" to judicial nominees, Trump pledged as a candidate that his appointees would "automatically" overturn *Roe v. Wade*, the Court's landmark abortion decision. "I am pro-life and I will be appointing pro-life judges," he promised in his final debate with Clinton.[70] Relying on suggestions from the conservative Heritage Foundation and Federalist Society, Trump already had released lists of judges from which he would choose his Supreme Court nominees, an unprecedented action by a presidential candidate. Evangelical Christians, who in many ways found the thrice-married casino owner and frequent guest on Howard Stern's raunchy radio programs objectionable, rallied to his support in the election based on his strong commitment to a conservative judiciary. Looming over nearly the entire election year, for the first time since George Washington, was the certainty that if Trump were elected, he would have an immediate opportunity to nominate someone to the Court. No sooner had Justice Antonin Scalia died on February 13, 2016, than Senate Republican leader Mitch McConnell vowed that the vacancy would remain unfilled until a new president was elected.

Partisan conflict over judicial nominations was hardly a new feature of American politics by the time Trump became president. Trump's two predecessors, Bush and Obama, had enjoyed great success winning confirmation for their nominees when their own parties controlled the Senate, but not later in their terms when the opposition party took control. Yet even as Senate Democrats removed the filibuster as a barrier to district and appeals court nominations in 2013, they left it unaltered for Supreme Court appointments. They also preserved the "blue slip" tradition that requires consent from both of a state's senators before the Senate judiciary committee will consider a nominee for a federal judgeship in that state. The result was that not just a Supreme Court vacancy but also the opportunity to fill more than a hundred seats on lower federal courts, left open by the Republican Senate during Obama's final two years, awaited Trump when he took office.

Because Scalia had been a leading conservative voice during his three decades as a justice, Trump's nomination of the equally conservative appeals court judge Neil Gorsuch to succeed him did not threaten to change the ideological balance on the Court. Gorsuch acquitted himself well during the confirmation process, demonstrating both a strong command of the law and a thoughtful demeanor. Even so, responding to continuing pressure from party activists, forty-five Senate Democrats opposed his nomination, enough to wage a filibuster that would kill it under existing Senate rules. Unanimous in their support of Gorsuch, Senate Republicans then changed the rules, extending the prohibition against filibusters to all appointments.

With three of the remaining justices in their late seventies or early eighties it seemed possible that Trump would have other opportunities to add new members to the Supreme Court. Two of the three, Ruth Bader Ginsburg and Stephen Breyer, are among the Court's liberals and the other, Anthony Kennedy, is a moderate conservative. Replacing any one of them with a Gorsuch-style strong conservative would move the evenly balanced Court to the right and provoke fevered opposition from Senate Democrats. But with the filibuster gone and Republicans in control of the Senate (and likely to remain so after the 2018 midterm elections, in which they will be defending only nine seats compared with the Democrats' twenty-five), Trump wields a strong hand in the politics of Supreme Court nominations.

The same is true of district and appeals court appointments. In contrast to his executive branch nominations, Trump was quick to send judicial nominees to the Senate, many of them not just conservative but also young. By mid-July, Trump was "on pace to more than double the number of federal judges nominated by any president in his first year."[71] When he took office, a majority of judges on nine of the thirteen federal courts of appeals were Democratic appointees, including the fourth and ninth circuit courts, the two that ruled against the travel ban. With many vacancies to fill and a Republican Senate that shared his judicial philosophy, Trump's prospects for altering the partisan balance on the federal courts were great.

In addition to the travel ban cases, during the president's first year a plethora of other lawsuits were filed challenging Trump administration actions, including his order to bomb Syria and a host of executive orders to reduce environmental regulations and cut off federal aid to "sanctuary cities" that refuse to help arrest undocumented immigrants. His ban on transgender individuals in the military was quickly challenged on constitutional grounds. In addition, Trump faced lawsuits filed by, among others, nearly two hundred Democratic members of Congress and the Democratic attorneys general of Maryland and the District of Columbia urging courts to force his businesses to stop accepting payments from foreign governments. The legal basis of the suits was the Constitution's emoluments clause, which forbids any "Person holding any office of Profit or Trust" from accepting "any present, Emolument, Office or Title, of any kind whatever, from any King, Prince, or foreign State."

The clause, which appears in Article I, section 9, is obscure at best and subject to a wide range of interpretations. It was dusted off by Democrats only because Trump chose neither to sell his businesses when he became president nor to put them into a blind trust. Instead he assigned his two adult sons to run them. Federal judges will have to decide whether, for example, foreign governments renting rooms in the Trump International Hotel in Washington are conferring emoluments on the president, as well as whether courts should rule on the issue rather than leaving it to Congress. As with the Supreme Court, who the judges that make those rulings will be is a matter of urgent interest for the Trump presidency. With twenty-eight states represented in the 115th Congress by at least one Democratic senator, the blue-slip tradition, like the filibuster, was in danger of extinction if it were used to keep Trump's judicial nominations from going forward.

STATES AND CITIES

State governments—at least the minority of them controlled by Democrats— and the larger cities within most Republican states, which are overwhelmingly Democratic—were a source of early and organized opposition to the new president. In 2016 Trump dominated rural counties and small cities while being trounced in the nation's metropolises, state capitals, and college towns. On the day after his election, the hastily organized Women's March protesting Trump's election drew not just a half million marchers to Washington, but another million and a half to Chicago, Los Angeles, and New York (and hundreds of thousands more to Boston, San Francisco, Madison, and scores of other cities). Other large-scale, multicity protests attacked aspects of Trump's presidency on a regular basis, including his unwillingness to release his tax returns and his order to ban transgender individuals from the military. In June alone, 532 anti-Trump protests and demonstrations were held across the country.[72]

Official acts of state and local resistance also marked Trump's first six months in office. Several dozen municipal governments declared themselves to be sanctuary cities whose police forces would not help federal authorities pursue undocumented immigrants. California negotiated a "green technology" agreement with China after Trump withdrew the United States from the Paris climate accord signed by Obama. More than three hundred mayors agreed to abide by the accord and "intensify efforts to meet each of our cities' climate goals."[73] Borrowing a tactic that Republican state attorneys general (including Pruitt) had used against various executive actions by Obama, Democratic state attorneys general filed the lawsuits that led courts to disallow the president's travel ban, as well as filing a suit to prevent Secretary of Education Betsey DeVos from freezing an Obama regulation that would erase the federal debts of students whose colleges had acted fraudulently. In July all but a handful of states—including most of those governed by Republicans—refused some or all of the Trump-formed Presidential Advisory Commission on Election Integrity's requests for information about their voters. Even Republican governors in the thirty-one states that had expanded Medicaid under Obama's Affordable Care Act resisted Trump-supported efforts to reduce federal spending on the program.

As in his dealings with the bureaucracy and the courts, Trump was unprepared for such resistance. Nothing in his long business career had required him to share power. With his absence of governing experience and lack of knowledge about American history, Trump had at best a dim understanding of the sharing of power mandated by the Constitution, both between the state and federal governments and among the branches within the federal government. Examples of his ignorance abounded. Andrew Jackson, Trump said, "was really angry that he saw what was happening in regard to the Civil War."[74] (Jackson died sixteen year before the war.) Speaking of Abraham Lincoln he asked, "Most people don't even know he was a Republican. Right? Does anyone know?"[75] (Yes.) "Frederick Douglass," Trump declared, as if speaking of a living person, "is an example of somebody who's done an amazing job."[76] After mentioning William McKinley to a crowd in Youngstown, Ohio, he wondered, "Does anybody know who the hell he is?"[77] President McKinley's birthplace was twelve miles away,

CONGRESS AND DOMESTIC POLICY

Trump was elected to a favorably disposed united party government, but the Congress with which he entered office was far from a rubber-stamp body. His victory had been narrow and carried no clear policy mandate. In the House, Republican leaders could afford only a twenty-three vote defection in the face of united Democratic opposition. The GOP's still narrower majority in the Senate allowed at most two defections on the limited number of bills, such as health care reform, that could be shoehorned into the filibuster-proof "reconciliation process." Even then, Vice President Pence would have to break tie votes. Other than appointments, most other measures required a nearly unattainable sixty-vote majority to overcome a Democratic filibuster. Depending on the issue, Republican defections might come from the GOP's small moderate "Tuesday Club" wing or, if that group's concerns were placated, from the ultraconservative and much larger "Freedom Caucus." Most Republican members in both chambers were economic conservatives who had been elected on a less populist platform than Trump; they certainly did not share his professed commitment to leave major entitlement programs untouched. As for Democrats, even those who may have preferred to vote for certain Trump-supported bills were hamstrung by party activists who insisted on unrelenting resistance. Like congressional Republicans during the Obama years, congressional Democrats became "the party of no."

In addition, Trump faced a Republican majority on Capitol Hill that was, like him, experienced in opposition but not in governing. The party won control of the House in the 2010 midterm election by opposing Obama; it captured the Senate by opposing him in 2014. In both elections, Republicans succeeded by attacking not just the president but also the entire federal government, which made supporting a legislative program of any kind all the more difficult. This included Trump's plans to build an expensive wall along the southern border; ramp up infrastructure spending on roads, bridges, tunnels, transit systems, waterworks, and airports; and "prime the pump . . . in order to get the economy going, and going big league."[78] "We were a ten-year opposition party," said Republican speaker Paul Ryan, "where being against things was easy to do. And now . . . we actually have to get 218 people to agree with each other on how we do things."[79] "We just simply don't know how to govern," echoed Representative Steve Womack of Arkansas.[80]

The Republicans' success in passing a flurry of Trump-supported deregulation bills in the early months of his presidency was the exception that demonstrates the rule. They won vote after vote on measures passed under the Congressional Review Act (CRA) of 1996. That act granted the new Congress sixty legislative days to revoke regulations issued by the executive branch during much of the previous year, with no Senate filibusters allowed. Until 2017 it had been used only once. But, seeing the CRA as a way of continuing to oppose Obama's policies even after he left office, Congress passed and Trump signed bills to repeal fourteen late Obama administration regulations, including one that would have prevented internet service providers from selling their customers' data and another that authorized state governments to offer retirement accounts to private sector workers. The tactic was entirely negative and served as a short-term expedient at best. On May 11, 2017—less than four months into Trump's term—the deadline for using the CRA was reached and its usefulness as a tool of presidential influence expired.

Midway through Trump's first year, Congress had yet to pass a single piece of major legislation, belying his blatantly inaccurate claim that "we've signed more bills—and I'm talking about through the legislature—than any president, ever."[81] Of the forty-two he did sign (fewer than the average number signed by his six most recent predecessors), most were minor, including one to rename a federal courthouse in Tennessee and another three to add board members to the Smithsonian Institution. To be sure, Republicans legislators united with the president in focusing relentlessly on their shared campaign promise to "repeal and replace" the ACA. As had been the case when Obama was president, Trump and his congressional party knew what they were against. Starting as soon as the Republicans won control of the House in 2010, that chamber voted to repeal or amend the ACA more than fifty times; when the Senate did so in 2015, Obama vetoed the measure, as they knew he would. During his presidential campaign Trump promised again and again "to end, terminate, repeal Obamacare and replace it with something really, really great that works."[82] But agreeing on what he and the Republican Congress were for was a challenge they were unprepared to meet, in part because they had not expected Trump to win the election.[83]

With little guidance from the administration, Republican House leaders began 2017 by writing a bill that the nonpartisan Congressional Budget Office (CBO) estimated would leave 24 million more Americans uninsured in ten years than if Obamacare remained on the books. Ryan canceled a scheduled floor vote on March 24 when it became obvious that the bill would not pass. He and his fellow party leaders modified the measure somewhat (only 23 million more would be uninsured) and on May 4 rammed it through the House on a 217–213 vote, with Democratic members unanimous in opposition. The bill then went to the Senate, where it was modified further under the guidance of Majority Leader McConnell (22 million more uninsured) but did not come close to uniting enough Republican senators to bring it to the floor. McConnell found that every moderate Republican vote he could attract by covering more people cost the bill several conservative Republican votes because of the added expense. Opposition from three conservative Senate Republicans doomed one version of the bill. When McConnell revised it to placate them, three moderate Republicans defected. Senate Democrats stood on the sidelines and, to a one, enjoyed watching the chamber's Republican majority refuse to cohere, leaving Obamacare intact. As for Trump, during the week that these efforts failed, he took four positions in three days: first he supported the McConnell bill, then he proposed repealing the ACA without replacing it, then he suggested that Republicans "let Obamacare fail" by doing nothing, and finally he pressured Republican senators to replace it after all.[84]

Desperate to pass something, McConnell brought three measures to the Senate floor during the last week of July. Republican defectors doomed all three. Nine Republican senators voted against a repeal-and-replace bill, seven against a repeal-only measure, and three against a "skinny repeal" bill that preserved Obamacare while abolishing the mandate that individuals have and large employers offer health insurance. Meanwhile, other much-touted Trump legislative priorities, such as tax reform, enhancing the nation's infrastructure, and passing a budget were weakly developed and stuck in traffic behind health care reform.

Congressional Republican futility in enacting a legislative program was aggravated by Trump's failure to provide effective leadership. He began by wasting the postelection transition period. Most new presidents use that time to develop detailed legislative proposals and staff the White House with at least some experienced veterans of Capitol Hill. Trump did neither. His interventions during the health care debate in the House were so clumsy ("I'm going to come after you," he emptily threatened House Freedom Caucus chair Mark Meadows, who had won his seat by a hundred thousand votes in 2016) that McConnell politely spurned his request to help out in the Senate.[85] Trump's public rhetoric was erratic, swerving from one petty complaint to another on Twitter instead of consistently rousing public opinion to support his policy proposals. Even when he did talk about health care, Trump veered from praising the House bill as a "great plan" that was "very, very, incredibly well-crafted" to condemning it as "mean" rather than "generous, kind, with heart."[86] Legislators seldom forget casting a tough vote in support of a president only to have him criticize them for it later.

As the author of *The Art of the Deal*, Trump prided himself on his ability to persuade others to do what he wanted and promised voters during the campaign that he would use his business acumen to make favorable deals for the American people. But as George Tsebelis has observed, the president can't deal with "an alternative Congress" the way a real estate developer can choose a different lender or contractor if the one he is negotiating with refuses to meet his terms.[87] As Trump's public approval rating quickly sank below 40 percent, his leverage on Capitol Hill further declined, despite his odd claim that "almost 40% is not bad at this time."[88] Reelection-seeking Democratic senators from states Trump carried handily, such as Joe Manchin of West Virginia and Heidi Heitkamp of North Dakota, breathed a sigh of relief when they saw how steeply his support in their states declined. Underlying all these sources of Trump's ineffectiveness with Congress was his lack either of factual knowledge about his own proposals or consistent guiding principles that could make up, as they did for Reagan, for this lack of knowledge. On Capitol Hill, Trump increasingly was neither feared nor loved.

COMMUNICATIONS

Trump's public communications during the 2016 presidential campaign were as brilliant as they were unorthodox. Most candidates for president, including Clinton and Trump's rivals for the Republican nomination, followed the standard campaign playbook: raise as much money as possible for paid media—that is, television, radio, and web-based advertising—so that they can control their message to the voters. In unscripted events, especially televised debates, the textbook strategy was to be as scripted as possible, delivering well-rehearsed sound bites regardless of the questions that are asked.

In sharp contrast, the Trump campaign downplayed paid media, partly because he rather than political donors was paying most of the bills and partly because he had no problem making the sort of news that attracted massive coverage—so-called earned media. Cable news networks televised many of his speeches live, responding to the ratings surge that occurred whenever they showed him. Trump, after all, in addition to being a business man, was a celebrity. Before entering politics in 2015 he had built a large audience as a bestselling author of braggadocious business books, a frequent talk-show guest, a fixture in tabloids for his many romances, a guest battler in WWE spectacles, and the star of the popular NBC television series *The Apprentice* and *Celebrity Apprentice*. Trump's debate appearances during the campaign, like his speeches, were freewheeling and spontaneous.

His main early rival for the Republican nomination, former Florida governor Jeb Bush, practically wilted when Trump branded him "low-energy" in one debate.

In addition to free television, Trump made masterful and unprecedented use of a relatively new social medium: Twitter. Within the constraints of the 140-character "tweet" format, he could send messages directly to millions of voters, who in turn forwarded them to millions more. Trump used tweets to proclaim ("MAKE AMERICAN GREAT AGAIN!"), to attack ("Hillary Clinton should have been prosecuted and should be in jail. Instead she is running for president in what looks like a rigged election."), and to defend ("For those few people knocking me for tweeting at three o'clock in the morning, at least you know I will be there, awake, to answer the call!").[89] "Without the tweets I wouldn't be here," Trump said after taking office.[90]

As a candidate Trump acknowledged that being president would be different than running for president. Concerning Twitter, he said, "I'll give it up after I'm president. We won't tweet any more. I don't know. Not presidential."[91] For a time, at least, Trump seemed to grasp the distinction between campaigning and governing. Campaigns are won by defeating a series of opponents. The words spoken by a candidate, however specific, have no direct effect on the conduct of government. Governing is about securing cooperation from other constitutional actors in a government of "separated institutions sharing powers."[92] Words, spoken no longer by a presidential candidate but by a president, often have important consequences.

By inauguration eve, Trump had forgotten the difference and changed his mind about tweeting. "I think I'll keep it. . . . It's working," he said.[93] He did keep it, averaging about five tweets per day during his first six months in office. As Michael Kruse has pointed out, Trump's tweets assumed a distinctive, almost genre-like form: "a one-sentence declaration, . . . followed usually by a one-word assertion of emotion: 'Weak!' 'Strong!' 'WIN!' 'Terrible!' 'Sad! 'BAD!'"[94] Sometimes these messages, however visceral, involved presidential-level public policy—for example, the ACA is "horrible," "imploding," "dead." More often, however, Trump's tweets were impulsive, petty, aimed at small targets, and distinctly unpresidential—not just undignified but also ineffective. His tweets tore down much more effectively than they built up. "Crooked Hillary" and "Fake News" took root in a way that "great healthcare" and "a great plan" did not.[95]

Trump was especially attuned to criticisms he heard during long stretches watching cable news programs. He often reacted in the moment. At 9:00 a.m. on June 28, for example, apparently while viewing *Morning Joe* on MSNBC, the president tweeted an attack on cohosts "low I.Q. Crazy Mika" Brzezinski and "Psycho Joe" Scarborough, adding that in a recent meeting Brzezinski "was bleeding badly from a face lift."[96] A few days later he retweeted a 2007 video of himself body-slamming WWE owner Vince McMahon at a WrestleMania event, with McMahon's head replaced by a CNN logo. These tweets were posted during the administration's planned "Energy Week," seven days in which Trump was urged by aides to direct the nation's attention to his policies promoting oil, gas, and nuclear production. He spent much of "Made in America" week tweeting attacks on Sessions.

Other targets of Trump's tweets included Arnold Schwarzenegger, comedian Kathy Griffin, *Saturday Night Live,* Germany, Sweden, Chicago, Nordstrom, the federal judiciary, "Cryin' Chuck Schumer," Barack Obama, the mayor of London, and, repeatedly, "Fake News CNN, . . . NBC, CBS & NBC, . . . the failing @nytimes & @washingtonpost. They are all Fake News." "Please just stop," an exasperated Republican senator Ben Sasse of Nebraska tweeted in response. "This isn't normal and it's beneath the dignity of your office." More than that, some of Trump's tweets provided fodder for judges ruling against the anti-Muslim bias of his travel ban and investigators looking into Russia's role in his election and his motives for firing FBI director James Comey. A former Central Intelligence Agency analyst even described Trump's tweets as "a gold mine for every foreign intelligence agency" because they provided direct evidence of his "stress level and state of mind" as well as his "preoccupations, personality quirks, and habits."[97]

To the extent that a strategy governed Trump's communications it was to solidify his base of supporters, the main consumers of his tweets. Trump's inaugural address, for example, painted a dystopian portrait of "American carnage" marked by "the crime and the gangs and the drugs," "the ravages of other countries," and closed factories "like tombstones"—similarly to his campaign speeches, but in sharp contrast to all fifty-seven previous inaugural addresses, each of which invoked deeply rooted American values and appealed for national unity. Further uprooting long-established traditions Trump bragged to the National Scout Jamboree about various states he carried in the election and urged naval personnel to contact Congress in support of his healthcare legislation. He was chastised by the Boy Scouts of America's chief executive for the first speech and by various military officers for the second.[98] Most of Trump's public speeches as president were stream-of-consciousness orations at campaign-style rallies held in states he carried in the election; not once did Trump deliver an address to the nation explaining and defending his major legislative priority, repealing and replacing Obamacare. His recurring attacks on the "MSM" (mainstream media) as "the enemy of the America People" were designed to discredit the information these outlets reported and steer his supporters to pro-Trump web sites and social media groups, as well as conservative talk radio and Fox News.[99]

FOREIGN POLICY

In matters of foreign policy, Trump took office with no experience, little knowledge, and hardly any connections with people who did have experience and knowledge. During the campaign he offered a series of bold statements whose theme was that although recent presidents had been inept and weak in their dealings with the rest of the world, he would put "America First," winning back jobs that had gone overseas, securing the nation's borders, avoiding feckless wars, and forging agreements with foreign leaders from a position of military strength. After his election Trump disdained the daily intelligence briefings that could have brought him up to speed on the issues for which he would be responsible as president. "You know, I'm, like, a smart person," he explained. "I don't have to be told the same things in the same words every single day for the next eight years."[100]

Trump talked with real relish during the campaign about applying his deal-making skills as a real estate developer to negotiations with other heads of government. In his first hundred days in office, he hosted sixteen meetings with foreign leaders and had phone conversations with forty-three, often placing or returning calls without being briefed by foreign policy specialists in his administration.[101] In many cases, these meetings and conversations led the president to change his mind. Chinese president Xi Jinping easily convinced Trump that his country was not, as Trump often had declared during the election, a "currency manipulator," and King Abdullah II of Jordan readily persuaded him not to keep his campaign promise to move the American embassy in Israel to Jerusalem, which Trump had vowed to do on "Day One" of his presidency.[102]

Trump quickly forsook other rashly made campaign promises as well. As a candidate he proclaimed that he was "psyched" to terminate NAFTA, "the worst trade deal maybe ever signed anywhere"; that "Islam hates us"; that NATO is "obsolete"; that it was "time to get out of Afghanistan"; and that the war in Iraq was "one of the great mistakes in the history of our country."[103] Yet early in his first year as president Trump decided to try to renegotiate rather than repeal NAFTA, described Islam as "one of the world's great religions," declared the United States would "strongly support NATO," authorized the secretary of defense to intensify the war in Afghanistan, and maintained the American military presence in Iraq.[104] He did, however, keep certain campaign promises that were consistent with his America First theme, such as withdrawing the United States from the Trans-Pacific Partnership and the Paris climate accord.

Trump's oscillations in foreign policy reflected his lack of considered opinions ("I like to think of myself as a very flexible person") and, more importantly, strong divisions among his advisors.[105] His foreign policy team consisted largely of generals and business leaders whom he admired for their success in war and commerce, domains that (in contrast to civilian government service) he regarded highly. Secretary of State Tillerson, Secretary of the Treasury Steve Mnuchin, and National Economic Council Director Gary Cohn came from the world of business. Secretary of Defense Mattis and National Security Advisor Michael Flynn were high-ranking generals in the Marine Corps and army, respectively. All but Flynn were internationalists who wanted to steer Trump away from unilateralism and isolation. When Flynn was replaced just weeks into the administration by H. R. McMaster, another army general, the team became uniformly internationalist. In addition to his high regard for these individuals and their views, Trump also delegated most military decisions to Mattis and, through the defense secretary, to the uniformed military. Early decisions to drop the largest conventional bomb in history on an ISIS bunker complex and to arm the Syrian Kurds were made by Mattis, who in turn empowered theatre commanders in Yemen and Somalia to launch strikes on their own authority.

The nationalists in Trump's administration were civilians concentrated mostly in the White House, notably political strategist Steve Bannon and policy adviser and speechwriter Stephen Miller. Their influence was based less on Trump's respect for their expertise or pre-governmental accomplishments than on the loyalty they displayed during the campaign and their fidelity to his America First theme. Presidential speeches often became battlegrounds between them and the internationalists. Trump's May 25 speech to NATO, for example, originally included a twenty-seven word statement pledging his country's "unwavering . . . commitment to the NATO alliance," which the internationalists wanted. But it was excised from the version Trump actually delivered by the nationalists.[106] In July, a major foreign policy address in Warsaw became a pastiche of nationalist and internationalist themes, embracing NATO but speaking darkly about the decline of the West and asking, "Do we have enough respect for our citizens to respect our borders? Do we have the desire and courage to preserve our civilization in the face of those who would subvert and destroy it?"

Some foreign policy issues were less matters of nationalist-internationalist conflict within the Trump administration than of the president's own confusion. During the campaign, Trump wondered, "If we could get along with Russia, wouldn't that be a good thing?"[107] Of Russian leader Vladimir Putin, he said, "I've always had a good instinct about Putin. . . . He's running his country and at least he's a leader, unlike what we have in this country."[108] What infuriated Trump was the great mass of evidence proving that Putin's government had covertly worked to help elect him by undermining Clinton, who had locked horns with the Russians several times as secretary of state. His reaction once in office was to oscillate between efforts to reach out to Putin and contradictory attempts to prove his independence by, for example, launching a cruise missile attack against the Syrian government, Russia's ally, when it used chemical weapons in its civil war. Nor did Trump ever let go of his anger at news stories and justice department and congressional investigations probing Putin's support for his election, which in Trump's mind were designed to devalue his victory. The day after his son Donald Trump Jr. released emails showing that the Russian government wanted Trump to win, the president strangely claimed that Putin "would like Hillary [because] she wants to have windmills" and "wouldn't have spent the money on military" that Trump was spending.[109] In the face of administration opposition Senate Republicans, long antagonistic toward Russia, and Senate Democrats, deeply antagonistic to Trump, put aside their differences and voted 98–2 in June for a bill that would impose new sanctions on Russia and require the president to seek congressional approval before lifting them. The House passed a similar measure in July by an equally veto-proof majority of 419–3.

Despite this troubled record, in one area of the world, Trump gave early signs of perhaps exceeding expectations. Unlike his recent predecessors in the White House, he took a purely transactional approach to the Middle East, putting aside concerns about democracy and human rights in the region that previous presidents had pursued ineffectively. He strengthened the American commitment to Israel, expressing indifference toward "two-state and one-state" solutions to the Palestinian question. "I like the one that both parties like," he said. "I can live with either one."[110] At the same time Trump forged a much stronger connection with Saudi Arabia and its allies than Obama had by focusing narrowly on their shared goals of defeating ISIS, which suffered serious military setbacks in spring and summer 2017, and reining in Iran. This sometimes put him at odds with his secretaries of state and defense, who were hoping to mediate a conflict between Saudi Arabia and Qatar when Trump intervened with a tweet labeling Qatar as a "funder of terrorism."[111]

REMOVAL

Challenges to Trump's constitutional legitimacy were an ongoing part of his presidency, starting the day after the election when protesters in several cities chanted "Not my president!" For weeks afterward, college administrators and faculty treated the results as a traumatic event for their students. On the eve of Trump's inauguration, the respected civil rights leader and sixteen-term Democratic congressman John Lewis of Georgia said that he did not regard Trump as a "legitimate president."[112] Nearly seventy Democratic members of Congress boycotted the inaugural ceremony after Trump tweeted that Lewis was "all talk, talk, talk—no action or results."[113] Grassroots party activists regarded Trump as a sexist, racist, unqualified bully who had both gamed the system by winning the Electoral College while losing the national popular vote and cheated it by colluding with, or at least benefiting from, the covert Russian campaign to defeat Clinton.

Efforts to find a way to remove Trump from office began almost immediately after he took the oath. Constitutionally, two mechanisms exist that allow a president's tenure to be ended against his will before the expiration of the four-year term. The first, impeachment, has been in the Constitution from the beginning. If a majority of the House of Representatives and, after a Senate-conducted trial, two-thirds of that chamber decide that the president is guilty of "Treason, Bribery, or other high Crimes and Misdemeanors," he is removed from office. The second, which took effect with the enactment of the Twenty-Fifth Amendment in 1967, concerns presidential disability. If the vice president and a majority of the heads of the fifteen cabinet departments decide that for reasons of mental or physical incapacity "the President is unable to discharge the powers and duties of his office," the vice president shall "immediately" become "Acting President" until such time as the president declares that "no inability exists." If the vice president and cabinet disagree with the president's claim to be able, Congress has twenty-one days to decide who is right, with a two-thirds vote in both houses needed to unseat the president. Anticipating that an "unable" president might fire the cabinet to keep it from meeting, the amendment also permits Congress to authorize some "other body" to act in the cabinet's place.

Historically, only two presidents have been impeached by the House, Andrew Johnson in 1868 and Bill Clinton in 1998. No president has been forced out by the vice president and cabinet on grounds of disability, nor has a vice president and cabinet ever tried to do so. Both Johnson and Clinton were charged with having committed various acts that violated their constitutional duty to "take care that the Laws be faithfully executed." Both survived the Senate trial, Johnson barely and Clinton handily. The one president who was driven from office through the impeachment process was Richard Nixon, who resigned in 1974 in the face of certain removal.

In Trump's case, impeachment talk moved from left-wing social media to mainstream telecasts and publications and the halls of Congress less than four months into his term, after he fired FBI director James Comey on May 9 for continuing to investigate possible criminal links between Russia and the Trump election campaign. As Trump publicly explained the firing two days later, "I said to myself, I said, 'You know, this Russia thing with Trump and Russia is a made-up story. It's an excuse by the Democrats for having lost an election that they should have won.'"[114] According to Comey, in a private meeting on February 14, the day after Flynn resigned as national security advisor, Trump told him, "I hope you can see your way clear to letting this go, to letting Flynn go. He is a good guy." Comey said he took the request "as a direction," greeted it with a noncommittal "he is a good guy," and continued the investigation.[115] Frustrated, Trump reportedly tried, again without success, to persuade national intelligence director Dan Coats and National Security Agency director Mike Rogers to deny publicly that there had been any collusion between his campaign and Russia and also to ask Comey to back off the Flynn investigation.[116]

Democratic leaders who had harshly attacked Comey during the election for criticizing Clinton's mishandling of classified emails when she was secretary of state now lionized him for standing up to Trump. On May 13 a prominent Democratic constitutional scholar, Laurence Tribe, argued in the *Washington Post* that Trump's expression of "hope" that Comey would drop the Flynn investigation and his subsequent firing of the director constituted obstruction of justice. This, Tribe argued, was an even worse "high Crime and Misdemeanor" than the ones that drove Nixon from office because it "involv[ed] national security matters vastly more serious than the 'third-rate' burglary that Nixon tried to cover up in Watergate."[117] On May 24, Representative Al Green, a Texas Democrat, announced that he was drafting articles of impeachment based on Trump's conduct toward Comey, and on June 12 Democratic representative Brad Sherman of California actually did so. Most Republicans either defended Trump or remained silent, but

Senator McCain said that the controversy was of "Watergate size and scale" and Representative Justin Amash of Michigan declared that Comey's allegations, if true, were grounds for impeachment.[118]

On May 17, eight days after Comey was fired, deputy attorney general Rod Rosenstein appointed former FBI director Robert S. Mueller III as special counsel to investigate the allegations about Russia and the Trump campaign. Rosenstein made the decision because Attorney General Sessions had recused himself from the matter on March 2 after it was revealed that during his Senate confirmation hearing he had failed to mention two meetings with the Russian ambassador. Then and later Trump was furious at Sessions for ceding control of the investigation. On July 19 he told the *New York Times* that if Sessions "was going to recuse himself he should have told me before he took the job and I would have picked somebody else."[119] For weeks afterward, Trump belittled Sessions in a series of tweets and interviews.

Mueller made clear that he would turn over any evidence that Trump had obstructed justice to Congress as part of a possible impeachment proceeding. Depending on the results of Mueller's investigation, as well as on continuing congressional and media revelations of other troubling presidential conduct, public opinion may turn so strongly against Trump as to persuade enough Republican members that it is politically safe to abandon him. Strong though Republican voters' early support for Trump was, a measurable number of them began leaving the party because they disapproved of him so strongly.[120] Trump's insistent unwillingness to admit that Russia had worked on his behalf gave the July revelation that Donald Jr. and Kushner had met with a Russian lawyer the previous June the appearance of a cover-up, even though the meeting produced nothing and did not include the candidate himself. Trump and Kushner took the meeting because they had been promised "official documents" that would "incriminate Hillary" as part of "Russia and its government's support for Mr. Trump."[121]

Any decision to remove a president is also, by implication, a decision to place someone else in the office, and many Republican members of Congress would be much happier with President Pence than President Trump. Pence remained unwaveringly loyal to Trump's policies but consistently distanced himself from controversial "stories about the time before he joined the ticket."[122] He even created a political action committee—the Great America Committee—to fund his political travel, something no previous vice president had done. Personal loyalty to Trump among Republican legislators, never great to begin with, was shredded by his disrespectful treatment of Sessions, as well as by threats to senators such as Dean Heller and Lisa Murkowski.[123] The Democrats may well take control of the House in the 2018 midterm election and, depending on the extent of Trump's unpopularity, conceivably could buck the odds and win the Senate. Such an outcome would make impeachment by a majority of the Democrat-controlled House likely and perhaps alarm enough Republican senators so that a two-thirds majority for removal could be forged in that chamber.

Finding the impeachment process too difficult to navigate, some critics who wanted Trump forced from office offered the Twenty-fifth Amendment as an alternate route. By the time Democratic representative Jamie Raskin of Maryland introduced a bill in June 2017 to remove the Trump-appointed cabinet from disability determinations and replace it with a "Commission on Presidential Capacity" consisting mostly of physicians and psychiatrists, a few conservative columnists, including Ross Douthat and George F. Will, and former Republican officials such as Eliot Cohen had already argued that Trump was unfit by reason of temperament, character, and mental health to be president. By July nearly sixty thousand self-identified "mental health professionals" had signed a petition declaring that "Trump manifests a serious mental illness" and "should be removed from office" under the terms of the amendment.[124]

To the extent that the disability approach was based on ease of accomplishment, it probably is misguided. Even if the cabinet was replaced by a medical board, the amendment cannot be used against an unwilling president without the vice president's agreement. And if the president were to appeal an adverse decision to Congress, as Trump certainly would, a two-thirds majority of both chambers, not just of the Senate, would have to vote against him. Even if they did, he could start the process all over again (and again) by claiming that his disability was ended. The premise of the amendment is that the president retains the office even when shorn of its powers and duties, and that these should be restored to him as soon as he is well.

The field of contenders for the 2016 Republican presidential nomination included seven governors and six senators, all of whose experience in high government office deeply embedded them in the talent pool from which nearly every recent president has been drawn. If any of them had been elected, however, he would have taken office facing problems similar to those Trump encountered. The governing coalition forged under Ronald Reagan was in the same late stage of regime decay that had limited previous presidents at similar moments in political time. In view of the close partisan division in the country, it is unlikely that any candidate would have been elected by a much larger margin or enjoyed a much more favorably disposed Congress than Trump. All of them would have suffered attacks on their legitimacy from the other party akin to those faced by Trump's most recent predecessors: Clinton, Bush, and Obama.

In all likelihood, Trump understood none of these things, any of which might have given him a more accurate sense of his precarious political status as a first-year president in 2017 than he actually had. During the seventeen months of his presidential campaign, the nearly three months of his transition from president-elect to president, and his first six months in office, Trump displayed virtually no knowledge of history, no awareness of the depth of fierce partisan opposition all presidents faced during the previous quarter-century, and no comprehension of how narrow his victory was. Trump actually thought that he had won the "biggest" electoral vote victory since Reagan (not even close), that he had outpolled Hillary Clinton in the national popular vote (false to an extent unsurpassed in American political history), and that the Russian government had tried to help get her elected president rather than, as was actually the case, helping him.[125]

As Paul Light has shown, a president's political influence usually declines over the course of the four-year term—but seldom, as Trump's did, during the first half of the first year. One reason Trump's political standing in Congress and the country was low from the start was the relentless hostility of Democratic officeholders and voters, spurred on by the party's grassroots activists. Another was that both he and the Republican Congress had been elected by attacking the federal government, not by advancing a positive agenda that could translate into legislative accomplishments. But the most important reason was Trump's own insensitivity toward anyone, in government or out, who disagreed with him about anything and his unwillingness to reach out, as most presidents do at least symbolically, to the unconverted. Trump's inaugural address, for example, violated all the traditions of unifying rhetoric that have marked inaugurals since George Washington first took the oath in 1789. So did his wild charge that President Obama "had my 'wires tapped' in Trump Tower just before the victory."[126]

Presidential effectiveness usually grows even as presidential influence declines. Presidents become more surefooted in the job by doing it. They get better because they cram during the transition period, surround themselves (sometimes sooner, but always later) with advisors experienced in government, and learn from their mistakes. Trump was arguably the first exception to all of these rules in the history of the presidency. Claiming that he makes great decisions "with very little knowledge other than the knowledge I [already] had, plus the words 'common sense' because I have a lot of common sense and I have a lot of business ability," he added: "I could actually run my business and run the government at the same time." "I'm president. Hey, I'm president," he marveled. "Can you believe it?"[127] "The president's new at this," said Speaker Ryan. "I think President Trump is learning the job," added Senate Republican leader McConnell, with (unintended?) condescension. Idaho congressman Mike Simpson was more blunt: "At first it was 'Well, this is the guy we elected. He'll learn, he'll learn. And you just don't see that happening."[128]

"We need a truly great leader," Trump said during the campaign. "We need a leader that wrote The Art of the Deal."[129] His confidence about his deal-making expertise was overweening. "I deal with Steve Wynn. I deal with Carl Icahn," he boasted, referring to two well-known businessmen. "I deal with killers that blow these [politicians] away. It's not even the same category. This [politics] is a category that's like nineteen levels lower."[130] Overconfidence blinded Trump to the reality that unlike the desire to make and maximize profits that animates the private economy, the motivations of legislators, judges, lobbyists, journalists, state and local officials, and other heads of government are varied, complex, and subtle. So is the reason these actors must be dealt with. The president cannot, for example, plausibly threaten to walk away when negotiations break down with Congress and find another legislature to deal with. Nor can he fire and replace the several million civil servants whom he must rely on to implement his decisions. Trump "never seems to recognize how much leverage he has or doesn't have, or what his negotiating partners might need," Michael Grunwald observed. "He just blurts out what he thinks should happen and then distributes the blame when it doesn't."[131] Midway through Trump's first year, having blown any chance for even a short honeymoon and failed to take advantage of a unified party government, not a single important piece of legislation that he supported had been enacted.

Trump's presidential candidacy came less than a quarter century after the independent campaigns launched in the 1990s by another celebrity business leader, Ross Perot. Perot, like Trump, led in the polls for a period of time. Like Trump, Perot caught fire with his appealing performances in debates. But like Trump, too, once Perot's snappy one-liners were exhausted, the shallowness of his understanding of the challenges a president faces and his unwillingness to learn more about them became all too apparent. Yet by spring 2017 Perot's unusual success as an independent candidate and Trump's election as the Republican nominee already had made at least two Democratic billionaires, hedge fund virtuoso Tom Steyer and Dallas Mavericks owner Mark Cuban, begin considering candidacies of their own in 2020.[132]

President of the United States of America, the most powerful office in the world, is not an entry-level government job. Appeals such as "I'm not part of that mess" or "My success in business (or academe or the media or some other realm) proves that I can lead the government" may sound good in an election campaign, but a candidacy built on them is ungrounded in reality. Presidents need certain skills if they are to lead the nation effectively.[133] Skills of political rhetoric and bargaining seem to be developed best by running for office and serving in government for a period of years. The same can be said of the subtle but vital capacity to sense the public's willingness to be led in different directions at different paces at different times. The challenges of administrative management are different in government than in the corporate sphere. Success in the private sector speaks well of a person and usually requires some of these skills, although Trump's lack of pre-presidential accountability to boards of directors and shareholders made his experience in the business world even less relevant to governing than that developed by the heads of publicly traded corporations. But only politics requires all of the skills and knowledge necessary to be an effective president in the first year and beyond.[134]

Fortunately for the country, not everything hinges on the president. The Constitution created a system of "separated institutions sharing powers" both among the three branches of the federal government and between the federal government and the states. It safeguarded the right of the people to speak, publish, petition, and assemble. From the resistance to Trump that emerged in Congress, the courts, the bureaucracy, the states and localities, the media, and the opposition party, he was taught the hard way what most of the country has rejoiced in for more than two centuries: that the American constitutional system is well designed "to counteract ambition" when ambition aspires to roam directionless and unrestrained.

NOTES

1. Ryan Grim and Danny Shea, "A Note about Our Coverage of Donald Trump's 'Campaign,'" Huffington Post, July 17, 2015, http://www.huffingtonpost.com/entry/a-note-about-our-coverage-of-donald-trumps-campaign_us_55a8fc9ce4b0896514d0fd66.

2. Natalie Jackson, "HuffPost Forecast Hillary Clinton Will Win with 323 Electoral Votes," Huffington Post, November 7, 2016, http://www.huffingtonpost.com/entry/polls-hillary-clinton-win_us_5821074ce4b0e80b02cc2a94; Sam Wang, "Is 99% a Reasonable Probability?" Princeton Electoral Consortium, November 6, 2016, http://election.princeton.edu/2016/11/06/is-99-a-reasonable-probability/; and Peter Baker, Obama: The Call of History (New York: Callaway, 2017), 290. Even FiveThirtyEight gave Trump only a 28 percent chance of winning. "Who Will Win the Presidency?" FiveThirtyEight, November 8, 2016, https://projects.fivethirtyeight.com/2016-election-forecast/.

3. Louis Jacobson, "Donald Trump's Electoral College Victory Was Not a 'Massive Landslide,'" PolitiFact, December 12, 2016, http://www.politifact.com/truth-o-meter/statements/2016/dec/12/donald-trump/donald-trumps-electoral-college-victory-was-not-ma/; and Rebecca Savrankly, "Trump Falsely Claims He Got Biggest Electoral College Win since Reagan," The Hill, February 16, 2017, http://thehill.com/business-a-lobbying/donald-trump-falsely-claims-biggest-electoral-win-since-reagan.

4. Two Trump-pledged electors defected, one to Ohio governor John Kasich and the other to former Texas congressman Ron Paul. Four Clinton-pledged electors in Washington and one in Hawaii cast three votes for former general Colin Powell, one for Vermont senator Bernie Sanders, and one for Yankton Sioux Nation leader Faith Spotted Eagle.

5. Aaron Blake, "Trump Claims None of Those 3 to 5 Million Illegal Votes Were Cast for Him. None," Washington Post, January 26, 2017, https://www.washingtonpost.com/news/the-fix/wp/2017/01/25/donald-trump-claims-none-of-those-3-to-5-million-illegal-votes-were-cast-for-him-zero/?utm_term=.12419deb439b.

6. "Trump Reversal on Obama Birthplace Conspiracy Stokes More Controversy," Chicago Tribune, September 16, 2016.

7. "Transcript: Donald Trump's Taped Comments about Women," New York Times, October 8, 2016, https://www.nytimes.com/2016/10/08/us/donald-trump-tape-transcript.html?mcubz=0.

8. Ben Schreckinger, "Trump Attacks McCain: 'I Like People Who Weren't Captured,'" Politico, July 18, 2015, http://www.politico.com/story/2015/07/trump-attacks-mccain-i-like-people-who-werent-captured-120317.

9. Paul J. Quirk, "The Presidency: Donald Trump and the Question of Fitness," in The Elections of 2016, ed. Michael Nelson (Washington: CQ Press, 2018), 189–216.

10. Nick Gass, "Trump Promises to Create 25 Million Jobs with Economic Plan," Politico, September 15, 2015, http://www.politico.com/story/2016/09/donald-trump-jobs-economic-plan-228218; Caitlin Yilek, "Trump: I Will Eliminate U.S. Debt in 8 Years," The Hill, April 2, 2016, http://thehill.com/blogs/ballot-box/presidential-races/275003-trump-i-will-eliminate-us-debt-in-8-years; "Here's Donald Trump's Presidential Announcement Speech," Time, June 16, 2015, http://time.com/3923128/donald-trump-announcement-speech/.

11. Melissa Chan, "Donald Trump Wants Military to Hatch Plan to Stop ISIS in 30 Days," Time, September 7, 2016, http://time.com/4481791/donald-trump-isis-30-days/.

12. "Here's Donald Trump's Presidential Announcement Speech."

13. "The CNN-Telemundo Debate Transcript, Annotated," *Washington Post*, February 25, 2016, https://www.washingtonpost.com/news/the-fix/wp/2016/02/25/the-cnntelemundo-republican-debate-transcript-annotated/.

14. Rob Crilly, "Donald Trump Finding Out That Winning as President Does Not Come Easy, as Dealmaker-in-Chief Comes Up Short on Healthcare," *Telegraph*, March 24, 2017, http://www.telegraph.co.uk/news/2017/03/24/donald-trump-finding-winning-president-does-not-come-easy-asdealmaker/.

15. Erwin C. Hargrove and Michael Nelson, *Presidents, Politics, and Policy* (Baltimore: Johns Hopkins University Press, 1984), 20–24.

16. Marc J. Hetherington, "The Election: The Allure of the Outsider," in Nelson, *The Elections of 2016*, 63–86.

17. James W. Ceaser, Andrew E. Busch, and John J. Pitney Jr., *Defying the Odds: The 2016 Election and American Politics* (Lanham, MD: Rowman and Littlefield, 2017), 170.

18. Rebecca Kaplan, "Trump's Immigration Comments Open Rift in GOP," *CBS News*, July 5, 2015, http://www.cbsnews.com/news/trump-immigration-comments-open-rift-gop/.

19. Miriam Valverde, "How Trump Plans to Build, and Pay For, a Wall along the U.S.-Mexico Border," PolitiFact, July 26, 2016, http://www.politifact.com/truth-o-meter/article/2016/jul/26/how-trump-plans-build-wall-along-us-mexico-border/; and Jenna Johnson, "Trump Calls for 'Total and Complete Shutdown of Muslims Entering the United States,'" *Washington Post*, December 7, 2015, https://www.washingtonpost.com/news/post-politics/wp/2015/12/07/donald-trump-calls-for-total-and-complete-shutdown-of-muslims-entering-the-united-states/?utm_term=.c61492de72c5.

20. Eugene Kiely, "Yes, Trump Said Bush 'Lied,'" FactCheck, March 17, 2016, http://www.factcheck.org/2016/03/yes-trump-said-bush-lied/.

21. Ali Vitali, "Donald Trump: 'Torture Works,'" *NBC News*, February 17, 2016, http://www.nbcnews.com/politics/2016-election/donald-trump-torture-works-n520086.

22. MJ Lee, "Donald Trump's Pledge: 'We're Gonna Be Saying Merry Christmas,'" CNN, October 22, 2015, http://www.cnn.com/2015/10/21/politics/donald-trump-iowa-rally/index.html.

23. Trevor Hughes, "Trump Calls to 'Drain the Swamp' of Washington," *USA Today*, October 18, 2016, https://www.usatoday.com/story/news/politics/elections/2016/2016/10/18/donald-trump-rally-colorado-springs-ethics-lobbying-limitations/92377656/.

24. Joshua Green, *Devil's Bargain: Steve Bannon, Donald Trump, and the Storming of the Presidency* (New York: Penguin Press, 2017), 117.

25. Thomas B. Edsall, "Hurricane Trump," *New York Times*, September 23, 2015; and "Here's Donald Trump's Presidential Announcement Speech."

26. "Exit Polls," CNN, http://edition.cnn.com/election/results/exit-polls/national/president.

27. William Safire, *Before the Fall: An Inside View of the Pre-Watergate White House* (Garden City, N.Y.: Doubleday, 1975), 116.

28. Light, *The President's Agenda: Domestic Policy Choice from Kennedy to Reagan* (Baltimore: Johns Hopkins University Press, 1991), 10.

29. Ibid., 36.

30. Paul Brace and Barbara Hinckley, *Follow the Leader: Opinion Polls and the Modern Presidency* (New York: Basic Books, 1993), chap. 2.

31. Light, *The President's Agenda*, 42.

32. Ibid., 52.

33. Mike DeBonis and Ed O'Keefe, "Republicans Increasingly Uncertain of a Legislative Victory before August," *Washington Post*, July 8, 2017, https://www.washingtonpost.com/

powerpost/republicans-increasingly-uncertain-of-a-legislative-victory-before-august/2017/07/08/2b13078a-631b-11e7-a4f7-af34fc1d9d39_story.html?utm_term=.1669222dfdd3.

34. Light, *The President's Agenda,* 37.

35. Amita Kelly and Barbara Sprunt, "Here Is What Donald Trump Wants to Do in His First 100 Days," NPR, November 9, 2017, http://www.npr.org/2016/11/09/501451368/here-is-what-donald-trump-wants-to-do-in-his-first-100-days.

36. Calculated from data in Harry Enten, "Six Months In, Trump Is Historically Unpopular," FiveThirtyEight, July 17, 2017, https://fivethirtyeight.com/features/six-months-in-trump-is-historically-unpopular/.

37. Scott Detrow, "Show's Over? Trump Pledges to Be So Presidential You Will Be So Bored," NPR, April 21, 2016, http://www.npr.org/2016/04/21/475126907/shows-over-trump-pledges-to-be-so-presidential-you-will-be-so-bored.

38. Mike Allen, "Playbook," Politico, March 10, 2016, http://www.politico.com/playbook/2016/03/trump-at-the-right-time-i-will-be-so-presidential-that-youll-call-me-and-youll-say-donald-you-have-to-stop-that-rubios-schoolyard-attacks-backfire-213129.

39. John Wagner and Jenna Johnson, "At an Ohio Campaign Rally, Trump Offers an 'Unfiltered' View of His Presidency," *Washington Post,* July 25, 2017, https://www.washingtonpost.com/politics/at-ohio-campaign-rally-trump-offers-an-unfiltered-view-of-his-presidency/2017/07/25/dbbf6792-7188-11e7-8839-ec48ec4cae25_story.html?utm_term=.a5f9ad2eb09b.

40. Alex Isenstedt, "Inside Chris Christie's Fall from Grace," Politico, November 19, 2016, http://www.politico.com/story/2016/11/chris-christie-fall-grace-trump-231659.

41. John P. Burke, *The Institutional Presidency: Organizing and Managing the White House from FDR to Clinton* (Baltimore: Johns Hopkins University Press, 2000).

42. Eliana Johnson and Andrew Restuccia, "Pence's Power Play," Politico, December 4, 2016, http://www.politico.com/story/2016/12/mike-pence-power-play-trump-transition-232151.

43. David A. Graham, "Trump: Middle East Peace 'Is Not as Difficult as People Have Thought,'" *Atlantic,* May 3, 2017, https://www.theatlantic.com/international/archive/2017/05/trump-middle-east-peace-is-not-as-difficult-as-people-have-thought/525267/; and Avantika Chilkoti, "With World Bank Initiative, a Change in Tone for Trump Administration," *New York Times,* July 19, 2017, https://www.nytimes.com/2017/07/19/us/politics/world-bank-initiative-multilateral-institutions.html.

44. Ryan Lizza, "Anthomy Scaramucci Called Me to Unload about White House Leavers, Reince Priebus, and Steve Bannon," *New Yorker,* July 27, 2017, http://www.newyorker.com/news/ryan-lizza/anthony-scaramucci-called-me-to-unload-about-white-house-leakers-reince-priebus-and-steve-bannon; and Julie Bykowicz and Jonathan Lemire, "Scaramucci's Profanity-Laced Tirade Brings Smoldering White House Tensions into the Open," *Chicago Tribune,* July 27, 2017, http://www.chicagotribune.com/news/nationworld/politics/ct-white-house-drama-scaramucci-20170727-story.html.

45. Jonathan Swan, "Government Workers Shun Trump, Give Big Money to Clinton," *The Hill,* October 26, 2017, http://thehill.com/homenews/campaign/302817-government-workers-shun-trump-give-big-money-to-clinton-campaign.

46. Johnson and Restuccia, "Pence's Power Play."

47. Eric Bradner, "Keith Ellison Prods Bernie Sanders to Help Out DNC," CNN, January 18, 2017, http://www.cnn.com/2017/01/18/politics/dnc-chair-debate-ellison-sanders/index.html.

48. Glenn Kessler, "President Trump's Claim His Nominees Faced 'Record-Setting Long' Delays," *Washington Post,* June 13, 2017, https://www.washingtonpost.com/news/fact-checker/wp/2017/06/13/president-trumps-claim-his-nominees-faced-record-setting-long-delays/?utm_term=.69094f18b506; and Carl Hulse, "Democrats Perfect Art of Delay While Republicans Fume Over Trump Nominees," *New York Times,* July 17, 2017, https://www.nytimes.com/2017/07/17/us/politics/senate-democrats-art-of-delay-trump-nominees.html?rref=

collection%2Fsectioncollection%2Fus&action=click&contentCollection=us&region=
stream&module=stream_unit&version=latest&contentPlacement=8&pgtype=sectionfront.

49. "Tracking How Many Key Positions Trump Has Filled So Far," *Washington* Post,
July 19, 2017, https://www.washingtonpost.com/graphics/politics/trump-administration
-appointee-tracker/database/?hpid=hp_hp-top-table-main_6months-tracker-1125am%3A
homepage%2Fstory; Michelle Cheng, "Trump Still Hasn't Filled Top Jobs, and He Has
(Mostly) Himself to Blame," FiveThirtyEight, July 3, 2017, https://fivethirtyeight.com/
features/trump-still-hasnt-filled-top-jobs-and-he-has-mostly-himself-to-blame/.

50. Calculated from data in Josh Dawsey, "Trump Badly Lagging Obama, Bush, Clinton
in Political Appointees," Politico, July 14, 2017, http://www.politico.com/story/2017/07/14/
trump-political-appointees-compared-to-obama-bush-240573; and Karen Yourish and Gregor
Aisch, "The Top Jobs in Trump's Administration Are Mostly Vacant: Who's to Blame?" *New
York Times,* July 17, 2017, https://www.nytimes.com/interactive/2017/07/17/us/politics/
trump-appointments.html?mcubz=0&_r=0.

51. Robert Costa, Abby Phillips, and Karen DeYoung, "Bannon Removed from Security Council as McMaster Asserts Control," *Washington Post,* April 5, 2017, https://www
.washingtonpost.com/politics/bannon-removed-from-security-council-as-mcmaster
-asserts-control/2017/04/05/ffa8b5d2-1a3a-11e7-bcc2-7d1a0973e7b2_story.html?utm_term=
.92ebcff3ea7a.

52. Michael Grunwald, Andrew Restuccia, and Josh Dawsey, "Trump Starts Dismantling
His Shadow Cabinet," Politico, May 1, 2017, http://www.politico.com/story/2017/05/01/
trump-starts-dismantling-his-shadow-cabinet-237819.

53. Cody Derespina, "Trump: No Plans to Fill 'Unnecessary' Appointed Positions," Fox
News, February 28, 2017, http://www.foxnews.com/politics/2017/02/28/trump-no-plans-to
-fill-unnecessary-appointed-positions.html.

54. Madeline Conway, "Trump: 'Nobody Knew That Health Care Could Be So Complicated,'" Politico, February 27, 2017, http://www.politico.com/story/2017/02/trump-nobody
-knew-that-health-care-could-be-so-complicated-235436 ; and Dana Milbank, "Lincoln Was
a Republican, Slavery Is Bad—and More Discoveries by President Obvious," *Washington
Post,* March 22, 2017, https://www.washingtonpost.com/opinions/lincoln-was-a-republican
-slavery-is-bad—and-more-discoveries-by-president-obvious/2017/03/22/3360c622-0f2c-11e7
-9b0d-d27c98455440_story.html?utm_term=.ac83910b328e.

55. Jeremy Diamond, "Trump: Defense Secretary Mattis Can 'Override' Me on Torture,"
CNN, January 27, 2017, http://www.cnn.com/2017/01/27/politics/donald-trump-defense
-secretary-override-on-torture/index.html.

56. Amanda Erickson, "Trump Thought China Could Get North Korea to Comply. It's
Not That Easy," *Washington Post,* April 13, 2017, https://www.washingtonpost.com/news/
worldviews/wp/2017/04/13/trump-thought-china-could-get-n-korea-to-comply-its-not-that
-easy/?utm_term=.ad965e5e1221.

57. Nolan D. McCaskill and Cristiano Lima, "Trump Reverses on NATO: 'It's No Longer
Obsolete,'" Politico, April 12, 2017, http://www.politico.com/story/2017/04/donald-trump
-nato-not-obsolete-237166.

58. Carol Morello, "Iran Nuclear Deal Could Collapse Under Trump," *Washington Post,*
November 9, 2017, https://www.washingtonpost.com/world/national-security/iran-nuclear
-deal-could-collapse-under-trump/2016/11/09/f2d2bd02-a68c-11e6-ba59-a7d93165c6d4_story
.html?utm_term=.7e49937d525c.

59. Christopher Mele, "Trump on Being President: 'I Thought It Would Be Easier,'" *New
York Times,* April 28, 2017, https://www.nytimes.com/2017/04/28/us/politics/trump
-interview-quotes.html?mcubz=0&_r=0.

60. Scott Clement and Dan Balz, "Poll Finds Trump's Standing Weakened Since Springtime,"

Washington Post, July 16, 2017, https://www.washingtonpost.com/politics/poll-finds-trump
-standing-weakened-since-springtime/2017/07/15/2decf03a-68d2-11e7-9928-22d00a47778f_
story.html?utm_term=.9ad8490a5509.

61. Lisa Rein, "Trump's Stark Priorities in Funding and Cutting Are Keenly Felt by the Federal Workforce," *Washington Post,* July 19, 2017, https://www.washingtonpost.com/politics/
trumps-priorities-in-funding-and-cutting-are-keenly-felt-by-federal-workforce/2017/07/19/
48e1ef08-6274-11e7-84a1-a26b75ad39fe_story.html?hpid=hp_hp-top-table-main_workforce
-1120am%3Ahomepage%2Fstory&utm_term=.b96d69192027.

62. Erin Seims, "Mueller, Sessions and Cuba: Trump News of the Week," *New York Times,*
June 16, 2017, https://www.nytimes.com/2017/06/16/us/politics/trump-news.html?mcubz=
0&_r=0.

63. David H. Becker, "Changing Directions in Administrative Agency Rulemaking: 'Reasoned Analysis,' the Roadless Rule Repeal, and the 2006 National Park Service Management
Policies," *Environs* 30 (December 2006), 66–99.

64. Lisa Friedman, "Court Blocks E.P.A. Effort to Suspend Obama-Era Methane Rule," *New
York Times,* July 3, 2017, https://www.nytimes.com/2017/07/03/climate/court-blocks-epa
-effort-to-suspend-obama-era-methane-rule.html?mcubz=0.

65. Adam Liptak, "Appeals Court Will Not Reinstate Trump's Revised Travel Ban, *New York
Times,* May 25, 2017, https://www.nytimes.com/2017/05/25/us/politics/trump-travel-ban
-blocked.html?mcubz=0.

66. Caitlin Dickerson, "Immigration Arrests Rise Sharply as a Trump Mandate Is Carried
Out," *New York Times,* May 17, 2017, https://www.nytimes.com/2017/05/17/us/immigration
-enforcement-ice-arrests.html?mcubz=0.

67. Farhana Khera and Johnathan J. Smith, "How Trump Is Stealthily Carrying Out His
Muslim Ban," *New York Times,* July 18, 2017, https://www.nytimes.com/2017/07/18/opinion/
trump-muslim-ban-supreme-court.html?ref=opinion.

68. Amy B Wang, "Trump Lashes Out at 'So-Called Judge' Who Temporarily Blocked Travel
Ban," *Washington Post,* February 4, 2017, https://www.washingtonpost.com/news/the-fix/
wp/2017/02/04/trump-lashes-out-at-federal-judge-who-temporarily-blocked-travel-ban/
?utm_term=.5bcff5d0b806; and David Jackson, "Trump Rips 'Disgraceful' Court Decision in
Immigration Ban," *USA Today,* February 10, 2017, https://www.usatoday.com/story/news/
politics/2017/02/10/donald-trump-travel/97735996/.

69. Brent Kendall, "Trumps Says Judge's Mexican Heritage Presents 'Absolute Conflict,'"
Wall Street Journal, June 3, 2016, https://www.wsj.com/articles/donald-trump-keeps-up
-attacks-on-judge-gonzalo-curiel-1464911442.

70. Ben Wolfgang and Stephen Dinan, "Trump Says His Justices Will Overturn Roe v.
Wade," *Washington Times,* October 19, 2016, http://www.washingtontimes.com/news/2016/
oct/19/donald-trump-says-his-justices-will-overturn-roe-v/.

71. Ronald A. Klain, "The One Area Where Trump Has Been Wildly Successful," *Washington Post,* July 19, 2017, https://www.washingtonpost.com/opinions/the-one-area-where
-trump-has-been-wildly-successful/2017/07/19/56c5c7ee-6be7-11e7-b9e2-2056e768a7e5_story
.html?utm_term=.380b0de90b68.

72. Calculated from data in Emma Chenowith, Devin Finn, and Jeremy Pressman, "More
People in the U.S. Protested in June Than in Any Month since the January Women's Marches,"
Washington Post, July 25, 2017, https://www.washingtonpost.com/news/monkey-cage/wp/
2017/07/25/more-people-protested-in-june-in-the-u-s-than-in-any-month-since-the-january
-womens-marches/?utm_term=.874d80036e03.

73. Lizette Alvarez, "Mayors, Sidestepping Trump, Vow to Fill Void on Climate Change,"
New York Times, June 26, 2017, https://www.nytimes.com/2017/06/26/us/mayors-trump
-climate-change.html?mcubz=0.

74. Jonathan Lemire, "Trump Makes Puzzling Claim about Andrew Jackson, Civil War," *Chicago Tribune,* May 1, 2017, http://www.chicagotribune.com/news/nationworld/politics/ct-trump-andrew-jackson-civil-war-20170501-story.html.

75. John Wagner, "Trump: Most People Don't Know President Lincoln Was a Republican," *Washington Post,* March 22, 2017, https://www.washingtonpost.com/news/post-politics/wp/2017/03/22/trump-most-people-dont-know-president-lincoln-was-a-republican/?utm_term=.3d2c8cfo9fe8.

76. Noah Bierman, "Trump Says Frederick Douglass Did 'An Amazing Job,'" *Los Angeles Times,* February 1, 2017, http://www.latimes.com/politics/washington/la-na-essential-washington-updates-donald-trump-says-african-american-1485966815-htmlstory.html.

77. Peter Baker, "'People Love You': For Trump, a Welcome Respite from the Capital," *New York Times,* July 25, 2017, https://www.nytimes.com/2017/07/25/us/politics/trump-ohio-rally.html?mcubz=0&_r=0.

78. Robert Draper, "Trump vs. Congress—Now What?" *New York Times Magazine,* March 26, 2017, https://www.nytimes.com/2017/03/26/magazine/trump-vs-congress-now-what.html?_r=0. Strangely, Trump claimed to have invented the phrase "prime the pump," which has been used frequently for more than a century. Max Ehrenfreund, "Behind Trump's 'Prime the Pump' Gaffe Is a Bunch of Real News," *Washington Post,* May 11, 2017, https://www.washingtonpost.com/news/wonk/wp/2017/05/11/behind-trumps-prime-the-pump-gaffe-is-a-bunch-of-real-news/?utm_term=.4c3004276648.

79. Karen Tumulty, "Trump Learns That Dealmaking Is Not the Same as Leadership," *Washington Post,* March 24, 2017, https://www.washingtonpost.com/politics/trump-learns-that-deal-making-is-not-the-same-as-leadership/2017/03/24/34953772-10c5-11e7-9b0d-d27c98455440_story.html?utm_term=.3f72824f9719.

80. Mike DeBonis, "It's Almost July, and House Republicans Still Can't Pass a Budget," *Washington Post,* June 27, 2017, https://www.washingtonpost.com/news/powerpost/wp/2017/06/27/its-almost-july-and-house-republicans-still-cant-pass-a-budget/?utm_term=.426d1e294fd9.

81. Michael D. Shear and Karen Yourish, ""Trump Says He Has Signed More Bills Than Any President, Ever. No, He Hasn't," *New York Times,* July 17, 2017, http://www.politico.com/story/2016/11/chris-christie-fall-grace-trump-231659.

82. Ryan Koronowski, "68 Times Trump Promised to Repeal Obamacare," Think Progress, March 24, 2017, https://thinkprogress.org/trump-promised-to-repeal-obamacare-many-times-ab9500dad31e.

83. Paul Kane, "One reason the GOP Health Bill Is a Mess: No One Thought Trump Would Win," *Washington Post,* July 6, 2017, https://www.washingtonpost.com/powerpost/one-reason-the-gop-health-bill-is-such-a-mess-they-didnt-think-trump-would-win/2017/07/06/bed6a8e0-624a-11e7-8adc-fea80e32bf47_story.html?utm_term=.ba8fc05ad0ed. "We didn't expect to be in this situation," said Republican senator Pat Toomey.

84. Julie Hirschfeld Davis, Thomas Kaplan, and Maggie Haberman, "Trump Demands That Senators Find a Way to Replace Obamacare," *New York Times,* July 19, 2017, https://www.nytimes.com/2017/07/19/us/politics/donald-trump-obamacare-health-care-republicans-senators.html.

85. Mike DeBonis, Kelsey Snell, and Robert Costa, "Trump to GOP Critics of Health-Care Bill: 'I'm Gonna Come After You,'" *Washington Post,* March 21, 2017, https://www.washingtonpost.com/powerpost/trump-arrives-on-capitol-hill-to-sell-house-gop-health-care-package/2017/03/21/e8ede3d2-0e2b-11e7-9b0d-d27c98455440_story.html?utm_term=.d5100fd0e372.

86. Thomas Kaplan, Jennifer Steinhauer, and Robert Pear, "Trump, in Zigzag, Calls House Republicans' Bill 'Mean,'" *New York Times,* June 13, 2017, https://www.nytimes.com/2017/06/13/us/politics/trump-in-zigzag-calls-house-republicans-health-bill-mean.html.

87. George Tsebolis, "This Is Why Trump's 'Art of the Deal' Doesn't Work in Politics," *Washington Post*, March 29, 2017, https://www.washingtonpost.com/news/monkey-cage/wp/2017/03/29/this-is-why-trumps-art-of-the-deal-doesnt-apply-to-politics/?utm_term=.7c881bac8ba1.

88. Donald J. Trump (realDonaldTrump), "The ABC/Washington Post Poll, even though almost 40% is not bad at this time, was just about the most inaccurate poll around election time!" July 16, 2017, 9:10 a.m., https://twitter.com/realDonaldTrump/status/886588838902206464.

89. "15 of Donald Trump's Most Popular Tweets," Twitter, November 7, 2016, https://twitter.com/i/moments/795695925566050304.

90. Michael Kruse, "I Found Trump's Diary—Hiding in Plain Sight," *Politico Magazine*, June 25, 2017), http://www.politico.com/magazine/story/2017/06/25/i-found-trumps-diaryhiding-in-plain-sight-215303.

91. Nick Gass, "Trump Says He Won't Tweet as President," Politico, April 25, 2016, http://www.politico.com/blogs/2016-gop-primary-live-updates-and-results/2016/04/trump-no-tweeting-president-222408.

92. The phrase is Richard E. Neustadt, *Presidential Power and the Modern Presidents: Presidential Leadership from Roosevelt to Reagan* (New York: Free Press, 1990).

93. Jennifer Calfas, "Trump to Continue Using @realDonaldTrump Account as President," *The Hill*, January 15, 2017, http://thehill.com/blogs/blog-briefing-room/news/314440-trump-to-use-personal-twitter-not-potus-account-as-president.

94. Kruse, "I Found Trump's Diary."

95. Emily Badger and Kevin Quealy, "Trump Seems Much Better at Branding Opponents Than Marketing Policies," *New York Times*, July 18, 2017, https://www.nytimes.com/interactive/2017/07/18/upshot/trump-seems-much-better-at-branding-opponents-than-at-marketing-policies.html.

96. Glenn Thrush and Maggie Haberman, "Trump Mocks Mika Brzezinski; Says She Was 'Bleeding Badly from a Facelift," *New York Times*, June 29, 2017, https://www.nytimes.com/2017/06/29/business/media/trump-mika-brzezinski-facelift.html?mcubz=0.

97. Mark Moore, "Trump Goes after 'Failing' New York Times Again," *New York Post*, June 28, 2017: http://nypost.com/2017/06/28/trump-goes-after-failing-new-york-times-again/; Liz Stark, "Ben Sasse Blasts Trump's Twitter Behavior: 'This Isn't Normal,'" *CNNPolitics*, June 29, 2017: http://www.cnn.com/2017/06/29/politics/sasse-trump-twitter/index.html; and Nada Bakos. "This Is What Foreign Spies See When They Read President Trump's Tweets," *Washington Post*, June 23, 2017, https://www.washingtonpost.com/outlook/president-trumps-twitter-feed-is-a-gold-mine-for-foreign-spies/2017/06/23/e3e3b0b0-5764-11e7-a204-ad706461fa4f_story.html?utm_term=.ec4a07481731.

98. David A. Farethold, "Boy Scouts Leader Apologizes for Trump Speech's 'Political Rhetoric,'" *Washington Post*, July 27, 2017, https://www.washingtonpost.com/politics/boy-scouts-leader-apologizes-for-trump-speechs-political-rhetoric/2017/07/27/374fefd4-72f4-11e7-8f39-eeb7d3a2d304_story.html?utm_term=.73c83975add7.

99. Amanda Erickson, "Trump Called the News Media 'An Enemy of the American People.' Here's a History of the Term," *Washington Post*, February 18, 2017, https://www.washingtonpost.com/news/worldviews/wp/2017/02/18/trump-called-the-news-media-an-enemy-of-the-american-people-heres-a-history-of-the-term/?utm_term=.859e287e801c.

100. "Donald Trump Explains All," *Time*, August 20, 2015, http://time.com/4003734/donald-trump-interview-transcript/.

101. Nolan D. McCaskill and Louis Nelson, "President Trump's First 100 Days: By the Numbers," Politico, April 29, 2017, http://www.politico.com/story/2017/04/29/donald-trump-first-100-days-by-the-numbers-237701.

102. Jack Moore, "Trump Delays U.S. Embassy Move to Jerusalem in Victory for Arab Leaders," *Newsweek*, June 1, 2017, http://www.newsweek.com/trump-delays-us-embassy-move -jerusalem-victory-arab-leaders-618968.

103. Alan Rappeport, "Trump Talks Tough on Trade, but His Team Is Treading Lightly," *New York Times*, June 1, 2017, https://www.nytimes.com/2017/06/01/us/politics/trump-trade -tpp.html; Meera Jagannathan, "Here Are All the Terrible Things President Trump Has Said about NAFTA—Before Deciding to Stick with It," *New York Daily News*, Aril 27, 2017, http:// www.nydailynews.com/news/politics/terrible-president-trump-nafta-article-1.3107104; "Trump's Middle East Reset," *The Week*, June 2, 2017; Mark Landler and Michael R. Gordon, "As U.S. Adds Troops in Afghanistan, Trump's Strategy Remains Undefined," *New York Times*, June 18, 2017, https://www.nytimes.com/2017/06/18/world/asia/us-troops-afghanistan -trump.html; and Michael D. Sheer, Julie Hirschfeld Davis, and Maggie Haberman, "Trump, in Interview, Moderates Views but Defies Conventions," *New York Times*, November 22, 2016, https://www.nytimes.com/2016/11/22/us/politics/donald-trump-visit.html.

104. Mark Landler, "From 'America First' to a More Conventional View of U.S. Diplomacy," *New York Times*, March 1, 2017, https://www.nytimes.com/2017/03/01/us/politics/national -security-foreign-policy-white-house.html.

105. Peter Baker, "The Emerging Trump Doctrine: Don't Follow Doctrine," *New York Times*, April 8, 2017, https://www.nytimes.com/2017/04/08/us/politics/trump-doctrine-foreign -policy.html?.

106. Susan Glasser, "The 27 Words Trump Wouldn't Say," *Politico Magazine*, June 6, 2017, http://www.politico.com/magazine/story/2017/06/06/trump-nato-speech-27-words -commitment-215231.

107. Michael Crowley, "Trump's Pursuit of Friendship with Putin Fulfills His Campaign Promise," Politico, July 7, 2017, http://www.politico.com/story/2017/07/07/trump-pursues -friendship-with-putin-240314.

108. Andrew Kaczynski, Chris Massie, and Nathan McDermott, "80 Times Trump Talked about Putin," CNN, n.d., http://www.cnn.com/interactive/2017/03/politics/trump-putin -russia-timeline/.

109. Aaron Blake, "Trump Contradicts His Son's Emails, Suggests Russia Preferred Hillary Clinton," *Washington Post*, Jul 12, 2017, https://www.washingtonpost.com/news/the-fix/ wp/2017/07/12/trump-contradicts-his-sons-emails-suggests-russia-preferred-hillary-clinton/ ?utm_term=.dd599545da76.

110. Madeline Conway, "Trump Says He Can 'Live With' Either Two-State or One-State Solution for Israel," Politico, February 15, 2017, http://www.politico.com/story/2017/02/ trump-two-state-one-state-solution-israel-235054.

111. Nicole Gaouetre, Dan Merica, and Ryan Browne, "Trump: Qatar Must Stop Funding Terrorism," CNN, June 10, 2017, http://www.cnn.com/2017/06/09/politics/trump-qatar -saudi-gulf-crisis/index.html.

112. Madeline Conway, "John Lewis: 'I Don't See This President-Elect as a Legitimate President,'" Politico, January 13, 2017, http://www.politico.com/story/2017/01/john-lewis-donald -trump-not-legitimate-president-233607.

113. Elise Viebeck, "Nearly 70 Democratic Lawmakers Now Skipping Trump's Inauguration," *Washington Post*, January 19, 2017, https://www.washingtonpost.com/news/powerpost/ wp/2017/01/16/more-than-30-democratic-lawmakers-now-skipping-trumps-inauguration/ ?utm_term=.337023e0e44b.

114. Mark Hensch, "Trump Says 'Made Up' Russia Story Part of Decision to Fire Comey," *The Hill*, May 11, 2017, http://thehill.com/policy/national-security/fbi/333056-trump-made -up-russia-story-part-of-comey-firing.

115. Martin Finucane, "Comey Testimony Includes Good News, Bad News for Trump,"

Boston Globe, June 7, 2017, https://www.bostonglobe.com/news/nation/2017/06/07/comey
-testimony-includes-good-news-bad-news-for-trump/YAxfv8SoiHnJoHo4fIrGbO/story
.html.

116. Adam Entous, "Top Intelligence Official Told Associates Trump Asked Him If He
Could Intervene with Comey on FBI Russia Probe," *Washington Post,* June 6, 2017, https://
www.washingtonpost.com/world/national-security/top-intelligence-official-told-associates
-trump-asked-him-if-he-could-intervene-with-comey-to-get-fbi-to-back-off-flynn/2017/
06/06/cc879f14-4ace-11e7-9669-250d0b15f83b_story.html?hpid=hp_hp-top-table-main_
usrussia-810pm%3Ahomepage%2Fstory&tid=a_inl&utm_term=.ec133185397e; and Adam
Entous and Ellen Nakashima, "Trump Asked Intelligence Chiefs to Push Back Against FBI
Collusion Probe after Comey Revealed Its Existence," *Washington Post,* May 22, 2017, https://
www.washingtonpost.com/world/national-security/trump-asked-intelligence-chiefs-to-push
-back-against-fbi-collusion-probe-after-comey-revealed-its-existence/2017/05/22/394933bc
-3f10-11e7-9869-bac8b446820a_story.html?tid=a_inl&utm_term=.37a148ff1680.

117. Laurence H. Tribe, "Trump Must Be Impeached. Here's Why," *Washington Post,* May 13,
2017, https://www.washingtonpost.com/opinions/trump-must-be-impeached-heres-why/
2017/05/13/82ce2ea4-374d-11e7-b4ee-434b6d506b37_story.html?utm_term=.b203a06aa2f2.

118. Anna Giaritelli, "McCain: Trump Scandals Have Reached 'Watergate Size and Scale,'"
Washington Examiner, June 15, 2017, http://www.washingtonexaminer.com/mccain-trump
-scandals-have-reached-watergate-size-and-scale/article/2623309; and Cristina Marcos, "First
Republicans Talk Possibility of Impeachment for Trump," *Hill,* May 17, 2017, http://thehill
.com/homenews/house/333803-first-republicans-talk-impeachment-for-trump.

119. Peter Baker, Michael S. Schmidt, and Maggie Haberman, "Citing Recusal, Trump
Says He Wouldn't Have Hired Sessions," *New York Times,* July 19, 2017, https://www.nytimes
.com/2017/07/19/us/politics/trump-interview-sessions-russia.html.

120. Brendan Nyhan, "Why Trump's Base of Support May Be Smaller Than It Seems," *New
York Times,* July 19, 2017, https://www.nytimes.com/2017/07/19/upshot/why-trumps-base-of
-support-may-be-smaller-than-it-seems.html.

121. Dan Balz, "A Revelation Unlike Any Other in the Russia Investigation," *Washington
Post,* July 11, 2017, https://www.washingtonpost.com/politics/a-revelation-unlike-any-other
-in-the-russia-investigation/2017/07/11/7985fa14-666b-11e7-8eb5-cbccc2e7bfbf_story.html?
utm_term=.85b9bdefi4ee.

122. Rebecca Savransky, "Pence Responds to Trump Jr., Emails: He's 'Not Focused
on Stories about the Campaign,'" *The Hill,* July 11, 2017, http://thehill.com/homenews/
administration/341473-pence-not-focused-on-stories-about-the-campaign.

123. Megan Trimble, "Trump Warns GOP Senator Over Obamacare Repeal," *USNews,* July
19, 2017, https://www.usnews.com/news/national-news/articles/2017-07-19/donald-trump
-warns-dean-heller-over-health-care-vote; and Erica Martinson, "Trump Administration
Threatens Retribution against Alaska over Murkowski Health Votes," *Alaska Dispatch News,*
July 26, 2017, https://www.adn.com/politics/2017/07/26/trump-administration-signals-that
-murkowskis-health-care-vote-could-have-energy-repercussions-for-alaska/.

124. John Gartner, "Mental Health Professionals Declare Trump is Mentally Ill and Must Be
Removed," Change.org, n.d., https://www.change.org/p/trump-is-mentally-ill-and-must-be
-removed.

125. Rachael Revesz, "Donald Trump Falsely Claims He Had "Biggest Electoral College
Win Since Ronald Reagan,'" *Independent,* February 16, 2017, http://www.independent.co.uk/
news/world/americas/donald-trump-news-electoral-college-ronald-reagan-biggest-win
-claim-a7584481.html; and "Donald Trump Says Vladimir Putin Wanted Hillary Clinton to
Win Presidency," *Guardian,* July 13, 2017, https://www.theguardian.com/world/2017/jul/12/
donald-trump-vladimir-putin-get-along-very-well.

126. Jana Heigl, "A Timeline of Donald Trump's False Wiretapping Charge," PolitiFact, March 21, 2017, http://www.politifact.com/truth-o-meter/article/2017/mar/21/timeline -donald-trumps-false-wiretapping-charge/.

127. Marc Fisher, "Donald Trump Doesn't Read Much. Being President Probably Wouldn't Change That," *Washington Post,* July 17, 2016, https://www.washingtonpost.com/politics/ donald-trump-doesnt-read-much-being-president-probably-wouldnt-change-that/2016/07/ 17/d2ddf2bc-4932-11e6-90a8-fb84201e0645_story.html?utm_term=.d4ce43172ac4; Shane Goldmacher, "Trump Refuses to Bend to the Office of President," Politico, January 11, 2017, http://www.politico.com/story/2017/01/trump-presser-highlights-not-backing-down-233488; and Shane Goldmacher, "Trump Savors Health Care Win: 'Hey, I'm President,'" Politico, May 4, 2017, http://www.politico.com/story/2017/05/04/trump-health-care-win-238005.

128. Rachel Bade, "Ryan Defends Trump on Comey: 'The President's New at This,'" Politico, June 8, 2017, http://www.politico.com/story/2017/06/08/ryan-defends-trump-on-comey -the-presidents-new-at-this-239298; Jeff Shesol, "Can President Trump Learn on the Job?" *New Yorker,* April 22, 2017, http://www.newyorker.com/news/news-desk/can-president-trump -learn-on-the-job; and Burgess Everett and Rachel Bade, "Republicans Lament an Agenda in 'Quicksand,'" Politico, July 20, 2017, http://www.politico.com/story/2017/07/20/gop -lawmakers-despondent-as-recess-approaches-240731.

129. Jane Mayer, "Donald Trump's Ghostwriter Tells All," *New Yorker,* July 25, 2017, http:// www.newyorker.com/magazine/2016/07/25/donald-trumps-ghostwriter-tells-all.

130. Green, *Devil's Bargain,* 239.

131. Michael Grunwald, "Trump's First 100 Days: What Mattered and What Didn't," *Politico Magazine,* April 26, 2017, http://www.politico.com/magazine/story/2017/04/26/trump-first -100-days-president-rating-accomplishments-215071.

132. Gabriel Debenedetti, "2020 Race Lures Sprawling Democratic Field," Politico, February 24, 2017, http://www.politico.com/story/2017/02/democrats-2020-presidential-field-235335.

133. Erwin C. Hargrove and Michael Nelson, *Presidents, Politics, and Policy* (Baltimore, Md.: Johns Hopkins University Press, 1984), chap. 4.

134. Michael Nelson, "Who Vies for President?" in *Presidential Selection,* eds. Alexander Heard and Michael Nelson (Durham, N.C.: Duke University Press, 1987), 120–54.

II ★ THE IMPORTANT FIRST YEAR

SETTING THE STANDARD

FDR's Extraordinary First Year

SIDNEY M. MILKIS

Every modern president has dwelled in the shadow of Franklin D. Roosevelt's extraordinary beginning amid the worst economic crisis in the nation's history. The confidence and energy with which he tackled the Great Depression during the critical early days of his presidency set the standard by which all subsequent presidents have been judged. FDR's emergency action to stanch the banking crisis was capped dramatically by his first fireside "chat" of March 12, 1933. He explained clearly in a warm, conversational tone what he had done about the banks and why he had done it. The country was dazzled.

Most first-year presidents cannot aspire to FDR-like leadership. Rare are the moments when presidents can successfully pursue what Alexander Hamilton described in Federalist Paper no. 72 as "extensive and arduous enterprises for the public benefit."[1] Yet no modern executive can avoid public expectations, encouraged by the mass media, to demonstrate during the first year that his or her elevation to the White House marks a new chapter in the country's history. "Someday a president-elect might feel that he could say to newsmen (and himself), 'There *won't* be any Hundred Days. . . . We *don't* yet understand how campaign pledges fit events and trends as yet unknown to us, that's what four years are for,'" Richard Neustadt, the dean of presidential scholars, wrote wistfully in his 1990 book, *Presidential Power and the Modern Presidents*.[2] It is very unlikely, however, that a president can afford to say, "wait until next year."

The first 365 days, including such key moments as the inaugural address, the staffing of the administration, and the first encounters with Congress and the bureaucracy, entail promise and peril that establish the cornerstone of a president's time in office. The most difficult task newly elected presidents confront is to balance the political demands of party leadership and the responsibilities of what FDR optimistically called "enlightened administration." Beginning with the Progressive-Era presidencies of Theodore Roosevelt and Woodrow Wilson and advancing dramatically with the New Deal, the White House became responsible for orchestrating domestic and foreign policy. The president, not the parties or Congress, was to be the principal instrument of American democracy—"the steward of the public welfare," in Theodore Roosevelt's alluring phrase.

Still, the Progressive conceit that "neutral competence" could transcend partisanship has never been a reality of modern American politics. The emergence of the president as steward of the people did not subordinate politics to administration. Rather, especially since Ronald Reagan posed the first fundamental challenges to the liberal state, administrative *politics* has been the norm. With the unraveling of what Arthur Schlesinger once called the "vital center" of the American political system, presidents have politicized more than managed the national security and welfare states. This has led not only to an emphasis on White House communication but also to the concentration of political and policymaking power in the hands of presidential staff members who do not have to be confirmed by the Senate.[3] In their 2012 book *The President's Czars,* Mitchel Sollenberger and Mark Rozell show that these influential staff positions have been a staple of the modern presidency since FDR created the Executive Office of the President.[4] But such posts grew dramatically during the George W. Bush and Barack Obama presidencies.

The politicization and centralization of administrative authority is at the heart of the modern presidential dilemma: the president occupies the most powerful position in the world, yet lacks the authority to direct events. Such audacious insularity—what Wilson called the "extraordinary isolation" of the president—was a major factor in the Obama administration's turbulent implementation of the new federal health insurance marketplace that was so crucial to the success of the Affordable Care Act. The West Wing—more specifically, the White House health care czar, Nancy-Ann DeParle—was in charge. But the nuts-and-bolts work fell largely to the Department of Health and Human Services, especially the Centers for Medicare and Medicaid. The result was a fragmented process that failed to establish essential connective tissue among White House planning, bureaucratic management, and construction of the project's technical underpinning. Adding to the chaos, although Congress and the states were expected to play a critical part in the development of insurance marketplaces, they were largely kept in the dark about controversial regulations and technical difficulties.

As Washington has become more polarized, and the president more likely at some point to face a Congress controlled by opponents, it has become especially difficult for new presidents to cultivate relationships with members of both parties. Indeed, the growing party divide has accentuated the pathologies of the modern presidency.

It remains to be seen, however, whether any new occupant of the modern executive office can truly view—and successfully navigate—this complex political terrain. George W. Bush promised to be a uniter, not a divider, and Obama's extraordinary elevation to the White House was fueled by his pledge to transcend red and blue America. In spite of these assurances, Bush and Obama—and now Donald Trump—presided over developments that have wrought the most polarized polity in modern American politics.

Our new executive-centered party system is characterized by high expectations for presidential leadership in a context of widespread dissatisfaction with government, strong and intensifying political polarization, and high-stakes battles over the basic direction of domestic and foreign policy. Furthermore, the common occurrence of divided government has greatly abetted executive-centered partisanship. Such interbranch divisions encourage presidents to make more frequent use of unilateral administrative power in the service of partisan objectives.

Of course, partisan polarization is not new. All major presidential transformations in American history have witnessed sharp party conflict; indeed, all of America's most important reform presidents either founded or refounded a political party. Yet partisan warfare proved temporary in these transformative moments, befitting a party system that was exceptionally decentralized and ideologically flexible. As each new political order took shape, a strong, relatively bipartisan consensus formed in support of the reform program of the new majority party. For example, Dwight D. Eisenhower, the first Republican president elected during the New Deal regime, bestowed bipartisan legitimacy on the liberal political order. Most significantly, in 1954, with bipartisan cooperation, Eisenhower pushed through Congress an expansion of Social Security that extended its benefits to many parts of society excluded from the initial 1935 statute, most notably occupations with large numbers of African Americans and women.

What was once episodic now seems routine. Contemporary Democrats and Republicans seem intractably—indeed, structurally—divided. During the past four decades, a more centralized, programmatic, and polarized form of partisanship has emerged that appears to defy compromise, much less consensus. President Obama agreed to many conservative concessions to his original health care legislation, including the sacrifice of its ambitious public option. But his acceptance of market exchanges failed to temper discontent on the right, and so the Affordable Care Act became the first major social welfare program to be enacted without a single Republican vote. After it became law, congressional Republicans began a long campaign to repeal what they called "Obamacare."

What can a first-year president do to negotiate the opportunities and hazards of the new party system? Recent history suggests that efforts to transcend partisanship are quixotic. With Democrats and Republicans engaged in a fundamental contest for the hearts and minds of a divided nation, artfully engaging rather than seeking to avoid partisan combat might better serve a new president.

More beholden to the Progressive Era tradition, recent Democratic presidents have been especially reluctant to assume the responsibility of party leadership. They have tended to sell themselves as leaders of a party devoted to problem-solving, not ideology. The argument favored by these presidents is that partisan confrontations are, as Obama suggested in words from 1 Corinthians in his first inaugural address, "childish things." Yet the view that major policies such as Obamacare were merely pragmatic responses to problems that transcend partisanship only rubbed salt in the wounds of a Republican Party increasingly hostile to the liberal vision of social and economic justice.

These observations are not meant to suggest that the president's first year should be consumed by partisan combat. One important task for any new president is to make partisan debate less ad hominem—to focus partisanship on competing principles rather than personal recrimination. As the Emory University political scientist Alan Abramowitz has noted, since the 1980s there has been a growing trend of "negative partisanship" in which party differences are overwhelmingly expressed through mutual antipathy between Democrats and Republicans.[5] These diatribes have focused especially on the president. The animating factor in mobilizing Democrats and activists during the George W. Bush years was their hatred of the Republican president; by the same token, the animus for rabid GOP partisanship during Obama's two terms was contempt for the Democratic president.

Might a new president and his or her political allies benefit from making partisan politics less personal? Facing this task when the polarizing personality of Andrew Jackson entered the executive mansion, Martin Van Buren—the architect of America's first mass-based party system—wrote to his comrade in arms Thomas Ritchie proposing that the great challenge in building a party was to substitute "party principle" for "personal preference."[6] Although the modern executive office can never be separated from personal image and character, any new president's rhetoric, staffing, and policy should be grounded in principles that explain the nature of the partisan contest that now consumes politics and governance in the United States.

An acknowledgment that partisan statesmanship involves, as Franklin Roosevelt claimed, "the redefinition of [constitutional] rights in terms of a changing and growing social order" might be an important step toward a more meaningful national partisan debate—one that is more substantive and civil than the existing contest between Democratic pragmatism and Republican conservatism.[7] No presidential candidate should promise, as many have, to carry out major policy changes on Day One of his or her presidency. Nor should any new president, sidestepping Congress, move quickly to pursue his or her agenda through unilateral executive action. Such a presidency-centered democracy risks embroiling presidents in policy controversies that diminish collaboration with Congress, roil the system of checks and balances, and erode citizens' trust in the competence and fairness of the national government. Paradoxically, our present discontents call for reconciling a more visionary leadership and purposeful partisan administration with presidential patience and acts of forbearance.

NOTES

1. "Federalist No. 72," Avalon Project at Yale Law School, Lillian Goldman Law Library, http://avalon.law.yale.edu/18th_century/fed72.asp.

2. Richard Neustadt, *Presidential Power and the Modern Presidents* (New York: Free Press, 1990), 258.

3. Arthur M. Schlesinger, Jr., *The Vital Center: The Politics of Freedom* (New York: Da Capo Press, 1988).

4. Mitchel Sollenberger and Mark Rozell, *The President's Czars* (Lawrence: University Press of Kansas, 2012).

5. Alan Abramowitz and Steven Webster, "The Rise of Negative Partisanship and the Nationalization of U.S. Elections in the 21st Century," *Electoral Studies* 41 (2016): 12–22.

6. Martin Van Buren to Thomas Ritchie, January 13, 1827, in Richard E. Ellis, *Andrew Jackson* (Washington, D.C.: CQ Press, 2003), 56–58.

7. Franklin Delano Roosevelt, "Campaign Address on Progressive Government at the Commonwealth Club in San Francisco, California," San Francisco, September 23, 1932.

THE PROMISE AND PERIL OF THE FIRST YEAR
The Value of Studying History

H. W. BRANDS

The different ways in which presidents enter the White House often shape their first-year prospects and agendas. Accidental presidents like Theodore Roosevelt and Lyndon B. Johnson typically feel obliged to assure the American people that they will seek to continue the work of their untimely departed predecessors. Presidents who win election by virtue of the continuing popularity of living predecessors—William Howard Taft and George H. W. Bush, for instance—experience similar pressure.

Presidents who enter office with decisive popular mandates—Warren Harding, Franklin D. Roosevelt, Dwight D. Eisenhower, and Ronald Reagan—enjoy unusual credibility. Presidents who are greeted by friendly Congresses—such as these four and Woodrow Wilson—have a head start on their policy agendas.

Finally, former governors—including Theodore Roosevelt, Calvin Coolidge, Jimmy Carter, Bill Clinton, and George W. Bush—have executive experience not possessed by former members of Congress, who nonetheless compensate with greater knowledge of the legislative process. Generals such as Eisenhower and business leaders such as Donald Trump bring their own distinctive sets of experiences that lie entirely outside the realm of elective politics.

Differences aside, first-year presidents face similar tasks, of which three stand out. First, they must form administrations. In particular, they must select cabinet secretaries and other individuals to fill the many top positions in the executive branch. Second, they must articulate and initiate domestic policy agendas. That is, they must tell Congress and the American people what they want to accomplish and take the first steps toward achieving their goals. Third, they must establish their leadership of the foreign-policy apparatus.

History suggests that first-year presidents should keep several considerations in mind as they take up these tasks. In selecting individuals for their administrations, presidents should balance their personal connections to appointees with appointees' experience of government. This is especially important for presidents with little personal experience in Washington. Carter's reputation as an outsider served him well as a candidate in the wake of the Watergate scandal, but the "Georgia mafia" with which he staffed the White House found Washington unfamiliar and, soon enough, unfriendly. Carter's presidency suffered as a consequence. Reagan, by contrast, created a "troika" consisting of two loyalists from California, Michael Deaver and Ed Meese, and Washington professional James Baker. Reagan's administration got off to a fast start and continued to run smoothly with Baker as chief of staff.

Incoming presidents must establish priorities. Some presidents have priorities thrust upon them: Abraham Lincoln had to deal with secession, Franklin Roosevelt to address the Great Depression, Harry S. Truman to finish World War II. But most presidents have leeway in deciding what to tackle first. Amid the crisis of the Depression, Roosevelt initially focused on rescuing the banking system and getting relief to unemployed workers and their families; measures with longer horizons, such as Social Security, were deferred until later. Johnson had big plans for his Great Society, but much of his first year was given to civil rights reform. Reagan devoted his first six months to cutting taxes and raising defense spending. Presidents without focus, by contrast, have often failed. The micromanaging Carter spread himself too thin to gain policy traction. Clinton ran on economic issues ("It's the economy, stupid") but wandered afield into a politically disastrous effort to reform health care.

First-year presidents must confirm their connection to the American people. Accidental presidents may have to do this for the first time. Most Americans knew little about Theodore Roosevelt beyond his service in the Spanish-American War. They knew that Calvin Coolidge disapproved of strikes by the police. They knew Truman wasn't FDR's first (or second) choice for vice president. They knew Johnson was from Texas. But elected first-termers have no less need to strengthen their connection with the public. Since Andrew Jackson's 1828 election, the presidency has been peculiarly the office of the people. No other elected official is answerable so directly to the nation at large. The most influential presidents have derived their power from the people. Lincoln embodied the national will (which was to say, the northern will) during the Civil War. Franklin Roosevelt employed radio to forge a link with the public during the darkest months of the Depression; the people responded by roundly endorsing the New Deal and resoundingly reelecting him. Reagan was to television what Roosevelt had been to radio; Reagan's televised speeches aroused public sentiment against Democratic opponents of his 1981 tax and spending plans.

Here again, the failures are exemplary. Herbert Hoover lost touch with the American people amid the stock market crash of 1929 and never regained it. Gerald Ford, already burdened with his lack of election to the presidency, undermined his credibility by pardoning Richard Nixon for his Watergate offenses.

Elected first-termers must recognize the difference between being a candidate for president and actually being president. The secret of the successful candidacy is the raising of expectations (the Obama campaign trademarked "Yes, we can," but the concept is as old as elective politics), whereas a secret of successful presidencies is the management of lowered expectations. Successful presidents, typically invoking priorities, artfully escape the less realistic promises they made when candidates. Franklin Roosevelt as a candidate pledged to balance the federal budget, but as president, citing the great needs of the Depression-ravaged country, he never came close. Less artful presidents suffer the consequences. George H. W. Bush promised not to raise taxes ("Read my lips: no new taxes"). When soaring deficits and Wall Street's consequent alarm impelled him to accept tax increases as the price of Democrats' agreement to trim spending, he was pilloried and mocked and then defeated for reelection.

If rigid attachment to campaign promises is the first casualty in a successful presidency, the second is devotion to principles that, although laudable in individuals, are dangerous to presidents. Friends ought to be loyal to friends, but presidents should be loyal only to the national interest. Andrew Jackson refused to fire his secretary of war, John Eaton, a man who had devoted years of his life to the service of Old Hickory. But Eaton's wife, Peggy, had a checkered background that scandalized the wives of the members of Jackson's cabinet. The kerfuffle paralyzed the administration for months. Jackson should have told Eaton to resign, but he was too loyal to his old friend. The nation suffered. Franklin Roosevelt understood what Jackson did not. Roosevelt's path to the White House had been smoothed by Louis Howe, who stood by FDR during the years when Roosevelt, afflicted by adult-onset polio, could not stand on his own. But upon election, FDR recognized that Howe's skill set was no longer useful. Gently but firmly, Roosevelt pushed Howe aside and proceeded with the nation's business.

First-year presidents must develop a working relationship with the leaders of Congress. This is comparatively easy, but not assured, when those leaders are members of the president's party and share the president's views. It is harder, but more necessary, when Congress is controlled by the other party or by dissenting members of the president's own party. Republican Dwight Eisenhower (birthplace: Denison, Texas) cultivated Texas Democrats Lyndon Johnson, the Senate majority leader, and Sam Rayburn, the speaker of the House of Representatives. As president, Johnson, facing opposition to civil rights reform from conservative southern Democrats, successfully appealed to Everett Dirksen, the Republican Senate minority leader, to help him muster the votes he required.

Presidents should profess belief in the sincerity and good intentions of powerful legislators, even when they have to lie through their teeth in doing so. Thomas Jefferson waved the olive branch after the ugly election of 1800; the first Republican president declared, "We are all Republicans; we are all Federalists." Jefferson didn't mean it, and no one believed him. But the gesture was graceful and may have kept some congressional Federalists from cutting off their noses to spite their faces when Jefferson asked for their support in the purchase of Louisiana. Reagan let on that he and Thomas P. (Tip) O'Neill shared an Irish bonhomie that came out over drinks at the end of long days battling over the budget. In reality it was an act (performed by the only president to enter the White House via Hollywood). Reagan distrusted O'Neill and bitterly complained in private that the speaker placed personal and partisan interests above the interests of the country.

One way of dealing with rivals and malcontents is to bring them into the administration. Abraham Lincoln gave William Seward, the original front-runner for the 1860 Republican nomination, the senior cabinet post as secretary of state. Franklin Roosevelt made John Nance Garner, a conservative skeptic of Roosevelt's welfare state policies, vice president. John F. Kennedy offered Lyndon Johnson the vice presidency, hoping the offer would impress Johnson's fellow Texans enough to keep them from voting Republican. Johnson may or may not have surprised Kennedy by accepting the offer, but the indisputable result was the elimination of Johnson as a rival for Democratic supremacy in Washington. Barack Obama vanquished Hillary Clinton in the 2008 primaries, then made her secretary of state.

First-year presidents should approach foreign affairs with caution. Seldom do candidates get elected for reasons of foreign policy. Voters are almost always more interested in domestic affairs, particularly those connected to the economy. For this reason, little can be gained by rushing to decide large matters of foreign policy—and much can be lost. New presidents quickly discover that the international context determines most of what they can do in foreign policy and that campaign promises become dead letters about the time presidents-elect receive their first classified briefings. Kennedy raked Eisenhower for the "missile gap" Eisenhower had let develop between the United States and Soviet Union; upon election, Kennedy was informed that there was indeed a missile gap but that it favored the United States. Carter, the first president elected after the American defeat in Vietnam, promised a foreign policy that allowed room for revolutionary ferment in the developing world, but after the Soviet invasion of Afghanistan, he proclaimed a personal epiphany and launched the great arms buildup for which Ronald Reagan received credit. Candidate Barack Obama campaigned to close the American prison at Guantanamo Bay; when he could not figure out what to do with the inmates, he left the prison in place.

A positive example of circumspection in foreign affairs is that of George H. W. Bush. Despite being elected as a proxy for a Reagan third term, Bush spent the first months of his administration conspicuously rethinking Reagan's policy toward the Soviet Union. The hiatus allowed Bush to gauge the growing resistance to communism in the Soviet belt of Eastern Europe and to formulate policies that helped guide Europe and the world to a soft landing after the Soviet engines of the Cold War flamed out.

Another reason for new presidents to be circumspect is that the unruly world repeatedly takes them by surprise. Woodrow Wilson was elected on a domestic platform in 1912. As he prepared to take his inaugural oath, he told an associate that it would be an "irony of fate" if foreign affairs figured largely in his presidency. A year and a half later, the largest war in history until then broke out, eventually engulfing Wilson's presidency. George W. Bush expected to be a domestic policy president until the terrorist attacks of September 11, 2001, pushed the Middle East to the top of his agenda.

Most first-year presidents should think small, rather than large. Truly transformative presidencies are rare because the American status quo resists change. This is partly because entrenched interests and practices are stubborn but also because the status quo has served America well for more than two centuries. Americans do not like to fix what is not broken. On those very unusual occasions when things are broken—the Civil War, the Great Depression—Americans allow presidents to rise to greatness. It is no coincidence that the two greatest presidents not named Washington—Abraham Lincoln and Franklin Roosevelt—presided over the two worst periods in American history.

Presidents who have pushed too hard against the status quo have often been frustrated. Wilson tried to lead America into a world government; the Senate slapped him down by rejecting the Treaty of Versailles and the League of Nations. Bill Clinton sought universal health care; Republican avatars "Harry and Louise" contended that things were fine the way they were, and Americans agreed.

A better model for incoming presidents is Theodore Roosevelt. The Rough Rider lacked neither imagination nor ambition, but he contented himself with reforming the status quo rather than overturning it. Roosevelt's success in busting trusts, regulating railroads, ensuring the safety of America's food and drug supply, protecting women and children from the perils of industrial labor, preserving America's wild beauty, and conserving the country's natural resources won him a spot in the presidential pantheon just below the triumvirate of Washington, Lincoln, and FDR. Absent undeniable national emergency, Theodore Roosevelt's record is about the best a president can hope for. To aim for more is to risk—and likely guarantee—achieving little or nothing at all.

First-year presidents who heed the foregoing advice are by no means assured of success. The presidency is a daunting job with competing and contradictory demands that no president, however gifted, can entirely satisfy. The most popular candidate will be harshly criticized as president, often sooner rather than later. Yet faint-hearts do not seek the White House, and new presidents always take up their task with big plans and high hopes. It is well that this is the case, for ambition and self-confidence are essential qualities in persons undertaking large endeavors of any kind. But so is attention to what has gone before, and first-year presidents who study their predecessors will increase their chances of becoming second-term presidents.

TEN LESSONS FROM PRESIDENTIAL ORAL HISTORY

MICHAEL NELSON

No previous experience fully prepares one to be president. The most important training presidents receive is on the job. But presidents and their aides can learn much about the first year from those who have gone before. What follows—drawn almost entirely from the Presidential Oral History Program of the University of Virginia's Miller Center—are ten lessons that any new president can apply, or at least be informed by, based on the experience of those who already have served in one or more administrations. The ten lessons are divided evenly between those that pertain to the postelection transition and those that inform the actual presidency.

LESSONS 1–5: THE POSTELECTION TRANSITION

1. Cultivate relationships with your party's members of Congress, even if they were not an important part of your election campaign.

The Carter presidency provides an object lesson in the price for not heeding this lesson:

> JIMMY CARTER, *president, 1977–81:* Very few of the members of Congress, or members of the major lobbying groups, or the distinguished former Democratic leaders, had played much of a role in my election. There wasn't that tie of campaign interrelationship that ordinarily would have occurred had I not been able to win the nomination by myself. I just didn't have that sort of potential tie to them, and I think they felt that they were kind of on the outside.

As a result of Carter's early detachment from Congress—which was dominated by his own party—his first-year domestic agenda faltered, as shown by his inability to secure the major legislation he wanted most, including welfare reform, tax reform, energy independence, and the repeal of a long list of public-works projects dear to influential legislators.

2. Choose a chief of staff who understands Washington.

Necessarily, and appropriately, new presidents tend to choose loyal, battle-tested members of the campaign team for important positions on the White House staff. The range of Washington constituencies with which the chief of staff must be familiar, however, requires a unique skill set.

> MICHAEL DEAVER, *deputy chief of staff to President Ronald Reagan, 1981–85:* Reagan did bring a lot of Californians, but in the middle of all those Californians he put someone who was the first among us who was a seasoned Washingtonian, a guy who knew his way around, [James Baker]. . . . I don't think Ronald Reagan would have been reelected if that hadn't happened. . . . He had a lot of counsel from Baker and people that Baker brought to the table who had been through other wars, who had been through fights with the Congress, who knew how to work with the Republican minority leadership and knew how you used OMB [Office of Management and Budget].

In contrast with Carter, Reagan was able during his first year to match political supporters with appropriate positions in the executive branch, secure major tax cuts and defense spending increases from a Democratic House of Representatives, and use the OMB to make detailed spending reductions in certain domestic and regulatory programs—all due in no small measure to Baker's knowledge of how Washington works.

3. Decide what the vice president's role is going to be—and make sure others in the administration understand that as well.

The vice president's usefulness to the president depends on a clear understanding between the two that is shared throughout the administration. And, considering that six of the nine vice presidents who have succeeded to the presidency have done so in the first year of a term, it is worth noting that the vice president needs to be prepared for that eventuality as well.

> ROY NEEL, *chief of staff to Vice President Al Gore and deputy chief of staff to President Bill Clinton, 1993–96:* [During the transition, President-Elect Clinton and Vice President–Elect Gore agreed that] there would be a weekly lunch set aside between Gore and Clinton and it would take precedence over anything else unless there was an emergency. There would be a senior Gore staffer placed on the National Security Council, on the Economic Policy Council, the Domestic Policy Council, and so on. . . .
>
> The most important thing was that Clinton took this one step further. We had the first cabinet meeting the day after the inauguration. The first thing he said was . . . if Gore called and talked to them, it would be the same as him. He went

further down through some of the points about Gore's senior staff, the same thing. They're to be treated as mine, and so on and so forth. He made it abundantly clear to all of them, and that set the tone within his own staff as well. . . .

What made it work was that the president continued to show trust and respect for the vice president.

As a result of Clinton's deciding at the outset what his vice president's role would be, and his making those decisions clear to the White House staff and the rest of the administration, Gore was able to function effectively as a senior presidential advisor in all areas of public policy and as Clinton's lead advisor on important matters such as technology policy and government reform.

4. Cabinet members should be partners in choosing their departmental teams.

The equal and opposite error of allowing cabinet members free rein in choosing their team is to impose a team on them. Roger Altman explains how he became deputy secretary to Secretary of the Treasury Lloyd Bentsen in the Clinton administration.

ROGER ALTMAN, *deputy treasury secretary to President Bill Clinton, 1993–94:* Bentsen had to be satisfied that this was something he wanted. It's really a bad thing to say to a senior cabinet officer, "Well, your deputy is—." . . . [It] just promotes disunity and so forth. So Clinton wisely determined that this was something that Bentsen ultimately had to make the call on. And Bentsen did make the call. . . . It's not the right move to inform a cabinet officer that his team is Mr. X, Miss Y, and Miss Z.

As Altman argues, consultation lies at the heart of an effective personnel strategy at the start of a new administration. Clinton succeeded by ensuring that both his staff and cabinet felt ownership in important subcabinet appointments.

5. "Campaigning is about addition, but governing is about selection."

"All of the above" is seldom on the governing menu, especially during the first year. Priorities must be set during the postelection transition period so that intelligent choices can be made.

WILLIAM GALSTON, *deputy domestic policy advisor to President Bill Clinton, 1993–95:* [Franklin D. Roosevelt's] Hundred Days and Lyndon Johnson's 1965–66 Great Society period are historical anomalies that no president is wise to rely on. Generally speaking, you cannot do that much. You cannot flood the zone and hope to complete very many passes. When you need to choose among elements of your agenda, make clean choices, as Bill Clinton did early in 1993, when he had to figure out whether to give the emphasis to public investment or to fiscal prudence. During the campaign he didn't think he was going to be faced with that choice, but circumstances changed. He had to adjust. He had to adjust by making a choice.

Clinton famously got off to a rocky start by making gays and lesbians in the military an immediate priority of his new presidency. But when it came to the most important issue on his first-year agenda—fixing the economy—Clinton made tough choices about which campaign promises to pursue ("fiscal prudence") and which to postpone ("public investment").

LESSONS 6–10: THE PRESIDENT TAKES OFFICE

6. Politics is part of policy, not its opposite.

Politics is about persuasion, an axiom that is no less true after the election than before.

> DAVID RUBENSTEIN, *domestic policy staff aide to President Jimmy Carter, 1977–81:* Early on, he was very much, "I only want to know what the best policy is and I'll worry about the politics of it later. You give me the best policy." Later on those kinds of bravado statements tended to disappear and he wanted to know what he could pass, what we could get through, what did this committee chairman want, what did this interest group want.

Carter learned from experience that policy and politics are intertwined. After his first year in office, he listened hard to his staff's congressional and interest group liaisons when shaping successful political strategies to secure approval of the Panama Canal treaty, civil service reform, and other controversial measures.

7. If painful decisions have to be made, make them in the first year.

The polls that matter are not conducted in the first year. The framers granted presidents a four-year term so that the long-range consequences of their sometimes difficult first-year measures would have time to emerge.

> ALTMAN: Remember, you're playing for four years, you're not playing for one year. . . . One of the oldest rules of presidential management is, take your pain upfront. . . . Nobody took more pain upfront than Ronald Reagan. I mean, the worst recession since the Great Depression occurred in 1981 and 1982 and in the fall of '82, in early August, Reagan was being described as Herbert Hoover, politically dead, gone, might as well already make his reservations back to Santa Barbara and so forth. And it turned around and by November '84, as you remember, it was "Morning in America" and he won 49 states. That's the way to do it.

GALSTON: No president can be indifferent to sustained political support, but at the same time achieving sustained political support at the cost of doing what needs to be done is a hollow victory. Staff people around the president have to be worried about feeding a president's desire for sustained high poll ratings. At some point, you have to say, "Mr. President, you're right. You're going to pay a price. We're all going to pay a price. But if we don't do this, we'll never get another chance and the country will be the worse for it."

Clinton had no desire to cut federal spending and raise taxes during his first year in office. Nor did Reagan welcome the deep recession of 1981–82. But they chose to act in confidence (justified, as it turned out) that their policies would help get the economy in strong shape by the time they ran for reelection.

8. Create a decision-making process so that routine matters don't reach you.

Every decision that lands on the president's desk should be one that only the president can make or actively wants to make. If the process for making other decisions is clear and fair, they can be safely delegated to the president's team.

STUART EIZENSTAT, *domestic policy advisor to President Jimmy Carter, 1977–81:* People knew that Carter was insisting on making every last decision. And so, if that's the case, take everything to him. What should have happened is the president should have said, Look, here is the [presidential review memorandum]. You've given me the basic issues, here are my decisions, now you go and settle it . . . and don't come back to see me."

RICHARD CHENEY, *chief of staff to President Gerald Ford, 1975–77:* If you don't trust the process, you're going to start looking for ways around it. . . . All of a sudden you have people freelancing, trying to get around the decision-making process because they feel the process lacks integrity. So it's very, very important when you set up the shop to make certain that you have a guaranteed flow—you know what's going in; you know what's coming out. You know when it goes in that it's complete, that everybody's got their shot at the decision memo. You know if there's going to be a meeting, the right people are going to be in the meeting, that the president has a chance to listen to all of that and then make a decision.

Contrary to lore, Carter did not stay up late assigning playing times on the White House tennis court. But he did go over the massive federal budget line by line. Focusing on the forest while allowing trusted OMB officials and White House staff members to tend to each individual tree would have served him better in persuading Congress to pass a budget that reflected his policy priorities.

9. Don't assume you're obligated to fight your predecessor's battles.

Everyone in Washington who is unhappy with a decision made in the years before the new president takes office will want to relitigate it. The first year should not be—and as Brent Scowcroft indicates below, need not be—filled with leftover issues. Working closely with Secretary of State James Baker, Scowcroft moved quickly to negotiate an agreement with Democratic congressional leaders that settled what had been a longstanding and contentious inter-branch fight over U.S. policy toward Nicaragua during the Reagan administration.

> BRENT SCOWCROFT, *national security advisor to President George H. W. Bush, 1989–93:* At the outset of the [Bush] administration, Central America loomed large. It had been a major preoccupation of the Reagan administration. I thought excessively so ... in this constant confrontation with the Congress [over policy toward Nicaragua]. It was not producing results, it was embittering everything, and nothing was getting done. I thought we ought to change that. I thought we ought to go up and try to coopt the Congress. And Baker, interestingly enough, the first time we talked about Central America, said the same thing. So that's what we tried to do.

Scowcroft served in an administration led by a president of the same party as his immediate predecessor. But even a change in partisan control of the White House can leave the new president with policies inherited from the congressional party. "We were absolutely deluged" with "pet legislation" from congressional Democrats when Jimmy Carter succeeded Republican president Gerald Ford in 1977, says Carter's legislative liaison Frank Moore. As a result, "we overloaded the circuits."

10. Foreign policy *is* domestic policy.

No matter the nature of the domestic and economic issues that may dominate the first year, world leaders will be taking the new president's measure based on how they are handled.

> WARREN CHRISTOPHER, *secretary of state to President Bill Clinton, 1993–97:* It's hard to overestimate the degree of credibility the president gained internationally by taking steps to balance the budget [in 1993], and I think he owed that to both his own determination but the presence of [Secretary of the Treasury] Lloyd Bentsen and [National Economic Council Chairman] Bob Rubin and [Office of Management and Budget Director] Leon Panetta steeled him to make that very difficult decision and changed the whole course of the administration, I think, and put it on a much sounder track.

Some senior foreign leaders were initially inclined to regard Clinton, whose pre-presidential experience was as governor of a small southern state, as an unimpressive statesman, especially compared with his globally surefooted predecessor, George H. W. Bush. Clinton's early resolve in the first-year budget battle caused these leaders to reassess him and, eventually, change their minds.

SUPREME COURT APPOINTMENTS IN THE PRESIDENT'S FIRST YEAR

BARBARA A. PERRY

Gerald Ford observed in his memoir that "few appointments a president makes can have as much impact on the future of the country as those to the Supreme Court."[1] Seven modern presidents—more than half of those who have served starting with Franklin D. Roosevelt—had the opportunity to nominate a member of the nation's highest court during their first year in office. Two of the seven successful first-year appointees were chief justices, and three were women—out of the 4 females who have served among the 112 total justices. One was the first Latina justice.

Reasons vary for why court vacancies occur so early in a presidential term. Sometimes the reason is coincidental, notably the sudden death of Chief Justice Fred Vinson in 1953 and Justice Abe Fortas's forced resignation over financial improprieties in 1969. Occasionally, a new president's whim creates a vacancy, as when Lyndon B. Johnson asked Arthur Goldberg to vacate his seat on the bench in 1965 to become U.S. ambassador to the United Nations. Goldberg did not want to leave the Supreme Court but, as he said regretfully when asked why he did so, "Have you ever had your arm twisted by Lyndon Johnson?"[2] Moving Goldberg to New York gave Johnson the chance to nominate his friend Fortas to the court.

The retirement of a justice who waits for a president of his party or ideology to occupy the White House presents a more predictable pattern. Justice Potter Stewart, appointed by Republican president Dwight D. Eisenhower, retired in 1981, shortly after Ronald Reagan, another Republican, became president. Justice Byron White, a Democrat nominated by John F. Kennedy, left when Democrat Bill Clinton took office in 1993. Although Justice David Souter had been placed on the court by Republican President George H. W. Bush, he frequently voted with liberal colleagues during his nearly twenty years on the bench and stepped down in 2009 after Democrat Barack Obama swept to victory. All three justices also knew that the president's party had a Senate majority that made confirmation of a likeminded successor probable.

Occasionally, other circumstances create a first-year vacancy. Republican Justice Owen Roberts became so uncomfortable with the judicial activism of Franklin D. Roosevelt's appointees that he retired during Harry S. Truman's administration. The new president, who had assumed the office after Roosevelt's death, made a bipartisan gesture by nominating his trusted friend from their Senate days, Republican Harold Burton, to replace Roberts. Chief Justice Earl Warren, the former Republican governor of California who, although placed on the court by Eisenhower, had led a liberal judicial revolution, told Johnson in the summer of 1968 that he would like to retire. Southern Democrats and conservative Republicans deployed the filibuster to deny Johnson's promotion of Fortas to chief justice in 1968. Warren stayed on for another term but reluctantly stepped down in the first year of Richard Nixon's presidency.

Because most justices in the modern era leave the court at the end of its term in early summer, even those who retire in an elected president's first year generally do so after he has been in office for at least six months. The unexpected openings created by Vinson's death and Fortas's resignation occurred in September and May, respectively. From Truman through Obama, no new president faced the consequential decision of whom to name to the Supreme Court until well after inauguration. Truman had three months after Roosevelt's death elevated him to the presidency to settle into the White House before Roberts retired. World War II still raged in the Pacific theater, and Truman thought it wise to exemplify bipartisanship by nominating Burton. In subsequent years, he maintained this pattern of naming longtime Washington friends for all four of his Supreme Court nominations, although his other nominees were Democrats.

Following its custom, the Senate voted unanimously for one of its own to cross First Street to sit in the "Marble Temple." Once on the court, Burton tended to practice judicial restraint. Although he usually disagreed with the more liberal wing of the court, he brought much-needed civility to its debates. He was not possessed of a superior intellect, however, and Court scholars have typically judged him a failed justice.[3]

When Chief Justice Vinson, another Truman friend and appointee, succumbed to a heart attack eight months after Eisenhower's 1953 inauguration, Eisenhower turned to a rival for the 1952 Republican nomination who had no judicial experience, Earl Warren. He had been a county prosecutor and the California attorney general before becoming governor of his state. He had also occupied the vice-presidential slot on the unsuccessful Republican presidential ticket with Thomas Dewey in 1948.

Eisenhower had spoken to Warren about the possibility of a Supreme Court nomination prior to Vinson's death; the president approved of the congenial governor's "basic philosophy," "high ideals," and "common sense."[4] The Senate confirmed the appointment by a unanimous voice vote, despite a nearly even split between Democrats and Republicans in the chamber. Although the president believed he had named a moderate to lead the court, Warren wrought a liberal revolution in civil rights and liberties that prompted "Impeach Earl Warren" signs to spring up throughout the conservative hinterlands. He was anathema in the South after his landmark *Brown v. Board of Education* rulings in 1954 and 1955, which ordered public schools to desegregate with "all deliberate speed." His leadership in broadening criminal rights provoked an equally vehement backlash. Warren's legacy continues to stir battles on the bench and in judicial appointments four decades later. Scholars rank him among the court's "greats."[5]

Arthur Goldberg, who was appointed by President Kennedy, had not even served three years on the court when President Johnson named him ambassador to the United Nations. Johnson was determined to place Fortas, his old friend and legal advisor, on the high court. If no opening occurred naturally, why not create one? Goldberg held what was then known as the court's "Jewish seat," previously occupied by Benjamin Cardozo and Felix Frankfurter. Johnson would simply trade Fortas, also Jewish, for Goldberg and perhaps garner credit among Jewish voters for choosing one of their coreligionists to represent the United States at the United Nations.

Fortas expressed unease with his nomination, preferring both his informal advisory role to the president and a lucrative law practice. He occasionally accepted pro bono assignments, as when he argued *Gideon v. Wainwright* before the Warren Court, winning the right for indigents to receive free legal counsel from states in noncapital criminal cases.

Only three conservative Republican senators (out of thirty-two) dissented from Fortas's nomination as associate justice. In little more than three years on the Court, he distinguished himself with landmark liberal opinions, especially involving the juvenile justice process. And he famously wrote in favor of free speech for students, arguing that they do not "shed their constitutional rights to freedom of speech or expression at the school house gate." Despite his truncated tenure and reason for leaving, Fortas is ranked by scholars as a "near great" justice.[6]

When Johnson's effort to promote Fortas to chief justice failed in 1968 and he resigned as associate justice in 1969, the next president had two positions to fill on the Court: the one abandoned by Fortas and the chief justiceship, which Warren had chosen to resign. Nixon had made the Warren Court's liberal rulings a prominent issue in the 1968 campaign, promising to name "law and order" justices. The new president also was looking for a way to advance the Republican Party's rising fortunes in the heretofore solidly Democratic South. His first two nominees to fill Fortas's seat, Clement Haynsworth of South Carolina and G. Harrold Carswell of Florida, were rejected by the Democratic Senate, in retaliation for Fortas's defeat the previous year and, in Carswell's case, because of a racist past. After publicly branding the Democratic Party hostile to southerners, Nixon nominated Harry Blackmun of Minnesota, who was easily confirmed but not until well into the second year of Nixon's presidency.

For chief justice, Nixon turned to Warren Burger, a conservative appeals court judge who had a middling résumé but certainly looked and sounded the part, as if central casting had hired an actor with chiseled features, a shock of thick white hair, and a basso profundo voice to preside in the majestic courtroom. Despite the Democrats fifty-seven to forty-three majority, the Senate approved Burger's nomination with only a trio of dissenters. The new chief justice went on to create a legacy that was more related to preserving the court's building and its history than to landmark judicial decisions. He disappointed Nixon's supporters by not leading a full roll-back of Warren-era rulings and by writing the unanimous opinion in *U.S. v. Nixon,* which forced the president to release the Watergate tapes and ultimately resign from his scandal-ridden presidency.

While visiting Arizona in the late 1970s, Burger met an impressive lawyer and politician, Sandra Day O'Connor. Several years later he escorted her down the marble steps of the Supreme Court as its newest member. During the 1980 presidential campaign, Ronald Reagan had developed a "gender gap" with polls indicating that women supported him at a lower rate than men did. Although Reagan staunchly opposed affirmative action policies, he announced during the campaign that one of his nominations to the Supreme Court would be a qualified woman—the first to serve on the tribunal.

Justice Stewart's retirement at the end of the Court's term in the summer of 1981 gave Reagan the opportunity to make good on his promise. Stewart was a moderate conservative, and Reagan's advisors found the perfect replacement for him in O'Connor, who was then serving as an Arizona court of appeals judge. With the Senate now in Republican hands, thanks to Reagan's coattails in the election, the first woman nominated for the Supreme Court sailed through unanimously.

In her near quarter century as associate justice, O'Connor became an icon for women around the world and made her mark with a moderate jurisprudence that vaulted her into the decisive "swing seat" on the closely divided Court. Like her mentor, Justice Lewis Powell, she would sometimes provide the deciding vote for the liberal bloc and at other times for the conservative wing. She voted nearly always for women's rights in abortion, affirmative action, employee benefits, military academy admissions, and sexual harassment cases.

Democrat-appointed justices who did not want to be replaced by a Republican president had to wait out the twelve years of the Reagan and Bush administrations before contemplating retirement. Byron White, a Kennedy nominee who reflected the president's moderate liberalism, had completed his third decade on the high court when he announced he would retire at the end of the term in June 1993. Newly elected Democrat Bill Clinton had his first opportunity to name a justice.

Initially, Clinton considered a politician in the Warren mold. When that plan foundered, he turned to federal appellate judge Stephen Breyer. Because Breyer was recovering from a bike accident, however, his interview with the president went poorly. Clinton then reached out to Judge Ruth Bader Ginsburg of the District of Columbia circuit, and she aced her interview with an inspirational narrative of how she had overcome gender discrimination. In one of the last uncontested

Supreme Court nominations, Ginsburg swept to confirmation with only three Republican nay votes in the Democrat-controlled Senate. Just the second woman on the Court, she has served nearly a quarter-century as a reliable liberal vote and leader for gender equality.

After postponing retirement during George W. Bush's two terms as president, Justice Souter, an introverted New Englander who had never been comfortable in Washington, happily left the court in 2009, President Obama's initial year. The first African American president made history by selecting the first Latina justice. Sonia Sotomayor's stellar education credentials and service on both federal trial and appellate courts, with appointments from Republican and Democrat presidents, made her an obvious nominee, especially to reward the 67 percent of Hispanics who had voted for Obama in 2008. The era of bipartisan support for Supreme Court nominees had ended, however, and only nine of forty GOP senators supported Obama's first nominee.

An active questioner at oral arguments, Sotomayor formed a solid liberal bloc with Justices Ginsburg, Breyer, and Obama's second appointee, Elena Kagan. When they are able to attract swing voter Justice Anthony Kennedy, a majority of the Court supports abortion rights, affirmative action, marriage equality, and church-state separation.

As Henry J. Abraham has observed, the historical criteria for Supreme Court nominees include merit, political and ideological compatibility, representative characteristics (religion, race, gender, and ethnicity), and personal or political friendship. Modern Supreme Court appointments in presidents' first years have reflected all of those considerations. Except for Truman's nomination of his friend Burton (a partisan anomaly during World War II), all recent nominees, like those of most presidents throughout history, appear to have shared a political and ideological kinship with the chief executive who named them. But their appointing presidents' ideological expectations were unmet by Warren, O'Connor, Souter, and, to some extent, Burger. Across the entire spectrum of appointment history, only about one-fifth of justices have disappointed the president who appointed them. In the cases of Warren and Burger, Eisenhower and Nixon misjudged the effects their chief justiceships would have. With O'Connor, another factor (in this case, gender) outweighed her moderation in Reagan's eyes. Ginsburg and Sotomayor combined both representative characteristics and ideological compatibility with Clinton and Obama. As with geography and religion in an earlier era, nominees' gender and ethnicity have sometimes guided recent first-year presidents in their efforts to reward constituencies who helped propel them to office or who, the presidents hoped, would help to reelect them.

In addition to bipartisanship, friendship determined Truman's court appointments, trumping merit. Ideology was responsible for the same result in Nixon's selection of Burger. Johnson's reliance on his friend Fortas to fill the Goldberg seat did not dilute merit as a criterion. Unfortunately, however, Fortas failed to overcome cronyism in favor of judicial ethics. Four other first-year appointees

(Warren, O'Connor, Ginsburg, and Sotomayor) were also highly qualified by virtue of education, experience, and intellect. They maintained their integrity on the bench.

When Chief Justice Charles Evans Hughes laid the court building's cornerstone in the midst of the Great Depression, he declared, "Our republic endures and this is the symbol of its faith." Fortunately, most of the successful first-year appointments in the past seven decades have enhanced that symbol.[7]

NOTES

1. Gerald R. Ford, *A Time to Heal* (New York: Harper and Row, 1979), 334.

2. Henry J. Abraham, *Justices, Presidents, and Senators: A History of U.S. Supreme Court Appointments from Washington to Clinton* (Lanham, Md.: Rowman and Littlefield, 1999), 213.

3. Ibid., 342.

4. Ibid., 192.

5. Ibid., 342.

6. Ibid.

7. Barbara A. Perry, *The Priestly Tribe: The Supreme Court's Image in the American Mind* (Westport, Conn.: Praeger, 1999), 10.

PRESIDENTIAL CONSTRAINTS

How the President Is Limited by Structural and Institutional Realities

DANIEL J. GALVIN

With the obvious exception of Franklin D. Roosevelt, the presidents remembered as our greatest did not enjoy exceptional political success during their first one hundred days in office. Abraham Lincoln certainly did not. In the week following his inauguration, the Congress of the Confederate States adopted a permanent constitution on behalf of the seven states that had already seceded. A month later, the Civil War commenced at Fort Sumter. And by the end of Lincoln's third month in office, four more states had seceded. No major legislation was passed during that time. Yet Lincoln is remembered as the greatest president of all.

Presidents are often advised to pay less attention to the hype surrounding the first hundred days and instead focus on building up a record of success and a reputation for winning. Practitioners encourage them (and scholars expect them) to think strategically: to work backward from four years out, score quick wins, collect favors from key players, and act unilaterally to rack up accomplishments.

To assert some measure of control over how their presidencies will unfold and how their historical legacies will take shape, presidents frequently are told to set smart priorities, work to develop forward-looking economic plans that will shape the nation's trajectory in the long term, and sequence the rollout of their initiatives strategically. Even if plans take a while to bear fruit, the president's ability to control the agenda and stick to the script is seen as essential.

Discipline is thus a highly valued trait. Ronald Reagan's White House was known for being controlled, restrained, and strategic. Reagan's staff would set a single message for each day. To ensure that the president did not overshadow his own agenda with off-topic remarks, his aides coached him to always stay on script. Bill Clinton, in contrast, was criticized for allowing controversial measures like "don't ask, don't tell" in his early months in office and several personal scandals throughout his presidency to hijack his policy agenda and detract from the popular economic message he sought to emphasize.

Discipline was not a trait associated with the Clinton presidency, or, for that matter, with Richard Nixon's. When candidate Barack Obama said in 2008 that

"Ronald Reagan changed the trajectory of America in a way that, you know, Richard Nixon did not and in a way that Bill Clinton did not," part of the contrast could be traced to the relative discipline, self-control, and strategic acumen exercised by each president.[1]

But even when presidents do stick to the script, control the agenda, and roll out their initiatives strategically, being remembered as "successful" or "great" is not always, or even very often, within their control. Presidents' capacity to bring about the changes they seek is severely constrained by structural forces and contextual conditions about which they can do little.

For starters, presidents are highly constrained by the constitutional system and the limited powers of their office, especially in relation to Congress but also to the courts and states. The framers of the Constitution limited presidential power and established a "separated system" on purpose. George W. Bush once quipped, "If this were a dictatorship, it would be a heck of a lot easier."[2]

To be sure, presidents can get a lot done unilaterally. After the Democrats lost control of both houses of Congress in 2014, Obama told his cabinet that even without congressional support, "I've got a pen, and I've got a phone," indicating that he would circumvent Congress by signing executive orders and rallying outside groups to help advance his agenda in nonlegislative ways.[3] But those strategies' limited ability to accomplish Obama's grand ambitions only reinforce the larger point. Presidents need support from Congress to accomplish their most significant goals.

Winning that support is not easy. Congress consists of 535 individual members, each with different constituencies, interests, time horizons, and policy goals. Staggered elections and varying and disjointed terms of office mean that each official is the product of an electorate that differs both *geographically* and *temporally* from everyone else's. Structurally, then, the incentives and interests of the president and members of Congress are never in perfect alignment.

Even when the president's party controls both congressional chambers, support for administration initiatives is not guaranteed. Despite the obvious appeal of unified party government, presidents often find that their ability to influence their fellow partisans in Congress is limited. The truth is, the larger the party's majority, the more heterogeneous it tends to be, and the more difficult it is for the president to get all factions to work together in concert.

The challenges Obama faced in lining up Democratic support for the Affordable Care Act in 2009 and 2010 offer perhaps the best illustration. Despite the Democrats' collective agreement that passing health care reform was vitally important for both the nation and the party, Obama had to carefully balance the interests and concerns of prolife Democrats, Democrats who sought greater state control of policy implementation, Democrats who preferred a single-payer system, and Democrats who sought a different set of enforcement mechanisms. Trying to "herd the cats" is a major challenge that all presidents face, whatever their political talents and skills.

A long tradition of scholarship has defined presidential leadership in precisely this way, as the struggle to enhance the president's "personal capacity to influence the conduct of the men who make up government."[4] Despite enjoying many years of unified party government during the twentieth century, Democratic presidents from Roosevelt to Jimmy Carter found their party's friendly majorities less friendly, and unified government less unified, than they had hoped. But this was not an experience specific to the Democratic Party. George W. Bush learned exactly the same lesson when the GOP won unified control of the federal government in the early 2000s. Such is the nature of political parties in a separated system of governing.

More importantly, the partisan makeup of government shapes the likely *content* of any legislation that is enacted. Scholars have found that presidents who face a Congress controlled by the opposition party ("divided government") still sign significant legislation into law at a healthy rate. But the content of that legislation will always be inferior, from the president's perspective, to what it would have been under unified party government.

Yet there is little evidence presidents can do much to affect the partisan composition of Congress. Yes, presidents can offer endorsements, campaign for fellow partisans, raise money for their campaigns, and offer other kinds of support. But as former Speaker of the House Thomas (Tip) O'Neill said, "all politics is local," and even the most popular presidents tend only to have a marginal influence on congressional races.

Considering structural factors in the larger political system such as congressional districts drawn for partisan purposes, unequal representation of population in the Senate, and staggered elections for members of Congress, presidents can try, but rarely succeed, in significantly altering the balance of party power in the legislative branch. And yet, the strength of their party in Congress matters more than just about anything else in shaping the president's likelihood of achieving legislative success.

Finally, as political scientist Stephen Skowronek has argued in this volume, presidents are also heavily constrained by their place in "political time," meaning their relationship to prevailing political narratives, ideational commitments, governing arrangements, and interest group coalitions. The challenges they face and their prospects for "success" hinge on the resilience of these inherited conditions. When a president's political identity is defined by, and inextricably tied to, a set of commitments that is still widely seen as credible and legitimate, the leadership task is different from that faced by a president who is tied to a set of commitments that are seen as more vulnerable. Presidents' goals matter too: Are they setting out to dismantle what exists and offer an alternative formulation? To deliver on received commitments without changing much at all? Or is their charge to hold together a rapidly fraying party coalition and follow through on a set of political commitments that has already lost much of its credibility? These contextual factors complicate the president's task and suggest that even the shrewdest chief executives have a difficult time navigating the political terrain they inherit.

Ronald Reagan, for example, set out to dismantle the New Deal order and usher in a new era of conservative governance. His task was one of repudiation and creative innovation. George W. Bush, in contrast, sought to "move the ball forward" on the same basic set of commitments—but to do so twenty years later, when there was far greater disagreement about what to do and how to do it, even among the most stalwart Republicans. Bill Clinton and Barack Obama, in contrast, sought to advance a very different set of priorities and commitments during the same era, but their alternatives did not enjoy broad or deep support. All four of these presidents had to contend with the same basic structural challenges—Constitution, party, policy—but what they were after and how much they were able to accomplish depended to a large extent on the relative strength of the prevailing ideas, institutions, and political supports during each moment in "political time."

In view of all this, it is clear that even the most ambitious and highly skilled first-year presidents face formidable structural, institutional, and political constraints. Try as they might to prioritize the right issues and alter the direction of the country through sound public policy, the constitutional system, the nature of political parties, and inherited political conditions make it extremely difficult for presidents to achieve their goals even in the best of circumstances. "Best," that is, from the president's perspective. Remember that the framers of the Constitution were less concerned with the president's ability to rack up legislative accomplishments in the first year, or at any point in their tenure, than with the stability and durability of the entire system—an objective they thought would be better advanced by *limiting* the president's powers.

Finally, it is worth contemplating the limited tools presidents have to affect the direction of the economy. Although the public certainly expects presidents to deliver economic growth and prosperity, their ability to alter the trajectory of the economy is actually quite limited. The president can use budget proposals to shape taxing and spending priorities, appoint members of the Federal Reserve Board, negotiate trade deals, and make other interventions that can affect economic growth, inflation, and unemployment rates. But altering the shape and direction of the national economy depends on the sustained, coordinated efforts of myriad interests, organized groups, and political actors working in concert on multiple levels (state, national, global, private) over long periods of time. Steering the national economy is a multifaceted, collective effort in which the president is only one—albeit an important—player.

Presidents are notorious for their oversized ambitions. Their sights are set higher and their purviews far wider than those of other political actors. They want to have a good first year but more than that, they want to have a lasting influence on the nation and often the world. They do not merely want to ride the currents of history but to steer them as well, thereby establishing a historical legacy of their own design. But in many ways, they are just along for the ride. They try their hardest and exploit the resources at their disposal, but most presidents most of the time find themselves effecting change, as political scientist George C. Edwards III has aptly put it, only "at the margins."[5]

NOTES

1. "In Their Own Words: Obama on Reagan," *New York Times,* http://www.nytimes.com/ref/us/politics/21seelye-text.html?mcubz=1.

2. George W. Bush, "President-Elect Bush Meets with Congressional Leaders on Capitol Hill," CNN, December 18, 2000, http://transcripts.cnn.com/TRANSCRIPTS/0012/18/nd.01.html.

3. Barack Obama, "First Cabinet Meeting of 2014," CBS News, January 14, 2014, http://www.cbsnews.com/news/obama-i-will-use-my-pen-and-phone-to-take-on-congress/.

4. Richard E. Neustadt, *Presidential Power* (New York: Wiley, 1960), 4.

5. George C. Edwards III, *At the Margins: Presidential Leadership of Congress* (New Haven, Conn.: Yale University Press, 1989).

HARNESSING THE ECONOMY

Lessons from Eight First-Year Crises from Adams to Obama

ROBERT F. BRUNER

Eight presidents confronted a major domestic financial crisis in the first year of their administrations—a sobering reminder that one can either harness the power of the nation's economy, or be run over by it.

Each crisis was unique, which means that a new president is unlikely to have to relive any of these particular nightmares.

JOHN ADAMS, PANIC OF 1797

Unbeknownst to Adams, a week before his inauguration, the Bank of England suspended payments in gold, which triggered a severe credit contraction in Britain and the United States. The contraction burst a bubble of speculation in land and bankrupted merchants and speculators. Adams took no specific action about the Panic of 1797, probably because there was scant precedent for a national government to rescue banks, relieve the unemployed, or stimulate economic growth. The midterm elections of 1798 produced growing tensions between the nascent Federalists and Democratic-Republicans. Adams's strategy was to steer a middle course between the parties, which doomed his chance for reelection in 1800.

MARTIN VAN BUREN, PANIC OF 1837

Weeks after Van Buren's inauguration, a bank panic broke out in New York and other eastern cities. Its roots were in rising interest rates in Britain, the falling price of cotton, and the policies of Van Buren's predecessor, Andrew Jackson. In May 1837, Van Buren called a special session of Congress, to convene in September. His proposal was to reorganize the U.S. Treasury to hold gold reserves in federal subtreasuries, rather than banks, around the country. Congress balked until 1840, when it approved the bill. Popular anger about the panic and subsequent depression echoed in the midterm elections of 1838, which enlarged the opposition party in Congress. Van Buren lost his bid for reelection in 1840.

JAMES BUCHANAN, PANIC OF 1857

Rising interest rates in England and the United States pierced a speculative bubble in land and shares of stock in new railroads. The collapse from August to October 1857 of institutions that had financed the speculation triggered bank runs and suspensions across the nation. The economic contraction sparked riots for bread and strikes by workers. Government tax revenues plunged. Buchanan's specific response to the crisis was to hold the states responsible for relief to unemployed workers; he said that the federal government was "without power to extend relief."[1] The panic aggravated debates about tariffs, homesteading, and slavery, and generally contributed to the widening gulf between the North and South. The midterm elections saw major losses for Buchanan's party. Buchanan retired from public life in 1861.

ABRAHAM LINCOLN, PANIC OF 1861

With the onset of the Civil War, Lincoln and his treasury secretary, Salmon P. Chase, strained to finance the military buildup. Congress approved new taxes and authority to issue bonds. In December 1861, the Treasury sold $150 million in bonds to banks, which were required to pay for the bonds in specie (gold and silver). This massive drain of specie, plus public disbelief in the stability of the banking system, prompted panic. The banks responded by suspending specie payments. The Treasury followed suit by suspending specie payments on its notes. In February 1862, Lincoln signed the Legal Tender Act, which sustained specie suspension by the federal government for two decades and launched the "greenback era" of fiat money. The Democrats made significant gains in the elections of 1862, attributable not only to the banking crisis but also to emancipation, suspension of habeas corpus, and endorsement of a military draft. In February 1863, Lincoln endorsed the National Banking Act, which reformed the financial system and introduced federal regulation of nationally chartered banks.

GROVER CLEVELAND, PANIC OF 1893

A few days before Cleveland's inauguration, a major railroad failed. This was followed within weeks by the bankruptcy of a large industrial trust. Then, on April 21, 1893, the gold reserves of the U.S. government fell below the prudent minimum, prompting a stock market crash. Runs on banks began as depositors feared the collapse of the government and the financial system. At the core of this crisis was the Sherman Silver Act of 1890, the unintended consequence of which was an arbitrage against the government's gold reserves, which canny traders exploited shortly after enactment. Cleveland summoned Congress to an emergency session in August 1893, aiming to repeal the provisions that created the arbitrage; Congress ultimately relented on November 1. Depletion of the Treasury's gold reserves continued through the balance of 1893 and 1894 owing to outstanding legal tender gold notes that had to be honored. In early 1895, Cleveland retained J. P. Morgan to issue bonds in Europe for the purchase of gold, under the authority of a little-known law passed during the Civil War. Morgan's syndicate successfully issued the bonds, the government purchased gold and shipped it to the United States, and confidence in the financial system returned. But the panic and subsequent recession split Cleveland's party and crushed his support in the following midterm and presidential elections.

HERBERT HOOVER, CRASH OF 1929

Almost eight months after Hoover's inauguration, the stock market began a spectacular crash, ultimately losing 85 percent in value. The Great Depression produced mass unemployment, widespread bankruptcies, and bank closings. Caught between progressives who insisted on government relief programs and conservatives who insisted on not responding, Hoover convened a high-level conference of business and government leaders in which he sought to gain voluntary commitments to maintain prices, wages, and employment. These commitments unraveled as the Depression deepened. Hoover signed the infamous Smoot-Hawley Tariff in 1930, in the belief that high tariffs would help to boost domestic production. He declined proposals to undertake a massive public works program or support relief for the unemployed. This, combined with his eviction of bonus marchers from Washington, D.C., fueled criticisms of presidential indifference to social distress. Eventually, Hoover agreed to sign legislation establishing the Reconstruction Finance Corporation, which would invest government funds in ailing firms. And in February 1932, he endorsed legislation to modify the supposedly inviolable gold standard and allow the Federal Reserve to discount a wider range of securities. In December 1932, Hoover signed the Federal Home Loan Bank Act, establishing a system to provide liquidity and oversight to building and loan associations. Yet his presidential activism was too little, too late. The Republican majority of 62 percent of House seat in 1928 fell to 28 percent after the election in November 1932.

FRANKLIN D. ROOSEVELT, PANIC OF 1933

A fresh wave of bank runs in the month before Roosevelt's inauguration heralded the renewed virulence of the Great Depression. FDR declined to embrace any of Hoover's policy proposals before his inauguration in March 1933. In his first inaugural address, Roosevelt set a tone of confidence, determination, and activism. Two days later, he issued a proclamation declaring a national bank holiday and calling Congress immediately into special session. What ensued was the famous "Hundred Days" in which Congress enacted fifteen pieces of major legislation, creating a government safety net stitched from stimulus spending, jobs programs, deposit insurance, bank resolution, and new regulations of the financial sector. Roosevelt led the United States off the gold standard. Through the Reconstruction Finance Corporation, the government became an active financier of last resort not only for banks but also industrial firms. Yet John Maynard Keynes criticized Roosevelt for emphasizing reform over recovery. Historians today debate whether FDR's response was so different from the direction in which Hoover had been heading in his final months. Roosevelt's congressional majority was sustained in the 1934 midterm election, and he was reelected to three more terms in office.

BARACK OBAMA, PANIC OF 2008–2009

The most recent of the eight crises climaxed in August through October 2008, with the collapse or bailout of financial institutions, a stock market crash, and financial distress of industrial firms. Regulators of the financial system—mainly the Federal Reserve and the Federal Deposit Insurance Corporation—intervened to stabilize the financial system through radical new monetary tactics and the exercise of a little-used provision of the Federal Reserve Act. In 2008, President George W. Bush's administration took various steps to quell the panic: stabilizing financial institutions and industrial firms, urging calm, and using existing powers in new and novel ways. But the flurry of interventions by the government triggered populist revulsion that eventually took shape as the Tea Party and Occupy Wall Street protest movements. The elections in November 2008 returned large Democratic majorities to Congress and sent a Democrat to the White House. Eight days after Obama's inauguration, on January 28, 2009, Congress passed the American Recovery and Reinvestment Act of 2009, a $787 billion economic stimulus plan. In 2010, Obama signed the Dodd-Frank Wall Street Reform Act.

Despite their heterogeneity, these eight crises yield six lessons.

1. The risk of a financial crisis is material.

Almost one in five presidents has confronted a major domestic financial crisis in the first year of his administration. Half of all presidents faced a major financial crisis at some point.

Barry Eichengreen, an economist at the University of California at Berkeley, wrote, "A crisis is a time when the pace of events seems to accelerate and when information is especially incomplete."[2] A severe financial crisis damages not only the financial system ("Wall Street") but also the real economy ("Main Street"), in the form of lost output, curtailed research and development, reduced capital investment, rising unemployment and bankruptcies, and the appearance of bread lines and civil unrest. According to one estimate, the economic output lost to a banking crisis amounts to 23 percent of gross domestic product, a massive setback.

A financial crisis can presage regime shift—a durable change in voting behavior. Populist anger toward elites is a regular response to major domestic financial crises, exemplified by the Tea Party after the Panic of 2008–9, William Jennings Bryan and the populists after the Panic of 1893, and the Whigs after the Panic of 1837. In the midterm elections following the eight crises discussed above, the median decline in House seats held by the president's party was 12 percent—twice the average loss of seats in the House in noncrisis midterm elections. Cleveland's party suffered a stunning 35 percent decline in the House, which remains the record. Roosevelt, however, experienced a gain of 2 percent in the House and 11 percent in the Senate. Regime shift can move either way, depending on how the president handles the crisis.

2. Presidents should save their leadership capital for only the largest financial crises.

Most financial crises are contained and have little long-lasting effect. The decline and bankruptcy of Enron in the fall of 2001—George W. Bush's first year as president—potentially threatened the stability of financial and energy markets just one month after the September 11 terror attacks. But Bush decided against any intervention. In 1998, when a run on Long Term Capital Management, a hedge fund, threatened the stability of the financial system, the Federal Reserve, not President Bill Clinton, used its influence to organize an orderly liquidation of the company. President George H. W. Bush declined to intervene in the crash of the junk bond market following the indictment of executives of Drexel Burnham Lambert in 1989. Various sharp but short stock market crashes in 1987 and 2010 elicited no presidential action. Thus, the staple response to smaller and more local events is for the president to do nothing and let the markets cure themselves, with appropriate regulatory oversight.

3. Presidents should focus on Main Street and on forestalling the next crisis.

Various federal laws empower agencies such as the Federal Reserve, the Federal Deposit Insurance Corporation, the Securities and Exchange Commission, the Consumer Financial Protection Bureau, and the Financial Stability Oversight Council to stabilize the financial system in a crisis. Their tools include auditing and investigating, imposing capitalization standards, managing interest rates, injecting liquidity and capital into the system, and implementing "circuit breakers" to suspend trading in financial markets that are spiraling out of control. All of these are time-honored responses but are not to be implemented lightly. The dilemmas are less about whether to implement these tactics and more about when and how.

Although powerful, the regulators are limited in the scope of their discretion. The president complements the agencies with other vectors of response. One vector entails initiating reforms of the financial system to enhance stability and forestall another crisis. Van Buren, Lincoln, Cleveland, and Roosevelt led such efforts. In June 2009, the Obama administration advanced regulatory reforms that ultimately emerged as the Dodd-Frank Act in 2010, the most significant change in financial sector regulation in seventy-six years.

A second vector is promoting transparency. During a crisis, decision makers and the public need to know what is going on. The president can promote transparency through executive orders, wise legislation, and study commissions. Transparency helps to relieve problems caused by information asymmetry. The National Banking Act of 1863; the Federal Reserve Act, which grew out of the Panic of 1907; Roosevelt's legislative agenda in 1933 and 1934; and the Dodd-Frank Act of 2010 all imposed new public reporting requirements on financial institutions. Sunlight may be the best disinfectant, but transparency comes with a cost, such as time-consuming reporting and bureaucratic oversight.

A third vector is relieving distress and stimulating the economy. Repairing the real economy is the province of the president, for which he or she has the full panoply of instruments: fiscal stimulus spending, social relief, executive orders, government contracts, antitrust and tax policy, and the "bully pulpit" for exhorting decision makers to action.

In response to the Panic of 2008, George Bush and Barack Obama deployed their administrations to nudge nearly $1.5 trillion in fiscal spending bills through Congress, stimulate the economy, bail out industrial firms such as General Motors and Chrysler, promote mergers of failing institutions, and assist distressed mortgage borrowers.

It was not always thus. Adams, Van Buren, Buchanan, Lincoln, and Cleveland did nothing in the way of relief and economic stimulus. The tide turned with Herbert Hoover. Today, voters are likely to expect some presidential intervention to address the damage to the real economy from a major financial crisis.

4. Quelling a financial crisis hinges on attributes of leadership.

Nobel laureate in economics Milton Friedman and his wife, economist Anna Jacobson Schwartz, wrote, "The detailed story of every banking crisis [is that] . . . in the absence of vigorous intellectual leadership . . . the tendencies of drift and indecision had full scope. Moreover, as time went on, their force cumulated. Each failure to act made another such failure more likely."[3]

Presidential leadership in a financial crisis is a matter of asserting priorities, mobilizing a coalition, and communicating well to other decision makers and to the public. Presidents are not in control of crisis-fighting. But they have immense influence and convening power to coordinate actions across the federal government. In addition to coordinating and motivating regulators, the president must work with Congress—often with the opposition party—on legislation involving fiscal stimulus and changes in financial regulation. Turning to Congress was among the earliest steps of Van Buren, Lincoln, Cleveland, Roosevelt, and Obama.

Engaging the opposition, however, is both expedient and fraught with danger, since the other party will certainly sense the potential for regime shift. Generally, presidential legislation responding to a financial crisis has garnered scant support from the opposition. Offering a response to the crisis that is partisan and polarizing is especially risky. Van Buren, Buchanan, and Cleveland all did this, and their parties suffered the consequences.

The potential for regime shift poses a stark choice: master the crisis or be mastered. "You never want a serious crisis to go to waste. And what I mean by that is an opportunity to do things that you think you could not do before," Rahm Emanuel, President Obama's first chief of staff, said in 2008.[4]

Lincoln, Roosevelt, and Obama made broad changes in financial regulations. Reagan significantly restructured the savings and loan industry. Roosevelt and Obama also harnessed their crisis momentum on behalf of social legislation.

5. Presidents should stay flexible.

A first-year first-term financial crisis calls for pragmatism and agility. Even though Van Buren campaigned on a continuation of Andrew Jackson's system of "pet bank" depositories for gold reserves, he swung his support to a subtreasury system after the Panic of 1837. FDR's platform in 1932 advocated a balanced budget, which he abandoned in 1934. He also campaigned against federal deposit insurance but later endorsed such legislation. Theodore Roosevelt, the trust-buster, endorsed a major merger in the steel industry to help quell the Panic of 1907. In the face of a run on the dollar in 1971, Richard Nixon abandoned the gold standard, famously saying, "I am now a Keynesian in economics."

Turning away from strong ideology or campaign promises is politically risky, although voters may forgive a pivot in the face of extreme circumstances, especially if the results are good.

6. Do no harm.

A concluding word of caution: Interventions risk making the financial system less nimble and more costly and can promote moral hazard. Government intervention in crises (large and small, systemic and local) may create an incentive for excessive risk-taking, which can amplify and accelerate the next crisis.

Also, the consequences of a financial crisis vary considerably by industry, region, and socioeconomic class. Industries such as health care; education; and food, beverage, and tobacco products actually grew in 2009 and 2010. By contrast, oil and gas exploration and automobile and furniture manufacturing fell sharply. In 1857, the manufacturing North suffered much more than the plantation South.

NOTES

1. James Buchanan, "First Annual Message to Congress on the State of the Union," Washington, D.C., December 8, 1857.

2. Barry Eichengreen, *Hall of Mirrors: The Great Depression, the Great Recession, and the Uses—and Misuses—of History* (New York: Oxford University Press, 2014), 380.

3. Milton Friedman and Anna Jacobson Schwartz, *A Monetary History of the United States, 1857–1960* (Cambridge, Mass.: National Bureau of Economic Research, 1964), 418.

4. Jack Rosenthal, "A Terrible Thing to Waste," *New York Times,* July 31, 2009.

DEAR MR. OR MADAM PRESIDENT

A Letter to the New President on Your First Year

PETER WEHNER

On the day before John F. Kennedy was inaugurated, President Dwight D. Eisenhower told him, "There are no easy matters that will ever come to you as president. If they are easy, they will be settled at a lower level."[1]

As a new president, you are about to discover that problems were easier to solve when you ran than they are once you take office. You will hear competing arguments that sound equally convincing. You will be expected to make consequential decisions on incomplete information in a compressed period of time, decisions whose outcome may well be determined by contingencies you cannot anticipate. That is just one of the reasons why presidents often age visibly during their tenures.

There is a great paradox at the heart of the presidency. It is, to be sure, the most powerful office in the world. But to assume events can be shaped like hot wax will set you up for an endless series of frustrations. To be psychologically prepared, you need to recognize from the outset that the constraints on your ability to shape events are far greater than you have anticipated.

Historically, the first year has been the easiest year to fulfill the goals of your campaign. Members of Congress tend to be more deferential to new presidents in the first twelve months than at any other time. You will want to take advantage of whatever goodwill there may be by having a very clear idea of what initiatives to pursue and the order in which to pursue them. Many issues will vie for your attention, and many will deserve it. But you need to make clear to Congress—and the country—what agenda items are first among equals. This will require discipline from you and your aides.

Political capital is limited. If you use it wisely, the success you have will build on itself. If you do not, you will be stunned at how quickly your power and influence can dissipate. President Jimmy Carter, for example, encountered significant setbacks in his first year that established the tone for his single term. The cornerstone of his legislative agenda, an energy bill, failed. He abruptly dropped support for a tax rebate after pressuring reluctant members of Congress to back it, infuriating many of them. His call to withdraw funds for water projects throughout the country further irritated legislative leaders. And his budget director and close friend, Bert Lance, was forced to resign over an ethics scandal. By the end of his first year, Carter was a wounded president, having experienced a dramatic loss in public support.

It is also important to govern in a way that aligns with how you campaigned. President Bill Clinton endured a rocky start to his administration because he felt he was losing control of his presidency, in the words of his former aide George Stephanopoulos.[2] Clinton ran as a New Democrat, focusing "like a laser beam" on the economy. Yet during his first months in office, he was seen as pursuing a liberal agenda (for example, allowing gays to serve in the military and pushing a gasoline tax increase). The early months of his presidency were discordant with what people expected. Unlike the Carter presidency, however, the Clinton presidency showed you can get off to a bad beginning and still correct course in plenty of time to win an easy reelection.

One of the least appreciated qualities in a successful president is nimbleness— the ability to assess circumstances and adjust to them. On one level, this skill will allow you to use unexpected moments to your advantage—for example, to signal resolve that leaves an impression on allies and adversaries. In the first year of Ronald Reagan's presidency, air traffic controllers went on strike. Reagan had warned that he would fire them if they did. He was true to his word—and that action was noticed as far away as the Kremlin. According to the Reagan biographer Edmund Morris, "Former Soviet apparatchiks will tell you that it was not his famous 'evil empire' speech in 1983 that convinced them he meant strategic business, so much as photographs of the leader of the air traffic controllers union being taken to jail in 1981."[3]

You will always want to seek to control events rather than be at their mercy. You will have a narrative in mind, but events may well intervene. Kennedy faced unanticipated crises in Cuba and Berlin. George W. Bush's presidency was transformed by the attacks on September 11, 2001. Barack Obama inherited a titanic financial crisis that occurred just before his election in 2008. Do not lament what you cannot control. Instead, adjust to crises. If at all possible, view them as opportunities. How you deal with them is likely to shape your legacy.

When people run for president, they tend to present the choices facing America in Manichean terms. Politics is often framed as a zero-sum game. Governing is different, and a good deal more complicated. "There are few things wholly evil or wholly good," Abraham Lincoln said. "Almost everything, especially of government policy, is an inseparable compound of the two, so that our best judgment of the preponderance between them is continually demanded."[4]

What this means is that you need to staff your White House with people who not only share your philosophy but also possess wisdom and prudence, the ability to apply principles to particular issues in particular circumstances. By all means use experts—but do not defer to them. The tendency toward deference will be particularly strong when it comes to the military. Recall that during the early phases of war, both Lincoln and George W. Bush relied on generals who were pursuing the wrong strategy. They kept looking until they found the right generals (Ulysses S. Grant in the Civil War and David Petraeus in the Iraq War). Once they were in place, the tides turned.

An important but overlooked first-year challenge is to gain control over the permanent bureaucracy that will carry out your policies—or not. Appointing effective cabinet members is one way to tighten your hold on the government. William J. Bennett was Reagan's secretary of education. Using an analogy to explain the early days of his tenure, Bennett said he gave orders, everyone saluted, and he turned the steering wheel of the ship (the Department of Education). But it kept going leeward, so he went below deck and found that the cables had been severed. In order to correct that, Bennett spent the early part of his tenure filling key posts with people who were committed to the Reagan agenda.

Beyond that, seek out the top experts in America to help you create an accountable management system that will translate your policies into action. As University of Maryland Professor Donald F. Kettl has put it, "You need a chief operating officer, someone who can look after the details when you are busy with everything else and speak for you when management muscle is needed."[5] Poor management can do tremendous damage to your presidency. Details matter.

When staffing your administration, you will naturally want to reward political loyalty. There is a place for that. But in the key posts you need people who were chosen above all for their excellence. By this I mean their intelligence, wisdom, and character, in addition to their qualifications and proven performance. Nixon, in selecting his initial cabinet, stressed the youth of his nominees. No one cared. You will be judged on results, and good results are the product of high competence. Everything else—political loyalty, years of service, years of friendship, who they know—needs to be subordinate.

James Baker was a superlative chief of staff for Reagan, yet Baker was originally a George H. W. Bush loyalist. Reagan showed he was willing to hire someone outside his inner circle to serve in a key post, and his presidency was better for it. Clinton hired his lifelong friend Thomas "Mack" McLarty to be his first chief of staff. Although he was a talented man, McLarty did not bring to the job the order and discipline needed to complement Clinton. Leon Panetta, who replaced McLarty in 1994, proved to be a much better fit.

You will need to guard against becoming dependent on or confined to a small group of advisors or experts, and to make sure people in whom you have confidence are present at key meetings and moments. If choke points develop, open things up. Your aides should understand that their job is to bring difficult decisions to you, not to protect you from them. There is a tendency among those who work for presidents to avoid arguing in front of you, to try to force a consensus in order to present a unified front. Make it clear that you are not afraid to hear vigorous debate; in fact, you welcome it. The message needs to go out to your senior advisors: if a genuine consensus does not exist, do not pretend that it does.

"The president wants to make decisions himself, not to preside over decisions made by staff," noted William Safire, an aide to President Richard Nixon.[6] After the Bay of Pigs fiasco, according to historian Arthur Schlesinger, Jr., Kennedy learned to "make greater use of generalists in whom he had personal confidence and remake every decision in his own terms."[7]

Learn from your predecessors' missteps but do not overlearn from them. There is a natural tendency to want to distance yourself from your immediate predecessor, especially if he was a member of the other party. That is understandable; you want to establish your own identity. But you will also discover that smart people preceded you. So sharply critiquing your predecessor should not trap you into reflexively rejecting previous policies.

Learn from your own mistakes, too. You will make some—and when you do, there will be tremendous internal pressure to downplay, ignore, or conceal them. Don't. If you figure out what went wrong, you are less likely to make a similar mistake in the future. The lessons Kennedy learned from the Bay of Pigs fiasco helped prepare him to succeed during the Cuban Missile Crisis.

Beware of advisors who, when a policy is perceived to be failing, tell you that you have a "communications problem." You may in fact have a real problem that creates a public relations problem. While serving in the White House, during a meeting about the Iraq War when things were going quite badly, one advisor said that we had a "communications problem" and needed a series of speeches to correct for it. I replied, "We don't have a communications problem. We have a facts-on-the-ground problem." Correcting the facts-on-the-ground problem will go a long way toward correcting your communications problem.

Every time your staff raises a problem, ask for a solution. Encourage a habit of mind in your senior aides that looks for answers and that is constantly and carefully thinking through the right response to the question, "What can we do to make things better?" And surround yourself with people who can think boldly, who are good at creating opportunities that others do not see. The President's Emergency Plan for AIDS Relief (PEPFAR), George W. Bush's global AIDS and malaria initiative, was a great moral achievement. There were aides who wanted to spend a fraction of what he eventually did. The president rejected their counsel, and as a result, more than a million lives were saved.

Even though it may seem as if there is no time to examine new ideas, keep the creative juices flowing. "The convictions that leaders have formed before reaching high office are the intellectual capital they will consume as long as they continue in office," Henry Kissinger has observed. "There is little time for leaders to reflect."[8] That is often the case, but you can fight it. You have the best minds in the world at your disposal—historians, scholars, public intellectuals, philosophers, theologians, and scientists. Make use of them. Set aside time in your schedule to think carefully and deeply on fundamental questions. Replenish your intellectual capital and use your experiences to refine your preexisting views. You can leave the presidency knowing a lot more than when you began it.

As president, your capacity to shape public opinion is considerable, while your capacity to change public opinion is less than you may think. Presidential scholars like George C. Edwards III have shown that the essence of successful presidential leadership is recognizing and exploiting existing opportunities, not in creating them through persuasion. Edwards makes a strong case that to avoid overreaching, presidents should be alert to the limitations of their power to persuade.[9]

Be prepared to change your mind when the facts warrant doing so—and be prepared to tell the American people you have done so. Most of them will accept it if you explain to them, in an honest and candid way, what you may have gotten wrong. The public will judge you on outcomes far more than they will on process. They want you to get decisions right, even if getting it right requires you to change your previous views. Nixon was known as a fierce anticommunist before he was elected. As president, he opened the door to communist China, which ranks among his greatest achievements.

You have an obligation to lead, but be careful that you don't force the pace beyond what circumstances allow. "A statesman who too far outruns the experience of his people will fail in achieving domestic consensus, however wise his policies," Kissinger wrote in his doctoral dissertation.[10] Be careful as well about overpromising. William Safire warned that the politicians who promise rain are held responsible for drought. And droughts will come.

Some journalists may give you the benefit of the doubt in the early days of your presidency, which will be helpful as you seek to shape public opinion. But many reporters will soon turn skeptical or hostile. When you know the inside story, you will realize how much of what is reported is incomplete, misleading, or outright false. You and your aides will be frustrated and even angry. But do not let yourself or your team view the press as the enemy. It feeds an attitude of paranoia that can imperil a presidency.

Do not tolerate people in your administration who mislead the press. In doing so, they are misleading the American people. I would even suggest that you embrace the press as an outside check on your administration. There is a tremendous temptation in the White House to automatically dismiss criticisms as ill-informed and unfair. Before you dismiss your critics, hear them out.

Beyond the press and the public, your administration will have to tend to Congress. Make sure your legislative affairs shop is attentive to members of both parties. The White House needs to show appropriate courtesy and deference toward the Hill—including, occasionally, with direct interactions from you. Treat legislators well even when they disagree with you. You may not have their votes now but you may get them in the future. The historian Douglas Brinkley said of Carter, "Often he wouldn't return phone calls of leading senators. There was a kind of an abrasive attitude he had towards them. He never showed them the respect. So they all eventually got bitter and turned on him."[11]

We live in an unusually polarized time, with both parties more ideological than has been historically the case. This makes working with Congress more challenging than in the past but certainly not impossible. President Lyndon B. Johnson is a good model in this respect. A quarter-century veteran of Congress himself, he was conversant in its ways and never forgot its importance to his administration.

How best to bring Congress and public opinion to your side? Speeches that do more to educate, rather than rally, will work to your advantage. Explain the various options you've considered and how you arrived at your decision. George W. Bush's first nationally televised speech was to announce his policy on stem-cell research. He laid out the competing arguments in an evenhanded way, and the audience did not know his position until the end. All speeches cannot follow that model—but more can than typically do.

It will not always be easy but try to retain a relatively charitable view of your political adversaries. "Remember, we have no enemies, only opponents," former Indiana governor Mitch Daniels, who worked as a political aide to Reagan, quotes him as admonishing his staff.[12] Keep in mind, above all, that you are the one person in public life who was elected to represent the entire nation. There will be a temptation to take the low road now and then. Resist it. Appeal to the better, not the darker, impulses of the American people. There is honor in doing so.

NOTES

1. John F. Kennedy Interview, December 17, 1962, American Presidency Project, http://www.presidency.ucsb.edu/ws/?pid=9060.

2. George Stephanopolous Interview, July 2000, PBS, http://www.pbs.org/wgbh/pages/frontline/shows/clinton/interviews/stephanopoulos.html.

3. Edmund Morris, *This Living Hand: And Other Essays* (Random House: New York, 2012).

4. Abraham Lincoln, *Lincoln's Words on Living Questions,* ed. H. S. Taylor and D. M. Fulwiler (Chicago: Trusty, 1900), 63.

5. Donald F. Kettl, "Ten Secret Truths about Government Incompetence," *Washington Monthly,* January/February 2015, http://washingtonmonthly.com/magazine/janfeb-2015/ten-secret-truths-about-government-incompetence/.

6. William Safire, *Before the Fall: An Inside View of the Pre-Watergate White House* (Garden City, N.Y.: Doubleday, 1975), 116.

7. Arthur M. Schlesinger, Jr., *A Thousand Days: John F. Kennedy in the White House* (Boston: Houghton Mifflin Harcourt, 2002), 296.

8. Henry Kissinger, *A White House Restored* (New York: Grosset and Dunlap, 1964), 329.

9. George C. Edwards III, *Predicting the Presidency: The Potential of Persuasive Leadership* (Princeton, N.J.: Princeton University Press, 2016).

10. Henry Kissinger, *A World Restored* (London: Weidenfeld and Nicholson, 1957), 329.

11. Douglas Brinkley Interview, "Jimmy Carter," *American Experience,* PBS, http://amextbg2.wgbhdigital.org/wgbh/americanexperience/features/transcript/carter-transcript/.

12. Mitch Daniels, "Governor Mitch Daniels Remarks at the Conservative Political Action Conference," Washington, D.C., February 11, 2011, https://www.c-span.org/video/?297974-3/governor-mitch-daniels-remarks.

III ★ NATIONAL SECURITY AND DIPLOMACY

JOHN F. KENNEDY
AND THE LESSONS OF
FIRST-YEAR STUMBLES

MARC SELVERSTONE

"Who would want to read a book on disasters?"

That was the question John F. Kennedy put to an aide in late 1961 when he heard that journalists were thinking about writing books on the first year of his presidency. As he knew full well, his previous twelve months had been filled with several foreign-policy missteps—the most notable and damaging being the failed invasion at Cuba's Bay of Pigs.

But, as Kennedy himself might have imagined, any book on that difficult year would have included his response to those "disasters," thereby offering something of a primer on how to make a course correction early in a presidency. Among its lessons would have been the need to: (1) rely on loyal and trusted advisors, (2) temper the urge to scrap existing administrative procedures, (3) insist on a full and frank discussion of policy options, (4) maintain open channels of communication with adversaries, and (5) allow those adversaries a dignified retreat. Many of these lessons derive in no small part from the Cuban fiasco, arguably Kennedy's worst blunder during his time in office.

Ironically, Cuba figured prominently in Kennedy winning the White House in 1960. Throughout the presidential campaign, the Democratic senator confronted Richard M. Nixon, the sitting vice president, on the Republicans' handling of Cuba. It was on the GOP's watch, Kennedy charged, that Fidel Castro engineered his revolution and cozied up to the Soviet Union. Kennedy chastised Republicans for failing to prevent Castro's consolidation of power and absorption into Moscow's orbit, criticizing President Dwight D. Eisenhower, and by extension Nixon, for insufficient vigor in meeting the communist threat.

Kennedy refrained from public comment on Cuba during the presidential transition as he shifted his efforts from campaigning to governing. But the narrow margin of his popular victory and the hawkish tenor of his rhetoric late in the contest narrowed his room for maneuver once he took office. Having laid the groundwork for a more assertive posture toward the Castro regime, Kennedy heightened the consequences of inaction if he failed to make good on his pledge of greater activism. The domestic politics of foreign policymaking, particularly for a Democratic Party still smarting from partisan battles over the Chinese communist revolution and the effects of McCarthyism, sustained the momentum toward anti-Castro military action.

The choices Kennedy made during this period concerning personnel, process, and priorities also conditioned his approach to Cuba and shaped the contours of his national security policymaking more broadly. Nowhere in this mix, however, was there any indication of which subjects Kennedy would tackle first as president or how he might sequence his agenda thereafter. Indeed, his national security advisor, McGeorge Bundy, acknowledged that the incoming administration would simply respond to external events as they arose, and that high-level planning would focus primarily on capabilities and tactics. Overarching statements of strategy were likely to be so broad as to be useless, and, if divorced from the budgetary process, would fail to meet the strategic imperative of matching means with ends.

Accordingly, Kennedy showed no interest in establishing a comprehensive and coherent national security strategy for his administration. He chose neither to review Eisenhower's basic national security policy during the transition nor to consider how the many threats facing the United States fit into a broader conceptual approach to national security. In fact, he never settled on a formal, articulated statement of security strategy during the entirety of his presidency. Although aides began the process of fleshing one out in 1961, it never received Kennedy's final sanction, not the least of reasons being the president's discomfort with such documents' potential for limiting his range of options.

If there was a strategic lodestar for the administration, it was the principle of "flexible response," which emerged in reaction to Eisenhower's perceived reliance on nuclear weapons for addressing all manner of enemy hostilities. A more nimble approach, Kennedy reasoned, would allow Washington to meet communist provocations with a range of responses, of graduating intensity, from the limited warfare of counterinsurgency, to the conventional warfare of battlefield maneuvers, to the nuclear option. Kennedy beefed up military capabilities in each of these areas, following a review of defense policy early in his new administration. The ensuing fiscal expansion threatened to undo the ties that Eisenhower stressed between balanced budgets and national security, but Kennedy viewed deficit spending as a stimulus package that would allow him to expand the arsenal while growing the economy.

To enact his defense programs, as well as his foreign and domestic initiatives, Kennedy assembled a "ministry of talent" to populate a bipartisan cabinet and White House staff. The group was composed of energetic, pragmatic policymakers—action-intellectuals, in the vernacular. "You can't beat brains," he would quip about Bundy; it was a comment equally befitting Defense Secretary Robert McNamara.[1] Preferring to act as his own secretary of state, though, Kennedy settled on the more taciturn Dean Rusk to lead Foggy Bottom.

Kennedy also revamped the machinery of national security, molding it to his operational style to allow for a more fluid policymaking environment. Facets of the National Security Council (NSC) that Eisenhower relied on to produce thoroughly vetted—and, to Kennedy, utterly stale—policy options and ventures were dismantled in favor of a leaner bureaucracy marked by a jumble of taskforces on regional and functional issues. As a result, the locus of energy in the administration, at least for its first year, remained at the tactical level, as Kennedy and his advisors developed bilateral and regional policies without systematically assessing their relative importance or their strategic coherence. Progressive innovations such as the Alliance for Progress, the Agency for International Development, and the Peace Corps remained in tension with the Cold War impulses suffusing them. Although such measures offered compelling rationales in isolation, each contributed to the missteps that were soon to come.

None was as traumatic or as consequential as the Bay of Pigs. Kennedy's first year included several low points—mounting troubles with communist forces in Southeast Asia; a testy exchange with Soviet premier Nikita Khrushchev in Vienna; and a heightened sense of crisis over Berlin, with the building of a wall separating that city's eastern and western residents, and a showdown with Soviet tanks at Berlin's Checkpoint Charlie. But all paled beside the failed invasion of Cuba's southern shore. Kennedy inherited a scheme to topple Fidel Castro from Eisenhower, and although leery of involving himself in actions held over from the previous administration, the new president nevertheless sanctioned ongoing planning for an assault. Success for the plan was hardly assured, but fearing that its design rendered the operation too "noisy" and thus too easily traceable to American sponsorship, Kennedy altered key elements of the proposed invasion, including the site of its landing and the scope of its air cover.

Compounding his troubles, Kennedy's national security team failed to conduct a meticulous evaluation of the revised plan and its chances for success, dooming the operation, now known as Zapata, to failure. Key principals never met with the president en masse to probe with sufficient rigor the veracity of guiding assumptions, the soundness of tactics, and the likely attainment of objectives. Senior defense officials never fully dissected the particulars of what had come to be a military operation run by the Central Intelligence Agency (CIA). Kennedy himself failed to grasp the mantle of the entire process and demand both full candor and a complete evaluation. Nor did the president gauge the consequences of the operation for his goal of better hemispheric relations and his support for postcolonial nations worldwide. The result was indeed a disaster. Not only did the operation fail, with over 100 members of the invasion force killed and more than 1,200 captured, but it came to be seen as an American project—the very outcome the president most sought to avoid. For Kennedy, the experience was shattering.

Although the president accepted blame publicly for the humiliation, privately he seethed at the malfeasance, incompetence, or mendacity of key members of his national security team. He judged himself equally culpable, wondering how he could have been so "stupid." But failure at the Bay of Pigs wasn't just the result of poor advice or bad judgment. It also stemmed from deficiencies within the machinery for national security policymaking. The compartmentalized taskforce arrangement failed to provide an adequate means of fully vetting the operation. Eisenhower's hierarchical NSC was not the right fit for the less-stratified Kennedy White House, but its emphasis on formal and systematic procedures might well have imposed the necessary rigor on the New Frontiersmen's less-deliberative process. Kennedy's own frenetic pace and style likely contributed to the disarray as well. In the aftermath of the crisis, Bundy complained to the president about how hard it had been to pin him down on specific matters and have him digest information in an orderly fashion. But failure in Cuba occurred at every stage of the process—managerial, operational, and analytic—with too little forethought, too much improvisation, and too few profiles in courage.

To conduct the operation's postmortem, Kennedy turned to retired general Maxwell D. Taylor, whose earlier writings had popularized the term "flexible response." Structural and personnel changes, even architectural ones, were soon in the offing. Bundy moved physically closer to the president, trading space in the Executive Office Building for a basement office in the White House. A new Situation Room adjoined Bundy's office, ensuring that classified information from the relevant national security agencies flowed uninterrupted to the national security advisor and his staff. Kennedy also reshaped his team, releasing or reassigning officials he deemed insufficiently loyal, supportive, or astute; these included top-tier policymakers at the State Department and the CIA. In time, Kennedy also replaced the army and navy chiefs of staff, and removed the chairman of the Joint Chiefs.

But merely swapping out one set of officials for another neither enhanced the quality of advice nor the frankness of those giving it. Kennedy therefore turned to men whose judgment he trusted. His increasing reliance on Special Counsel Ted Sorensen and even more on his brother Robert F. Kennedy, the attorney general, brought new voices into discussions of national security. Alongside Taylor, who now served the president as his military representative and mediated between the president and the Joint Chiefs, Robert Kennedy became a catalyst for the newly created Special Group coordinating counterinsurgency activities. The president thus shrewdly placed those closest to him in positions where they could lobby increasingly hard for the more activist elements of administration policy, which arguably were those he deemed most important.

These changes and others conditioned Kennedy's handling of national security for the remainder of his presidency. More formal procedures for managing policy took root following the Bay of Pigs. In addition to the Special Group and its offshoots, an NSC standing committee assumed coordination of interdepartmental activities, stepping in to provide leadership where the State Department had proved wanting. Improvisation remained, however, and episodically to the good, as an executive committee of the NSC, known as ExComm, labored to resolve the Cuban Missile Crisis and other matters into 1963. In terms of personnel, Kennedy's vow never to rely on the "experts" left him wary of recommendations from military and intelligence officials, stiffening his reluctance to intervene in Laos and his resistance to an American combat role in Vietnam, and leading him to delay the use of lethal force in resolving the missile crisis. Likewise, Kennedy settled the Berlin tank crisis in October 1961 by using his brother Robert and a secret backchannel, and with an awareness of the need for American as well as Soviet leaders to avoid escalation and humiliation; it was a lesson Kennedy would heed twelve months later when faced with Soviet missiles in Cuba. In addition, Kennedy's willingness to establish a personal relationship with Khrushchev through a "pen pal" correspondence in late 1961, during a period flush with bellicose public rhetoric and dramatic confrontation, may also have aided in the peaceful resolution of the missile crisis.

But these lessons were offset by less salutary measures Kennedy took both before and after his early Caribbean misadventure. With public statements first rejecting the idea of a "missile gap" in Moscow's favor and then acknowledging Washington's superiority in nuclear weapons, administration officials openly needled Khrushchev and laid bare the reality of the strategic balance. The administration's continued agitation for Castro's ouster further threatened Soviet interests, particularly at a time when Moscow was competing with Beijing for leadership of the communist world. No one was more hawkish on Cuba than Robert Kennedy, whose value to the president in the wake of Zapata should not mask his contribution to the frictions that culminated in the placement of Soviet missiles on that embattled island.

These provocations suggest that the ends and means of administration policy, along with the policies themselves, were often in tension with each other. They highlight the contradictions, for instance, between Kennedy's support for the developing world and his opposition to revolutionary nationalism. Likewise, his courting of African leaders and Latin American regimes collided with Cold War concerns about Marxist reforms and troublesome governments, often leading him to trade economic, social, and political progress for local and international stability. Although willing to treat with neutral nations and nettlesome figures, and frequently impatient with the dogmas of the era, Kennedy operated in a zero-sum environment in which mere perceptions of communist gains could prompt fears of falling dominoes. As a result, the president resorted—selectively—to subversion and a heavy hand, the better to ensure that modernizing and emerging nations would not fall prey to instability and a potential lurch leftward.

Kennedy's approach also reveals that his sensitivity to rifts within the communist world failed to shape policy in ways that moderated the belligerence of great power adversaries. Although his emerging detente with Moscow and isolation of Beijing contributed to the desired hardening of the Sino-Soviet split, the near-term benefits of the rift to Washington likely shrank with Kennedy's escalation of the conflict in Vietnam. The influx of American military aid to Saigon helped to galvanize increasing Chinese and, eventually, Soviet support for Hanoi, as the two communist powers competed for influence and prestige in Southeast Asia and in the socialist world at large.

The collective weight of these developments suggests that much of Kennedy's national security policymaking played out in an atmosphere of almost unrelenting crisis. In the wake of the missile showdown, Robert McNamara's apocryphal remark that there was "no longer any such thing as strategy, only crisis management," captures the sense that events were outpacing the relevance of broader conceptual planning.[2] The administration, however, had never tried to articulate a comprehensive and systematic strategy, and arguably had been engaged in crisis management since its first days in office. It may be that all presidential administrations are fated to do likewise—especially during the first year—as they respond to threats and opportunities both seen and unforeseen. But a failure to undertake a more comprehensive strategic review denied Kennedy the chance to establish priorities, evaluate the coherence of proposed initiatives, and consider more rigorously the implications of policy options.

NOTES

1. Ivo H. Daalder and I. M. Destler, *In the Shadow of the Oval Office: Profiles of the National Security Advisers and the Presidents They Served—From JFK to George W. Bush* (New York: Simon and Schuster, 2009), 34.

2. Coral Bell, *The Conventions of Crisis: A Study in Diplomatic Management* (London: Oxford University Press for the Royal Institute of International Affairs, 1971), 34.

RONALD REAGAN'S DYSFUNCTIONAL FIRST-YEAR TEAM— AND HOW HE FIXED IT

HAL BRANDS

In 1977, Richard Allen, a foreign-policy advisor, asked Ronald Reagan for his theory of U.S.-Soviet relations. "Here's my strategy on the Cold War," Reagan replied. "We win, they lose."[1]

Reagan's statement reveals a crucial insight that new presidents need to grasp: they must have core strategic ideas in place to orient their early policies. Of course, presidents always have to adapt to crises as they arise. But success in times of crisis often depends on having a few clear, guiding ideas that can help them set their administration's course and navigate through the inevitable troubles that arise.

Reagan's first year in office also contains three other vital lessons that he learned the hard way:

1. Presidents must select advisors who are compatible with their management style;
2. Presidents must have a strong, fully empowered national security advisor to facilitate effective decision making and implementation;
3. Presidents must be willing to drop ineffective personnel and revisit flawed administrative arrangements early on, even when such changes can be embarrassing.

By the time he became president in 1981, Reagan had spent decades formulating the core tenets of his approach to the Cold War. Like many conservatives, Reagan was alarmed by the Soviet military buildup of the 1960s and 1970s, as well as by recent Kremlin advances in the Third World. Yet he also viewed communism as inherently unsustainable, and he perceived that Soviet military strength cloaked profound economic, political, and ideological decay. During his pre-presidential years, Reagan had argued that concerted pressure could turn the tide of the Cold War and restore American leverage over a declining rival. That leverage, in turn, could be used to facilitate more advantageous arms control agreements and begin reducing superpower tensions on favorable terms.

Before and during the 1980 campaign, Reagan had also begun to spell out specific initiatives to realize this aspiration. He advocated a multiyear military buildup, along with greater efforts to resist communist expansion and contest recent Soviet gains in the Third World. He called for an economic warfare campaign against the Soviet bloc and other initiatives to encourage Soviet dissidents and underscore the internal rot of the system. These measures, Reagan argued, were essential to restore American strength and establish the conditions for successful East-West diplomacy. Although Reagan often appeared an unrepentant hardliner, he had long favored the reduction, if not outright elimination, of nuclear weapons, and he argued that Washington could safely become more aggressive in arms control once it had created a stronger negotiating position. "If you look at [his pre-presidential writings and speeches]," one advisor later noted, "you can see the whole . . . conceptual understructure of the Reagan administration right there."[2]

Ideas are one thing—putting them into action is another. When Reagan took office, the context for turning his "conceptual understructure" into a coherent set of policies looked promising. Democrats ruled the House of Representatives, but Republicans controlled the Senate for the first time in a quarter century. Partisanship aside, there was increased domestic and congressional receptivity to hawkish policies, largely because of Soviet overreach in recent years. And in response to that overreach, the Carter administration had begun its own Cold War offensive in 1979–80, laying the initial groundwork—in areas from strategic modernization of the American military to support for anticommunist insurgents—for the policies that Reagan would pursue.

In 1981, this context—and Reagan's overarching conceptual framework—helped the administration take several crucial first steps. The administration secured passage of a major defense authorization bill, initiating a multiyear buildup that would ultimately raise real defense spending by more than 40 percent through 1986 and fund an array of conventional and nuclear programs. The seeds of the Reagan Doctrine were also planted when the CIA initiated lethal support to anti-communist rebels in Nicaragua and continued Carter-era aid to the anti-Soviet jihad in Afghanistan. Reagan himself launched what would be a sustained ideological offensive against the Soviet regime, vocally declaiming its failures in order to highlight its internal weaknesses and impair its moral legitimacy at home and abroad. Finally, even though measures to pressure Moscow took priority in Reagan's first year, in November 1981 the administration began to unveil a longer-term diplomatic agenda by offering the "zero option"—a proposal to completely prohibit all intermediate-range nuclear forces in Europe—as a political counterpart to its planned deployment of Pershing-II and Tomahawk missiles in NATO countries.

Each of these initiatives—the military buildup, the Reagan Doctrine, the ideological offensive, and the zero option—would ultimately play crucial roles in

Reagan's Cold War statecraft, and each flowed logically from the strategic mindset that Reagan brought to Washington. In this sense, Reagan's first year affirmed the value of having core strategic ideas to catalyze and guide early action.

But despite these bold first steps, Reagan's first year was hobbled by institutional failings and policy deadlocks. Within the administration, "hardliners," who favored sharp confrontation with Moscow and doubted the value of diplomacy, quarreled endlessly with "moderates," who worried about alienating allies and favored blending strength with early negotiations. The resulting discord caused mixed messages and dueling leaks that discombobulated and often disturbed allied governments.

The discord within Reagan's national security team also generated obstacles to effective decision making on a range of important issues. Despite prolonged deliberations, the administration failed to establish a position on East-West economic relations or economic warfare toward the Soviet bloc. Zero option notwithstanding, 1981 also ended without the administration forging a concrete proposal for the broader Strategic Arms Reduction Talks (START) that Reagan had proposed. Most notably, the administration made virtually no headway toward what should have been a crucial early objective—issuing a comprehensive strategy statement that would translate Reagan's ideas into a formal set of priorities and actions. Certain pieces of Reagan's policy took shape in 1981, but the overall impression was of an administration spinning its wheels.

In part, this disappointing debut reflected Reagan's primary emphasis on his domestic economic program. Yet more important was the nature of his foreign-policy decision-making process. In organizing his administration, Reagan made two crucial decisions. First, he weakened the national security advisor, depriving that position of direct access to the president and demoting it from the cabinet level to a more modest, second-tier staffing role. Second, Reagan focused less on achieving cooperation or cohesion within his inner circle than on populating the cabinet with strong-willed individuals who would advocate for the diverse positions and organizations they represented. Alexander Haig at State, Caspar Weinberger at Defense, William Casey at the CIA, Jeane Kirkpatrick at the U.S. permanent mission to the United Nations, and other aides all fit this mold.

These decisions had their logic. Weakening the national security advisor would ensure that no one aide dominated the interagency process (as Henry Kissinger had done under Richard M. Nixon and Gerald Ford). Likewise, Reagan's personnel decisions would give both the hawkish and more moderate factions of the GOP stature within the administration, engender robust debates, and allow the president to set the basic lines of policy and then delegate implementation to strong lieutenants. It is worth noting, moreover, that this model did work in some respects. Group-think was never a problem in the administration, and the mixed nature of the cabinet enabled Reagan—whose Cold War vision encompassed both confrontation and negotiation—to interact with officials who favored each of these approaches. And Reagan's method of empowering trusted aides as policy entrepreneurs sometimes proved productive. Weinberger vigorously spearheaded the defense buildup from the Pentagon, for example, and Casey started to turn the president's desire for a Third-World offensive into the covert programs that would comprise the Reagan Doctrine.

In retrospect, however, two severe liabilities of Reagan's model contributed to the travails of his first year. One was that Reagan's most prominent appointee, Alexander Haig, refused to work within the president's intended administrative setup. Reagan wanted his lieutenants to be assertive yet also to coexist peacefully with their colleagues and understand that the president ultimately sets the administration's direction. Haig was spectacularly ill-suited to this role. "CINCWORLD," as the imposing former White House chief of staff and Supreme Allied Commander Europe was dubbed by his rivals, saw himself as a Kissinger-type figure who should overshadow all others in the administration—Reagan included—on national security matters. Predictably, Haig's approach quickly poisoned the climate in Reagan's inner circle, ensuring that the early innings were often consumed with bureaucratic turf wars rather than efforts to assemble and codify a coherent strategy.

The other liability was that the combination of a weak national security advisor (Richard Allen) and a cabinet full of strong-willed individuals was a recipe for trouble. Vigorous debate is a sign of a healthy process, but without a strong manager to adjudicate disputes, force decisions, and ensure implementation, debate can turn into paralysis. This was what happened in 1981. Allen, who lacked bureaucratic stature or a close relationship with Reagan, was totally overmatched as Haig did battle with more hardline advisors—Casey, Weinberger, and Kirkpatrick—over issues large and small. Intrigue and infighting were a constant; important issues from arms control to economic warfare to overall strategy languished without resolution; decisions were often relitigated internally or through the press. National Security Decision Directives (NSDD)—the administration's guiding documents on foreign-policy issues—were issued infrequently and on few important matters. The machinery of government was clogged, with Allen unable to break the jam and Reagan—who disliked personal confrontation with his subordinates—not willing to do so on his own.

"The entire first year and a half of the administration passed in an atmosphere of unremitting tension," National Security Council (NSC) staffer Richard Pipes later wrote.[3] Although 1981 was not a wasted year, it was less productive than Reagan had hoped. The president had good and prescient ideas about Cold War strategy. But his administration was doomed to sputter as long as it lacked the supporting personnel and administrative procedures needed to turn good ideas into a comprehensive program of action.

Only as the administration learned from these shortcomings did it gradually become more effective. In mid-1982, Reagan eased Haig out of the State Department, replacing him with a new secretary—George Shultz—who was far better attuned to the president's strategic instincts and operating style. Earlier that year, Reagan accepted Allen's resignation. He replaced him with William Clark, who possessed little substantive foreign-policy experience but had a strong relationship with Reagan and a mandate to improve the policy process. Reagan also restored the national security advisor's position to cabinet-level status, gave Clark direct access to the president, and thereby ensured that the national security advisor could take a stronger role in coordination and implementation.

To be sure, neither these changes nor any others ever solved the problems of bureaucratic infighting and intrigue within the administration. But when it came to constructing and articulating a more complete Cold War strategy, the changes served their purpose. In 1982–83, Clark's NSC staff coordinated the issuance of dozens of NSDDs on important policy issues, including two documents—NSDD-32 and NSDD-75—that provided comprehensive statements of Reagan's strategy. In particular, NSDD-75 codified the approach that Reagan had long advocated— the idea that confrontation could ultimately enable diplomacy—and contained subordinate guidance on specific issues from Afghanistan to Central America to U.S. relations with China. At the same time, the administration finally achieved a unified position on East-West economic relations and advanced a bold START proposal, and Reagan used his newly empowered NSC staff to develop signature initiatives—the National Endowment for Democracy and the Strategic Defense Initiative, for example—that would play crucial roles in his Cold War statecraft.

Not least, despite lingering State-NSC tensions, in 1983 Shultz and NSC staffer Jack Matlock gained approval of a four-part diplomatic agenda for engaging Moscow over the long term. After a slow start, the administration was now assembling and integrating the policies that would help alter the course of the Cold War and ultimately facilitate the diplomatic breakthroughs that began moving the conflict toward its successful conclusion.

Reagan's experiences underscore the value for new presidents of bringing core strategic principles to office. Whatever his other failings, Reagan had developed a perceptive and well-formed worldview during his pre-presidential years, and these ideas framed the initiatives his administration did manage to roll out in 1981. The first year of any administration is difficult and perhaps somewhat chaotic. Thinking through basic strategic concepts beforehand can help a president orient early initiatives—and recover from early mistakes.

Reagan's experience also shows that new presidents must choose advisors who are compatible with their intended administrative style. This is not to say that advisors must agree with the president on all substantive issues; that is a recipe for sycophancy. But there must be a clear understanding of how each aide will relate to the president and to the broader administration. Reagan's unhappy experience with Haig demonstrates how a mismatch between personality and process can inject dysfunction into decision making.

Additionally, the Reagan years affirm the need for a strong, fully empowered national security advisor to oversee the policy process. "Oversee" does not mean "dominate," and vigorous debate is the lifeblood of smart policy. But a president needs a strong manager to adjudicate disputes, force decisions on crucial issues, and ensure prompt and effective execution. Allen's inability to play this role during Reagan's first year was a major source of grief for the president.

Finally, Reagan's experience underscores that presidents must be willing—even at the cost of bad publicity—to revisit flawed administrative procedures and dismiss advisors who are not fitting in to the team. It can seem costly to make such alterations early, because any new president is understandably loath to admit unforced errors. There is also the loyalty that presidents feel toward their close advisors. But because so few administrations get the organizational issues entirely right the first time around, not making needed changes can be far more damaging. It was only when the Reagan administration took steps to mitigate early internal dysfunction that its Cold War strategy really began to get on track. This willingness to learn from mistakes, and to change course accordingly, represents an important lesson for any first-year president.

NOTES

1. Richard Allen, "The Man Who Won the Cold War," *Hoover Digest,* no. 1 (2000), http://www.hoover.org/research/man-who-won-cold-war.

2. Hal Brands, *What Good Is Grand Strategy?* (Ithaca, N.Y.: Cornell University Press, 2015), 106–7.

3. Richard Pipes, *VIXI: Memoirs of a Non-Belonger* (New Haven, Conn.: Yale University Press, 2003), 153.

HIPPOCRATIC DIPLOMACY

George H. W. Bush's First Year

JEFFREY A. ENGEL

The first year of the George H. W. Bush administration demonstrates that less can be more. More happened on the international stage during those first twelve months than for any other president in American history. A democratic tsunami overwhelmed European communism. The Berlin Wall fell. The Cold War effectively ended. Tiananmen Square transformed from a place to an event. Coups failed in Panama and the Philippines, the first due to American indifference and the second because of American action. All this in a single year, and from Washington's perspective, save for events in China, nearly all positive.

Matters were not guaranteed to work out that well. Profound changes carry incalculable dangers. Collapsing states frequently bring ethnic violence and retribution for historic affronts. Mass protests can lead to crackdowns, civil war, or coups, the condemnation of which brings diplomatic problems of its own. As Robert Gates frequently noted from his post as Bush's assistant national security advisor, never before in history had a great power collapsed without an ensuing great power war. Never before had nuclear weapons been involved. Peacefully navigating the potential rocky shoals of the Soviet Empire's disintegration meant avoiding or at least tempering scenarios that historically had brought devastating results.

Officials of the Bush administration navigated these shoals because they declined to act decisively when clear policy choices did not present themselves. Theirs was a Hippocratic approach to diplomacy, predicated on first doing no harm. Convinced of the appeal of American ideas and the inherent power of the U.S. economy and military, and more fundamentally certain that world affairs generally were moving in democracy's direction, they strove above all to do nothing that might jar the international system off its positive course.

Bush did not intervene in the Soviet bloc's travails, for example, even when short-term domestic political gain seemed ripe for the taking with just a few short words of support for prodemocracy rallies. Awful images of Tiananmen Square remained fresh in Bush's mind when hope for democratic change quickly turned to desperation and death once Chinese officials decided they had heard enough from protesters and their supporters around the world. Bush's mild support of the

prodemocracy rallies did not trigger the crackdown in Beijing. But Chinese officials nevertheless employed his words to justify their actions as a defense against
foreign interference. The crowds that formed in East Germany only a few months
later therefore raised fears within the administration of similar treatment, not least
because the East German government had made a point of inviting Chinese police
officers to teach them "crowd control" techniques. History, Bush feared, seemed
about to replay.

Bush felt that the best odds of democracy's success would come from his simply letting events play out. Warning Beijing against cracking down had done nothing. Thus similar warnings were never issued to East Germany. More importantly,
Bush refrained from too overtly praising the protesters no matter how much he
sympathized with their cause.

"I keep hearing critics saying we're not doing enough on Eastern Europe," Bush
explained to his diary. "Here the changes are dramatically coming our way, and
if any one event—Poland, Hungary, or East Germany—had taken place, people
would say this is great. But it's all moving fast—moving our way—and [yet]
you've got a bunch of critics jumping around saying we ought to be doing more.
What they mean is, double spending. It doesn't matter what, just send money,
and I think it's crazy." Furthermore, he continued, "If we mishandle it [Eastern
Europe], and get way out looking like [promoting dissent is] an American project,
you would invite crackdown, and . . . that could result in bloodshed."[1]

Written the night before the Berlin Wall fell, the timing of these sentiments is
particularly illuminating. No one expected the breach to occur. The wall opened
largely by accident, and the faltering East German regime lacked the power to
close it. Bush consequently got what he wanted—greater democratization in
Eastern Europe—without doing or saying anything that might have thwarted this
desire, because he rightly perceived that events already were "moving our way." He
reasoned that when the stream of history carries the ship of state in your preferred
direction, you should let it.

"We're seeing it move, aren't we?" Bush quickly retorted when a reporter asked
for the umpteenth time why his White House was not doing more to openly
support the region's democratic transition. "We're seeing dynamic change, and I
want to handle it properly."[2] Pundits and legislators could propose almost anything without consequence. He was ultimately responsible, and he knew that
"the United States can't wave a wand and say how fast change is going to come to
Czechoslovakia or to the GDR [East Germany]."[3]

Not acting precipitously did not mean not acting at all, as two examples from
Bush's first year demonstrate. First, although Bush did nothing to precipitate the
Berlin Wall's collapse, he did much behind the scenes in its aftermath, engaging in marathon telephone diplomacy with European leaders, including Mikhail
Gorbachev, to ensure that each strove to keep any ensuing chaos at bay. With the
stream of history moving in his direction, Bush paddled hard to avoid the rapids,
working quietly and largely without public notice when others might have sought

greater credit. "I'm not going to dance on the Berlin Wall," Bush told aides in response to critics who charged he should do more to celebrate this apparent Cold War triumph. The last thing he wanted to do was "stick a finger in Gorbachev's eye" and catalyze a communist backlash.[4]

Bush's team also used the first months in office to think. Most administrations want to hit the ground running, showing their mettle or righting all the wrongs they had been elected to fix. Even though his administration followed a Republican president into office, Bush's team did not think of itself as Ronald Reagan's third term. "This is not a friendly takeover," James Baker, Bush's eventual secretary of state, announced soon after his friend's election, demanding resignations from every one of Reagan's appointees so Bush would have free rein to make his own appointments. Bush's inner circle also thought Reagan's team had been too trusting of Gorbachev and potential Soviet reforms. "Don't you think you all went too far?" Baker asked during his first visit to Foggy Bottom.[5]

Bush did not immediately change course, however, instead initiating a lengthy "pause" in Soviet-American relations while launching a top-to-bottom review of the nation's foreign policies. "The jury is still out" on whether or not the United States should really trust in *perestroika,* Bush said, as well as on whether Gorbachev's new spirit of cooperation was genuine or merely a Machiavellian "peace campaign" designed to wean Western Europe from Washington's sphere of influence without firing a shot.

The pause worked, providing time to think and assess, leading ultimately to a reversal of Bush's own uncertainty. "Look, this guy IS *perestroika,*" Bush told his staff in the fall.[6] He consequently instructed them not to do anything to make Gorbachev's life harder, finding ways to help the Soviet leader without exacerbating the rising opposition the Russian faced at home. The events of November 1989 in East Germany seemed to validate Bush's earlier conclusion. Watching once-unfathomable televised images of the Berlin Wall's breach, Bush turned to Brent Scowcroft, his national security advisor, and said, "If they are going to let the Communists fall in East Germany, they've got to be really serious."[7]

One should not conclude that Bush was incapable of action merely because he so effectively demonstrated restraint during his first year in office. This was the president, after all, who subsequently moved more than half a million troops to the Middle East to reverse Saddam Hussein's invasion of Kuwait. "I feel great pressure, but I also feel a certain calmness," Bush wrote of that decision. He knew "what can be done and how long it will take." Ultimately, because he had a clear option before him, because the moral and political issues at stake seemed clear, and because, unlike the prodemocracy movement in Eastern Europe, the situation in the Middle East would not resolve itself without American leadership, Bush concluded, "I know I am doing the right thing."[8]

Taken together, Bush's first year in office offers any incoming president three lessons:

First, do no harm.

Second, take time to reassess policy, rethink convictions, and reshape the national security bureaucracy to your liking.

Third, take additional time before implementing solutions. Bush's team bungled a series of crises in its first year, most famously the failure to provide even minimal support to Panamanian plotters eager to remove Manuel Noriega from power. Information was stove-piped and jealously guarded, leaving crucial bits of data unavailable to some in the decision-making loop, and ultimately forcing Bush to wonder about Noriega's fate for a full six hours after Defense Secretary Dick Cheney and Joint Chiefs Chairman Colin Powell knew that he had returned to power.

Critics howled at the administration's apparent incompetence, demanding the removal of Cheney or Powell, perhaps both. Bush refused to fire anyone, however, instead giving them time to refine their organizations for future crises while emboldening Scowcroft to streamline the administration's overall approach to emergency management. Having taken the time to select good people as subordinates, Bush believed it was important to give them the opportunity to learn how best to work with each other.

In the final analysis, Bush's example teaches prudence. Prudence requires caution, judgment, experience, and patience. It does not preclude action. Neither does it allow for reckless decisions. Rather, the prudent leader realizes that less is more when the world is moving the right way, and that action, when necessary, is best taken consciously and intentionally. It means allowing good people time to think and do their jobs, as well as recognizing that the best leadership can come from doing nothing at all. Or, as Bush noted in his diary as his one-year anniversary in office neared, "The longer I'm in this job, the more I think prudence is a value and experience matters."[9]

NOTES

1. George H. W. Bush, *All the Best, George Bush: My Life in Letters and Other Writings* (New York: Scribner, 2013), 441, 442.

2. George H. W. Bush, "The President's News Conference, October 31, 1989," in *Public Papers of the Presidents of the United States: George Bush, 1989, July 1 to December 31, 1989* (Washington, D.C.: U.S. Government Printing Office, 1991), 1427.

3. Ibid.

4. Christopher Maynard, *Out of the Shadow: George H. W. Bush and the End of the Cold War* (College Station: Texas A&M University Press, 2008), 42; Roman Popadiuk, *The Leadership of George Bush* (College Station: Texas A&M University Press, 2009), 119.

5. Lawrence S. Wittner, *The Struggle against the Bomb* (Stanford, Calif.: Stanford University Press, 2003), 3:425.

6. Michael Beschloss and Strobe Talbott, *At the Highest Levels: The Inside Story of the End of the Cold War* (Boston: Little, Brown, 1993), 73.

7. Robert Harvey, *A Short History of Communism* (New York: St. Martin's Press, 2004), 363.

8. Bush, *All the Best*, 477.

9. Ibid., 442.

IT'S NOT JUST THE ECONOMY, STUPID

Bill Clinton's Distracted First-Year
Foreign Policy

JEREMI SURI

Running for president in 1992, Governor Bill Clinton wanted his campaign to focus on domestic reforms. With world affairs looking so favorable to American interests—the Soviet empire had collapsed, Eastern Europe was free, a great allied coalition had defeated Iraq in the Persian Gulf War—Clinton did not challenge George H. W. Bush on foreign policy. "It's the economy, stupid," his campaign manager, James Carville, famously exclaimed.[1] The electoral strategy worked, and Clinton entered the White House with a clear domestic agenda to increase jobs and economic growth.

Within months of becoming president, however, Clinton learned that the world would not cooperate with his domestic-focused agenda. In Clinton's first year, Washington confronted a cascade of small challenges abroad that threatened American regional interests and called on the nation's humanitarian conscience. During the early fall of 1993, the president had to respond to the death of eighteen American soldiers in Somalia, the failure of an American military vessel to dock in Haiti because of protesting crowds, open military conflict between Russian president Boris Yeltsin and the democratically elected parliament of his country, and rising tensions on the Korean peninsula as the dictatorship in Pyongyang pursued a nuclear arsenal. Civil war and ethnic cleansing intensified in the former Yugoslavia, and Iraqi leader Saddam Hussein continued to defy international sanctions by rebuilding his military, tightening his grip on power, and rewarding the families of terrorists in Israeli-occupied territories. Terrorist threats to American citizens, soldiers, and allies also increased during this period, with numerous sponsors—including an emerging network around a wealthy Saudi radical, Osama bin Laden.

Clinton's domestic preoccupations left his administration unprepared for these multiplying challenges. Like John F. Kennedy before him, Clinton intended to rely on his instincts rather than on organized planning or preparations for foreign crises. He believed his predecessors had succeeded when they "made it up as they went along."[2]

But Clinton's first year proved that even the most talented politician cannot improvise a clear and effective foreign policy. To lead abroad, a president must begin with a disciplined effort to define interests and goals, anticipate threats, link resources and objectives (that is, means with ends), and organize appropriate resources across a labyrinth of U.S. government agencies. Clinton's inattention to these strategic issues during his first months in office set him back significantly. He had respected and knowledgeable advisors, but he allowed them to operate without clear guidance or a disciplined policy process. They were each making it up as they went along, rather than working together toward common foreign-policy goals.

What were the priorities for American security in 1993? What were the emerging threats and how could the United States best protect itself against them? Clinton did not demand clear answers to these questions. With his focus on domestic economics, and his desire to avoid other hard choices and distractions, Clinton encouraged continued foreign-policy superficiality during his first year. "Soft" security issues—including drug trafficking, free trade, and environmental protection—became backdoor routes for giving more attention to domestic needs than traditional international concerns.

The avoidance of geopolitics started with the president's inaugural address. Clinton famously explained to the nation: "There is no longer a clear division between what is foreign and what is domestic."[3] Although that was true, he framed the observation to justify shaping foreign policy around popular concerns at home. Trade policy was a primary example. Clinton created the National Economic Council (NEC) to act as a counterpart to the National Security Council (NSC). The NEC worked with Secretary of Commerce Ron Brown to promote American manufacturing and exports abroad. Opening markets to help American companies and workers was, during Clinton's first year in office, his primary foreign-policy goal. It served domestic American interests but not necessarily the needs of allies and developing states with struggling economies of their own. The president's basic assumption was that a cultivation of prosperity at home would, more than anything else, elicit prosperity abroad as the U.S. model shined beyond its boundaries. "Our greatest strength is the power of our ideas, which are still new in many lands," Clinton said in his inaugural address on January 20, 1993. "Across the world we see them embraced, and we rejoice."[4]

The international sources of resistance to these ideas evaded clear analysis during most of Clinton's first year because the president wanted to trumpet the seamless global benefits of his domestic program, and he did not want to address geopolitical challenges to it. He did not make a major statement about international inequality, ethnic conflict, or terrorism during his first year, despite the prevalence of these challenges, especially in southeastern Europe and the Middle

East. The president also ignored rising threats from what his NSC advisor later called "backlash states"—Iraq, Iran, and North Korea, in particular.[5] Clinton preferred to talk about markets, democracy, and civil society.

All of Clinton's foreign-policy advisors understood the president's willful optimism, and many shared it in the afterglow of communism's collapse in Russia and Eastern Europe. They sought to champion American liberal, capitalist values in different ways, refusing to contemplate the possibility that these ideas and practices might not work in other regions. They ignored the accumulating evidence that religious and ethnic sectarianism trumped democratic alternatives in Slobodan Milosevic's Serbia, Hafez al-Assad's Syria, and countries under military rule such as Haiti and Burma.

Undisciplined wishful thinking made the United States reactive at best—and crisis-prone at worst. The Clinton administration did not match capabilities to goals. What was the plan for spreading democracy in poor, authoritarian regions? What role would the American military play? How would the administration align trade policy, aid efforts, public diplomacy, and force? Instead of coordinating the tools available to the White House for effective action, the administration repeatedly assembled ad hoc responses to conflicts it had not anticipated. This happened over and over again during the unfolding civil war in the former Yugoslavia and the emerging crises in Somalia, Rwanda, and Haiti.

Presidents cannot predict crises, but they can formulate a coherent framework to integrate the nation's resources for maximum achievement of objectives. Without such a framework, the Clinton administration spent its first year either running to place bandages on international wounds or denying that such wounds existed. This reactive approach allowed small international actors to become the agenda-setters in southern Europe, Africa, and many other regions.

Beyond disorganization and distraction, the Clinton administration suffered from a very vague conceptualization of its goals. What kind of world did it want to help create? How did it expect to get there? Abstraction increases confusion when it elides rather than elucidates difficult policy choices.

Civil wars in Yugoslavia, Somalia, and Rwanda proved the vagueness of the Clinton administration's thinking and its harmful effects. Candidate Clinton accused President Bush of doing too little to address post–Cold War ethnic conflicts, but in each of these cases, the Clinton administration was unable to marry its rhetoric about democracy with peacekeeping initiatives that encouraged favorable outcomes. In Yugoslavia, the Serbs and Croats expanded their ethnic cleansing efforts, and the White House failed to orchestrate an effective, multilateral response. In Somalia, Clinton inherited a humanitarian intervention, under United Nations direction, that exposed U.S. army rangers—deployed as protectors for aid workers—to urban guerilla warfare that resulted in eighteen American combat deaths and few positive results. Scarred by the events in Somalia, six months later President Clinton refused to deploy force when Hutu militias in Rwanda killed more than 500,000 Tutsi and Hutu citizens.

Market democracy and multilateral peacekeeping seemed to mean very little as ethnic conflicts triggered civil wars in Europe, Africa, and other areas. National Security Advisor Anthony Lake defended the administration for being "principled about our purposes but pragmatic about our means."[6] No one within government, however, could explain what that meant in practice. Vagueness contributed to confusion about American foreign-policy aims. Without direction, it was impossible to allocate the nation's resources effectively.

The diplomats and soldiers involved in Yugoslavia, Somalia, and Rwanda felt this confusion, and by early 1994 relations among the White House, State Department, and Defense Department had reached a low point. The Clinton administration was not isolationist, but its behavior and behind-the-scenes comments made its internationalism thin, self-serving, and ultimately ineffective. The combination of idealistic rhetoric and strategic uncertainty turned vague words into frustrating sources of disillusion.

Clinton's troubled first year teaches that new presidents must prepare themselves and their closest advisors to enter the White House with a clear set of realistic foreign-policy goals based on core national interests, a rigorous assessment of threats, and a disciplined process for aligning resources. The president must formulate a coherent agenda for a complex international landscape very quickly, or else a multiplication of foreign demands will end up defining administration policy. The president must then use the first year to apply and adjust strategy through a continual process, which he or she directly manages, for reassessing interests, goals, threats, and resources.

Foreign-policy appointments are among the most important that the new president makes because the commander in chief needs trusted advisors who can help assess numerous threats and implement goals, despite contrary pressures. Most important, rigorous, high-level thinking about foreign-policy goals is necessary early in an administration to set a favorable course, signaling to government agencies the goals they should pursue and the programs they must prioritize. Clinton's disappointing first year is a warning against the perils of a presidential transition that assumes the focus of the successful election campaign—in which issues are separated and simplified—is the same as the focus for successful national leadership, in which integration and management of complexity are crucial.

NOTES

1. Michael Kelly, "The 1992 Campaign: The Democrats—Clinton and Bush Compete to Be Champion of Change; Democrat Fights Perceptions of Bush Gain," *New York Times,* October 31, 1992, http://www.nytimes.com/1992/10/31/us/1992-campaign-democrats-clinton-bush-compete-be-champion-change-democrat-fights.html.

2. James D. Boys, *Clinton's Grand Strategy: US Foreign Policy in a Post–Cold War World* (London: Bloomsbury, 2015), 82.

3. Bill Clinton, "Inaugural Address January 20, 1993," American Presidency Project, University of California at Santa Barbara, http://www.presidency.ucsb.edu/ws/?pid=46366.

4. Ibid.

5. Anthony Lake, "Confronting Backlash States," *Foreign Affairs* 73, no. 2 (1994): 45–55. doi:10.2307/20045918.

6. Anthony Lake, "From Containment to Enlargement," speech, Washington, D.C., September 21, 1993, https://www.mtholyoke.edu/acad/intrel/lakedoc.html.

TRUST BUT CLARIFY

George W. Bush's Rivalry-Ridden National Security Team

MELVYN P. LEFFLER

Upon taking office in 2001, President George W. Bush quickly turned his attention to his domestic agenda—lowering taxes, reforming education, and implementing a strategy of compassionate conservatism through faith-based initiatives. But he faced a real challenge: his foreign policy advisors were saying contradictory things.

"For the first time in decades," commented Secretary of Defense Donald Rumsfeld in March 2001, "the country faces no strategic challenge. . . . We don't have to wake up every morning thinking something terrible is going to happen."[1] Two months later, George Tenet, director of the CIA, warned Condoleezza Rice, Bush's national security advisor, that "100 percent reliable information" suggested an impending "spectacular" terrorist attack against American or Israeli interests. "This is real. . . . We are going to get hit," he told skeptics within the administration.[2]

Nonetheless, in mid-July, when Rice asked State Department officials to begin drafting the administration's national strategy statement, they slighted the terrorist threat, noted the absence of any global rivals, stressed America's "unparalleled strength," and heralded a "time of opportunity." Rumsfeld was otherwise preoccupied. On September 10, before a large audience at the Pentagon, he declared, "The topic today is an adversary that poses a threat, a serious threat, to the security of the United States of America. . . . It attempts to impose its demands across time zones, continents, oceans, and beyond. . . . It disrupts the defense of the United States and places the lives of men and women in uniform at risk." That adversary, Rumsfeld pronounced, was the "Pentagon bureaucracy."[3]

These vignettes reflect the Bush administration's discord and lack of urgency during its first few months. Although ambiguity and uncertainty are not uncommon in newly installed presidencies, the first year of the Bush administration illustrates how important it is for a president to impose his own imprimatur on the nation's foreign-policy goals and priorities, and how essential it is to bring together a team of advisors who embrace those goals, trust one another, and share confidence in their own decision-making machinery. These advisors must also think strategically, rigorously assessing and ranking threats, delineating priorities, and linking tactics and goals.

Bush's presidential campaign got off to a good start in 1999. A Texas governor and former businessman, Bush did not have much knowledge of foreign policy or national security, and he knew it. So he invited Condoleezza Rice, a former Russia expert on his father's national security staff, to tutor him and to put together a team to formulate overall policy direction. The group, known as the Vulcans, included Paul Wolfowitz, Richard Armitage, Robert Zoellick, and Dov Zakheim, among others.[4]

The team fashioned several excellent speeches for candidate Bush and prepped him for his debates with Al Gore, the Democratic candidate. In these campaign speeches and debates, Bush emphasized the importance of military strength yet wanted the United States to act with humility and empathy. The United States, Bush declared, must not withdraw and must not drift. "America must be involved with the world," he said. It must rebuild its military capabilities. But military action must not be "the answer to every difficult foreign policy situation" or "substitute for strategy. American internationalism should not mean action without vision, activity without priority, and missions without end." Bush stated his priorities clearly: work with strong democratic allies in Europe and Asia; promote democracy in the Western Hemisphere; defend "America's interests in the Persian Gulf and advance peace in the Middle East," with a secure Israel; check the spread of weapons of mass destruction; and promote free trade.[5]

To carry out this foreign policy, Bush appointed people of great experience and immense stature. His vice presidential running mate was Richard Cheney, a former chief of staff to President Gerald Ford and former secretary of defense. His secretary of state was General Colin Powell, a former national security advisor to Ronald Reagan and former chair of the Joint Chiefs of Staff. Donald Rumsfeld was his selection for secretary of defense, a former ambassador to NATO, secretary of defense under Gerald Ford, presidential envoy for Ronald Reagan, and chairman of a national advisory study on ballistic missile defense during the Bill Clinton years. Rice, who was not only Bush's foreign policy mentor but also had become his trusted friend, was appointed national security advisor. Her task was to coordinate, not to operate; to reconcile divergent views, not to impose her own agenda. Bush prided himself on his managerial and leadership skills: pick exceptional people, stress teamwork, and delegate responsibility.

But the process did not cohere and a clear strategy did not emerge. The postelection transition was delayed because of the controversy over the election's outcome. Appointments came slowly. The exceedingly laborious confirmation process handicapped planning and complicated coordination.

From the outset, Bush's foreign policy principals did not agree with or even trust one another. Bush did not appoint a secretary of defense or a secretary of state he knew well. And Rumsfeld and Powell did not hit it off; their staffs sniped at one another, as did those of the secretary of state and the vice president. The president mostly stayed aloof from these disputes.

Coordination was difficult, despite Rice's efforts and those of her assistant, Steve Hadley. Vice President Cheney and his staff played a key role in national security matters, yet Cheney mostly voiced his views privately to the president and not to others. Meetings of deputies and principals were frustrating. Powell did not say much; Rumsfeld liked to ask questions and pose options rather than state his own clear preferences. Rice struggled to establish her authority, failed to garner the full respect of the principals and deputies, and futilely sought consensus when there was none. She knew the president was capable of making tough choices, yet cabinet secretaries and their staffs remonstrated against her reluctance to present the president with divergent options.[6]

Frustration abounded and disarray ensued. For example, establishing better relations with Mexico was a presidential priority. Less than a month after taking office, Bush visited the ranch of Vicente Fox, Mexico's president. The aim was to highlight Mexico's importance and America's humility. But during the first press conference, everyone's attention was distracted by news of an American attack on Iraqi air defenses close to Baghdad. The unplanned American action was precipitated by Iraqi efforts to challenge the no-fly zones imposed by U.S. air power. The news disrupted the meeting; it was a "disaster," Rice acknowledged. She blamed herself.[7]

Less than two weeks later, Kim Dae-jung, the South Korean president, came to visit Washington. Bush wanted to convey privately that his administration did not favor the South Korean's conciliatory policy toward North Korea, an approach that the Clinton administration had broadly endorsed. Yet during the visit, Secretary of State Powell said that the United States would continue the approach of his predecessor. Bush was furious and asked Rice to get Powell to issue a correction. Powell complied, but Rice recognized that "the public perception of Colin Powell being reined in by the White House lingered and festered."[8]

At almost the same time came a terrible flap over the Kyoto Protocol on climate. The president wrote a public letter to four Republican senators categorically announcing the administration's opposition. Rice read a draft and knew it would alienate European allies. Wanting to modify the language, she went to the president and learned that Cheney was already delivering the letter to Capitol Hill. She was "appalled," she later wrote, that Cheney moved ahead without her assent or that of the secretary of state. She knew the letter would sour relations and damage America's reputation abroad; it did, as do most changes in policy that are not carefully rolled out.[9]

Then came a real crisis with China, when an American espionage plane collided with Chinese aircraft and had to land on Hainan Island. A Chinese pilot was killed in the crash, and China's government demanded an apology. Since the American plane was flying in international airspace when the incident occurred, defense officials dug in their heels while their counterparts at the State Department wanted to talk. The Chinese were "testing" us, Rumsfeld insisted.[10] Bush deferred to Powell, and the crisis was resolved by smart diplomacy and mutual accommodation. Rice acknowledged that "this was not the way we'd hope to start off our relationship with Beijing."[11] But the unexpected always happens, and knowing one's priorities is critical to fruitful policy.

More successful were relations with Russia. From the outset of the administration, Bush made clear that ballistic missile defense was a priority. To achieve it, the United States had to disentangle itself from the Anti-Ballistic Missile Treaty of 1972. Although Russian president Vladimir Putin was opposed, Bush communicated this priority to him at their first meeting in June 2001 and successfully prepared the groundwork at home.

Yet all these matters paled in comparison to the indecision over what do with Saddam Hussein's Iraq and how to deal with the threat posed by the Islamic terrorist group known as al-Qaeda, headquartered in Afghanistan and led by Osama bin Laden. Contrary to popular myth, Bush's advisors entered office with no plans for military action against Iraq. They wanted regime change, but their real focus was on how to handle the erosion of sanctions and the protection of aircraft enforcing the no-fly zones. Deputies and principals met repeatedly to discuss options, with very few concrete results. "The effort to make the sanctions smarter was maddeningly slow," conceded Rice in her memoir.[12] The bickering and indecision infuriated Rumsfeld, although he posed options rather than offering solutions. Paul Wolfowitz, the deputy secretary of defense, wanted to topple Saddam but suggested no precise plan. Rumsfeld himself was far more interested in reforming the Pentagon than in transforming Iraq. Bush provided little leadership.[13]

Nor was there any clarity on the threat posed by al-Qaeda. Richard Clarke, the counterterrorism expert on the NSC staff, was held over from the Clinton administration, as was George Tenet, the director of the CIA. Both men virtually screamed about the threat posed by al-Qaeda. "The threat from terrorism is real, it is immediate, and it is evolving," Tenet told the Senate Armed Services Committee in March 2001.[14] The director of the Defense Intelligence Agency said the same thing: the immediate threat for the next twelve to twenty-four months "was a major terrorist attack against the United States either here or abroad."[15] Clarke protested to Rice and Hadley that they needed to move quickly, and Tenet pounded on the desk of his friend Richard Armitage, the deputy secretary of state, and warned of an imminent attack. Yet Rice and Hadley felt that a regional strategy needed to be designed before directly tackling the al-Qaeda threat. They postponed meetings of deputies and principals until such a strategy was scripted yet pushed ahead with the appropriate work. Papers were prepared and meetings were scheduled for September.[16]

President Bush was not indifferent to the terrorist threat. He asked for a presidential daily briefing on the topic, which took place on August 6. But he did not dwell on the matter either before or after that briefing. He did not ask for subsequent meetings and did not convey interest commensurate with the strong warnings from his CIA director and chief White House counterterrorism expert. These men carried little influence within the administration. They were Clinton holdovers in an administration steadfastly committed to changing direction from anything linked to Clinton. Moreover, Clarke was viewed as a self-promoting bureaucratic entrepreneur, inclining his colleagues to minimize his admonitions, especially when those warnings became more muted in the late summer of 2001. Homeland security, Rice believed, was not her domain; it was the FBI's. Nor was there sufficient reason for her to be concerned with the matter, she thought.[17]

Rice and Hadley wanted a regional strategy, including Afghanistan and Pakistan, to deal with al-Qaeda. Their colleagues in the vice president's office, including Eric Edelman and Scooter Libby, felt that what the administration really needed was an overall global strategy, with a clear delineation of worldwide threats and a set of national goals and regional priorities.[18] Yet the principals and deputies rarely, if ever, discussed broad strategy or priorities. The president and vice president continued to focus mainly on their domestic agenda.

In the summer of 2001, Rice asked the State Department policy planning staff to draft an overall strategy paper. The priorities were remarkably similar to those of the George H. W. Bush and Clinton administrations: promoting open trade and more freedom in the world. The main goals were to collaborate with America's democratic allies; preserve America's superior power; forge "realistic" relations with Russia and China; and alleviate poverty, disease, corruption, and tyranny in the world. The principal "impediments" to these goals were possible disputes with democratic allies, anticipated renewal of great-power competition, and endemic poverty and corruption in parts of Asia, Africa, and Latin America. The draft included a passing allusion to the threat of terrorism but did not mention al-Qaeda. American interests were not clearly defined; means and ends were not reconciled; regional strategies were still to be designed.[19]

Incomplete, the overall strategy—regarded primarily as a bureaucratic exercise to comply with a legislative mandate—was not vetted among the principals or discussed at NSC meetings. President Bush showed little interest in it. Nor did Secretary Powell; he preferred to react to ongoing challenges and especially wanted to deal with Palestinian-Israeli strife. Rumsfeld focused on reforming the Pentagon, advocating ballistic missile defense, fighting the entrenched Pentagon bureaucracy, and circumventing many top military officers, several of whom detested him. Cheney was deeply interested in security, intelligence, and energy policy, but he shared his thoughts only with the president. Tenet and Clarke were obsessed with the terrorist threat, but the Joint Chiefs showed no special interest in such matters.

In these initial months, notwithstanding the president's hopes, there was much bickering, poor teamwork, and incessant badmouthing. The president did not pay much attention to these problems, engaging selectively on some issues but providing little broad direction. Although he effectively led meetings, he did not demand the teamwork and accountability he prized. Nor did he underscore the authority that Rice needed to do her work successfully. He made little effort to discuss over-all strategy, shape a consensus about priorities, and think seriously about means and ends. He did not grapple with the effects of domestic initiatives like tax cuts on national security goals, such as military transformation and rearmament. Pol-icy was not shaped by a tough assessment of threats. Warnings from Clintonian holdovers were minimized.[20]

After September 11, the president did take command, riveted his attention on national security policy, and launched the global war on terrorism. His priority was set: destroy terrorists with a global reach and the regimes that accorded them safe haven. The initial mission, he insisted, should be Afghanistan, not Iraq. But the defense department and the CIA continued to dispute tactics. Frustrated, on October 10, 2001, Rumsfeld lashed out again at his subordinates: "We have tens of thousands of dedicated, talented, creative people. . . . But something is fundamen-tally wrong in the department. . . . I am seeing next to nothing that is thoughtful, creative or actionable."[21] Nonetheless, soon thereafter, the Taliban were defeated by creative actions of CIA operatives, U.S. air power, and the Northern Alliance inside Afghanistan.

The administration embraced the victory with enormous satisfaction. But victory was self-defeating because it nurtured hubris and reduced incentives to reflect on a decision-making process that remained flawed. Nor did it lead to a clear strategic overview about subsequent priorities and actions, other than an inchoate consensus that the greatest threat to American security was the nexus of state actors, terrorists, and weapons of mass destruction. Rice hired a trusted non-governmental confidant, Philip Zelikow, to rework the administration's national security strategy statement. The paper, carefully perused by the president, was not vetted thoroughly through the various agencies or discussed among the principals or deputies.[22] Subsequently, there was no meeting to address the pros and cons of waging an invasion of Iraq, and the planning for the posthostilities Iraqi regime was wracked with confusion, indecision, and overlapping chains of command among the newly created Coalition Provisional Authority, the Defense Depart-ment, the State Department, the national security advisor, and the White House.[23]

What can be learned from this experience? National security decision making requires strategic thinking that integrates threat perception, reconciles domes-tic and foreign-policy priorities, and links means and ends. It requires teamwork among decision makers, clear lines of authority, a respected and tough-minded national security advisor, and a broadly understood process among the decision makers themselves. Most of all, it requires a strong, focused, and inquisitive presi-dent, inclined to assess and rank threats, think strategically, discuss overall goals and tactics, and articulate priorities. While delegating responsibility, the com-mander in chief must also be attuned to and ready to resolve differences among advisors. When priorities are agreed upon, as was the case with ballistic missile defense, effective policy may ensue. But precipitous changes without careful delib-eration and systematic implementation will be harmful, as was the case with the president's unilateral renunciation of the Kyoto initiative on climate or his desire to change course regarding Korea.

Bush's first year shows how daunting the challenges of national security can be even for a president who has chosen advisors of great stature and vast experience. Of course, presidents do learn and recalibrate. It would be even better if they thought through these matters before assuming the great responsibilities that await them.

NOTES

1. Richard B. Myers, *Eyes on the Horizon: Serving on the Front Lines of National Security* (New York: Simon and Schuster, 2009), 140.

2. George Tenet, *At the Center of the Storm: My Years at the CIA* (New York: HarperCollins, 2007), 149, 154.

3. Donald Rumsfeld, "Remarks as Delivered by Secretary of Defense Donald H. Rumsfeld," September 10, 2001, A Government of the People, https://agovernmentofthepeople.com/2001/09/10/donald-rumsfeld-speech-about-bureaucratic-waste/.

4. Elaine Sciolino, "Bush's Foreign Policy Tutor: An Academic in the Public Eye," *New York Times,* June 15, 2000, http://www.nytimes.com/2000/06/16/world/2000-campaign-advisor-bush-s-foreign-policy-tutor-academic-public-eye.html; James Mann, *The Rise of the Vulcans: The History of Bush's War Cabinet* (New York: Penguin, 2004); Dov S. Zakheim, *A Vulcan's Tale: How the Bush Administration Mismanaged the Reconstruction of Afghanistan* (Washington, D.C.: Brookings Institution Press, 2011).

5. George W. Bush, "A Distinctly American Internationalism," speech, Simi Valley, Calif., November 19, 1999, https://www.mtholyoke.edu/acad/intrel/bush/wspeech.htm.

6. George W. Bush, *Decision Points* (New York: Broadway, 2010), 87–88; Condoleezza Rice, *No Higher Honor: A Memoir of My Years in Washington* (New York: Crown, 2011), 13–22; Donald Rumsfeld, *Known and Unknown: A Memoir* (New York: Penguin, 2011), 324–30.

7. Rice, *No Higher Honor,* 26–29.

8. Ibid., 36–37.

9. Ibid., 41–42.

10. Rumsfeld, *Known and Unknown,* 312–15.

11. Rice, *No Higher Honor,* 46.

12. Ibid., 32.

13. Zakheim, *A Vulcan's Tale,* 39, 54–55, 63; Zalmay Khalilzad, *The Envoy: From Kabul to the White House, My Journey through a Turbulent World* (New York: St. Martin's Press, 2016), 96–99.

14. George J. Tenet, "Worldwide Threat 2001: National Security in a Changing World," statement, Senate Select Committee on Intelligence, Washington, D.C., February 7, 2001, https://www.intelligence.senate.gov/sites/default/files/hearings/107-2.pdf.

15. Thomas R. Wilson, "Global Threats and Challenges through 2015," statement, Senate Armed Services Committee, Washington, D.C., March 8, 2001, http://fas.org/irp/congress/2001_hr/s010308w.html.

16. Rice, *No Higher Honor,* 65–70; Richard A. Clarke, *Against All Enemies: Inside America's War on Terror* (New York: Free Press, 2004), 236–38; Khalilzad, *The Envoy,* 99–100; interviews with Richard Armitage and Richard Clarke.

17. Rice, *No Higher Honor,* 66–70; interviews with Eric Edelman.

18. Interviews with Eric Edelman and Scooter Libby.

19. Melvyn P. Leffler and Jeffrey W. Legro, eds., *In Uncertain Times: American Foreign Policy after the Berlin Wall and 9/11* (Ithaca, N.Y.: Cornell University Press, 2011), 211n13.

20. See Rice, *No Higher Honor;* Rumsfeld, *Known and Unknown;* Clarke, *Against All Enemies;* Tenet, *At the Center of the Storm;* Bush, *Decision Points.*

21. Donald Rumsfeld to Dick Myers and Pete Pace, October 10, 2001, http://library .rumsfeld.com/doclib/sp/86/2001-10-10%20to%20Myers%20Pace%20re%20What%20will %20be%20the%20Military%20Role%20in%20the%20War%20on%20Terrorism.pdf.

22. See Philip Zelikow, "U.S. Strategic Planning in 2001–2002," in Leffler and Legro, eds., *In Uncertain Times,* 110–14.

23. See Melvyn P. Leffler, "The Foreign Policies of the George W. Bush Administration, Memoirs, History, Legacy," *Diplomatic History* 37(April 2013): 190–216.

BEST PRACTICES

Eight Lessons for Navigating National Security

MICHÈLE A. FLOURNOY

Much can be learned from how presidents have managed national security issues in their first year in office. There are best practices to be emulated and mistakes to be avoided. Historical insights are complemented here by my own observations as a participant in the national security decision-making process under two presidents and five secretaries of defense.

1. Come into office with a clear assessment of U.S. national security challenges, opportunities, goals, and priorities, and a strategy to align the administration's efforts in the first year.

The president does not have the luxury of waiting until after the election is held and the official presidential transition begins. The two and a half months between Election Day and Inauguration Day are simply not enough time to do this work well. Rather, each candidate should empower a team to begin working before the election to assess the national security environment, develop a strategic framework and set of guiding principles, and articulate a clear set of priorities that will inform the administration's early actions. Specifically, each should assign a senior team to draft an early version of a first National Security Decision Directive (NSDD) that would outline in detail the governance, structure, and assumptions of the national security process and deliberations. This initial work should be further refined during the transition, with the aim of having it ready to shape the administration's earliest national security decisions and initiatives as well as its response to any crises that may arise once it is in office.

2. Choose a national security team based not only on individual experience, expertise, and qualifications but also on how effectively the group will work together.

Given the wide array of challenges the United States faces, there is little room for learning on the job. Presidents need experienced cabinet members who are deeply knowledgeable about the issues, know how to get things done in government, understand the strengths and limits of the interagency policymaking process, and can lead and manage large institutions effectively. For national security positions at the White House, the president should make prior service in one of the national security agencies and experience participating in the interagency process a prerequisite.

Beyond their individual attributes, National Security Council (NSC) principals and deputies should be chosen based on how they will work as a team. Do they share the president's national security vision and priorities? Do they accept the president's view of their role and responsibilities? Do they have the requisite skills individually and collectively to be successful in accomplishing the president's goals?

Presidents should certainly put a premium on excellence and experience but also on diversity, collegiality, and chemistry. In the business world, it is increasingly well understood that teams with greater diversity of perspective and experience make better decisions and create higher-performing organizations. In addition, teams composed of people who are willing to speak up and offer their best advice and counsel, including respectful dissent, perform better than those that get mired in bureaucratic turf battles and personality conflicts.

In 2008, the Obama Transition Team hung a banner in the main transition office that read, "No ego, no drama, this is not about you." This adage should guide the selection of the principals (and their deputies), who will meet together for countless hours in the windowless Situation Room to help the president make difficult, high-stakes decisions.

3. Start with a clean sheet of paper and redesign the NSC staff and process.

In both the Obama and George W. Bush administrations, the NSC staff grew larger than the historical norm. It also went beyond its traditional writ of helping the president develop strategy, set policy priorities, and define the limits that should guide execution. Instead, it became more engaged in managing the day-to-day details of how agencies execute national security policies and programs. New presidents should clarify the roles and responsibilities of the national security advisor, the NSC principals, and the NSC staff, and create an effective and efficient interagency process.

The first step is to clarify the role of the national security advisor and his or her staff vis-à-vis the principals who sit on the NSC, particularly the secretary of defense, the chairman of the Joint Chiefs of Staff, the secretary of state, and the secretary of the treasury. Historically, different presidents have relied on different models, with mixed results. Most historians and practitioners would agree, however, that one of the most effective NSC models was the Scowcroft NSC. National Security Advisor Brent Scowcroft, who served under Presidents Gerald Ford and George H. W. Bush, saw the role of the advisor and his staff as that of an honest broker, developing and assessing options for decision making, ensuring that the president had the benefit of the full range of perspectives when making decisions, and then, once a decision was made, providing oversight to ensure that it was executed by agencies according to presidential intent.

In this model, all of the principals on the NSC were empowered to (1) participate in the development of strategy and options for the president, (2) provide their best advice and counsel to the president before he made a decision, and (3) employ the resources of their agency to execute the president's policies within the policy parameters set by the White House. Accountability was exercised not by micromanaging agency execution from the White House but by ensuring transparency and holding principals accountable for their performance as presidentially appointed, Senate-confirmed leaders of their respective agencies.

Presidents should adopt such a model, which involves centralized policy decision making and largely decentralized execution. The president needs to convey to the White House staff and cabinet that he or she intends to act more like a chief executive officer than a chief operating officer.

Accordingly, the president should direct the national security advisor to refashion the NSC staff to be smaller, more strategic, and staffed by more senior and experienced professionals. He or she should also be explicit with NSC principals, individually and as a team, concerning expectations of their respective roles, responsibilities, decision-making rights, and accountabilities. The president should aim for the maximum clarity possible, recognizing that some authorities may be shared to avoid precious time and energy being wasted on adjudicating unclear lines of responsibility. The principals, in turn, should empower their subordinates to make and execute decisions that are clearly within their respective lanes of responsibility.

The NSC process should emphasize transparency and accountability to enable the NSC and the president to regularly monitor progress, make course corrections as necessary, ensure interagency coordination, and hold agency heads accountable for performance. But it should take pains to avoid bringing execution decisions into the White House. Falling prey to the temptations of micromanagement only diverts attention from more strategic decisions and, ironically, draws risk to the president, as opposed to protecting him or her. Only a more empowered and decentralized approach to decision making and execution will enable the president to cope with the complexity and speed of international events and compressed timelines for response.

4. Pay immediate and close attention to any ongoing or imminent military or intelligence operations, particularly those that put Americans in harm's way.

On the first day of the transition, the president should receive briefings on all ongoing military operations and intelligence activities broadly defined, as well as on any diplomatic and development activities that pose significant risk to the American personnel involved. Understanding the operational landscape—including what authority has been delegated to individuals serving below the president and even below the principals—is critical to preparing to step in as commander in chief and avoid being unpleasantly surprised. The president must know what is being done around the world in his or her name. A comprehensive review of operations is a critical first step. In addition, each new president would be wise to borrow a best practice from the Bush-Obama transition and conduct a tabletop simulation involving both departing and incoming NSC members to familiarize the new team with existing procedures for crisis response and increase their readiness for crisis management.

5. Given the volume and complexity of the national security agenda, set aside time for regular engagement with the team to set direction, monitor execution and outcomes, course correct, and learn.

The president needs to pay attention not only to setting strategy and monitoring its implementation but also to whether the NSC process is functioning properly and serving his or her needs, as well as to how successfully key people are performing. One of the lessons of previous administrations is the importance of being willing to make process and personnel changes as necessary in the first year to improve performance. Too often, presidents are asked to accept or manage difficult or poorly performing personalities; this should be deemed unacceptable. Cabinet officials should be expected and empowered to make hard personnel decisions.

The president should protect time on the schedule not only for regular NSC meetings but also for meetings with key principals in the Oval Office, both individually and in small groups. These more informal discussions are vital to "norming and forming" the team and to ensuring its members understand presidential vision and intent when executing policy. In addition, the president should make time to engage important stakeholders—particularly anyone responsible for implementing the president's national security priorities—to listen to their ideas and generate a greater sense of ownership of the new administration's policies and initiatives. Scheduling habits develop early and can be hard to change; the president should think carefully about how he or she will use different meeting venues, from the President's Daily Brief to formal NSC meetings to more informal interactions, to engage and align the national security team and get business done.

6. Develop an initial agenda of initiatives and actions to signal renewed American leadership internationally and communicate the administration's strategic priorities.

The president's strategic framework should be used to determine the priorities for diplomacy and engagement in the first months of the administration, from the initial travel schedules of key principals to the invitations sent by the White House to foreign leaders to changes made to the previous administration's budget requests to routine military exercises and freedom of navigation operations. These and other details will be scrutinized by foreign governments for indications of changes in priorities and policy direction; the new president should use them to send clear signals internationally.

7. Ensure that the national security team invests in a healthy civil-military relationship.

Most presidents, and many on their national security teams, come into office without any personal military experience or even experience working with the military. In some cases, they may have no clear concept of how civil-military relations should work; in other cases, they may arrive with misconceptions about how their military counterparts think and behave. Similarly, on the military side, senior officers may come to the table with unrealistic expectations about how the civil-military relationship is supposed to work (too often based on theories taught in war colleges that may have little grounding in reality). This state of affairs sets up both parties for frustration and disappointment. Presidents should invest in training civilian appointees on how to work effectively with the military; by the same token, senior military officers should be included in the efforts to norm and form the new national security team.

8. Invest in the people on the national security team, whether political appointees, civil servants, foreign service officers, intelligence professionals, or military officers.

One surefire way to increase a team's performance is to invest in its human capital—the recruitment, training, professional development, and retention of its people. Yet in government, taking care of one's people is too often seen as ancillary or even irrelevant to the main mission and practically impossible given the frenetic pace and long hours. The president should impress on his or her direct reports the importance of a "stewardship mindset."

Specifically, the president should start by having the transition team develop a human capital strategy before coming into office. The president should also increase the resources available to the Presidential Personnel Office and the White House Personnel Office to ensure that the best practices are used to find, recruit, and vet in a timely manner the best talent for appointed positions. The president should make clear to the national security advisor and NSC principals that each of them is expected to invest in the training, professional development, and mentoring of their staffs.

POLICY ENGINEERING, NOT POLICY GUESSWORK

PHILIP ZELIKOW

Imagine a new president who sets a tone of governance among a team of top-flight senior managers, who in turn are determined to restore the confidence and trust that Americans once had in their great public institutions.

Imagine that this president is working to build alliances in Congress well before Inauguration Day.

Imagine a president doing all this with a radically smaller White House staff that actually increases the president's own influence, simultaneously empowering departments and agencies yet holding them more accountable.

Imagine a president focused on policy execution with policy development linked to the budget process.

Imagine all those things and you would be imagining a changed American government. Yet none of these goals is unattainable. All have been achieved before, and can be again, as adapted to twenty-first century needs.

1. Prepare to govern.

When running for office, politicians master the art of judging what stands to take on issues and how best to represent these choices to key audiences. None of that stops when a candidate becomes president. But that skill is radically insufficient for governing.

It is worth reflecting on just how the core skills of governance are different from the core skills of electoral politics.

To govern is to:

- ▶ define concrete, operational definitions of success;
- ▶ work through alternative strategies for how to attain those objectives;
- ▶ design the many actions needed to make such strategies real and assemble the requisite coalitions;
- ▶ follow through; and
- ▶ review constantly and make adjustments as plans encounter reality.

True, some of the skills of governance overlap with the electoral campaign worlds of field organization, scheduling, and media buys. But in campaigns, the speech is often the end point. In governance, the speech is usually just the starting point. And the power to get anything done is always, always shared among various people and institutions.

All successful presidents undergo a shakedown period. It is when they figure out how to compose and lead a team that is good at governance. There is usually tension between the former campaign staff and those brought in to help make policy. Members of the winning campaign staff are wary of anyone who tries to profit from "their" victory without having fought the election battle. As presidential scholar Richard Neustadt once observed, "A golden haze of brotherhood descends at the moment of election on the campaigners and on their winning candidate, but on no one else."[1]

Yet the skills for high-quality policy work, for policy engineering, are special. People who are good at high-level governance are rare. The craft is rarely taught anymore. Such people are both choreographers and orchestra conductors. They have a zoom lens that can range quickly from the broad view of a landscape to a precise focus on a detail within it. They have a mastery not only of the general subject but also of the characteristics of various channels for taking actions.

One reason why Franklin D. Roosevelt, Dwight D. Eisenhower, and George H. W. Bush were all reasonably successful at governance was simple. They understood policy craft and respected it, because they all had substantial experience at it before becoming president.

No one possesses all the needed talents for governance. A president's task is to compose a team. Or, to put it more accurately, he or she must assemble a team of teams to blend the needed strengths. The president's attitude toward governance sets the tone.

2. Build policy partnerships in Congress, even before the inauguration.

Practically all briefing papers for new presidents concentrate on the White House and the executive branch. Congress is usually treated as a fortress to be assaulted.

Yet, on a good day, Congress can be an invaluable source of policy knowledge. There are usually committee (and some personal) staff members who have been cultivating issue expertise for years. They often have draft legislation filed away. Some early and carefully selected partnerships with them can provide a basis for quiet planning.

In 1989, as Bush took office, the largest open wounds in relations with Congress were constant battles—more than a decade old—over U.S. policies in Central America. Those battles, as they erupted in the Iran-Contra scandal of 1986–87, had nearly brought down the Reagan administration.

Even before Bush took office, Secretary of State–designate James Baker and his team made a major effort to forge understandings with Congress that would defuse this contentious issue. Revisiting the Central America controversy would allow Bush and Baker to focus on other priorities (like, say, ending the Cold War).

The effort extended to the Republican administration's nomination of a centrist Democrat, Bernard Aronson, as the State Department's assistant secretary for Latin America. And the effort was successful. After more than a decade as a fault line in American politics, Central America became a little-noticed area of regular bipartisan cooperation and policy success.

For a contrast, look at what happened in 2009, when President Barack Obama set out to close the Guantanamo Bay detention camp—a worthy goal. He used an executive order at the outset of his administration. His aides never worked with congressional leaders who might have become allies—including Obama's just-defeated opponent, John McCain. Obama's executive order failed to think through and specify where the transferred prisoners would end up.

Therefore, instead of being opposed by the congressional delegation of just one unlucky state, Obama's executive order was opposed by representatives from one end of the country to the other. All quickly issued "NIMBY" statements to reassure their constituents that their state or district would not be hosting imprisoned terrorists. The politics of the issue soon became poisonous for the administration. Eight years later, Guantanamo Bay was still open.

The big point is this: few major policy issues can be tackled solely by executive branch initiative. Yes, executive initiatives are essential. But none of these issues is likely to be meaningfully addressed in an administration's first year if work on them is deferred until January 20. All the possible solutions require months of staff work and policy development. That work is much more likely to be done in congressional offices than in campaign-managed transition processes.

Another reason for congressional partnership is to get help with updating and managing critical institutions. Most advice for new presidents assumes that the government machine works; the advisors—many of them outside the machine—just argue about how to steer it. Big mistake.

Significant portions of the government are so beset by out-of-date institutional designs, and they are so badly maintained as to be profoundly dysfunctional. They have become so dysfunctional that they cannot be relied on to perform many basic tasks. It may not matter where the new president wants to steer the car if the tires are flat and the engine is coughing. If a new team wants to fix national institutions, partnership with Congress is a must.

3. Treat good policy development—written staff work—as a matter of life and death.

Top officials and their staffs often know a lot about general subjects. They may be canny in their grasp of bureaucratic processes. But, in general, they are not trained to do policy analysis or related staff work to explain their analysis, crisply articulate key assumptions, and delineate the choice of operational objectives.

Americans once knew how to translate ideas concisely into operational alternatives. Arguments and choices were carefully noted and clearly communicated to those who needed to know. Relevant assumptions—about foreigners and our own side—were rigorously tracked.

The American policy professionals of the 1940s and 1950s managed colossal efforts at a high level of professionalism with staffs that are tiny by today's standards (and with no computers or email). To anyone who reads the historical records from these years, the quality of the paperwork is often strikingly good, identifying issues and clarifying arguments. Top officials, from the president on down, were accustomed to reading, critiquing, and sometimes composing detailed policy papers.

In recent decades, however, the quality of substantive policy staff work across much of the government cannot be favorably compared to the paperwork routinely found in the archives even as late as the 1960s and 1970s.

An oft-given reason for not doing good written work is the fear of leaks. This is a risk that must be taken. The Roosevelt war years, for example, experienced some leaks that were extremely serious. But at no time did the president or his key advisors abandon the staff work habits that they regarded as vital to guiding the efforts of a vast government.

An insistence on quality work must start at the top, with the president. No national security advisor can enforce quality and timeliness controls if the president does not provide backup, and with some heat. If the president is content to ruminate, or sits still for unilluminating PowerPoint bombardments, or does not pay attention to written details, those examples will set the tone for the rest of the team.

When the quality of written staff work is mediocre or worse, the symptoms include more staffers who actually accomplish less, as they meet more often with ill-focused purpose. These symptoms are currently rife. The bureaucracy is slowed by an interagency process that consumes more and more time in less and less consequential meetings. These meetings become something the better officials wish to avoid.

The White House then adds more staff to watch the executive agencies, a kind of American version of the old Soviet commissar school of management: announce the party line, monitor the functionaries carefully as they interpret their "guidance," and shoot a few to encourage the others.

The result may strengthen the White House staff, yet it does not strengthen the president (the two are not synonymous). It certainly does not encourage quality staff work from senior managers. Instead, it reduces them and their teams to being, well, functionaries. And the downward spiral just gets worse.

4. Link policymaking to budgeting.

The process for guiding and coordinating policy implementation has substantially broken down.

Viewed historically, the last time the National Security Council (NSC) handled program coordination reasonably well was in the Eisenhower administration. A principal reason for this, which hardly anyone understands today, is that this generation of officials—very much including Eisenhower himself—was formed by the habits of wartime staff work, influenced by British practices, including the way the British managed their War Cabinet.

So, for program oversight, Eisenhower had an Operations Coordination Board in the NSC to perform this function, allocating resources as he cut defense spending requests and prepared the government to wage a long Cold War. Eisenhower's NSC also had an innovatively designed Planning Board.

In the Eisenhower system, the NSC sat atop what officials then half-jokingly called "Policy Hill." Policy papers traveled through the interagency committees, shepherded by the Planning Board, to the top of that hill. They were considered in the council with Eisenhower actively chairing, and then were escorted down the other side of the hill, through the Operations Board's committees, to the departments and agencies.

To improve the current situation, a mix of options can be considered, including reviving an Eisenhower-style system. Another option could be to have a deputy national security advisor concentrate on policy implementation.

Another essential ingredient, however, should be a rebuilt link between policymaking and budgeting. Since every senior manager of an agency or business knows that you manage with your budget, this weakness in the NSC system (after 1960) is remarkable.

The NSC rarely does any budget work. This is left to a separate process led by the Office of Management and Budget (OMB). In fact, partly because of the way information is distributed in the government, the NSC staff rarely has much insight either into the budgets or the operations of any agency—except the poor State Department.

Leading OMB officials should become core participants in the national security policymaking process, as they once were. As any manager of a large enterprise knows: manage the money and you manage what is done.

The NSC must somehow figure out how to engage meaningfully with defense budget planning (which dominates national security spending). Waiting until the gigantic cake has already been baked in the very complex Defense Department process will be too late. Just adding or cutting the top line is too stupid. There are ways to do this that involve White House engagement in bodies with names like "joint requirements council" and the like. There are various historical precedents that can be consulted from the pre-1960 era. Analogous suggestions could be considered for the intelligence community budgeting process overseen by the director of national intelligence.

In sum, the message is that to govern, policy is more than a slogan. The U.S. government is now organized more for policy guesswork than for policy engineering with foreseeable results, including declining public confidence. To preserve the institutions of our republic, presidents must do better.

NOTE

1. Charles O. Jones, ed., *Preparing to Be President: The Memos of Richard E. Neustadt* (Washington, D.C.: American Enterprise Institute Press, 2000), 167.

CONFRONTING INTERNATIONAL FINANCIAL INSTABILITY

JEFFRY FRIEDEN

International finance is likely to present any new president with some of the most difficult challenges of the first year. The challenges will come in the form of growing financial instability around the world, with a buildup of the sort of macroeconomic imbalances that led to the Great Financial Crisis of 2008–9. But opportunities may also present themselves as the United States and its trading partners attempt to stabilize the global financial system and steer the world economy back toward growth.

International financial developments have a way of blindsiding American policy makers—as the administration of George W. Bush found out to its chagrin. If international financial risks materialize, the president and administration will quickly learn that confronting international financial instability requires cooperation among the world's principal centers of economic activity. This is bound to pose not just a diplomatic challenge but a domestic one as well, for the measures needed to limit the costs to the United States of financial crises abroad may be controversial at home.

FINANCIAL INSTABILITY

Financial crises have buffeted the world continually since the 1980s. The Latin American debt crisis of that decade gave way to the Mexican crisis of 1994, then to the East Asian crisis of 1997–98. Argentina, Russia, Turkey, and other dominoes fell in the following years. Then came the global financial crisis that began at the end of 2007, the most serious economic collapse since the Great Depression of the 1930s. The effects of this crisis continue to be felt around the world. Europe remains mired in the aftermath.

The first year of a new administration is precarious. The already-weak European recovery was thrown into disarray in 2016 when the United Kingdom voted to leave the European Union. Emerging markets such as Brazil already were in deep trouble. The Chinese financial system has sometimes appeared to be teetering on the brink of a full-blown crisis.

Certain macroeconomic policies almost certainly contribute to the fragility of international financial conditions. Cuts to corporate and personal taxes, along with large-scale spending on infrastructure, for example, would substantially increase the budget deficit and act as a fiscal stimulus. This in turn would trigger large capital inflows and—along with shifting Federal Reserve policy—increased interest rates. The result would be a stronger dollar—good for American consumers (though not for its manufacturers) but a problem for other countries, especially in emerging markets. This is because higher interest rates put pressure on their economies, American international borrowing sucks capital out of the rest of the world, and a stronger dollar increases the real debt burden of these countries—all of which could lead to financial volatility, and perhaps financial crises, in a range of emerging and even developed economies.

COSTS OF CRISES

Financial crises are dangerous for many reasons. First, they are extremely expensive: They burn up, on average, three to five years' worth of economic growth. They are not only dangerous to the country in which the crisis originates but are easily transmitted around the world. This was strikingly apparent in 2007–8, as problems in a relatively minor segment of the American housing market sparked a panic of global proportions. Contagion is now common. The recent crisis in the Eurozone started in one of its smallest members, Greece, but quickly implicated all the countries that were members of the currency union, and many that were not.

The economic costs of financial crises are far greater than those of cyclical recessions because recovery from a debt crisis takes a very long time. A financial crisis leaves the countries affected with a "debt overhang," a burden of accumulated debts. Creditors with a portfolio of bad, or potentially bad, loans are reluctant to lend. Debtors struggling to service their debts have to restrict their spending.

In the aftermath of a financial crisis, banks don't lend and consumers don't spend, which is why the average recovery takes from five to seven years, as opposed to a few months in the case of a "normal" cyclical recession. The Eurozone needed nine years to claw its way back to the level of economic activity prevailing before this most recent crisis hit.

Financial crises have political costs as well. The Obama administration, for example, found in its first year in office how seriously the crisis it inherited impinged on all other policy issues. Financial crises lead to major political conflict, often upheaval. Debtors have to tighten their belts to service their debts, while creditors have to rebuild their portfolios to recover from the bad debts on their books.

Debtors and creditors fight over the distribution of the burden of adjustment, as they did in the first year of the Obama administration. Creditors want to be repaid in full; debtors want their obligations to be reduced or restructured to share the pain. When, as is common, the financial ties are international, conflict occurs among countries, with creditor countries arrayed against debtor countries. Within such countries, groups battle to shift the costs of the crisis onto others. Who makes the sacrifices necessary to rebuild the nation's finances: taxpayers, bankers, government employees?

The economic and political costs of financial crises can be incalculable: The debt crises of the 1930s led almost directly to the rise of fascism in Central and Eastern Europe. The most recent debt crisis in Europe inflamed extremist passions throughout the continent, shattered the cohesion of the European Union, and, some believe, threatened the stability of democracy in some of its member states. Macroeconomic problems in the emerging markets have contributed to political instability in countries ranging from South Korea to Brazil.

CAUSES OF CRISES

We know how costly financial crises are. If we are to avoid them, we need to know what causes them. Three interrelated factors come together to create the conditions for crisis. The first is globe-straddling financial markets that can quickly move trillions of dollars around the world. International finance is welcome when it moves money from where it is less needed to where it can be used productively. It is less appealing when it transmits panic around the world within hours.

Global financial integration might be less troubling if there was global financial regulation, but instead there are dozens of competing regulatory systems among the major financial centers. The second factor that challenges financial stability is the existence of fundamentally different ways of regulating financial markets, when these differences can create conditions for regulatory evasion and eventual volatility.

Third, the differences in the macroeconomic policies of the major economic powers can create the conditions for financial insecurity. When one country is stagnant and another is growing rapidly, capital moves away from stagnation and toward growth. Taken together, the combination of differences of this sort, financial integration, and regulatory fragmentation can lead to massive capital flows as money sloshes from one place to another. These "global macroeconomic imbalances" were the cause of the American financial crisis of 2007–8, as well as of the Eurozone crisis that began then. Such forces create the conditions for cycles of boom and bust, with bubbles bursting that leave societies to clean up ever greater financial messes.

Ever more global finance, and ever larger international financial markets, also create tremendous opportunities. They make enormous sums available to emerging markets and other productive investments around the world. But the larger and more encompassing international finance becomes, the greater are the threats of larger and more damaging financial crises. The crisis of 2007–8 came very close to bringing the world economy to a terrible halt and risked a collapse worse than the Great Depression of the 1930s. The next crisis may be even bigger. America and the world need to devise measures to prevent, or limit the effects of, the next global crisis. But how?

WHAT CAN THE PRESIDENT DO?

The first year of a new administration often gives the president the opportunity to undertake difficult initiatives. International financial initiatives are always difficult because the public has little understanding of, or interest in, the topic. And today's global financial markets are not going to be unwound. Nor should they be: they serve important purposes.

That leaves the other two sources of financial instability: inadequate and fragmented regulation, and uncoordinated macroeconomic policies. Specialists and policymakers in money and finance have long recognized the desirability of harmonizing financial regulations and coordinating macroeconomic policies for decades. Governments have even taken some steps toward harmonizing financial regulations. Under the auspices of the Bank for International Settlements, regulators from the major financial centers have agreed on some common standards. The effort has been only a qualified success, and a great deal more work is needed before financial regulation is both adequate and consistent enough to avoid some of the regulatory nightmares that have surfaced.

It has been much more difficult to get governments to coordinate relevant macroeconomic policies. It is never easy for a government to subordinate national policies to abstract notions of international cooperation, especially when economic growth is at stake. The demands of macroeconomic policy cooperation can be severe. It can mean reining in an economic expansion, running a budget deficit, or raising taxes. In other words, almost by definition, macroeconomic cooperation requires governments to do things they would not otherwise do. And the benefits can be hard to measure—and even harder to justify to constituents. Difficult as it is to harmonize macroeconomic policies among nations, however, the inability to do so has been at the root of most of the economic upheavals of the past quarter century.

CAN IT BE DONE?

The obstacles to progress are political. Powerful special interests can block cooperative efforts, and electoral pressures can make them risky for politicians who want to stay in office. Financial regulation everywhere is a thicket of special-interest pressures. In normal times, only financial institutions care enough, and know enough, to influence the design and implementation of financial regulation. When banks fail or a crisis hits, voters become painfully aware of the flaws in the regulatory architecture, blame politicians for them, and insist that they be repaired. But attention flags quickly, and soon the regulatory playing field is again full only of special interests. The challenge to any new president, therefore, is to overcome popular opposition or apathy and interest-group influence to make regulatory progress both domestically and internationally.

Coordinating macroeconomic policies is, if anything, more difficult. Governments from China to Germany jealously guard their monetary and fiscal policy autonomy. Again, the size and centrality of the United States gives it a unique opportunity to lead the way. But Americans are no different from anyone when it comes to an unwillingness to subordinate national economic goals to international considerations.

In the years before 2007, international financial institutions and others voiced plenty of warnings about the dangers of the macroeconomic imbalances, and in particular the massive foreign borrowing spree that the United States embarked on after 2001. But the Bush administration had little incentive to slow a rapidly growing economy, even if the housing bubble became increasingly obvious. Such action would have required real economic foresight and political statesmanship.

In the first year of a new administration, major opportunities are available to take the lead in addressing global financial regulation and macroeconomic policy cooperation. In a way, the first year of the first Obama administration provides some guidance as to what might be feasible and where there may be obstacles.

Both financial regulation and international policy cooperation were central to economic policy in Obama's first year or so in office. True, it took a year and a half for the administration to actually propose the Dodd-Frank Act's massive overhaul of the nation's financial system, but the reform was in the works long before that. Still, most observers regard it as successful in at least focusing attention on the desirability of more regulatory attention to new financial instruments.

By the same token, the major economic powers came together quickly when the global crisis hit in 2008. The first year of the Obama administration saw a surprising degree of macroeconomic policy cooperation among the member states of the Group of Seven, and even in some instances of the Group of Twenty. The threat of a truly epochal shutdown of global financial markets, and the prospect of the most serious recession since the 1930s, seems to have focused the minds of policymakers enough that, domestic politics or not, they worked hard to devise a common response to the crisis.

Yet even the most positive appraisals of the Obama administration's first-year efforts on financial regulation and macroeconomic policy coordination would have to concede that the efforts were not sustained. The implementation of Dodd-Frank quickly degenerated into traditional special-interest pleading for favored treatment, and it is unclear which aspects of the act will be preserved. The Groups of Seven and Twenty just as quickly degenerated into the ineffectual talking shops they had been before the crisis.

The lesson would seem to be that progress in these international economic policies is possible for a new administration. But progress will be fleeting—and its consequences very limited—unless the administration can create enough political and institutional momentum to sustain these efforts past the first year. The immediate political incentives to do so may be weak, but the risks of inaction are enormous.

IV ★ THE DOMESTIC AGENDA

BE LIKE IKE

Eisenhower and the Interstate Highway System

PETER NORTON

Nineteen months into his first term, President Dwight Eisenhower, quoting an unnamed former college president, advised a public audience: "I have two kinds of problems, the urgent and the important. The urgent are not important, and the important are never urgent."[1]

In warning his successors that they've "got one year" to get their program through Congress, President Lyndon B. Johnson was arguing for the urgency of the important. Eisenhower, whom his vice president, Richard Nixon, said was always "the coolest man in the room," pursued his most important objectives with little sense of urgency.

Eisenhower's greatest domestic policy achievement came in his fourth year. But he laid the groundwork in his first year. The Federal-Aid Highway Act of 1956 launched the most ambitious infrastructure project ever undertaken. Success in 1956, however, depended on a strategy Eisenhower began implementing soon after his electoral triumph of November 4, 1952.

During the next four years, Eisenhower showed how a president can use the first year to achieve legislative success later in the first term, at a time that will best contribute to reelection, even when the opposing party has majorities in both houses of Congress.

- ▸ Year 1: Organize a strategy led by trusted insiders who command respect in and out of the White House.
- ▸ Year 2: Use these leaders to build coalitions of business groups and governors and unite them behind a plan.
- ▸ Year 3: Present the united plan to Congress, negotiating to find common interests that cross party lines.
- ▸ Year 4: Reap the legislative reward.

Although an extraordinary achievement by any standard, the interstate highways—especially their urban segments—were (and remain) controversial. In private, Eisenhower agreed with critics who warned that urban interstates would tear cities' social fabric. Together, Eisenhower's private reservations about the urban segments of the interstates and his public cautions about undue business influence on public policy suggest that if he could have done his first year over, he would have made one important change: to maintain control of the policy agenda and keep the weeds of opportunism from crowding the crops of policy.

THE GENERAL

Eisenhower's years as an army officer taught him the value of three virtues: organization, planning, and patience. In his first year in the White House, Eisenhower institutionalized them, and they served him well.

Eisenhower was an organizer. Following his election, the new president, in his own words, was determined to "organize the White House for efficiency." He admitted that "organization cannot make a genius out of an incompetent," but "on the other hand, disorganization can scarcely fail to result in inefficiency and can easily lead to disaster."[2] He organized his White House accordingly. A relatively lean and durable staff, many of them former military officers (including six generals) who had known Eisenhower for years, maintained close working relationships with members of Congress. To Eisenhower, organization was the necessary preparation for successful planning.

Eisenhower was also a planner. As supreme commander of the Allied Expeditionary Force, he famously restrained his less risk-averse colleagues Field Marshal Bernard Montgomery and General George Patton. Such restraint was evident in 1953 as well. Although interstate highways were among Eisenhower's highest domestic political priorities, he gave them little attention in his first year. Bryce Harlow, a congressional liaison for the Eisenhower White House, explained, "A president cannot have too many congressional issues that are 'presidential' at one time. Otherwise none of them are presidential, and all of them suffer."[3] To Eisenhower, success required a sustainable pace, executed in accordance with a plan.

Eisenhower was above all patient. Privately, he feared "the inability of men to forego immediate gain for a long time good."[4] Both as supreme commander and as a civilian commander in chief, he earned a reputation for caution and for preparing carefully before acting. D-Day followed more than a year of planning. Eisenhower did little to further his infrastructure agenda in his first year. His priorities lay in foreign affairs, and above all in Korea. But Eisenhower invested the time into organizing and planning. The strategy paid off.

YEAR 1: THE TEAM

To Eisenhower, success required a disciplined White House organization of trusted insiders to whom he could delegate assignments. They worked outside of cabinet departments and so were not subject to Senate confirmation. They built coalitions with powerful business groups, governors, and segments of the general public. Once these alliances were in place, the president could take his agenda to Congress from a position of strength.

Eisenhower did not ignore Congress in his first year. To the contrary, he believed relations with key members had to be cultivated before he could depend on them. Eisenhower did not land major legislative proposals on the shores of Congress until he had organized the operation and prepared the objective. This was the responsibility of his White House congressional liaison staff, led by Wilton "Jerry" Persons. Eisenhower had known Persons for more than twenty years, and they were close; indeed, Eisenhower painted Persons's portrait as a gift to him. Through the congressional liaisons Persons managed, the Eisenhower administration negotiated with Congress discreetly and almost continuously, without undue pressure on the president himself. He thereby avoided open confrontations with a Congress his party did not control after his first two years.

YEAR 2: THE COALITION

Eisenhower opposed "New Dealism," distrusted politicians and bureaucrats, and demanded executive control. These values guided him in his coalition-building effort and led him to depart from the strategies of his predecessors.

Federal aid for paved interstate motor roads began in 1916. Responsibility lay in the Bureau of Public Roads, housed usually in the Commerce Department. Its dynamic early chief, Thomas H. MacDonald, was a zealous advocate of good roads and adept at building business support for his agency. Consistent with most of the interest groups behind interstate roads, MacDonald opposed tolls, preferring "free" roads.[5] Under Franklin D. Roosevelt, MacDonald's agency proposed an ambitious network of toll-free interstate highways. The bureau's major reports went directly to Congress. Through the Federal-Aid Highway Act of 1944, Congress approved a bureau proposal for an interstate network and authorized funds, but actual appropriations were slow in coming. Meanwhile, as rail and transit systems were neglected and suburbs proliferated, pro-highway interest groups cited the popularity of the automobile, traffic congestion, and traffic fatalities as evidence that more highways were urgently needed.

Eisenhower had taken a personal interest in better roads when he crossed the country in an army convoy in 1919, witnessing poor conditions firsthand. As a candidate in 1952, Eisenhower told the Hearst newspapers: "The obsolescence of the nation's highways presents an appalling problem of waste, danger and death."[6]

But an interstate system would have to be funded, and any funding method would compete with states' mechanisms for funding their own roads. Most governors were suspicious of such federal intrusion. Unlike MacDonald, Eisenhower, who ran in 1952 on a platform of spending cuts and tax reduction, favored toll roads where possible. Other interstates would be funded through bond issues. To shield the national debt, gasoline tax revenues would go into a special off-budget fund that would continuously pay off the bonds.

Thus, Eisenhower abandoned precedents set by Roosevelt and Harry S. Truman, who had let MacDonald direct the federal-aid road effort. MacDonald left the Bureau of Public Roads two months after Eisenhower took office. Eisenhower's interstate highway effort would be led from the White House, would be less bureaucratic, and would consider tolls. But some powerful pro-highway groups opposed tolls. Fiscal conservatives saw the proposed highway fund as an accountant's trick to conceal debt, and many governors did not want federal gas taxes competing with their own state gas taxes. Despite broad interest in highways, such divisive matters threatened any particular program.

Before Eisenhower could go to Congress with a program, therefore, he had to build a strong coalition. He began with the states. In July 1954, he sent Vice President Nixon to the annual governors' conference to deliver the president's appeal to "recommend to me the cooperative action you think the federal government and the 48 states should take . . . so that I can submit positive proposals to the next session of Congress."[7] To coordinate governors' advice and to secure business support, Eisenhower—consistent with his usual methods—put a trusted military friend in charge of a special committee. As chairman of the President's Advisory Committee on a National Highway Program, General Lucius Clay put together a plan for federal bond issues that would be paid off by gas tax revenues.[8]

YEAR 3: CONGRESS

Eisenhower faced a Congress he could not count on. Even in 1953 and 1954, when the Republicans held slim majorities in both houses, he faced significant Republican opposition to his agenda. For all eight years, Eisenhower depended on bipartisan support for the success of his programs. In 1953, he wrote privately: "The particular legislators who are most often opposing Administration views are of the *majority* party."[9]

Eisenhower compensated by exploiting his popularity. "Eisenhower was so popular," Lyndon Johnson said, that "whoever was supporting him would be on the popular side."[10] But Eisenhower could not rely on his popularity alone. By the time his highway agenda reached Congress, Clay's plan was in trouble. Pro-highway groups saw it as a grab for more gas tax money with no guarantee that the revenues would be committed solely to highways. Fiscal conservatives saw it as an expansion of the federal budget and tax power. In the summer of 1955, Eisenhower's first proposed highway bills died.

During the next year friends of the interstate highway program worked together to find another way. To appease fiscal conservatives, no bonds would be issued. Instead, gas tax revenues would be spent directly on roads on a "pay as you go" basis through a "Highway Trust Fund." The federal share of spending to build interstate highways would rise from 50 percent to 90 percent, overcoming states' reluctance to accept a greater federal role by reducing their costs. To appease the critics of tolls, the interstate system would permit tolls only on those segments of the network that were already toll roads, and even then, only if a toll-free alternative route existed. Meanwhile, the Bureau of Public Roads published a book of maps plotting promised urban interstates in cities in forty-two states, distributing the work to all members of Congress.[11] The compromises worked, and the 1956 highway bill won broad bipartisan support. On June 29, Eisenhower signed the Federal-Aid Highway Act of 1956.

THE HAZARDS OF SUCCESS

Although Eisenhower's practice of delegating authority to trusted associates worked well for him, there was a cost. His well-organized White House system could run so smoothly that he did not have to monitor it closely. Left on its own, however, it could take a course the president disapproved of, forming alliances of expediency that shifted authority away from him.

The president's advisors had his confidence to such an extent that they sometimes acted on his behalf without consulting him. To Eisenhower, such initiative was a valuable benefit of delegation. It was not only a practical convenience; the president's health emergencies, and particularly his prolonged convalescence following his 1955 heart attack, made it a necessity.

But Eisenhower was sometimes angered to discover that his subordinates, to win the support they needed, made decisions in his name that he opposed. In 1955, the president's own Bureau of Public Roads drafted urban interstate routes that would cut through dozens of cities. They were expensive, disruptive, and controversial. But the president was apparently unaware of these urban highway plans. Once the demolitions to make way for these routes began, many local residents, intellectuals, and the popular press were outraged.

In 1959, Eisenhower put yet another general in charge of a committee to look into the matter. General John Bragdon warned the president that the urban interstates served local more than national needs and were too expensive. Eisenhower agreed. Bragdon took up the matter with the Bureau of Public Roads, where his recommendations were not well received. The controversy simmered. Finally, in April 1960, the president met with Bragdon and bureau leaders. The imprecise minutes indicate that Eisenhower was angry about the urban segments, but it was too late to thwart them.

THE EISENHOWER COROLLARY TO THE
JOHNSON FIRST-YEAR DOCTRINE

Eisenhower and Johnson were among the most dissimilar leaders ever to serve as presidents. Johnson was a partisan politician, a legislative leader, and a demanding negotiator. Eisenhower was a general with an aversion to partisan politics, a managerial executive, and a coalition builder. It is unsurprising, therefore, that Eisenhower's variant of Johnson's doctrine that legislative success can only come in the first year is substantially different—yet no less valid.

Eisenhower's administration demonstrates that a president who invests the first year of the first term in developing and implementing a strategy for success can reap major legislative victories late in the term. This Eisenhower corollary to the Johnson first-year doctrine has practical advantages. As Johnson's own example demonstrates, a president who excels in the first year may lose momentum when his record of accomplishment tails off. In 1964–65, Johnson's approval ratings were among the best ever recorded and never fell below 60 percent. But they eroded steadily thereafter, hovering stubbornly in the low forties by 1967–68. Eisenhower's first-term approval ratings were durably high, beginning at about 70 percent and staying near there all four years. The Federal-Aid Highway Act contributed to Eisenhower's overwhelming reelection victory in 1956, when he earned 57 percent of the popular vote.

Despite facing a Congress controlled by the opposition party, despite prioritizing foreign policy in his first year, despite a commitment to limit bureaucracy and the federal budget, and despite a personal distaste for congressional politics, Eisenhower achieved, in his first term, one of the most ambitious domestic policy triumphs of any presidency.

NOTES

1. Dwight D. Eisenhower, "Address at the Second Assembly of the World Council of Churches," Evanston, Ill., August 19, 1954.

2. Valerie Adams, *Eisenhower's Fine Group of Fellows: Crafting a National Security Policy to Uphold the Great Equation* (New York: Lexington Books, 2006), 41.

3. Quoted in Stephen Hess, *What Do We Do Now? A Workbook for the President-Elect* (Washington, D.C.: Brookings Institution Press, 2008), 40.

4. Robert Griffith, "Dwight D. Eisenhower and the Corporate Commonwealth," *American Historical Review* 87, no. 1 (1982): 87–122.

5. U.S. Department of Transportation Federal Highway Administration, *Highway History: Thomas H. MacDonald on Toll Roads* (Washington, D.C.: U.S. Department of Transportation, 1947).

6. "Ike Understands Road Problem We're Facing," *Road Builders' News*, November–December 1952, 7.

7. Richard Nixon, "Address of Vice President Richard Nixon to the Governors' Conference," Lake George, N.Y., July 12, 1954.

8. Advisory Committee on a National Highway Program. *A Ten-Year National Highway Program: A Report to the President* (Washington, D.C.: U.S. Government Printing Office, 1955).

9. Dwight D. Eisenhower, *Mandate for Change* (New York: Doubleday, 1963), 193.

10. Jean Edward Smith, *Eisenhower: In War and Peace* (New York: Random House, 2012), 648.

11. U.S. Bureau of Public Roads, *General Location of National System of Interstate Highways, Including All Additional Routes at Urban Areas Designated in September, 1955* (Washington, D.C.: U.S. Government Printing Office, 1955).

PRESCRIPTION FOR SUCCESS
Enacting Medicare and Medicaid

GUIAN MCKEE

The passage of Medicare and Medicaid represented one of the most significant accomplishments of Lyndon B. Johnson's Great Society. Careful review of the process the Johnson administration used to shepherd the legislation through Congress offers important lessons for any new president about to take office.

When Johnson took over the presidency in November 1963, critical shifts had already taken place in the debate about health care policy in the United States. Following the defeat of President Harry S. Truman's proposals for national health insurance at the hands of congressional conservatives allied with the American Medical Association (AMA), reformers focused on achieving health coverage for elderly Americans, rather than for the population as a whole. The elderly represented an inherently sympathetic constituency, and the Social Security system provided a familiar mechanism for their coverage. Meanwhile, during the 1950s, labor unions, corporations, and commercial insurers expanded employer-based health insurance. By the early 1960s, roughly 70 percent of Americans had some form of coverage through this "insurance company model," a development that further reduced pressure for national health insurance.

Yet the elderly, no longer in the workforce and poor risks for insurance companies, remained largely outside this private coverage system. In 1960, House Ways and Means Committee chairman Wilbur Mills and Senator Robert Kerr sponsored a limited measure that provided federal matching grants to the states to cover low-income seniors. Not all states took up the program (popularly known as Kerr-Mills), and its effectiveness remained limited. During the 1960 presidential campaign, John F. Kennedy called for a Social Security–based program of federal health insurance for the elderly, an idea that his campaign referred to as Medicare.

Lesson 1: Use early policy defeats to build future legislative opportunities.

In January 1962, late in the first year of his presidency, Kennedy submitted his Medicare proposal to Congress. Known as the King-Anderson bill after its chief sponsors, Kennedy's Medicare bill covered hospital and nursing home expenses for Social Security's old age and disability recipients but did not include coverage of physicians' fees. Mills, one of the most influential figures in Washington, opposed the bill. The Kerr-Mills Act had just taken effect, and Mills did not want to undermine it by passing Medicare. He also feared that financing the new program through the payroll tax might jeopardize the long-term fiscal viability of the existing Social Security system. The AMA, meanwhile, remained uncompromising in its opposition and launched an all-out lobbying campaign, which included the distribution of anti-Medicare recordings made by actor Ronald Reagan. The Ways and Means Committee held hearings but never voted on King-Anderson. This pattern repeated itself when the administration reintroduced the bill in 1963.

The Kennedy administration used these defeats strategically, publicizing the nature of the AMA's opposition and seeking to build public support for a renewed effort later in the president's term. Significantly, Kennedy also influenced new appointments to the Ways and Means Committee by insuring that all new members either supported Medicare or would at least vote to report it to the floor. One potential lesson for a first-year president thus rests in Kennedy's role in Medicare's ultimate passage: even in defeat, look for ways to create future legislative opportunities.

Taking office after President Kennedy's assassination, Lyndon Johnson followed a similar strategy. In 1964—what might be called Johnson's "first first year"—the president made an intensive push for Medicare but ultimately fell one vote short of a majority on Ways and Means. Along with White House congressional liaison Lawrence O'Brien and Assistant Secretary of Health, Education, and Welfare Wilbur Cohen, Johnson worked extensively during this period to win over Wilbur Mills. In part, Johnson did this by suggesting that Mills would receive the credit for passing a Medicare bill but also by indicating that the administration would be open to options other than King-Anderson. Mills feared that because King-Anderson as written covered only hospital and nursing home costs, seniors might be disappointed when they discovered that Medicare did not cover doctors' bills—and that they would blame the Democratic Party. As early as January 1964, Mills suggested the addition of physicians' fees to Medicare. In June 1964, Mills and Johnson discussed a package that would combine hospital and physician coverage with the existing Kerr-Mills program.

This would be the ultimate model for the legislation that, nine months later, created both Medicare and Medicaid. Although the Johnson administration lost the 1964 debate, the president and his team created conditions that would facilitate later success on an even grander scale than the original proposal.

Lesson 2: Find ways to appeal to opponents' interests—or seek to isolate them.

President Johnson's support for Medicare, which a majority of the public now supported, contributed to his landslide victory in the 1964 election. The president's lengthy coattails also brought large Democratic majorities to Congress. The Ways and Means Committee now had a clear majority in favor of a Medicare bill.

When Johnson took the oath of office for his "second first year," Medicare's passage seemed certain, but its exact form remained unclear. The 1965 amendments to the Social Security Act constituted the battleground for the bill: the administration initially proposed the standard King-Anderson package of hospital and nursing insurance financed by an additional Social Security payroll tax. Moderate Republicans, desperate to recapture the political center after their party's massive defeat in the 1964 election, attacked Medicare for its lack of coverage for physician services (as Mills had anticipated). Wisconsin Representative John Byrnes, the ranking minority member on Ways and Means and a widely respected Social Security expert, offered a proposal that the Republicans dubbed "Bettercare." It provided coverage of both physicians' fees and drugs, with participation voluntary. Financing would be entirely outside the Social Security system, through general tax revenues and participant contributions. Bettercare sought to break the Republican identification with the AMA and to peel off the votes of moderate and conservative Democrats.

Meanwhile, the increasingly desperate AMA sought to stave off both Medicare and Bettercare with a more limited proposal to extend the Kerr-Mills program for low-income seniors. The AMA designated their program as "Eldercare." The AMA also relaunched its standard attack on Medicare as "socialized medicine," but by 1965, the doctors' organization had lost much of its former influence. The public had come to see it as simply an interest group, rather than as the authoritative voice of medical science, and no longer responded to AMA warnings about creeping socialism.

At a more strategic level, the AMA's continued intransigence so irritated Mills that he refused even to consult its representatives in closed sessions of the Ways and Means Committee. Some doctors began to defect from their professional organization's position, both because they saw little real harm in providing medical coverage for the elderly and because they had become comfortable with accepting payments from commercial insurers. Finally, even the AMA's supposed allies in the insurance industry were not really with them. Although the Health Insurance Industry of America (HIIA) still officially opposed the Medicare legislation, its member companies were happy to offload an unprofitable industry segment (offering health insurance to illness-prone senior citizens) onto the federal government. The nonprofit Blue Cross plans had begun negotiating years before for a role administering an eventual Medicare program, and the rest of the industry joined that effort as passage seemed likely in early 1965. As a result, the HIIA publicly supported the AMA position but never fully mobilized against Medicare.

The positions of the AMA and HIIA suggest a principle that first-year presidents should continually pursue: whenever possible, search out ways to appeal to opponents' own interests, and failing that, seek to isolate them.

Lesson 3: Be ready to shift plans in new directions.

With the Republican bill gaining traction in the House, Wilbur Mills made a dramatic move during closed Ways and Means Committee hearings. Previously, the Republican, AMA, and administration bills had all been assumed to be mutually exclusive, even though they covered different aspects of medical care. Mills mused, "Well now, let's see. Maybe it would be a good idea if we put all three of these bills together."[1] He ordered Wilbur Cohen to draft such a bill by morning. This "three-layer cake," as it came to be called, formed the basis for the modern Medicare and Medicaid systems.

The move stunned veteran observers of Ways and Means. Historians disagree over whether Mills and Johnson had secretly planned the three-layer-cake strategy. Yet they discussed the prospects for such a combination in June 1964, and Mills later recalled that "we planned that, yes."[2] Although this comment likely overstates the level of direct coordination between Mills and the White House, Lyndon Johnson had clearly indicated that he would accept new solutions to the Medicare challenge. When Mills saw the opportunity, the president felt free to take it.

Cohen and other Social Security experts immediately redrafted the bill according to Mills's instructions. The King-Anderson bill became Medicare Part A, covering hospital and nursing home charges through a new payroll tax (as well as a broadening of the wage base on which the payroll taxes are levied). Mills tried to ensure clear actuarial soundness for the overall program and also insulated Social Security from Medicare by creating a separate trust fund for the latter.

As passed, Medicare and Medicaid reflected the ideas not only of the administration but also of Wilbur Mills, moderate Republicans, and even the AMA. This suggests that first-year presidents can develop new policy opportunities if they remain open to changes in approach, particularly through the cooptation of opponents' ideas.

Lesson 4: Consider the long-range fiscal consequences of short-term political compromises.

Medicare and Medicaid represent two of Johnson's most important legacies. Medicare in particular has done more than any other federal policy to lift seniors out of poverty and assure dignity and a modicum of comfort in old age. But the program also created long-term budgetary challenges that have plagued every president since Johnson. Today, health care represents one of the largest and fastest-growing sources of federal spending. A 2010 Peterson Foundation report on the long-term fiscal crisis emphasized that "any long-term plan to stabilize the national debt as a percentage of the overall economy will depend on successfully controlling the costs of federal health programs."[3]

Medicare and Medicaid are expensive because they are intertwined with the larger American health care system, whose cost vastly exceeds those of other developed countries (Medicare actually has somewhat lower cost levels than private insurers). This outcome reflects Johnson's and Mills's choices about the basic structure of the program. Seeking to avoid further alienation of the AMA, Medicare did not provide effective controls on physicians' fees. Instead, it left the determination of reasonable charges up to physicians in conjunction with insurance companies (which gained a profitable role in Medicare claims administration).

Hospitals received a similar degree of pricing deference. Over time, this latitude contributed to the excessive rate of cost inflation in the wider health care system. Such costs threaten the actuarial soundness of Medicare and Medicaid as well as the overall federal budget.

In 1965, Johnson and Mills lacked the long-range forecasts that the Congressional Budget Office now provides. Nonetheless, both understood that Medicare and Medicaid would have significant and unpredictable long-range costs, but they chose to emphasize the short-run affordability of the programs.

The immediate costs would be manageable; the problem lay in the way that Medicare and Medicaid embedded the larger system's cost structure in its basic incentives and financial architecture. This suggests that politics aside, first-year presidents must consider the long-range fiscal consequences of health care policy choices. The real benefits of such policies must be balanced against the problems they will generate for future presidents.

Lesson 5: Find your Wilburs and rely on them.

Although Republicans in the House still preferred John Byrnes's plan (and came within twenty-three votes of passing it during a late tactical maneuver), most did not oppose the final three-layer cake of Medicare and Medicaid. Mills's endorsement, in turn, secured the votes of many conservative southern Democrats. The bill cleared the Ways and Means Committee and passed in the House by a vote of 313 to 115 on April 8, 1965. The Senate passed a version with expanded benefit levels that added $800 million in costs to the bill, but Mills led a coalition of fiscal conservatives that knocked out most of these amendments in conference committee.

On July 27, both the Senate and House passed the conference committee bill. Three days later, President Johnson signed it in the presence of Harry Truman at the former president's library in Independence, Missouri—paying tribute to the president who had proposed the first federal health insurance legislation nearly two decades before.

Lyndon Johnson did not micromanage this legislative process. Instead, he deferred details to knowledgeable surrogates such as Cohen, who in turn worked with Mills to craft both strategy and specific legislative provisions. This allowed the president to exert his influence when needed while providing a useful degree of separation from the immediate pressures of the policy process.

The passage of Medicare and Medicaid demonstrates the importance of identifying and relying on key personnel both inside and outside the administration.

On an inside basis, the first-year president should find a Wilbur Cohen (prefera- bly along with a Lawrence O'Brien): talented and knowledgeable subordinates to manage the details of the legislative and policy development process, allowing the president to save direct interventions for critical moments. Outside the admin- istration, the first-year president should find a Wilbur Mills: pragmatic congres- sional leaders, some of whom may even begin in opposition, with the credibility to bring their colleagues into line and an openness to building long-term alliances.

Lesson 6: Prioritize issues that meet real public needs.

The persistence of the Kennedy and Johnson administrations in pushing Medi- care year after year, despite repeated failures, contributed to building the political conditions that won over Mills and the Ways and Means Committee to the Medi- care cause. More than just persistence, this effort reflected the manner in which Medicare met a pressing need among the American people. This suggests another lesson for new presidents: identify issues and policies that appeal to real areas of concern among the broad public and then do not give up.

Through these techniques, the Johnson administration created conditions under which Mills could move the legislation forward by incorporating both the Republican and AMA positions in a way that made it difficult for either to block the final bill. This produced a more expansive program and a historic first-year victory for the president. Like all such achievements, the passage of Medicare reflected the particular historical contingencies of its time. The broad principles of its success, however, can nonetheless be useful for any first-year president.

NOTES

1. Rick Mayes, *Universal Coverage: The Elusive Quest for National Health Insurance* (Ann Arbor: University of Michigan Press, 2004), 69.

2. Wilbur Mills Interview, March 25, 1987, Wilbur Mills Oral History, Interview II, Lyndon Baines Johnson Library Oral History Collection, https://www.ssa.gov/history/pdf/mills2.pdf.

3. Peter G. Peterson Foundation, "State of the Union's Finances: A Citizen's Guide," April 2010, https://www.slideshare.net/PGPF/pgpf-citizens-guide2010.

PRESIDENTIAL PRECEDENTS

Recent Approaches to Fostering Opportunity

MICHAEL NELSON

Equal opportunity is the core American value that animates the American dream of upward mobility. All four presidents from Jimmy Carter to Bill Clinton whose administrations' histories have been published as part of the Miller Center's Presidential Oral History Program either faced a challenge or launched an initiative during their first year in office relating to the expansion of opportunity in the service of greater social and economic mobility.

These challenges and initiatives involved opportunity and mobility policies ranging from food stamps to AIDS to disability rights to health care reform. The range of cases below includes some issues that were foreseeable as early as the election campaign that brought the new president to office and others that arose unexpectedly after the inauguration. How the four presidents handled these situations illuminates the range of possibilities that any new chief executive may face.

JIMMY CARTER AND THE FOOD STAMP ACT

The food stamp program (today called the Supplemental Nutrition Assistance Program, or SNAP) was launched in 1964 on the premise that adequate nutrition is a prerequisite for seizing opportunities to advance in society. By Carter's first year, a problem in the program's design had become evident, which he and his administration decided to fix. For a newly elected Democratic president entering office after eight years of Republican administrations, addressing a core Democratic program such as food stamps—especially one that he believed in deeply—was a matter of some urgency.

SECRETARY OF AGRICULTURE ROBERT BERGLAND: I think our [department's] total budget was $25 billion or something, of which easily half went into feeding programs, school lunches, WIC [Women, Infants, and Children], food stamps, and these things. Every year in Carter's budget, that budget went up, on my recommendation and with his strong support. He believed in that. He figured it was the decent thing to do. On one occasion I provided him some documentation. So he saw the cost-benefit analysis. He was impressed by that, but that wasn't what drove him. His instincts on these social programs were purely humanitarian. I think it was really his test. . . .

We had a problem in that there was a lot of cash that was transacted and would change hands. This person would get certified as being eligible for food stamps, but they have to put up 25 percent. So if they are eligible for $100 in food stamps, they had to come up with $25. . . .

What we wanted to do was get rid of the purchase requirement so that instead of this person paying $25 for this book of coupons and having all the trouble we had with handling that money that got stolen, we just say, "We will reduce your food stamp benefits. Instead of paying us $25 and getting a $100 book, you don't pay us anything, and we'll give you $75. . . ."

So we eliminated the cash. I went up to [House Agriculture Committee] chairman [Tom] Foley and some of the people on the House side, and they've known about this purchase requirement problem for a long time. They said, "Yes, this makes sense. This is the smart thing to do." I went over to see Chairman [Herman] Talmadge and the more conservative senators, and they just had a fit. They said, "What? You are going to give these things away free? Free food stamps? It's a mistake. The president ought to have his head examined." I said, "The president doesn't know about this. . . ."

So I met with the president, and he looked over the evidence after he had read all the papers. He said, "Go ahead, we'll take the heat."

Part of Carter's achievement in reforming the food stamp program involved a willingness to act in defiance of a powerful congressional leader, something that a first-year president may only be willing to do when it involves an important commitment that engages his or her core values.

RONALD REAGAN AND AIDS

HIV/AIDS was first diagnosed in the United States in 1981 during Reagan's first year as president. Across the country, fears verging on panic were rampant about how the then-fatal disease was spread, with resulting discrimination against AIDS sufferers. The Reagan administration was criticized by many who felt that both the president and relevant agencies of the executive branch were slow to take the health crisis seriously because most of its victims were gay men. In time, federal research and prevention programs were launched, but a moment came when the president decided to use the symbolic authority of his office on behalf of the victims.

SECRETARY OF HEALTH AND HUMAN SERVICES OTIS BOWEN: [The organizations] that gave me the most trouble were the AIDS groups thinking they were getting shortchanged all the time—even though the budget would go up and up and up. They had good points. It was a very, very serious thing, and I think, earlier, the administration didn't think it was as important as it really was. . . . And in the AIDS area, you didn't dare, in that administration, talk about the use of condoms. The only program that the administration would permit was "Just don't."

WHITE HOUSE PHYSICIAN JOHN HUTTON: The president had always been curious about the science of medicine and wondered if our researchers were making any progress with identifying the infectious agent. I volunteered that Dr. [Robert] Gallo [of the National Institutes of Health] had isolated a hitherto unknown virus for which man seemed to have no defense.

The president replied, "You mean like the measles virus, but one that won't go away, that arouses no immune response?" He understood my explanation and its implication.

I'm not sure with whom he discussed this disease entity, but he soon learned of the patients being studied at NIH, and of implications for panic from ignorance of how the disease was being spread. He asked if it would help with the awareness of the disease if he went out to NIH and visited with patients—especially with the children who had contracted the disease from their mothers.

How well I remember the afternoon when our motorcade took us to NIH, and we were escorted to the ward that housed these patients. He fully understood the routes of communicability of this disease, and in an effort to lend a calmness and understanding to the nation, he moved from room to room, visited with the mothers in his most congenial way, picked up the children as would any father, all to the satisfaction of the medical staff and photographers, and hopefully the curious and concerned citizens of our country.

Within a week an advisory committee was created, initially chaired by a member of the Mayo Clinic faculty and then by a former chief of naval operations.

The president has attempted to enlighten the world about this threat, and at the same time to assuage their fears about the contagious nature of this most dangerous disease from which no one had yet survived.

Most presidential initiatives involve tangible action—legislation proposed, executive orders issued, or appointments made. Certainly the fight to address the AIDS crisis involved all of those things. But Reagan also showed that the power of the president to alleviate public fears through personal, highly visible conduct is important as well.

GEORGE H. W. BUSH AND THE AMERICANS WITH DISABILITIES ACT

Removing barriers to full participation in American life for people with disabilities was one of Bush's stated goals during his presidential campaign and his first year in office. Finding a way to achieve that goal without placing undue burdens on job-creating employers was the challenge. Working, sometimes contentiously, across party lines with Senator Edward M. Kennedy and others, Bush achieved passage of landmark legislation. The Americans with Disabilities Act (ADA) was enacted during Bush's second year in office, but only because his administration had laid the foundation during his first year.

WHITE HOUSE CHIEF OF STAFF JOHN H. SUNUNU: This is a president that believes in a set . . . of fundamental conservative principles of minimizing government involvement, of free market, . . . and of a kinder, gentler (remember that phrase?) set of policies that deal with individual needs and recognizing that different people have different needs. That was the president's broad philosophy. . . . It is embodied in ADA, recognizing that a segment of our society wasn't able to participate because of handicaps and trying to give them an avenue to participate without creating a club or a sword that is used to hamper the capacity of the private sector to function. . . .

During the election of '88 what are we going to campaign on as domestic issues? . . . Campaigned on a concern for all Americans and out of that concern for all Americans grew, I think, his commitment to the civil rights bill and the ADA. . . .

On the domestic side, there were two things that were a priority: Number one, let's start doing something about the budget and the deficit, had to get a hold of that. And number two, start to create the interactions on issues . . . like civil rights and ADA, that gets us to the point where we get them passed. We may not pass them this year, but you have to start this year. . . .

The first ADA bill looked like it had 110 senators supporting it out of a hundred. Nobody had read anything but the title and how could you vote "no" for a piece of legislation called the Americans with Disabilities Act? But the first bill was terrible, the first draft. It created about a hundred new entitlements, slight exaggeration but only slight.

SENATOR EDWARD M. KENNEDY, *chairman of the Senate Education and Labor Committee:* I asked to go down to see his chief of staff, John Sununu. It was in the late summer, and he was decent to see me, but he was very abrupt and to the point. He said, "Look, we're not going to support any social legislation. . . ."

But Bush walked by where we were, and I asked if I could go in and see him. He said fine. I went in. . . . And I said why I was down here, and he said, "Well, that's of some interest to me, and I'll talk to John further about it. . . ."

I went down to see Sununu some weeks later; this was when we sat in his office and he said, . . . "What is this going to mean in New Hampshire at the Sunapee Ski Resort? Somebody comes up in a wheelchair and wants to be able to go to the top of the mountain. What are we going to have to do? Are we going to have to retrofit every chair?" I said, "No, no we're not going to have to do that." He said, "What are we going to have to do?"

I said, "We're going to have to make reasonable accommodation." He said, "Well, what's reasonable—every tenth, every hundredth?" I said, "We make the decision based on how many people in wheelchairs want to go, what the cost is. It's going to have to be reasonable."

SUNUNU: It was a very hard kind of negotiations because . . . we're struggling to build into it provisions that the business community was desperately coming to us with concerns about. But over time it evolved, and it evolved primarily because of the chairman, Kennedy.

KENNEDY: One of the final meetings we had on disability—now that it was all worked out, and the Republicans wanted to get their stamp on it—was with [Senate Republican leader Bob] Dole up in his leadership office.

SENATE MINORITY LEADER ROBERT J. DOLE: [ADA is] a great piece of civil rights legislation. . . . I had a strong interest because of my disability. . . . [Attorney General Richard] Thornburgh has a son, of course, who had a very severe disability.

ATTORNEY GENERAL RICHARD THORNBURGH: The ADA act was signed on July 26, 1990 . . . and it was a triumphant day when that bill was signed. . . . And the president's speech was marvelous. He ended it with a call, "To let these shameful walls of exclusion finally come tumbling down," a reference to the Berlin Wall. It was neat, a good exercise. That's the way the system ought to work.

Bridging partisan divides is never easy in Washington. But the likelihood of success is greater when, as with the rights of the disabled, the issue is not one that traditionally separates the parties and when the work of coalition-building begins in the first year, with the midterm election still a year away and the next presidential election three years in the future.

BILL CLINTON AND HEALTH CARE REFORM

Not every first-year initiative is successful. Clinton's ambitious plan to extend health care to all as a necessary condition for economic advancement and social mobility was grounded in his oft-stated governing values of "opportunity, responsibility, and community." But it foundered on the shoals of complexity traceable in part to the flawed legislative design process he created.

DEPUTY DOMESTIC POLICY ADVISOR BRUCE REED: [In our first year] we wanted to flood the circuits. We figured that Congress would slow-walk enough things as it was, so that we didn't have to make it any easier for them. One of the areas where we ran into the most difficulty was that the congressional system is not well set up to handle a couple of high priorities at the same time. Bill Clinton actually wanted to pursue welfare reform and health care at the same time, because he felt that they were intrinsically related as policy and that they spoke to different anxieties of the electorate. Unfortunately, they went through the same committees. And even worse, the House wanted to do health care and not welfare reform, and the [Senate] Finance Committee wanted to do welfare reform and not health care.

HEALTH CARE ECONOMICS ADVISOR DAVID CUTLER: [There] was a fateful meeting on health care [during the transition] in Little Rock. . . . It's with the president. The first lady is there. She sat in the back of the room, quiet.

SECRETARY OF HEALTH AND HUMAN SERVICES DONNA SHALALA: It's a famous meeting because . . . the president talked about how he was going to run the health care reform process with his own staff [rather than my department]. . . .

There was no way I could turf fight over that. . . . It was screwy, but when the president and the first lady decide they want to do something first on, unless it's illegal you support it.

HEALTH CARE ADVISOR CHRIS JENNINGS: I think in fairness it was more of an illustration of the importance of the issue to the president, I think, on Capitol Hill and elsewhere. "Well gee, he's willing to put her out there and put their capital on the line. He must really care about this issue."

DEPUTY DOMESTIC POLICY ADVISOR WILLIAM GALSTON: To be direct—the way the leadership of that effort was constituted did not invite a lot of vocal dissent. If you really wanted to screw up things with the first lady (and arguably with the president as well), expressing doubts about the health care process or its product was a damn good way to go about it.

COUNCIL OF ECONOMIC ADVISORS MEMBER ALAN BLINDER: Anyway, the idea was to bundle the health care reform into [the congressional budgetary] reconciliation [process], on the grounds that you needed only fifty-one votes and that might be the only way they could get the health care bill through the Congress . . . one humongous bill that can't be filibustered.

As one, to a man and woman, the economic team went nuts over that idea, for a variety of reasons. But the simplest of which, and the most compelling to me, was there was no way in hell we were going to have a health care plan ready by the middle of February [1993, when Congress would be acting].

OFFICE OF MANAGEMENT AND BUDGET DIRECTOR LEON PANETTA: I can remember spending a lot of time in the [first lady's health care] taskforce saying, "You've got to have a simple way to explain things, and it's not just to the American people, but to a member of Congress. If you take more than two sentences to explain what's in a piece of legislation, chances are you're going to lose them. . . ." I kept saying, "This thing is like a Rubik's Cube in the sense that no matter how you talk it through, you become so immersed in the detail of it that you can't say, 'What does this mean for the average citizen on the street in terms of what the impact is going to be?'"

CUTLER: Even if you look at when the president gave his speech in September [1993], he said there were six principles—not three, not one, not two, but six. Nobody will remember six principles.

Clinton's campaign for health care reform helped prepare the way for passage of the Affordable Care Act sixteen years later. In that sense, it was successful but premature. But as a first-year initiative in 1993, it was hobbled in several ways by the president's haste to get things done, which led him to develop the proposal within the White House without adequate departmental consultation. It overwhelmed a crowded congressional agenda, and the White House failed to arrive at clear and comprehensible ways of explaining a very complex program to the American people.

CREATING A NEXT-GENERATION ECONOMY

MARGARET O'MARA

What can a president do to build a next-generation economy? How can economic growth widen opportunity for all Americans, not just a privileged few? Every modern American president has wrestled with some version of these two questions during his first year in office. History provides powerful lessons and debunks popular myths of where innovation comes from.

The nation's extraordinary record of invention and technical achievement—from the cotton gin to the transistor to the self-driving car—is not just a story of ingenious entrepreneurs and free markets. It is a story of moral leadership from the White House, both in setting grand challenges and pushing for policies to meet them. These actions fall into three large categories, each with its own lessons for a new president.

INVESTMENT

Innovation and opportunity have bloomed when political leaders make foundational, long-range investments in people, ideas, and audacious technologies for which there is not yet a market.

Consider President Dwight D. Eisenhower. The former military man came into office at a moment of high public anxiety and geopolitical instability. "We live," said Eisenhower in a May 1953 radio address, "not in an instant of danger but in an age of danger."[1] At the same time, the mounting costs of the conflict in Korea demonstrated how unsustainable it would be for the United States to engage in serial conflicts in every global hotspot. Instead, Eisenhower proposed a "New Look" military that, among other things, used technological strength—in nuclear weapons, aerospace, and electronics—to deter potential conflicts. One result was a massive mobilization of scientific people and institutions rather than a massive mobilization of soldiers.

Eisenhower set in motion an era of dazzlingly rapid American technological achievement. In the San Francisco Bay area, for example, large defense contracts became the bedrock for a small-electronics industry. Defense contractor Lockheed was the largest employer in the region that later became known as Silicon Valley. Hewlett-Packard, a company that also counted the federal government as a big customer, became the second largest. In the first years after its 1957 founding, Fairchild Semiconductor—the plucky venture-backed startup that was the training ground for future leaders of many iconic valley companies—got 80 percent of its business from government contracts. And federal money turned Stanford University into a research juggernaut and astoundingly fertile intellectual hub for innovators in both high-tech and biotech.

These developments went into overdrive after another first-year president, John F. Kennedy, declared that America would reach the moon within the decade, creating a fresh harvest of federal contracting opportunities for companies making transistors, circuits, and components. Government investment gave entrepreneurs an incentive to develop blue-sky technologies and offered the security of doing business with a patient and deep-pocketed customer.

Are Eisenhower's military spending and Kennedy's moon shots good models for the current age of austerity and its accompanying political pressure to cut public spending and lower tax burdens? Yes. Eisenhower and Kennedy faced similar pressures (including considerable opposition in Congress), but they still made a case for bold action and sustained investment.

What is more, a first-year president does not need to start from scratch. We still have the extraordinary research complex that the Cold War and space race built. However, it is in a fragile position, partly because too few recognize the foundational role that public policy continues to play in the high-tech economy.

To keep the pipeline flowing with new ideas, presidents need to prioritize sustained and increased investment in the national research agencies. To ensure that the United States has the world's most highly skilled, innovative workforce, they must lead a national reinvestment in higher education that sustains excellence in all disciplines while lowering college costs for students. The golden age of the American high-tech industry did not come from applying market models to research and education. It came from the willingness to make very long-term investments in basic research and talented people.

INTERNATIONALISM

It is no coincidence that the United States became the global command-and-control center of the high-tech industry at the same historical moment that the nation opened its borders to a broad range of nationalities and ethnicities. Throughout human history, innovation has grown in open societies with open borders, where economic and educational opportunities draw in new migrants from across the globe.

During President Harry S. Truman's first year, as the United States emerged from World War II and into the Cold War, Senator William Fulbright, a Democrat from Arkansas, led the charge to establish international educational exchange programs that brought thousands of foreign students and scholars to our shores. The expansion of the Fulbright and other such programs over the years by leaders of both political parties turned American colleges and universities into destinations for the world's best and brightest—and helped make our higher-education system the strongest in the world.

At the same time, the Truman administration kept the nation's doors open to refugees from war-torn Europe, a humanitarian act that paid huge economic dividends for the United States. Those who came included some of the world's leading scientists and thinkers as well as people whose potential was not clear at the time. One was Andy Grove, a penniless nineteen-year-old Hungarian who stepped off a boat in New York in 1946 and went on to cofound the legendary microchip maker Intel two decades later.

Borders opened wider—and welcomed an even more diverse range of people—when President Lyndon B. Johnson signed the Hart-Cellar Immigration Act of 1965. Johnson acted in the name of civil rights, as the bill lifted racist quotas that had restricted immigration from most of the world (especially Asia and Latin America) for generations. At the time, he and the bill's supporters believed it was mostly a symbolic gesture rather than something that would radically alter immigration patterns. But Hart-Cellar did not just alter them—it transformed them entirely, and transformed the nation in the process.

The post-1965 immigrant wave altered the economy as well, and there is no better place to see this than in Silicon Valley. Indian- and Chinese-born entrepreneurs were at the helm of 24 percent of the technology enterprises started between 1980 and 1998, a formative and hugely lucrative time for high-tech. The economic upside of open doors has been clear to the most successful occupants of the Oval Office. "Our strength," declared Ronald Reagan during his first year, "comes from our own immigrant heritage and our capacity to welcome those from other lands."[2]

New presidents must remember that an innovative economy relies on open borders and a willingness to make bets on all sorts of newcomers, whether they have a Ph.D. or less than a high school education. An increase in the number of visas for highly educated workers—something Silicon Valley tech companies strongly support—is a critical piece of an innovation-focused immigration policy. But so is keeping our doors open to political refugees and providing amnesty to the undocumented immigrants already here. It is not only the right thing to do; it makes economic sense. Immigrants are more likely than American-born workers to become business owners. Indeed, immigrants' rate of business formation is more than twice that of those born here.

INCOME SECURITY

Ideas and growth industries blossom when a society is stable and secure enough to become a place of hopeful possibility, imagination, and willingness to take risks. In the case of the United States, the emergence of a world-dominant tech industry came out of the remarkable twenty-five years of rising incomes and education levels that began after World War II. The expansion of economic security and opportunity during that period formed the bedrock for subsequent decades of technological breakthroughs and entrepreneurial success.

How did this happen? Presidential commitments to broad-based economic security—from Social Security to the G.I. Bill to Medicare and Medicaid—worked in tandem with public investments in research and development and in infrastructure to raise incomes and expand educational and professional opportunities. These efforts gave people the opportunity to apply their raw intelligence and entrepreneurial energy to create new companies, markets, and industries.

Most of the people who founded iconic tech companies were not born rich. They were middle-class kids whose families rode that wave of twentieth-century upward mobility. Steve Jobs's father was a machinist who did not finish high school. Intel co-founder Robert Noyce was the son of a small-town Iowa clergyman. Another legendary microchip-industry CEO, Jerry Sanders, was a street-fighting kid raised by his grandparents on Chicago's South Side. Growing up during a moment of political commitment to expanded opportunity and prosperity, these men benefited from policies that widened opportunities for college education, invested in science and math programs and built computer labs in schools, and broke down some old prejudices about religion, ethnicity, and pedigree.

Policies that create opportunity, like publicly backed venture funds or targeted grants to underrepresented individuals, are one way to enlarge the pool of tech entrepreneurs. But presidents also can and should lead the way in broadening the definition of entrepreneurship itself—beyond tech and toward all sorts of small businesses. Through both moral leadership and policy action, the president must make the case to the American people that public investments to ensure overall prosperity—for the many, not just the few—are foundational to the next-generation economy.

LONG-TERM INVESTMENTS WITH FEW STRINGS ATTACHED

Unlike other countries, American public-sector spending on innovation is often indirect—flowing through contracts to private industry or universities, regulatory institutions, or the tax code. Where investments are more obvious, as in appropriations to the National Science Foundation or the National Institutes of Health, they are part of a long game. Because research investments take a long time to pay off, their returns are not immediately obvious to either political leaders or the public.

But the indirect, almost stealthy nature of public spending has been absolutely critical to the ascendance of the American high-tech economy. The government invested, and then it got out of the way. The result was many centers of innovation across public, private, and nonprofit sectors. Size mattered, too. Sure, there were big federal research labs. But there also were plenty of contracts to small private companies that created an incentive to be entrepreneurial, to push technological boundaries, to innovate and grow. Contracts have likewise been a way for Washington to encourage the private sector to adopt certain behaviors, whether relocating from areas deemed prime targets for nuclear bombs in the 1950s or encouraging firms to hire more women and minorities in the 1970s.

To keep the bedrock of opportunity firm, first-year presidents should not be afraid to push for long-term direct investments in research and education. To keep this world-class entrepreneurial economy churning and enlarging its reach, presidents should deploy the contracting system to create private-sector incentives that tackle particular social problems and bring a more diverse workforce into tech.

UNINTENDED CONSEQUENCES?

The most powerful American "innovation policies" have not been top-down, command-and-control initiatives to boost particular kinds of industry. In fact, their greatest benefits often have come through the unanticipated consequences of policies designed with broader and different goals in mind.

Dwight Eisenhower never once declared that he would build a science city, tech park, or innovation district. In fact, the massive growth of government-sponsored science under his watch made him fearful about the future of American ingenuity. In the same farewell address of 1961 in which he gloomily assessed the reach of a new "military-industrial complex," the president lamented that the innovative landscape had changed. "The solitary inventor, tinkering in his shop, has been overshadowed by task forces of scientists in laboratories and testing fields," he declared. "A government contract becomes virtually a substitute for intellectual curiosity."[3]

Eisenhower was dead wrong. But he was right in setting bold priorities in his first year in office that turned the American military into a more high-tech fighting force. The extraordinary outlay of federal spending on scientific research and development during his administration helped build the ultimate "science city," Silicon Valley. Although regional economic development was not something he or other political leaders of that era had in mind when they authorized new defense and space programs, the extreme geographic concentration of these investments created dynamic regions that today are the undisputed global capitals of tech.

Eisenhower's example, and that of his successors, is a helpful one for all new presidents. Policies that support great public education can have the unintended consequence of identifying and nurturing the next Steve Jobs. Policies to keep borders open and welcoming to immigrants and refugees can draw in the next generation of inventors, creators, and company founders. Along the way, these presidential moves can rebuild the economic security that propelled the American innovation economy forward in the first place.

NOTES

1. Dwight D. Eisenhower, "Radio Address to the American People on the National Security and Its Costs," Washington, D.C., May 19, 1953.

2. Ronald Reagan, "Statement on United States Immigration and Refugee Policy," Washington, D.C., July 30, 1981.

3. Dwight D. Eisenhower, "Farewell Address," Washington, D.C., January 17, 1961.

CENTURY OF CITIES
Urban Infrastructure and Economic Growth

MASON B. WILLIAMS

The twenty-first century will be a century of cities. Long the engines of American innovation, cities are supplying fresh ideas and vital economic growth, and in an interconnected world, they are working collaboratively across national boundaries to deal with big issues such as economic development, environmental sustainability, and terrorism.[1] But to lead America into the twenty-first century, cities will need an infrastructure capable of serving as a platform for sustainable development and one that functions for everyone.

To appreciate how American cities are built on infrastructure, consider public water systems. Until the mid-nineteenth century, clean drinking water was scarce and sewer systems were nonexistent. Widespread contamination contributed to frequent outbreaks of disease, and the scarcity of water made it difficult to douse fires—a major scourge of early American cities. In 1837, following outbreaks of yellow fever and cholera and the Great Fire of 1835, New York City reached into rural Westchester County to collect fresh water via the Croton Aqueduct. Other big cities followed suit. Complex systems of reservoirs, aqueducts, filtration facilities, tunnels, and pipes helped big cities overcome imposing barriers to urban development, especially contamination, epidemic disease, and fire. Water infrastructure has become such a fundamental part of American life that we seldom think about it—until it fails us. The recent water crisis in Flint, Michigan, highlights just how essential infrastructure is to urban life.

But if infrastructure has made the modern city possible, it has also contributed to some of the most severe problems facing American cities today. After World War II, massive federal investment in highways helped many white, middle-class Americans—and many businesses—move out of cities into surrounding metropolitan regions, leaving behind a legacy of racial segmentation, inner-city disinvestment, and fragmentation. The same interstate highways that helped drive national economic growth starting in the late 1950s tore through working-class urban neighborhoods, displacing hundreds of thousands of residents and countless small businesses, and subjecting those who stayed to environmental degradation. The challenges facing many American cities today are in no small measure the consequences of patterns of metropolitan development underpinned by automobile-centric infrastructure.

Prior to the 1930s, most infrastructure projects within cities were carried out by local governments. Only during the Great Depression did the federal government and cities begin to collaborate in the development of urban infrastructure. In 1933, Congress and President Franklin D. Roosevelt created the Public Works Administration (PWA), which offered local governments grants-in-aid for large, capital-intensive construction projects; two years later, Roosevelt established the Works Progress Administration (WPA), which paid unemployed Americans to work on projects designed by local governments.

Working together, cities and the federal government were able to do things that neither was capable of on its own. "We would have been awful damned fools," WPA director Harry Hopkins remarked, "if we thought for a minute that we have either the power or the ability to go out and set up 100,000 work projects . . . without the complete cooperation of local and state officials. We couldn't do it if we wanted to."[2] For enterprising local leaders such as New York City mayor Fiorello La Guardia, the New Deal represented, as one official put it, "a challenge and an opportunity . . . to have done those things which make our cit[ies] more beautiful and useful, and which [we] on [our] own behalf would hardly ever be financially able to do."[3] In the span of a few years, the PWA and WPA helped build a staggering amount of infrastructure: airports, bridges, tunnels, subway extensions, parkways, schools, public beaches, college campuses, health centers, and public radio broadcast facilities.

The initiatives of the 1930s established a new model of collaboration between the federal government and local authorities. In the postwar years, Congress replaced the New Deal agencies with a variety of targeted grant-in-aid programs (notably, to support the construction of hospitals and airports). The federal government also took on the role of supporting the nation's water systems through regulation, quality assurance, and assistance. In the 1960s, it began to support the development of mass transit.

At its best, midcentury liberalism strengthened urban neighborhoods by building a social infrastructure that made city life more decent and enjoyable. But some elements of the New Deal's vision were at odds with the very form of the dense, crowded industrial city. Starting in the 1930s, the federal government actively supported suburban single-family homeownership. Two decades later, Cold War spending on research and development funneled resources to new research complexes located on the outskirts of cities, such as Boston's Route 128 corridor and the San Francisco Bay Area's Silicon Valley. As suburbanization and corporate relocation drained older cities of residents and revenue, the federal government used infrastructure spending to try to help cities beat suburbia at its own game. New urban superhighways connected downtowns to outlying residential areas, and federally supported "urban renewal" projects flattened neighborhoods to create space for middle-class housing, commercial establishments, and hospitals,

university campuses, and cultural facilities. These projects offered little to established neighborhoods and their residents; indeed, inner-city communities paid
the price for urban renewal, in the form of dislocation and environmental degradation.[4] Planners also frequently routed new highways through communities of
color and not infrequently used infrastructure to reinforce boundaries between
white and nonwhite communities.

Since the 1960s, public investment has largely been on the decline. Citizens
responded to the excesses and inequities of urban renewal with intense protests,
leading to more rigorous permitting and approval processes. At the same time,
suburbanization and corporate relocation made it harder for city governments to
fund essential projects while also prompting them to chase private investment for
sports stadiums, convention centers, and other commercial facilities. Total public
spending on transportation and water infrastructure topped out in the first half
of the 1960s as a share of gross domestic product; it has been falling ever since,
although it revived temporarily following passage of the 2009 American Recovery
and Reinvestment Act. Both federal spending on infrastructure and federal contributions to cities have declined sharply since the end of the 1970s.

Increasingly, cities have found it difficult to maintain existing infrastructure, let
alone build new projects. When New York's La Guardia Airport opened in 1939,
its namesake thanked President Roosevelt for helping to build "the greatest, the
best, the most up to date, and the most perfect airport in the United States . . . 'the'
airport of the New World." In 2014, Vice President Joe Biden likened La Guardia
Airport to "some third-world country."[5]

Fortunately, however, infrastructure is the rare issue that today commands
bipartisan support. "We've spent $4 trillion trying to topple various people,"
Republican presidential candidate Donald Trump said in a primary debate. "If we
could've spent that $4 trillion in the United States to fix our roads, our bridges and
all of the other problems . . . we would've been a lot better off." In 2016, Democratic
presidential nominee Hillary Clinton promised to fill America's "infrastructure
gap" through a five-year, $275 billion federal commitment.

What does the history of city building tell us about how to approach the challenge of urban infrastructure?

▶ *Infrastructure should not be exclusively a profit-making enterprise.* Private investors can play a constructive role in infrastructure by bringing needed discipline
   to the selection of projects; there are plenty of examples of bridges to nowhere
   that are a product of politically driven funding decisions rather than economically rational ones. But having private investors drive public spending choices
   limits the kinds of infrastructure we can have to projects that produce returns
   in the form of profit rather than human well-being. The Progressives and New
   Dealers supported both kinds of projects. We need to set up funding systems
   today that take care of both.

▶ *Infrastructure should connect people, not keep them apart.* At its best, infrastructure has expanded access and opportunity for all Americans. At its worst, it has simply reinforced the advantages enjoyed by the well-to-do at the expense of the marginalized, as the history of highway building suggests. In setting priorities, presidents should emphasize infrastructure projects that expand access to opportunity, information, and resources. This may take the form, for instance, of a large-scale push to expand access to high-quality internet service or new transit initiatives to mitigate the "spatial mismatch" between urban residents and suburban jobs.

▶ *Local governments must be active partners in rebuilding America's infrastructure.* Historically, local authority has been associated with racism and other forms of social marginalization, and has often been captured by business interests. Yet local democracy is still the best way to make sure that the federal government supports projects that communities actually want. The lesson of urban renewal is that we need institutions that allow local citizens to be heard so we can build projects that our people want, rather than ones that governments and investors say they need.

NOTES

1. Richard Florida, "What If Mayors Ruled the World?" *Atlantic,* June 13, 2012, http://www.citylab.com/politics/2012/06/what-if-mayors-ruled-world/1505/.

2. Jason Scott Smith, "New Deal Public Works: People or Projects?" in *Building New Deal Liberalism: The Political Economy of Public Works, 1933–1956,* ed. Jason Scott Smith (New York: Cambridge University Press, 2006), 105.

3. Mason B. Williams, *City of Ambition: FDR, La Guardia, and the Making of Modern New York* (New York: Norton, 2013), 153.

4. Mindy Fullilove, *Root Shock: How Tearing up City Neighborhoods Hurts America, and What We Can Do about It* (New York: One World/Ballantine, 2009).

5. Williams, *City of Ambition,* 198.

LEADING IN THE ANTHROPOCENE

WILLIS JENKINS

The politics of nature are rapidly shifting. Natural systems are increasingly integrated within social systems. The phenomenon is so dramatic that many scientists and observers see a new epoch of geological history dominated by human influence emerging—the "Anthropocene Epoch."

In the Anthropocene, the political question is no longer how humans should use nature, but what nature itself will become. What should the president say to the public about the medical capability not only to read the human genome but to edit out particular traits? How would the president present an initiative to combat the Zika virus by releasing genetically modified mosquitos?

Beyond policy decisions and funding recommendations, leading in the Anthropocene entails developing capabilities of governance for actively directing evolutionary systems. Whether basic systems of life should be changed by humans is moot. The question now is, Whose ideas and initiatives will shape nature? The first year of a new administration offers an opportunity to set out a framework that can get in front of the dizzying changes in the human relationship to the natural world and engage the new politics of nature in multiple practical domains.

BACKGROUND

In the broad span of evolutionary history, the decisions made by any one administration matter relatively little. The time periods relevant to government do not even register in the geological epochs that mark the unfolding of planetary life. And yet, in a way probably without precedent, basic processes of life have become entangled with political time. On both genetic and planetary scales, the paths taken during a single presidential administration will inscribe themselves in evolutionary systems.

When scientific and cultural observers refer to this coupling of political and evolutionary time as the Anthropocene Epoch, the name suggests not only that Earth's geological history is passing out of the Holocene but also that it is in fact passing out of "natural history" altogether. Within multiple systems basic to supporting life, humanity has rapidly become the most significant dynamic of change.

Not only is most of Earth's land surface terraformed by civilizations, but the nitrogen content of waterways, the chemical composition of the atmosphere, the surface temperature of the planet, and the pH of the oceans are all now shaped by the integration of ecological systems with social systems. Integration of social and biological systems is also intensifying at the genetic scale, as breakthroughs in gene editing have accelerated the possibilities for precision medicine, genetic modification, and synthetic biology. Nature, including human nature, is being remade—and it is happening at the speed of political time.

Atmospheric chemist Paul J. Crutzen's proposal to imagine anthropogenic climate change from the perspective of a new epoch has catalyzed public discourse.[1] Whether or not Earth has officially left the Holocene and entered the Anthropocene is up to the Royal Geological Society, which is currently studying whether there is sufficient stratigraphic evidence to designate a new geological epoch. Yet whatever the Royal Society decides, the frame has already been adopted by many observers to depict a new cultural condition: pervasive anthropogenic influence through many natural systems and human responsibility for the future of nature.

The basic shift represented by the idea of the Anthropocene is that, instead of imagining societies as embedded in nature with obligations not to disrupt its balance, it now makes more sense to imagine nature as embedded in societies, which have increasing responsibility for what nature becomes. The shift in frame has already transformed the politics of nature across multiple domains, most critically in geoengineering and genetic engineering.

GEOENGINEERING

The Anthropocene idea reframes the political imagination of climate change. If humans are pervasively, even if unthinkingly, influencing planetary systems on a geological scale, it may not be feasible to withdraw the influence; perhaps it is time instead to engineer systems to function for political goals. Crutzen proposes that humanity should prepare to avoid the adverse consequences of global warming by dispersing sulfur particles in the upper atmosphere to deflect incoming solar energy.[2] Other proposals for climate engineering generally would either manage solar radiation or enhance carbon capture. The basic argument for these proposals is that, because humans already influence the climate clumsily and dangerously, we should prepare technology to influence the climate system precisely and responsibly.

Climate engineering is controversial because the prospect of technological solutions seems to divert attention from strengthening international emissions agreements. Moreover, such approaches raise the prospect of nations deploying engineering strategies in ways that further their own interests or threaten the interests of others. Criteria for responsible deployment of any scheme remain unclear. Yet the Anthropocene concept has already influenced climate politics. In Anthropocene conditions, any policy response to climate change (including the policy of doing nothing) must be seen as a form of managing the atmosphere, which is an unprecedented political undertaking.

Divisive political conflicts concerning climate change arise in part from the cultural uneasiness involved in coming to terms with such tectonic changes in the human relation to the earth. What ideas and narratives make sense of that change? The president's administration should recognize that, above and beyond climate debates, the grand tension of this moment in history is how cultures will reckon with the changed human relationship with nature.

GENETIC ENGINEERING

Genetic modification of nonhuman organisms has been possible since the 1970s and commercially widespread since the 1990s. Until recently, however, modifying the genetic makeup of organisms has been costly and laborious, which has limited the extent of the technology. A breakthrough technique, using an element of a prokaryotic immune system known as CRISPR, has recently made modification so cheap, efficient, and accurate that almost any laboratory can edit DNA. Meanwhile, other initiatives are developing ways to construct genomes synthetically, in effect writing codes of life on a blank page.

There are three major areas of application. The most controversial is genomic medicine, sometimes called precision medicine. Made possible by the sequencing of the human genome, precision medicine identifies genetic sources of certain diseases and makes modifications to correct or prevent them. Some modifications—those affecting germ-line cells—would be passed on to the offspring of the patient, changing the DNA inherited by future generations.

To call attention to ethical responsibilities involved in editing human nature, and perhaps galvanized by headlines that Chinese researchers had already attempted germ-line editing in human embryos, in late 2015, American, British, and Chinese academies of science and medicine convened the International Summit on Human Gene Editing. Observing potential and risks, the summit noted that genetic editing raises the prospect of directing evolution by design. It promises to improve, correct, and perhaps even escape inherited natures.

Although many technical distinctions must be carefully made, the basic vocabulary used to describe what is going on is critical. What counts as a "mistake" in nature? Which genetic differences may be "corrected" or "improved"? And how do those interventions differ from optional "enhancement"? Are the lexical metaphors of "reading," "editing," and "writing" human genomes the most appropriate way to imagine genetic engineering? Is "engineering" even the right vocabulary?

Considerations of language and imagination also apply to the other two major applications of genetic editing. Genetic modification of nonhuman organisms, already common in agricultural staples, has become much easier with CRISPR-derived techniques. Before long we can expect hundreds of new kinds of organisms, constructed by humans for human goals. Some of those modifications offer techniques for intentionally altering ecosystems by genetically modifying certain organisms to function differently. For example, imagine modifying ticks so they cannot carry disease, or plants so they sequester more carbon.

Longstanding global distrust of genetically modified organisms demonstrates the mistake in deferring discussion of basic ideas to international summits and presidential commissions. The range of concerns expressed in public about these matters is much more expansive than the near-term balance of benefits and risks typically discussed in official summits. Public debate should include concerns about inequality, relations between science and business, appropriate forms of agriculture, and—most basically—how humans should relate to nature.

STEWARDSHIP

In previous presidential administrations, stewardship has been the moral concept most often used to frame responsibilities for nature. Popular for its acceptability to many political philosophies and its resonance with several religious traditions, the idea of stewardship connotes accountability for an inherited trust. Stewardship has been helpful to presidents navigating environmental debates because it implicitly authorizes the use of nature while also suggesting that those uses should be consistent with a responsibility to protect nature for the future.

Critics of stewardship object that the idea cloaks environmental exploitation with moral dignity. They worry that stewardship moralizes violence to land and people by making it seem that nature is perfected by wealth-producing mastery.

Anthropocene conditions shift the basic frame of stewardship. As nature must be imagined less as an inherited trust and more as a designed product or an engineered system, stewardship can no longer be about protecting nature from human interference, or even about perfecting nature through the pursuit of wealth. Stewardship now entails managing coupled human-natural systems. When scientists call for active planetary stewardship, they are calling for forward-looking design for basic systems of life. How are we to think about political goals in the midst of turbulent change to those systems? Here are three broad strategies:

1. Learn what makes systems resilient.

If humans have made themselves responsible for evolutionary systems, one way to find criteria for managing them well is to learn lessons from what makes certain systems succeed or collapse. In particular, what permits systems to persist and succeed amid dramatic change?

The lexicon of resilience offers ways of thinking about political involvement in complex systems. Resilience thinking happens in many disciplines and is not strongly associated with a particular cultural worldview. The basic political goal is security. Resilience could offer a conceptual platform for funding initiatives to break academic research out of silos and organize collaborations that include defense, infrastructure, and technology sectors.

2. Engage new threats to political freedom.

The legacy of eugenics, endorsed heartily by the federal government a century ago, shadows confidence in genetic projects today. One fear of genomic medicine is that it seems an easy, profit-incentivized slide from insured parents having access to repairs of genetic "mistakes" to the affluent having access to private enhancements for their offspring. Biology could intensify social conflict. What will prevent inscription of wealth inequality and social prejudice into the human genetic line?

That sort of fear bears on responses to planetary change as well. A major theme of Pope Francis's encyclical on the environment, *Laudato Si,* was concern that the powerful will respond to global environmental problems in ways that increase their advantages over the poor and vulnerable. Technological management of the planet, he argued, would likely intensify inequality and inscribe injustice into natural systems.

In both cases, the concern is with the power of governmental policy to change conditions of life in ways that threaten human dignity and political freedom. And again, in both cases, withdrawing government from the politics of nature is no longer an option. The question is, Whose power will govern the changing conditions of life?

A stewardship frame can engage fears of naturalized inequality by taking up that question. If citizens fear that social systems are rewriting nature in ways that threaten freedom, an administration with populist roots should directly engage those fears with ideas and initiatives that focus on roles for sustaining democratic values within redesigned evolutionary systems.

3. Foster democratic deliberation.

In the midst of rapid, unsettling changes in systems of life, an uncertain, pluralist society needs wide democratic deliberation about the values, goals, and priorities at stake in human management of natural systems. Leaving the debate to experts is likely to alienate the public whose good is at stake in these changes, and possibly create distrust of the branches of science most crucial to understanding Anthropocene challenges.

An indispensable role for cultural arguments about various integrations of human and natural systems lies in testing metaphors and experimenting with language to develop cultural wisdom. "Engineering" is not the only or best way to imagine a human role with genomes and atmospheres; "cultivating" or "designing" or "repairing" or "protecting" will seem better to some citizens, and each would give rise to different initiatives for shaping nature.

In meeting Anthropocene challenges, the politics of nature is also cultural policy. How people experience nature, including their own bodies and their relation to future generations, is uniquely at stake in this political time.

NOTES

1. Paul J. Crutzen, "Albedo Enhancement by Stratospheric Sulfur Injections: A Contribution to Resolve a Policy Dilemma?" *Climatic Change* 77, nos. 3–4 (2006): 211–20. doi:10.1007/s10584-006-9101-y.

2. Ibid., 212.

A DEMOCRATIC
OPPORTUNITY AGENDA

WILLIAM A. GALSTON

Equal opportunity is America's promise. From the beginning of the nation's existence, we have told ourselves and the world that in the United States, unlike so many other countries, where one begins does not determine where one ends up. One's religion does not matter. Nor does race, ethnicity, or parentage. Talent and character shape one's destiny.

Americans have never measured up entirely to our own standards, of course. But over time we have gotten closer, both by tearing down barriers to the promise and by doing what was necessary to help everyone participate in it. We need to keep moving down this road. Not to do so would be to stop short of fulfilling the promise we have made, not to some but to all.

This is the moral argument for the opportunity agenda. But there is a political argument as well. The American Dream is in peril. Too many Americans have come to doubt that their talent and character can yield a rising standard of living, no matter how hard they work. They have lost confidence in a better future for their children. Majorities believe that their children's lives will be worse, not better, than their own. This is a dagger aimed at the heart of the American Dream.

There is also an economic argument. When opportunity is unequal, many Americans are prevented from putting their talents to their best use, reducing productivity and economic output below the levels they would otherwise reach. When the labor force was growing rapidly, high economic growth could be achieved despite the drag of unequal opportunity. But in coming decades, the labor force will expand at only one-third the rate experienced in the closing decades of the twentieth century.[1] The price of preventing individuals from making their best contribution—or even excluding them from the labor force altogether—is rising steadily. Each individual will matter more than ever before.

And finally, there is an empirical argument. For some decades we have known that economic resources are distributed less equally in the United States than in most other advanced democracies. Counterbalancing this, it was believed, was a higher degree of social mobility in the United States. Europe was regarded as static and class-bound, while the United States was open and fluid. To become an American was to choose this package of inequality and mobility.

Our belief is mistaken. If someone is born in the United States to parents of low or modest means, his or her odds of becoming well-off are lower than in many other advanced democracies.[2] The proportion of children born on the bottom rung of the ladder who rise to the top as adults in the United States is 7.5 percent—lower than in the United Kingdom (9 percent), Denmark (11.7), and Canada (13.5).[3]

Behind these aggregate statistics are even more disturbing facts about differences among groups of Americans.[4] African Americans born to families in the lowest fifth of the national income distribution have a 51 percent chance of ending up there, compared to a meager 3 percent chance of rising to the top. Of white Americans born at the bottom, by contrast, only 23 percent remain there as adults, while fully 16 percent rise to the top. Put differently: only 22 percent of African Americans born in the bottom fifth rise to the middle class or better as adults, compared to 58 percent of whites. When it comes to equal opportunity, the United States still has a ways to go.

Equal opportunity is not the product of an invisible hand. Laws that establish and safeguard formal equality of opportunity are not sufficient; policies that promote substantive equality of opportunity are needed as well. Low-income families are less able to provide high-quality childcare and education for their sons and daughters, for example, and are less likely to belong to networks that link young adults to jobs. If equal opportunity is to be more than a hollow promise, then government must act to level the playing field—not to produce equal outcomes but to give every child a fair chance to succeed.

WHY OPPORTUNITY IS UNEQUAL: PIECES OF THE PUZZLE

Understanding the multiple dimensions of unequal opportunity helps specify the building blocks of an opportunity agenda. The list includes the following:

- Low-income families typically find it harder to provide the kind of nurturance that infants and toddlers need to thrive. On average, the schools available to lower-income children are less likely to offer the quality of education and training these students need to succeed. This helps explain why the level of adult skills in the United States is well below the Organization for Economic Co-operation and Development (OECD) average.
- During the past three recoveries from economic downturns, economic growth has been concentrated in fewer and fewer locations, mainly metropolitan areas with high levels of technology and professional services. Smaller towns and rural areas have been left behind. Although we are less aware of rural than of urban disadvantage, it too is becoming more prominent in the overall phenomenon of unequal opportunity.
- Research has documented a decades-long decline in geographical mobility. Low-income adults in areas with poor job prospects are more likely to remain there than they were as recently as the 1980s. Some are stuck in houses they

cannot sell. Many lack the means to leave for other jurisdictions. Most have lived their lives within the confines of a single neighborhood and lack the connections and confidence to move. Within cities, decades of underinvestment in metropolitan public transportation have made it difficult for low-income people to get from their homes to work and back again.

▸ The U.S. prison population per capita is five times the OECD average. A record of incarceration bars many young adults, mostly male and minority, from access to employment in other than the most menial and episodic jobs.

▸ Because the United States does less than many other advanced democracies to help women balance work and family responsibilities, the female labor force participation rate peaked in the late 1990s (60 percent in 1999) and has been declining ever since. In 2016, it stood at 57 percent.

▸ Employment discrimination persists, albeit at lower levels than a generation ago. Studies have shown, for example, that employers are less likely to interview job candidates from racial and ethnic minorities than white candidates with identical qualifications.[5]

▸ Licensing requirements imposed by states make it more difficult to work in occupations such as beauty salons that traditionally offer paths to upward mobility for individuals without high levels of formal job skills. Relatedly, increasing regulatory burdens in tandem with decreased access to capital have made it harder for entrepreneurs to start small businesses, another traditional route of social mobility. In recent years, the number of new small businesses has fallen below the number going out of business, a period of entrepreneurial decline that may be without precedent in our history.

THE LEGISLATIVE RESPONSE: AN OPPORTUNITY AGENDA

These obstacles to full opportunity for all Americans require a legislative response, in four broad categories:

1. We should do more to ensure adequate education and training for all.

For children ages zero to three from disadvantaged families, this means access to programs, such as regular home visits from trained personnel, that improve parents' ability to provide the nurturance that infants and toddlers need. Starting at age three, children should have the opportunity—backed by means-tested funding—to attend prekindergarten programs until they enter public schools.

Three decades of K–12 education reform have overwhelmed teachers and school administrators, with modest results. Another wave of top-down reform would not be productive. On the other hand, failing to complete high school has become an economic death sentence. Efforts to increase high school graduation rates have made progress, and we need to double-down with a crash program to raise them farther and faster. We should bolster twenty-first-century skills training in high schools and community colleges in partnership with private sector employers.

2. We should reduce barriers to employment.

Where discrimination in hiring still exists, we should use the federal government's powers of investigation and enforcement to fight it. We should work in partnership with the states to reduce occupational licensing and other regulatory obstacles to entering the workforce. Paid parental leave would ease the conflict between employment and care of newborns that induces many parents—especially women—to drop out of the paid workforce. We should help unemployed workers trapped in communities with few job prospects move to places where opportunities exist. And working with the states, the federal government should reduce employers' disincentives to hire ex-felons.

3. We should make work work for more Americans.

Expanding the Earned Income Tax Credit (EITC) to cover more low-income employees would encourage individuals at the margins of the workforce to enter it and would reduce their dependence on other means-tested programs. The outdated system of unemployment insurance should be redesigned to help workers make the transition from declining to expanding sectors of the economy. A contributory program of wage insurance should be instituted to cushion the financial fall of displaced workers whose new jobs pay substantially less than the jobs they lost. Employers should be encouraged to respond to declining demand by sharing work among their employees rather than dismissing a large percentage of them outright.

4. We should expand opportunity by boosting job creation.

One way to do this is to attack the problems—such as access to capital, burdensome regulations, and the cost of tax compliance—that recently have reduced small business formation, a prime source of new jobs. At the same time, we should overcome the fiscal, regulatory, and political forces that have impeded adequate investment in infrastructure for more than three decades. In the here and now, increased investment means more jobs that pay well and cannot be exported. Over time, it will boost economic efficiency and productivity, necessary preconditions for sustainable wage growth.

WHERE TO BEGIN? A FIRST-YEAR LEGISLATIVE PACKAGE

Any first-year president should lead with the parts of the opportunity agenda that are most likely to be enacted quickly. This means choosing items that enjoy substantial bipartisan support; will not get bogged down in multiple, overlapping congressional committees; and do not plunge the administration into the complexities of intergovernmental relations in the federal system.

These criteria dictate postponing portions of the opportunity agenda to a second phase of legislative activity. For example, states are principally responsible for occupational licensing, and nudging them to expand access into over-regulated professions will not be easy. Similarly, nearly 90 percent of prisoners are incarcerated in state rather than federal correctional institutions, so the states will have to play a significant role in easing ex-felons' reentry into the workforce.

Other portions of the opportunity agenda meet the criteria for inclusion in a first-year legislative package. For example:

- ▶ Numerous surveys show overwhelming support across party lines for paid parental leave, an idea whose time has clearly come.
- ▶ Employers are seeking, but often not finding, workers with the skills a twenty-first-century economy requires. An agreement across party lines to boost investment for job training in community colleges is within reach, especially if there is a formal mechanism for coordinating the development of new courses and programs with employers' needs.
- ▶ The EITC has long enjoyed bipartisan support, and leaders in both political parties are open to expanding it to cover currently excluded portions of the workforce, such as single male workers.
- ▶ Both parties are concerned about the declining pace of small business formation. Proposals to simplify the challenge of complying with the dizzying array of regulations small businesses face and to increase their access to capital would be well received.
- ▶ As geographical mobility has decreased in recent decades, too few workers are moving to new opportunities across state lines. Policy experts have recommended assisting workers in leaving communities with few job openings to take advantage of better employment prospects elsewhere, and many members of Congress seem likely to agree.
- ▶ The Great Recession that began in 2008 revealed the obsolete nature of the unemployment insurance system created in the 1930s in response to the Great Depression. The current model—income support for workers experiencing temporary unemployment in cyclical downturns—does not reflect today's workplace. Both parties want to modernize the system and reorient it toward retraining workers displaced by structural changes in the economy.
- ▶ To expand opportunity, we need to end the chronic underfunding of our infrastructure. The states can do more, and many are beginning to, but they find it difficult to agree on projects that cross state lines. We need to find innovative ways of mobilizing investment—including private capital—for this purpose. A well-crafted proposal to this effect would help break the congressional logjam in this area.

A CAUTIONARY TALE

Throughout his first presidential campaign in 1992, Bill Clinton called for "ending welfare as we know it" by shifting the program's basic thrust from providing open-ended income support to facilitating long-term recipients' entrance into the workforce.[6] There was every reason to believe that welfare reform would be the centerpiece of his first-year domestic policy agenda. But at the last minute, funding for welfare reform was removed from the first budget he submitted to Congress less than a month after taking office, a decision that may have delayed the passage of reform legislation by more than two years.

The moral of the story: in forging a first-year legislative agenda, the president should make sure the administrations' economic and domestic policy teams collaborate to produce a budget that reflects his or her policy priorities. Congress is unlikely to adopt any budget submission unchanged, of course, but members will be quick to seize on the signals it sends. If the new president does not propose funding for the administration's proposals, Congress is likely to conclude that he or she will not fight very hard for them.

NOTES

1. "The Budget and Economic Outlook: 2016–2026," Congressional Budget Office, January 2016, https://www.cbo.gov/.

2. Raj Chetty, "The Impacts of Neighborhoods on Economic Opportunity: New Evidence and Policy Lessons," Brookings Institute, 2015, https://www.brookings.edu/.

3. Raj Chetty et al., "Where Is the Land of Opportunity? The Geography of Intergenerational Mobility in the United States," *Quarterly Journal of Economics* 129, no. 4 (2014), 1553–1623.

4. Richard V. Reeves, "Saving Horatio Alger: Equality, Opportunity, and the American Dream," Brookings Institution, August 20, 2014, http://csweb.brookings.edu/content/research/essays/2014/saving-horatio-alger.html#.

5. David Francis, "Employers' Replies to Racial Names," National Bureau of Economic Research, 2016, www.nber.org.

6. H.R. 3734, 104th Cong., U.S. G.P.O. (1996) (enacted).

A REPUBLICAN OPPORTUNITY AGENDA

PETER WEHNER

The concept of an opportunity society, the chance to pursue the American Dream, is fundamental to America's self-conception and has deep roots in the nation's history.

The United States has always been a beacon for people looking for a fresh start and has always offered to those who do not begin the race of life with an advantage the hope that they can nonetheless succeed and prosper. The animating ideals of our founding documents include the proposition that we are all created equal and endowed by our "Creator with certain unalienable Rights, that among these are Life, Liberty and the pursuit of Happiness." The greatest interpreter of the founders, Abraham Lincoln, spoke of a government "whose leading object is to elevate the condition of men—to lift artificial weights from all shoulders, to clear the paths of laudable pursuit for all, to afford all an unfettered start and a fair chance, in the race of life."[1] So this idea of opportunity is one that has deep resonance with the American people; it is a thread running through our history.

WHERE THINGS STAND

For a variety of complicated reasons, the United States has badly fallen short of this "leading object" of government. Some of the reasons have to do with structural economic changes such as globalization and advances in technology, community dysfunction, and family instability. Some have to do with the failure to modernize institutions to adapt to contemporary challenges. And some have to do with misguided policies and missed opportunities by both the Democratic and Republican Parties.

Whatever the precise explanations and apportionment of blame, many European countries now have as much social mobility as, and more opportunity than, the United States. In the United States, a child's future depends on parental income more than it does in Canada and parts of Europe.

Middle-class Americans have been working harder and longer hours, yet their wages are stagnant. The median family income, adjusted for inflation, was lower in 2013 than it was in 1989, and in 80 percent of the counties in America, the median income is lower today than it was at the start of the century.[2] Many Americans have experienced a rise in the cost of living, particularly in the areas of health care (which doubled in constant dollars from 1988 to 2016) and college tuition (which tripled during the three decades from the mid-1980s to the mid-2010s). In sum: the middle class in America has been losing ground for a generation.

Younger workers are finding it more difficult to launch their careers than ever. For example, in 2014, more than a third of Americans between the ages of eighteen and thirty-one were living in their parents' home.[3]

As for the poor, in 2016, 14 million people lived in extremely poor neighborhoods, 5 million more than before the economic downturn of 2008 and more than twice as many as in 2000. Of those residents, 6.3 million were themselves poor. "Put differently," according to one study, "13.5 percent of the nation's poor population faced the double burden of being poor in a very poor place"—an increase from the last decade.[4] "If you are born poor [in America]," note Isabel Sawhill and Ron Haskins of the Brookings Institution, "you are likely to stay that way."[5]

WHY A FIRST-YEAR PRIORITY

Clearly there is a cognitive dissonance between where the United States is and how Americans like to think of themselves—as the land of opportunity. As a result, many are feeling frustrated and uneasy, insecure and pessimistic.

When thinking about an opportunity agenda, the place to start is with economic growth. After a forty-year period of high growth—averaging 3.5 percent per year from 1960 to 2000—the United States has seen a rapid deceleration. During Barack Obama's two terms in office, not one year of 3 percent gross domestic product growth occurred. Tepid growth is the enemy of an opportunity society.

Getting Americans on the right track requires several things, beginning with remaking a tax code that impedes growth by penalizing investment and innovation and encouraging cronyism. We need to broaden the tax base, flatten and lower the rates, clean out and get rid of many existing deductions—excluding mortgage interest and charitable giving—and lift burdens off middle-class families.

Immigration has always been part of the American recipe for growth but can only remain so with serious reforms. The definition of family reunification needs to be rethought, as it is currently too expansive. There needs to be a greater emphasis on visas for the high-skill workers our economy requires. The United States should model its approach after Canada and Australia, whose immigration policies advance their economic interests. David Brooks of the *New York Times* explains how we should approach the issue: "The immigration system should turn into a talent recruiting system, a relentless effort to get the world's most gifted and driven people to move to our shores."[6]

The United States is experiencing what Walter Russell Mead calls "the energy revolution of the 21st Century," which he argues has the capacity to be a genuine game-changer based on new discoveries and new technologies, including hydraulic fracturing and other extraction technology. "The United States is better supplied with fossil fuels than any other country on earth," according to Mead. "Canada and the United States are each richer in oil than Iraq, Iran, and Saudi Arabia combined."[7]

This energy revolution has the potential to launch a jobs revolution, including substantial growth in high-income jobs for blue-collar workers. Alongside investments in alternative energy sources, we need to pursue policies to keep this "energy revolution" going—such as lifting the ban on American crude-oil exports, allowing more fossil-fuel exploration on federal lands, and encouraging investment in our oil and gas transportation infrastructure.

The kind of economic growth that reforms like these could encourage is an essential prerequisite for a revival of opportunity in the United States. But it is only a beginning. To help those most in need to benefit from growth, much more is required.

Education must lie at the heart of a renewed opportunity agenda. Too few students are being well-served by the current education system, but students from poor families are suffering by far the most. Those in greatest need of a good education are stuck in the worst-run and most dysfunctional schools and denied any promising alternatives.

Some combination of public-school reform and private-school choice is essential to ending the intergenerational cycle of poverty and failure. There should be more choice and variety, greater accountability and merit pay, more options in school curricula, greater transparency, and expanded online learning opportunities and home schooling. Teacher preparation programs should be reformed, principals should be empowered, and the policy of "last in, first out" for teachers should be abolished.

Authors like Chester E. Finn, Jr., and Michael Brickman argue for further innovations, such as choices among individual school courses and course providers, tax-sheltered scholarship programs to cover private-school tuitions, and even debit card–style savings accounts that parents can tap for their children's education.[8] K–12 education is not primarily a federal responsibility, but the federal government can help lift obstacles to such reforms, and this must be a high priority.

The federal government has a greater part to play in higher education, especially given its role in helping millions finance their tuition. A college degree remains a crucial ticket to the middle class. Yet the higher-education system is fundamentally broken—outmoded, far too expensive, and much too difficult to access.

The goal must be to subject the higher-education system to the kinds of consumer pressures that would compel it to offer better choices at lower costs. What does that mean concretely? Along with investments in skills training and alternatives to college, there should be more flexibility in accreditation to let more players onto the field; more data about outcomes to enable consumers to make better informed choices; and reforms of the student loan system to restrain the inflationary pressure that drives up costs and allows failures to survive. Rather than being a big bank that funds ever-higher tuition costs, the federal government should be seen as an enabler of dynamism and constructive competition.

When it comes to helping less-skilled Americans who find it difficult to find meaningful work and raise a family, Michael Strain of the American Enterprise Institute makes a persuasive case for four proposals:[9]

▸ Expand earning subsidies like the Earned Income Tax Credit (EITC), including to childless workers, as a way to increase the rewards to work, increase the workforce participation rate, and reduce poverty.
▸ Dramatically expand child tax credits to help working families offset the burdens of paying (through taxes) for entitlement programs for the elderly by allowing them to keep more of what they earn.
▸ Provide relocation subsidies to the long-term unemployed that will finance some significant part of the cost of moving to a part of the country with a better labor market.
▸ Cut the profoundly regressive payroll taxes and gradually fund more old-age entitlement programs from general revenue in order to shift resources from the elderly to younger workers.

The eligibility rules for a number of our key public-assistance programs, especially Medicaid but also the EITC, are designed in ways that discourage higher-paying work, since benefits diminish or disappear abruptly as income rises. They therefore discourage investments in the kind of self-improvement often necessary to obtain such work. These and other social programs must be structured to encourage recipients to make more productive use of their talents.

Scott Winship of the Manhattan Institute recommends ways to extend the lessons of the 1990s welfare reform to the rest of the federal safety net by block-granting means-tested programs and sending them to the states, thereby encouraging independence, experimentation, and flexibility while requiring work and time limits for most—but not all—beneficiaries.[10]

"Poverty produces family instability," the political scientist Robert D. Putnam has written, "and family instability in turn produces poverty."[11] If America had the same lower percentage of single parents today as we did in 1970, the child poverty rate would be 30 percent less. Encouraging family formation and marital permanence is something government has a very poor record in doing. Many things have been tried; few have succeeded. But there are some steps worth taking.

At a bare minimum, marriage penalties in the tax code and disincentives to marry in welfare programs should be removed. To narrow the "growing marriage divide" between less-educated and better-educated Americans, the scholars William Bradford Wilcox, Charles E. Stokes, and Nicholas H. Wolfinger encourage experimenting with a range of public and private strategies. They claim that some relationship-education programs—for example, the Oklahoma Marriage Initiative and Supporting Father Involvement—have improved the quality and stability of low-income parents' relationships and the emotional welfare of children whose parents have participated in them.[12]

Local civic initiatives designed to strengthen family life already exist, such as First Things First in Chattanooga, Tennessee, a promising local civic initiative that teaches about marriage, fatherhood, and parenting. "Programs like this need to be scrutinized and, if they prove to be effective, replicated across the country," according to Wilcox, Stokes, and Wolfinger.[13]

The same can be said about programs such as the Nurse-Family Partnership, in which nurses visit first-time, low-income mothers to provide information on nutrition and parenting as a way to increase school readiness for at-risk kids.

There are other matters to look at, including criminal justice reform, encouraging financial literacy and mentoring for low-income families, improving infant and child health, and supporting public-service campaigns to discourage teen pregnancy and encourage what has been called the "success sequence": education, work, marriage, and parenthood in that order. An agenda geared to enabling economic growth, improving education, and strengthening our safety-net programs would be a strong start on the path to greater opportunity.

NOTES

1. Abraham Lincoln, "First Message to Congress, at the Special Session," Washington, D.C., July 4, 1861.

2. Neil Irwin, "The Typical American Family Makes Less Than It Did in 1989," *Washington Post,* September 17, 2013, http://www.washingtonpost.com/.

3. Richard Fry, "For First Time in Modern Era, Living with Parents Edges out Other Living Arrangements for 18- to 34-Year-Olds," Pew Research Centers Social Demographic Trends Project RSS, May 24, 2016, http://www.pewsocialtrends.org/.

4. Elizabeth Kneebone and Natalie Holmes, "U.S. Concentrated Poverty in the Wake of the Great Recession," Brookings Institution, March 31, 2016, https://www.brookings.edu/.

5. Isabel Sawhill and Ron Haskins, "Five Myths about Our Land of Opportunity," *Washington Post,* November 1, 2009, http://www.washingtonpost.com/wp-dyn/content/article/2009/10/30/AR2009103001845.html.

6. David Brooks, "The Working Nation," *New York Times,* October 23, 2014, https://www.nytimes.com/2014/10/24/opinion/david-brooks-the-working-nation.html.

7. Walter Russell Mead, "The Energy Revolution and Its Biggest Losers," Global Warming Policy Foundation, October 7, 2012, http://www.thegwpf.org/.

8. Charles E. Finn, Jr., *Charter Schools at the Crossroads: Predicaments, Paradoxes, Possibilities* (Cambridge, Mass.: Harvard Education Press, 2016).

9. Michael R. Strain, "A Jobs Agenda for the Right," *National Affairs* 18 (2014), https://www.nationalaffairs.com/publications/detail/a-jobs-agenda-for-the-right.

10. Scott Winship, "Why the 1996 Welfare Reform Benefited Poor Children," *National Review Online,* September 1, 2016, https://www.manhattan-institute.org/html/why-1996-welfare-reform-benefited-poor-children-9215.html.

11. Robert D. Putnam, *Our Kids: The American Dream in Crisis* (New York: Simon and Schuster, 2015).

12. William Bradford Wilcox, Charles E. Stokes, and Nicholas H. Wolfinger, "One Nation, Divided: Culture, Civic Institutions, and the Marriage Divide," *Marriage and Child Wellbeing Revisited* 25 (2015): 111–27.

13. Ibid., 122.

V ★ RACE AND IMMIGRATION

RELUCTANT REFORMER
Lyndon B. Johnson and Immigration Reform

DANIEL TICHENOR

Nearly every new president of the modern era has viewed the nation's immigration policies as deeply flawed. Yet few of these modern executives have been willing to make immigration reform—one of the most controversial issues in American politics—central to their agenda. Even fewer have had much success doing so. The most dramatic and successful of all—Lyndon B. Johnson's landmark 1965 reform—itself followed a pattern of steep political costs with uneven policy results. Yet his achievement also captures the transformative possibilities of remaking immigration law for countless newcomers and larger national interests.

Today, as in the past, efforts to significantly revise immigration laws and policies have produced fierce political divides that explode even the most unified party coalitions and that make straightforward problem definition a pipedream. Campaigns for sweeping reform regularly have followed a tortured path of false starts, prolonged negotiation, and frustrating stalemates. When lightning has struck for passage of nonincremental reform, enactment has hinged on difficult compromises among rival goals and interests.

The result has been legislation that is typically unpopular among ordinary citizens, compels stakeholder groups to swallow bitter pills, draws fire from determined opponents, and places new and often competing policy demands on the government. These dynamics—intraparty conflicts, elusive problem definition, difficult compromises, and unpopular outcomes—have led most American presidents to proceed with caution.

Johnson was well aware of these challenges as a first-year president, yet he forged ahead knowing the fight for sweeping immigration reform would be far more taxing and unpredictable than nearly all of the other legislative proposals on his immense agenda. He did so recognizing that failing to spearhead an immigration overhaul would significantly undercut his civil rights, social justice, and geopolitical goals. The Johnson administration learned that major reform required the formation of "strange bedfellow" alliances that are unstable and demand painful concessions. But his White House also understood that the levers of immigrant and refugee admissions both reflected and served larger visions of nationhood, and it refused to let nativists continue to monopolize those terms to codify their ethnic, racial, and religious animus.

Johnson ultimately expended far more political energy on this issue than anyone on his team anticipated, with bedeviling twists and turns on the path to major reform. Furthermore, his remarkable legislative achievement had dramatic unforeseen consequences, including an unprecedented change in the country's demographic landscape. Yet it also enabled Johnson to upend xenophobic policies that had prevailed for a half-century, and to project very different ideals at home and abroad. Johnson's battle for reform underscores the alluring capacity of immigration policy to be a potent tool for nation-building, one that naturally appeals to presidents committed to higher forms of statecraft.

For all of its possibilities to reshape the nation's social, economic, and political life, immigration reform has made most modern presidents decidedly uneasy. Franklin D. Roosevelt assiduously avoided clashes with immigration restrictionists in Congress during the 1930s, a period when draconian national origins quotas from the 1920s barred entry for most newcomers and nativist demagogues blamed unemployment on past arrivals. Decades later, presidents such as Ronald Reagan and Bill Clinton pursued a cautious, reactive strategy toward immigration reform, one in which they responded opportunistically to congressional initiatives on the issue. The Obama administration shelved immigration reform when it became clear that nearly every Republican member of Congress (and some Democrats) would derail legislation. When pressed, Barack Obama eventually followed precedents begun by Harry S. Truman and Dwight D. Eisenhower by taking unilateral executive action to provide deportation relief and economic benefits to particular undocumented immigrants, most notably young people who entered the United States as children (and later their parents, a move blocked in the courts). Donald Trump aimed much of his rhetorical fire at undocumented immigrants during his successful 2016 presidential campaign.

Reticence on this issue, let alone avoidance, will be all but impossible for future presidents. Going it alone via executive action will be viewed at best as a stopgap measure that satisfies few, or at worst as a crassly partisan maneuver that is constitutionally suspect and worthy of harsh congressional, judicial, and popular sanctions. In short, the pursuit of major immigration reform will be both daunting and nearly inescapable. However, this challenging effort need not be as illfated or politically damaging as those of Jimmy Carter, who pursued employer sanctions-amnesty legislation, and George W. Bush, who hoped for comprehensive immigration reform.

As an unexpected first-year president, Johnson stands out as a reluctant champion of immigration reform who ultimately won passage of the landmark Immigration and Nationality Act (INA). Despite enormous legislative advantages, the Johnson administration's battle for the INA was anything but easy. Indeed, it provides an especially instructive example of the formidable hurdles, painful compromises, and transformative consequences of significant innovation in this contentious policy arena.

Although Johnson pledged to fulfill the agenda of his slain predecessor, and no other president was more closely identified with liberal immigration reform than John F. Kennedy, Johnson initially made it clear to White House advisors that he wanted nothing to do with the issue. For years, he had been whipsawed by immigration policy in the Senate, where Democrats were deeply divided between southern conservatives opposed to any opening of the gates and northern liberals committed to dismantling national origins quotas that reserved about 70 percent of visas for immigrants from just three countries: Great Britain, Ireland, and Germany. According to reporters, during the 1950s, when serving as Senate majority leader, Johnson exploded with invective when asked about holdups to progressive immigration reform. Although Kennedy described immigration reform as "the most urgent and fundamental" item on his New Frontier agenda, he got nowhere with his plans to alter immigration law because of potent opposition from conservative Democrats like Senator James Eastland of Mississippi and Representative Michael Feighan of Ohio, who controlled the immigration subcommittees of both houses. These lawmakers stood atop a bipartisan coalition that favored immigration restriction in the name of national security, job protection, and ethnic and racial hierarchy.

As a new president, Johnson told advisors that the issue was a political buzz saw that lacked public support and could hurt other reform plans. Yet numerous aides argued that the persistence of national origins quotas for selecting immigrants contradicted Johnson's goals at home and abroad. These draconian quotas were inconsistent with his civil rights agenda "to eliminate from this Nation every trace of discrimination and oppression that is based on race or color," and they provided, as Senator Philip Hart, a Democrat from Michigan, put it, "grist for the mills of Moscow and Peiping."[1] Johnson became a late convert to immigration reform.

Johnson's first State of the Union Address in 1964 buoyed the hopes of immigration reformers. In this speech, he outlined a civil rights agenda that championed for all citizens access to public facilities, equal eligibility for federal benefits, an equal chance to vote, and "good public schools." Then he added, "We must also lift by legislation the bars of discrimination against those who seek entry into our country." An administration bill was soon introduced that would increase annual immigration to 165,000 and replace discriminatory per-country quotas with a preference system allocating 50 percent of visas on the basis of special occupational skills or education that benefited the nation's economic interests. Remaining visas would be distributed to refugees and those with close family ties to American citizens or legal permanent residents.

One week after his address, Johnson held a press conference at the White House that included members of the House and Senate immigration subcommittees as well as a broad and diverse set of advocacy group leaders favoring reform.

As the restriction-minded Eastland and Feighan looked on uneasily, Johnson went before a phalanx of reporters and television cameras to urge Congress to make immigration law more egalitarian. He reminded lawmakers that every president since Truman believed that existing immigration policies hurt the nation in its Cold War struggle with the Soviet Union. Johnson then invoked the language of Kennedy's inaugural address, urging a meritocratic admissions policy that asked immigrants, "What can you do for our country?" "We ought to never ask," he added, "'In what country were you born?'" Leading congressional sponsors of the administration's bill, including Senator Hart and Democratic representatives Emanuel Celler of New York and Peter Rodino of New Jersey, praised the measure. When they finished their statements, Johnson caught Eastland off guard by asking him to address the assembled journalists and policy activists. A surprised Eastland told the gathering that he was prepared to look into the matter "very carefully and very expeditiously." After a series of tense Oval Office meetings with Johnson in 1964, Eastland stunned Washington observers by agreeing to temporarily relinquish control of his Immigration Subcommittee to the freshman senator from Massachusetts, Edward Kennedy. Johnson's unusual influence over Eastland removed a formidable impediment to the Hart-Celler bill, but major legislative hurdles remained.

As chair of the House immigration subcommittee, Feighan made headlines in 1963 by charging that the CIA was riddled with Soviet spies and that the actor Richard Burton should be banned from entering the country for having an "immoral" affair with Elizabeth Taylor. A year later, Feighan mobilized restrictionists in both parties to block Johnson's immigration bill. Instead, Feighan proposed a rival bill that promised to preserve preferences for northern and Western Europeans, exclude nearly all Asians and Africans, favor immigrants with family ties under existing quotas, and maintain exclusions for ideology and sexual orientation. This maneuver ensured that no action would be taken until after the 1964 election.

The Johnson team renewed its push for immigration reform in 1965, yet Feighan and his allies held two months of hearings in which they peppered administration officials with questions about a new merit-based preference system and its potential effects on the number and diversity of newcomers. "How about giving the welfare of the American people first priority for a change?" Feighan asked proponents of progressive reform.[2]

Frustrated by Feighan's roadblocks, Johnson and House Democratic leaders successfully moved in the spring of 1965 to expand the immigration subcommittee by adding Johnson loyalists like Texan Jack Brooks as crucial swing votes. Despite this tactical blow, Feighan privately told antireform lobbyists that he enjoyed enough bipartisan backing to seriously limit radical policy change. Yet Feighan also understood that Johnson and the reformers now had sufficient political momentum to overcome delaying tactics, so he entered tough negotiations with the White House.

In the end, Feighan and his allies agreed to dismantle the national origins quota system and the so-called Asiatic Barred Zone if Johnson sacrificed the administration's emphasis on immigrant merit and skills. Feighan was convinced (incorrectly, as it turned out) that reserving most visas for immigrants with family ties to American citizens and legal permanent residents would decidedly favor European applicants and thus maintain the nation's ethnic and racial makeup. The new legal preference system in the administration's bill established four preference categories for family reunification, which were to receive nearly three-quarters of total annual visas. Spouses, minor children, and parents of citizens over the age of twenty-one were granted admission without visa limits. The revised bill left roughly a quarter of annual visas for economic-based admissions and refugee relief.

Along with the legal preference system, the "non-quota status" of Mexican immigration in particular and Latin American admissions in general were a prominent concern for restrictionists in both houses of Congress during the legislative wrangling of 1965. The notion of a cap on Western Hemisphere immigration was adamantly denounced by Secretary of State Dean Rusk and other foreign policy advisors, who argued that taking such a step would be a huge setback to relations with Central and South American countries. The administration's stand on Western Hemisphere immigration came under withering attack in the Senate, however. In particular, southern Democrats, led by Sam Ervin, Jr., of North Carolina, threatened to stall action in the Senate immigration subcommittee unless concessions were made. Facing a major logjam, Johnson and pro-immigration lawmakers compromised with Ervin and his restriction-minded colleagues on an annual ceiling for Western Hemisphere immigration. As Johnson's congressional liaison Lawrence O'Brien explained, "Listen, we're not going to walk away from this because we didn't get a whole loaf. We'll take half a loaf or three-quarters of a loaf."[3]

Even by the outsized standards of Lyndon Johnson and his Great Society juggernaut, the Immigration and Nationality Act of 1965 was monumental. The new law marked a dramatic break from immigration policies of the past by abolishing eugenics-inspired national origins quotas that barred nearly all but northern and Western Europeans. In their place, the INA established a preference framework that continues to guide immigrant admissions, with family ties receiving highest priority followed by occupational skills and political refugee status. Although few historians believe that the INA's champions anticipated how profoundly it would change the nation's demographic landscape, Johnson recognized that its passage was especially significant—enough so that he oversaw the staging of an elaborate signing ceremony at the base of the Statue of Liberty. True to form, White House staffers were given strict instructions by the president to physically block political rivals like New York governor Nelson Rockefeller from the cameras assembled on the dais at Liberty Island. Hinting at the INA's potential consequences, Johnson predicted that the new law would "strengthen us in a hundred unseen ways."

Lyndon Johnson stands apart for successfully shepherding landmark immigration reform through Congress. In various respects, he enjoyed many exceptional advantages in championing the INA, including its close association with his martyred predecessor and broader civil rights reform; a near consensus of foreign policy experts that reform served national geopolitical interests; a strong economy; and an electoral landslide in 1964 with, concomitantly, huge gains for his party in Congress. That these especially favorable circumstances did not make the Johnson administration immune to an arduous legislative struggle underscores the enormously daunting political barriers that usually emerge when major immigration reform is at stake. The INA was decades in the making, and its enactment in 1965 was trying and uncertain despite being attached to Johnson's Great Society juggernaut.

It is equally revealing that in the end, Johnson's success in winning passage of the INA depended significantly on painful compromises, including cross-cutting reform packages that both expanded and restricted immigration opportunities in new ways. Whether one celebrates or condemns the INA, it is clear that this law defies simple characterization precisely because it is an intricate statute with multiple meanings. The INA marked a monumental watershed in immigration policy by ending a draconian national origins quota system that was explicitly rooted in eugenicist notions of northern and Western European superiority. That it took twenty years after the defeat of Nazi Germany for Congress to remove these barriers from American immigration law speaks to how effectively Cold War nativists knitted together racial hierarchies and national security fears. This history made it especially fitting that the Johnson administration coupled the INA with the Civil Rights and Voting Rights Acts.

It is equally true, however, that opponents of diverse immigration left their imprints on the INA by winning new limits on Western Hemisphere immigration and by making family ties rather than individual skills the keystone of the legal preference system. In the final analysis, the INA is a reflection of the arduous struggles among Johnson, reformers, and congressional stalwarts over its form and substance. The dramatic and unanticipated demographic shifts that these restriction-minded provisions helped spur underscore the INA's transformative, yet variegated, influence on American life.

NOTES

1. Lyndon B. Johnson, "President Lyndon B. Johnson's Address before a Joint Session of the Congress," Washington, D.C., November 27, 1963; Tyler Anbinder, *City of Dreams: The 400-Year Epic History of Immigrant New York* (Boston: Houghton Mifflin Harcourt, 2016), 512.

2. Daniel Tichenor, "The Overwhelming Barriers to Successful Immigration Reform," *Atlantic*, May 25, 2016, https://www.theatlantic.com/politics/archive/2016/05/replicating-lbjs -immigration-success/483908/.

3. Ibid.

AMERICAN APARTHEID

Why Blacks Are Central to but Excluded from America's Identity

ORLANDO PATTERSON

Two profound paradoxes lie at the heart of contemporary American race relations. The first is evident to anyone who keeps abreast of the news: It is that in the final year of the nation's first black president's administration, there was growing pessimism and outrage about race in the nation. This was reflected in the Black Lives Matter movement, demonstrations against racism on campuses, outrage over the repeated killing of black youth by police officers, and a general sense that racial progress has stalled and may even be moving in reverse. A Kaiser Foundation study reported that almost two-thirds of the public (64 percent) said racial tensions had increased in the country in the 2010s.[1]

What happened to the optimism and triumphalism about American democracy and racial progress that greeted the historic election of President Barack Obama in 2008? How, of all times since the 1960s, could the nation find itself in anguished discussions, with popular works such as Ta-Nehisi Coates's *Between the World and Me* little more than cries of hopelessness about America's racial failures?

This first paradox—call it the Obama Paradox—must be seen in terms of a broader and deeper contradiction. After centuries of exclusion, black Americans have been almost wholly accepted into the public sphere of American life and are central to the nation's definition of itself as a political and social community. And yet, at the same time, black Americans remain extraordinarily excluded from most regions of the nation's private sphere: they are as segregated as ever, have remarkably few intimate friendships with nonblacks, and are the most endogamous group in the nation. This apartness from the nation's private sphere—two eminent sociologists have labeled it "American apartheid"—has worsened even as black Americans' public integration has greatly increased. A black man was twice elected to the presidency; blacks have occupied the nation's major public offices: senators, governors, secretaries of state, attorneys general, the chairmanship of the Joint Chief of Staff; and they are a major presence at all levels of the nation's cultural life. And yet at the private level, they are still a largely excluded group, the great majority living in hyper-segregated neighborhoods of concentrated poverty, misery, and violence, or else in picket-fenced, middle-class communities that are best described as gilded racial ghettos.

One striking expression of the view that blacks are outsiders was the insistent belief by a significant segment of the population that the black president was not born in America but was instead a foreigner who had stolen "our nation" which "we want back."

The other side of our paradox is the persisting poverty and apartness of most nonelite blacks from the nation's private life. Moderate absolute growth in black median household income occurred between the 1960s and the 2010s, but compared with income change among white Americans the gap remained the same. In 1967, black median household income was 65.5 percent of the median white household income; in 2013 the same was true. The staggering growth in inequality negatively affects all but the wealthiest Americans, but the black poor have suffered disproportionately. The poverty rate for blacks, having declined during the Clinton administration years from 32.9 percent in 1992 to 21.2 percent in 2000 (the lowest on record), climbed to 24.5 percent in 2007 and now stands at 27.4 percent—compared with 9.9 percent for whites.[2] Early childhood poverty is now recognized as a reliable predictor of later poverty and social maladjustment, so it is alarming that 46 percent of black children under age six are living in poverty.[3] The top-down nature of the nation's economic gains is most strikingly reflected in the fact that inequality among blacks is substantially greater than it is among whites. Among blacks, the mean household income of the top fifth is twenty times that of the poorest fifth, compared with a multiple of twelve in the nation at large.

In light of all these profound social contradictions, what should a newly inaugurated president do?

▸ Early in the first year, a new president should give a major address, preferably at the National Museum of African American History and Culture, aimed at stanching the growing sense of pessimism about race that dominates public discourse. The president should point out that the achievements of the civil rights movement are real and should be celebrated. Dr. Martin Luther King, Jr., and the heroic leaders of the civil rights movement did not toil and give their lives in vain. America, the president should also say, can claim to have a more genuinely diverse society than any other majority white nation in the world, one that continues to integrate outsiders better than any other society. At the same time, the president should acknowledge the special hardships that African Americans have suffered, and continue to suffer, in spite of their disproportionate contribution to the nation's cultural, economic, and political development. He or she should thus commit the administration to policies that will improve the condition of black Americans.

▸ In less dramatic fashion, but with no less urgency, the president should move swiftly to undo the national disgrace that the United States has incarcerated more of its citizens than any other nation in the history of the world. The president should build on the bipartisan consensus that has already emerged about this tragedy. A related initiative would be for the president to initiate the process of restoring the right to vote for the thousands of ex-felons who have served their time and paid the price for their misdeeds. America is the only modern society that lacks this practice and that instead commits an egregious violation of a basic right.

▸ The president should vigorously pursue nascent efforts toward a complete reform of America's police training, practices, and culture. The recommendations of Obama's Task Force on 21st Century Policing clearly laid out what needs to be done: greater transparency; community policing; an end to racial profiling; respect for and a protective rather than adversarial attitude toward blacks and all other citizens; and the use of violence as a last resort.

▸ The reintegration of disconnected black youth into society should be a major policy goal. Many federal and state programs already exist, such as the Youth ChalleNGe Program of the National Guard and midnight basketball leagues that have been shown to be effective in reducing the attractions of gang membership and the underground economy. The president should make the invigoration and expansion of these programs a major policy priority.

▸ Remedying the persisting problem of residential and school segregation should be a major long-term policy objective of the president. Sociologists have long known that concentrated poverty in hyper-segregated communities has been among the gravest sources of black (and increasingly Latino) disadvantage, excluding them not just from good schools but also from the social and cultural capital essential for mobility in America. The next president should aggressively pursue a policy of desegregation through the imaginative use of housing and educational vouchers.

▸ Closely related is a policy that strongly prioritizes federal backing for programs that support families of all ethnoracial groups, but especially minority families in need. The evidence is now overwhelming that the most cost-effective federal welfare and social programs are those focused on highly subsidized pre-K, early childhood education, and afterschool programs that not only provide desperately needed relief to single parents but enhance the educational chances and broader socialization of disadvantaged children and youth. However, this proposal should be one component of a wider program aimed at cultural and social change within the black community. Since every president but Obama has been a white person, this effort must be handled with great discretion and respect. The president should be absolutely clear that no attempt is being made to promote or influence the family life or gender relations of African Americans (that's something blacks alone must seek to change among themselves). Such an effort was attempted by the George W. Bush administration and was a nearly complete failure. Rather, the goal should be to improve the condition of single mothers and the care and education of their children.

Steps such as these would represent crucial movement toward completing the thwarted black struggle for equality. For most of the twentieth century, that effort focused mainly on the exclusion from the public sphere of politics, law, work, and popular culture, or the discrimination blacks experienced within those few corners of the economy where their presence was tolerated. The civil rights movement marked the triumph of these efforts. In less than a generation, the institutional infrastructure of Jim Crow was dismantled, and the legal system came to support blacks in a "rights revolution" that had enormous implications for other major disadvantaged groups, especially women, Latinos, and gays. Accompanying these changes was a fundamental liberalization in the attitudes of the vast majority of whites toward blacks.

The movement, however, was in most respects a top-down revolution that largely benefited the middle and upper classes of whites and blacks alike. In this regard, it made the American class system unique among the white-majority societies of the world. No other diverse society, especially those with black minorities, comes close to America in the degree of integration of its elite, especially in the public sphere.

This fragile economic base—along with persisting, though declining, labor market discrimination; residential and marital isolation; a reversal in educational attainment; as well as internal cultural problems persisting from slavery but reinforced by modern circumstances—accounts for a second stunning recent development: massive intergenerational downward mobility from the black middle class. A recent Pew Research Center study reported that "a majority of black children of middle-income parents fall below their parents in income and economic status," and fully half have fallen to the very bottom of the income ladder![4]

The paradox of public inclusion and ongoing, indeed increasing, private separation is most glaringly revealed in the persistence of large-scale residential segregation in America. Segregation levels vary by region in quite unexpected ways, compounding the paradox. They are highest in those regions where blacks have achieved the greatest levels of public integration: the metropolitan regions of the Northeast and Midwest. New York, the liberal heartland of America where blacks have, arguably, achieved the strongest presence and influence in public life, ranks near the bottom of the nation's metropolitan areas in residential integration.

Nowhere is the paradox of public inclusion and private separation more starkly found than among black American youth, especially poor males. On the one hand, they are the most segregated segment of the nation's population and face the most formidable socioeconomic problems. They have the highest rates of dropping out and delinquency in the nation. Although the great majority are law abiding, and homicide rates are at a fifty-one-year low, violence has remained endemic among a disconnected 20 percent of these youth.[5] Delinquency, combined with draconian laws and an unfair justice system that targets all black youth, rather than the 20 percent who are disconnected, has resulted in a horrendous incarceration rate in which blacks constitute nearly a half of this country's 2 million prisoners.

Those not incarcerated face unemployment rates above 20 percent among those still seeking work. And yet this same group is the creator of a powerfully vibrant popular culture, one that has had an outsized influence on the broader national culture and is perhaps the most potent force in the globalization of American popular influence. White American youth avidly consume the hip-hop productions of black ghetto youth—their music, fashion, poetry, dance, lifestyle, and language.

How do we explain this paradoxical state of racial affairs?

Surprisingly, the negative reaction of whites to the gains of blacks can only be understood in light of the genuine liberalization in racial attitudes of the great majority of whites. From the early 1940s, when most whites considered blacks racially inferior and approved of laws prohibiting intermarriage and forbidding the sale of homes to blacks, white American attitudes have evolved to the point that the great majority—approximately 80 percent—claim to hold genuinely liberal views regarding racial equality. How then do we explain the resistance to policies aimed at helping blacks, and just as importantly, the fact that so many blacks— over 50 percent according to a recent Kaiser Foundation study—report experiencing racial discrimination and avoidance in their daily encounters with whites?[6]

One explanation is what Harvard social science professor Lawrence D. Bobo calls laissez-faire racism.[7] Whites, while committed to the principles of racial equality and integration, nonetheless resist supporting policies that benefit blacks if they are perceived as harming their own interests. The classic examples of this are hostility to affirmative action, school busing, and changing zoning laws to facilitate the desegregation of society.

Another explanation is what I call "the 20 percent conundrum." Although the great majority of whites may genuinely claim to have liberal racial views, surveys and experiments indicate that a stubborn 20 percent of them are outright racists in their stereotyping of blacks and belief in their racial or cultural inferiority. The extreme wing of this group was on display in the violent rhetoric unleashed during the 2016 election campaign. The nation's white population, including Hispanic whites, amounts to 246.6 million, or 77 percent of the total population, while blacks, those who identify as mixed, and black-identified Latinos amount to 42 million, or 14 percent of the total. What this means is that for every black American, there is more than one outright white racist. To complicate matters, a disproportionate number of this racist minority of whites are likely to be in positions of institutionalized power, such as police officers, security guards, and small employers. Hence the conundrum whereby the great majority of whites can genuinely claim that they and their friends are not racists in the traditional sense while the great majority of blacks experience racist aggression in their daily lives.

So far, I have emphasized the exogenous factors in black-white relations, especially those springing from personal and institutional racism. But there also are endogenous factors that partly account for the persisting plight of blacks and that also spill over into black-white relations, especially in regard to white perceptions of blacks.

The most important of these is the growing number of children being raised by single, usually female, parents—now over 70 percent of black children.[8] Sociologists have thoroughly demonstrated the deleterious consequences of single parenting. These include a high probability of such children being poor and their much greater risk of remaining poor as adults, becoming single parents themselves, and falling into delinquency and violence.

Somewhat related is another major problem: the high rate of violence within black communities. This is in part a function of poverty, poor schools, unemployment, overconcentration, and a chemically toxic environment. However, the street culture of thuggery, individual and gang violence, and engagement in the underground economy of illegal drugs cannot be wholly explained in terms of disadvantaged circumstances. As W. E. B. Du Bois documented in his sociological works near the end of the 1800s, black communities have long been plagued by violence. Violence is in part the persistence of responses to the violence of slavery and Jim Crow and to the problems of being brought up in single-parent families without the resources or the time to nurture and socialize children, especially boys.

Noting these internal sources of economic and social insecurity is not to blame the victim, as is often claimed, or to support the racist view that blacks are culturally inferior. Contrary to right-wing views that the state can and should do nothing to help heal these problems, the fact that they are the historic result of state-sponsored slavery and institutionalized racial exploitation dictates the moral imperative that the American state do all in its power to alleviate the worst effects of these internal problems.

NOTES

1. Kaiser Family Foundation and CNN, *Survey of Americans on Race,* November 2015, http://files.kff.org/attachment/report-survey-of-americans-on-race.

2. U.S. Census Bureau, Historical Poverty Tables, table 2: Poverty Status of People by Family Relationship, Race, and Hispanic Origin, September 1, 2016, http://www.census.gov/data/tables/time-series/demo/income-poverty/historical-poverty-people.html.

3. Economic Policy Institute, *State of Working America Data Library,* http://stateofworking america.org/fact-sheets/poverty/.

4. Pew Research Center, *Pursuing the American Dream: Economic Mobility Across Generations,* July 2012, http://www.pewtrusts.org/~/media/legacy/uploadedfiles/pcs_assets/2012/pursuingamericandreampdf.pdf.

5. Pew Research Center, *Gun Homicide Rate Down 49% since 1993 Peak; Public Unaware,* May 7, 2013, http://www.pewsocialtrends.org/2013/05/07/gun-homicide-rate-down-49-since-1993 -peak-public-unaware/.

6. Kaiser Family Foundation and CNN, *Survey of Americans on Race.*

7. Lawrence D. Bobo, "Laissez-Faire Racism, Racial Inequality, and the Role of the Social Science," in Charles A. Gallagher, *Rethinking the Color Line: Readings in Race and Ethnicity* (New York: McGraw-Hill, 2011), 148–57.

8. Pew Research Center, *Parenting in America,* December 17, 2015, http://www.pewsocial trends.org/2015/12/17/parenting-in-america/.

OBAMA'S LESSONS

Rethinking the President's Approach to Racial Issues

MICHAEL ERIC DYSON

Despite the election of our nation's first black president in 2008—and in some ways, perhaps because of it—America, in the realm of race, remains embroiled in crisis, controversy, and catastrophe. That need not be the case if we as a nation are willing to learn hard lessons from the Obama era and move forward with renewed determination to contend with our tattered racial legacy.

During his two terms in office, President Barack Obama often was loath to lift his voice on race lest he be relegated to a "black box." His reluctance deprived the nation of his wisdom and starved black folk of the most visible interpreter of their story and plight. His silence often sent the wrong signal that race, and black concerns, did not count as much as other national priorities.

Questions of race—explicit and implicit—suffused the Obama presidency, for obvious reasons. Early in his tenure, the first black president was confronted with a test of how he would engage on what became the signature racial issue of his presidency—police treatment of African Americans. After Cambridge, Massachusetts, police arrested black Harvard professor Henry Louis Gates, Jr., for disorderly conduct in 2009, Obama said the officers "acted stupidly."

Gates had returned home from a trip to China to discover that his door was jammed, and as his driver helped him gain entry to his house, a passerby called the police, thinking it might be a break-in. The ensuing conflict between Gates and the police officer who responded to the call led to Gates's arrest and a national debate about race and law enforcement.

Obama's comment—as tepid as it would come to appear in contrast to the police misconduct controversies that ensued later in his administration—was harshly criticized. The Gates confrontation made Obama deeply hesitant to speak on race and led him to three fateful conclusions:

► Never speak of race in a way that holds whites even partially responsible for black suffering. The subject of white guilt of any sort—even in circumstances of clear white culpability—is to be avoided at all costs. This is another way of saying that race is primarily the business and burden of blacks.

▶ Although they read it quite differently, both white and black communities were eager for Obama to excoriate perceived black error—for instance, in his warning in a 2013 commencement speech to Morehouse College graduates against using racism as an excuse for failure—and to damn black pathology, such as absentee fathers. In black life, such gestures are often read as tough love; in white America, they are seen as heroic battles against black deficiency.

▶ When the structural features of black suffering cannot be ignored, it is best to soften the blow with ample mentions of black criminality or black moral failure.

A single event smoked Obama out of his presidential cubbyhole of racial nonengagement and thrust him into his bully pulpit to, in part, define, and then defend, black people—really to represent them, an extraordinary feat in itself.

It was the epic grief that gripped black America with the 2013 not-guilty verdict in Sanford, Florida, in the trial of self-styled neighborhood watchman George Zimmerman for the fatal shooting of black teen Trayvon Martin. That verdict, and the persistent injustice it highlighted, contrasted sharply with the broadly accepted narrative equating Obama's ascent with the end of racial problems and tensions in America.

Obama spoke about Martin to explain to white Americans why so many black folk were enraged over the verdict. Many white conservatives viewed Obama's "one-sided" explanation of black suffering—a radical departure from the tough blows he had thrown black people's way in most of his public pronouncements on blackness—as a surly betrayal of a "racial agreement" implicitly accepted by the president. Some whites believed that agreement was as follows: do not speak much on race, and when you do, go after your own kind, as well as offering the blandest platitudes possible about racial progress and the work that remains to be done.

The rash of racial crises during Obama's presidency—from the Henry Louis Gates affair to a white supremacist's murders in June 2015 of nine black people in a Charleston, South Carolina, church—led to calls for presidential leadership from the office's bully pulpit, and yet Obama was often slow to command the rostrum to address race. "I've found in this position that it's not always true that an incident automatically triggers a useful dialogue," he told me, in an interview. "What you have to do is be able to create a place where people are willing to look at things in new ways and the media is willing to look at things in new ways. As president that means I've got to pick and choose my spots effectively."[1]

Obama's record of effectively picking and choosing his spots was hit-or-miss; he often sabotaged his own standards with rhetoric that was far from organic or surprising, perhaps because it grew from controversies that compelled him to react. It is understandable that Obama preferred being seen as the black *president* rather than the *black* president. But his refusal to address race except when he had no choice—a kind of racial procrastination—left him little control of the conversation. When he was boxed into a racial corner, often as a result of black social unrest sparked by claims of police brutality, Obama was mostly uninspiring: he warned (black) citizens to obey the law and affirmed the status quo.

Yet Obama energetically peppered his words to blacks with talk of responsibility in one public scolding after another. When Obama upbraided black folk while barely mentioning the flaws of white America, he left the impression that race is the concern solely of black people, and that blackness is full of pathology. Obama's reprimands of black folks also undercut their moral standing, especially when his eager embrace of other minorities like gays and lesbians validated their push for justice. Obama was fond of saying that he was the president not of black America but of the entire nation. This reflected his faith in universal rather than targeted remedies for black suffering: blacks will thrive when America flourishes.

Obama's views on race featured three characteristics, in various combinations: *strategic inadvertence,* in which racial benefit is not the expressed intent but the consequence of policies geared to uplift all Americans, in the belief that they will also help blacks; the *heroic explicit,* whereby he carelessly attacked black moral failure and poor cultural habits; and the *noble implicit,* in which he avoided linking whites to social distress or pathology—or moral or political responsibility for black suffering—and spoke in the broadest terms possible, in grammar both tentative and tortured, about the problems we *all* confront. It was an effort that drew false equivalencies between black and white experiences and mistook racial effects for their causes.

Obama's successors in the presidency must quickly and directly address the racial crises we confront and acknowledge them as the product of a malevolent history of racism that has tarnished our national will and robust experiment in democracy.

For instance, after the Charleston church murders in 2015, former secretary of state Hillary Clinton, in a speech before a mayors' conference in San Francisco, directly addressed the swirling racial currents that flooded Charleston and the nation in the ugly sweep of violent animus—what Clinton later called "racist terror." Clinton said that, tragically, despite our devotion to human rights and diversity, "bodies are once again being carried out of a black church," and that, once again, "racist rhetoric has metastasized into racist violence." Clinton argued that "it is tempting to dismiss a tragedy like this as an isolated incident, to believe that in today's America, bigotry is largely behind us, that institutionalized racism no longer exists. But despite our best efforts and our highest hopes, America's long struggle with race is far from finished." She acknowledged that race is a difficult issue to talk about; that "so many of us hoped by electing our first black president, we had turned the page on this chapter in our history"; and that "there are truths we don't like to say out loud or discuss with our children," but that "we have to," because it is "the only way we can possibly move forward together."[2]

Clinton laid out the facts: blacks are nearly three times more likely than whites to be denied a mortgage; the median wealth owned by black families is $11,000, while for whites it is $134,000; nearly half of black families have lived in poor neighborhoods for two generations, compared to just 7 percent for whites; black men are more likely to be stopped and searched by police, charged with crimes, and sentenced to longer prison terms than white men (10 percent longer for federal crimes); black students suffer from the vast resegregation of American schools; and black children are 500 percent more likely to die from asthma than white children. Clinton's remarkable oration was steeped in black culture and charged with sophisticated analysis. It was an extraordinarily honest reckoning by a major American politician with both intimate and institutional racism—racism of the heart and racism in the systems of society.

Future presidents must clearly and consistently use the bully pulpit to offer such analyses, encourage the nation to engage our brutal racist legacy, and together find a way forward. They must reject the adherence to strategic inadvertence and craft public policy that grapples with the specific features of black suffering. Obama believed that mainstream American ideas of equal opportunity are the catalyst, along with race-neutral goals, for improving the plight of minorities. His belief that universal programs provide a better outcome for minorities rested in part on political expediency: Whites will embrace these programs only if they offer everyone the potential to succeed. But the time has come to reject such an outlook and adopt a race-specific approach to black suffering.

Some of the most prominent advocates of Obama's approach have seen the light. In 1990, sociologist William Julius Wilson argued in his article "Race-Neutral Policies and the Democratic Coalition" that Democrats, in their effort to expand the party's base, should not emphasize race-specific policies like affirmative action but should instead embrace race-neutral policies that overwhelmingly serve poor minority communities. Wilson has more recently changed his mind:

> In my previous writings I called for . . . policies that would directly benefit all groups, not just people of color. My thinking was that, given American views about poverty and race, a color-blind agenda would be the most realistic way to generate the broad political support necessary to enact the required legislation. I no longer hold to this view.
>
> So now my position has changed: in framing public policy we should not shy away from an explicit discussion of the specific issues of race and poverty; on the contrary, we should highlight them in our attempt to convince the nation that these problems should be seriously confronted and that there is an urgent need to address them. The issues of race and poverty should be framed in such a way that not only is a sense of fairness and justice to combat inequality generated, but also people are made aware that our country would be better off if these problems were seriously addressed and eradicated.[3]

Any new president would be wise to follow suit. One size does not fit all; one solution cannot possibly apply to all cases.

Finally, the president must resist the temptation of the heroic explicit by not heedlessly and incautiously attacking perceived black moral deficiencies and harmful cultural habits, and forgo whatever short-term political benefit may derive from embracing the noble implicit and thereby failing to speak honestly about, and grapple with, racial transgressions in the white mainstream. The president must offer meaningful rhetoric that acknowledges and challenges white privilege while also rejecting the notion of white innocence and ignorance about the vast reaches of racial injustice in our society—especially police brutality and the relentless death of unarmed black and brown people at the hands of white police.

The most effective way to accomplish this in the near future would be to explicitly address the Black Lives Matter movement and some of the most salient underlying causes for its existence: flawed racial practices in law enforcement; the continuing racial inequality that mocks both true democracy and racial justice; the failure to wrestle with the interlocking forces of racial, gender, class, and sexual oppression; and the persistent racial animus that flares with alarming violence as it did against Trayvon Martin and in the church in Charleston. An executive order in support of the recommendations of the President's Task Force on 21st Century Policing, submitted in 2015—coupled with a national address in the first months of the term underscoring the need for vigilance in defending the rights of black and brown American citizens in the face of dispiriting assaults and deaths—could powerfully move the nation forward.

Any first-year president is destined to face grave and difficult racial problems. But if the president is willing to directly confront them through enlightened public policy, and is willing to offer fresh thinking about how the social forces that blight the American scene are interrelated and vividly intersect, we have the best chance of making progress on race, which remains the most damning and enduring problem we face as a nation.

NOTES

1. Michael Eric Dyson, *The Black Presidency: Barack Obama and the Politics of Race in America* (Boston: Houghton Mifflin Harcourt, 2016), 155.

2. Hillary Clinton, "Remarks to U.S. Mayors on Charleston Massacre and Systemic Racism in America," San Francisco, June 20, 2015.

3. William J. Wilson, *More Than Just Race: Being Black and Poor in the Inner City* (New York: Norton, 2010), 141.

RACIAL PIONEER?
New Presidents and Racial Dialogue

DOUGLAS A. BLACKMON

American presidents historically have had limited power over the policies that affect race and discrimination, and rarely have they used their direct influence in ways that were helpful to African Americans. For nearly two hundred years, presidents made domestic stability for the majority white population a far higher priority than ensuring civil rights or equal opportunity for nonwhites.

But presidents also have a long history of employing moral persuasion when they had no formal power over crucial issues—especially in times of crisis. And in modern times, presidents have been able to dramatically—and in some cases swiftly—help the American people constructively reimagine and reshape deeply entrenched attitudes in areas such as the rights of women, minorities, gays, and others.

In order to be "president for all Americans," the president must establish four critically important symbolic messages:

- ▸ That he or she understands how past economic "rising tides" that left behind millions of working-class whites also injured even higher percentages of African Americans.
- ▸ That he or she acknowledges the unique economic and social barriers that African Americans and other minority groups have faced, including misconduct by the police, and that a message of restoring the "greatness" of the past reads to black citizens like a return to times of deep discrimination.
- ▸ That he or she unequivocally renounces all organizations or individuals that advocate any belief in the superiority of one ethnicity over another.
- ▸ That he or she recognizes that resolving generations of racial discord is a necessity for unlocking the full talents of the American people, rather than a favor done for African Americans.

Slavery and the extended racial divisions it spawned are a vein of cruelty and immorality inextricably embedded in the bedrock of American history. George Mason—one of the principal architects of the Bill of Rights—correctly identified slavery as a "slow poison . . . daily contaminating the minds and morals of our people."[1] The challenge posed to presidents by that poisoned history has evolved through three great eras. First came chattel slavery from the colonial period to the Civil War; then the century of legally mandated segregation that followed; and, most briefly, the modern era in which the civil rights of all races are acknowledged in the law but ongoing discrimination and vestiges of past conduct still deform American society.

There were, of course, certain presidents remembered heroically for bold action on race: Abraham Lincoln most of all, for declaring an end to antebellum slavery and holding the nation together through the Civil War; Franklin D. Roosevelt for opening federal jobs to African Americans in the 1940s; John F. Kennedy for endorsing legislation to end Jim Crow segregation in 1963; and Lyndon B. Johnson for fulfilling Kennedy's vision and then extending to African Americans rights and assistance far greater than Kennedy could have imagined.

But during most of American history, it was astonishingly rare for presidents to take any action related to race, in the first years of their terms or any other. When presidents did act, it was overwhelmingly bad for African Americans or other minorities.

This is for a simple reason: one-third of American presidents served during the era of antebellum slavery, during which eight chief executives personally owned slaves, including George Washington, Thomas Jefferson, James Madison, James Monroe, and Andrew Jackson. Although Jefferson and others at times expressed reservations about the morality of slavery, the early presidents all accepted that their only legitimate role in relation to race was extraordinarily narrow. Until the late 1850s, there were no "issues" related to race beyond the question of whether or not slavery would expand into new territories. Furthermore, almost every president viewed slavery less as a question of morality or a test of American principles than of whether even to debate slavery threatened the unity and stability of the still-young nation. Because slavery was critical to a national economy hugely reliant on agriculture—and cotton production in particular—to challenge slavery was to challenge the preservation of the nation. By that harsh logic, a patriot was compelled to accept the institution of slavery as an ethical necessity to protect the United States.

In 1837, for example, President Martin Van Buren used his inaugural address to endorse a policy adopted by his predecessor, Andrew Jackson, that banned anti-slavery literature from delivery through the U.S. postal service and attempted to suppress most other abolitionist activity. Those who sought to preserve slavery were, Van Buren argued, like the founding fathers, "humane, patriotic, expedient, honorable, and just," while those who pushed to limit or end slavery were the "wicked."[2]

In the century after the Civil War, most presidents failed to preserve the hard-won rights of former slaves. A cynical agreement to settle the disputed presidential election of 1876 awarded the White House to Republican Rutherford B. Hayes in return for ending Reconstruction in the South by removing Union troops. Hayes's first year began decades of the federal government turning a blind eye as whites in the former Confederate states systematically reasserted their political and economic subjugation of African Americans.

This failure of national will and presidential leadership ushered in another eighty years of excruciating dispossession in which huge numbers of African Americans remained in a state of "neoslavery." Forced labor as court-ordered punishment for sometimes minor crimes became as central to the resurrection of the cotton economy as antebellum slavery had been a generation earlier.

In the first years of the twentieth century, President Woodrow Wilson allowed Jim Crow segregation practices to be adopted by the federal government, dramatically reducing the number of African American appointees to federal offices; he also did virtually nothing to blunt the wave of lynchings and civil terror that followed the efforts of black military men to vote or assert economic independence after returning home from World War I. Nearly two decades before his election in 1912, Wilson had written that the resubjugation of blacks after the Civil War was "the natural, inevitable ascendancy of the whites."[3] He never retreated from such views.

The Democratic Party already was openly the party of white supremacy, but the Republican Party—which had once proudly claimed its mantle as "the party of Lincoln and of emancipation"—also was turning its back on African Americans. In his inaugural address in 1909, Republican President William Howard Taft applauded how whites in the South had successfully engineered new voting restrictions to prevent almost all blacks from voting—thwarting the "danger of . . . an ignorant electorate."[4]

In the 1930s, before Roosevelt opened federal jobs to African Americans, he brokered passage of his New Deal programs partly with promises to southern senators that the programs would never challenge segregation. After World War II— as newly invented farm equipment and chemicals began to eliminate the need to employ millions of black laborers in the fields of the South—the continued oppression of African Americans slowly became less necessary to the preservation of the Union. That allowed for the first time since the Emancipation Proclamation the possibility of presidential actions that might meaningfully benefit black citizens.

In the early 1960s, not long after President Dwight D. Eisenhower sent troops to enforce school integration in Little Rock, Arkansas, Kennedy ordered federal troops to Mississippi to enforce the court-ordered desegregation of a state university. Moved by the terrible violence being unleashed on civil rights workers in the South in 1963, Kennedy gave a national address promising a new law to end racial segregation and guarantee the economic and political rights of African Americans.

Before the Civil Rights Act was passed, however, Kennedy was assassinated. His successor, Lyndon B. Johnson, once again demonstrated the power of moving swiftly and against expectations. In stark contrast to his past profile as a vulgar Texan from a state with a long history of extreme racial oppression, Johnson demanded swift action on Kennedy's civil rights bill and forged an unorthodox coalition of northern Democrats and moderate Republicans to pass it. Despite his recognition that enacting the law would likely sever from his party "the South for a generation," as he reportedly told an aide, Johnson signed the Civil Rights Act on July 2, 1964—the signature achievement of his first year in office.

By moving quickly in the earliest days of his presidency, and leveraging the grief of American voters, Johnson achieved a legislative victory long thought impossible, and one with vast tangible benefits for African Americans. The Civil Rights Act would become one of the most consequential laws in American history.

Kennedy and Johnson also surmounted a president's limited powers to affect race by using the prestige and moral authority of the White House to engage in day-to-day developments related to the civil rights movement, as well as to coerce and cajole local officials into reforming their own behavior. Both men directly called southern governors and other officials to demand protection for civil rights activists.

In August 1965, for example, Johnson instructed aides to become involved when local funeral homes in Alabama refused to transport the body of slain civil rights activist Jonathan Daniels, a young white priest from New Hampshire who had been gunned down by an Alabama deputy sheriff.

Seven presidents, beginning with Richard Nixon, held the White House during the half-century after the final dismantling of legally mandated segregation. The first four—Nixon, Gerald Ford, Jimmy Carter, and Ronald Reagan—governed in an era in which discussions of race were dominated by debate over legislation directly derived from the civil rights movement and its constitutional reinterpretations, notably funding for private schools, the use of federal powers to intervene in segregated neighborhoods, and whether Dr. Martin Luther King, Jr., should be honored with a national holiday.

Since the administration of George H. W. Bush began in 1989, however, presidents have faced an increasingly elusive challenge in guiding the nation on race. Opposing overtly discriminatory laws, or combating self-proclaimed hate groups, has been replaced by debates over measuring economic progress, the sources of social ills, and, most explosively, interactions between police officers and African American citizens. Meanwhile, Supreme Court rulings have undercut the once-certain symbolic reauthorizations of vital federal civil and voting rights statutes.

Despite a generally more tolerant atmosphere toward race, presidents have continued to be reticent about embarking on dramatic initiatives early in their terms. One result is that, more often than not, presidential engagement has come, as so often in history, only at the height of civil crisis.

In 1992, Bush became the first modern president to confront the power of citizens and the media recording what appeared to be police misconduct toward a citizen, when grainy video of four Los Angeles police officers beating motorist Rodney King triggered days of massive riots. Bush condemned the actions of police and urged calm on the part of citizens, but he was unable to stem a tide of violence that spread to Atlanta and other cities.

His successor, President Bill Clinton, struggled to address outrage over New York police mistreatment of Haitian immigrant Abner Louima. Clinton's national Advisory Panel on Race was widely viewed as remote and ineffective. George W. Bush attempted to shift discussion about the struggles of minorities away from a focus on past discrimination and toward expanded opportunity and improved public schools. But his signature No Child Left Behind education initiative came to be seen as widely ineffective, especially for poor and minority children.

President Barack Obama, as the first African American to occupy the White House, entered office with an explicit promise to heal the divisions within American society. Yet his tenure was characterized by a spike in racial tensions and multiple episodes of questionable police conduct followed by civil disturbances.

Both Clinton and Obama—arguably the two modern presidents most popular among African Americans—were applauded for resonant, sweeping oratory about race, but each struggled to find genuine traction or influence after racially tinged events that galvanized the public. Their calls for a "national dialogue on race" never moved beyond rhetoric. Both the Clinton and Obama presidencies ultimately left many black citizens with a deep sense of unfulfilled promise.

Obama's successors have the chance to learn from their predecessors by setting a new and unexpected civil rights agenda, and moving quickly and confidently to help their followers see the shared interests of all who have been "left behind" by the nation's troubling racial history. It could be a president's most historic achievement.

NOTES

1. Robert A. Rutland, ed., *The Papers of George Mason* (Chapel Hill: University of North Carolina Press, 1970), 173.

2. Martin Van Buren, "Inaugural Address," Washington, D.C., March 4, 1837.

3. Ronald Pestritto, *Woodrow Wilson and the Roots of Modern Liberalism* (New York: Rowman and Littlefield), 45.

4. William Taft, "Inaugural Address," Washington, D.C., March 4, 1909.

VI ★ MANAGING THE EXECUTIVE

THOMAS JEFFERSON AND THE PEACEFUL TRANSFER OF POWER

ALAN TAYLOR

As the first American president to wrest power from an opposing party, Thomas Jefferson had to balance the demands of his fellow Republicans for radical change against the risk that extreme measures would revive the defeated Federalists. In particular, Jefferson had to decide whether to preserve or abolish new national institutions created by the Federalist administrations of George Washington and John Adams. By preserving the Bank of the United States, honoring (but paying down) the national debt, and preserving (while shrinking) the navy and army, Jefferson conciliated moderate Federalists. By sharing credit with congressional leaders for successful legislation, Jefferson sustained his Republican coalition despite formidable factional tensions. By these two balancing acts, Jefferson consolidated his popularity through his first term, setting an example that any subsequent administration could profitably emulate.

Americans celebrate Jefferson's election to the presidency in 1801 for setting the great precedent of the peaceful transfer of power between rival political parties. That selective memory, however, slights the nation's peril and constitutional crisis in early 1801, when the incumbent Federalists risked plunging the nation into civil war rather than surrender power to a despised opponent. Although Jefferson did win the presidency, the electoral crisis of 1801 informed his first year in office, when he sought to unite a bitterly divided nation while still altering federal policies to advance the philosophy of his own party. On the one hand, Jefferson offered soothing rhetoric and avoided a rapid and complete purge of federal officeholders. On the other hand, he pushed Congress to reduce taxes, bolster civil liberties, and liberalize the naturalization of immigrants as citizens. Enhancing his popularity, Jefferson ruined the Federalist opposition, which rapidly declined into futility in national politics. By pursuing popularity as the font of republican power, Jefferson gained leverage with Congress.

ELECTORAL CRISIS

In the election returns of late 1800, Jefferson and his fellow Republican candidate, Aaron Burr of New York, secured most of the electoral votes: seventy-three versus sixty-five and sixty-four respectively for the Federalists John Adams and Charles Cotesworth Pinckney. But Republican Party discipline proved too good, for every one of its electors cast a vote for Jefferson and a second for Burr, leaving the two candidates tied in the Electoral College returns. Under the original terms of the Constitution, the electors could not distinguish between votes for president and vice president. The Constitution also stipulated that, in the absence of a majority in the Electoral College, the House of Representatives would choose the president. But it would vote by state delegation with each state casting one vote, which meant that Jefferson needed to capture at least nine of the sixteen delegations. In early 1801, Republicans controlled eight delegations, the Federalists six, and two states were evenly split.

In the lame-duck Congress, the Federalists favored Burr, a clever opportunist who seemed open to making a deal. "It is much safer to trust a knave than a fool," a Federalist reasoned to explain his preference for Burr over Jefferson.[1]

The Federalists hoped to entice the northern Republicans to defect from Jefferson and provide the winning margin to the New Yorker. If not, the Federalists sought to sustain a prolonged deadlock until inauguration day in March, when, in the absence of an elected president, they might govern through a president pro tempore chosen by the Senate.

Through six days and thirty-five votes, the House remained deadlocked at the end of Monday, February 16. To keep one side from exploiting any temporary absence of the other, the congressmen hunkered down in greatcoats on cots and had meals brought in. The Republicans were resolved to never yield.

During the bitter suspense, Federalists and Republicans muttered about preparing for civil war. A Pennsylvania Republican, John Beckley, warned that the day that the Federalists denied the presidency to Jefferson would be "the first day of revolution and Civil War."[2] The Republican governors of Virginia and Pennsylvania prepared to mobilize state militiamen to put Jefferson in office. If denied the presidency, Republicans also threatened to stage a constitutional coup by convening their own convention to rewrite the Constitution along Republican lines.

As the crisis dragged on, Federalists grew more uneasy. As conservative nationalists, they dreaded disabling the federal government. Jefferson noted that they would "prefer yielding to the wishes of the people rather than have no government."[3] On Tuesday, February 17, a moderate Federalist, James Bayard, broke the deadlock in favor of Jefferson by abstaining. Bayard believed that he had Jefferson's commitment to preserve the Federalist system of public finance, which included a national bank and a fully funded national debt. Bayard added that "it was admitted on all hands that we must risk the Constitution and a civil war or take Mr. Jefferson."[4] As Delaware's only congressman, Bayard could swing an entire state, and his example inspired the Vermont and Maryland Federalists to give up the fight by also abstaining, shifting their states into Jefferson's camp, giving him ten delegations. Burr had to settle for the vice presidency and Jefferson's bitter distrust. A relieved congressman noted that, had the Federalists denied the presidency to Jefferson, "What other result would follow but civil war?" In that event, "his head would not have remained on his shoulders for twenty-four hours afterward."[5]

Sobered by the constitutional crisis over the election, Republicans in the new Congress crafted the Twelfth Amendment. Ratified by the states in 1804 in time for the next presidential election, the amendment obliged each member of the Electoral College to cast one vote for president and the other for vice president. Thereafter, the president and vice president would almost certainly belong to the same party. The framers of the Constitution had sought to preclude partisan divisions, but the Twelfth Amendment assumed their inevitability. Jefferson still hoped, however, "to obliterate the traces of party & consolidate the nation, if it can be done without abandonment of principle."[6] He later explained that a president's primary duty was "to unite in himself the confidence of the whole people . . . and point them in a single direction, as if all constituted but one body and one mind."[7]

Jefferson overstated the possibility of uniting diverse Americans in one big consensus, but he understood that a president's power depends on sustaining popularity. He rejected the approach of his Federalist predecessors, Washington and Adams, who wanted the presidency to temper and control the popular impulses manifest in Congress. Rather than react against and restrain congressional initiatives, as Washington and Adams had done, Jefferson sought to rally public opinion as public capital and then to lead and goad Congress toward passing his program.

In his private correspondence, Jefferson indulged in provocative statements drawn from his political philosophy, but in office his pursuit of popular consensus compelled a careful attention to pragmatism. Shortly after taking office, he assured a political ally, "No more good must be attempted than the nation can bear."[8] During his first term as president, Jefferson displayed an uncanny sense of how much good the public could abide.

DISTINCTIVE STYLE

In public statements, Jefferson struck a conciliatory tone, famously declaring in his first inaugural address, "We are all Republicans—we are all Federalists."[9] But Jefferson preached moderation as the means to ruin the Federalist Party forever. With soothing rhetoric, he wooed moderate voters to abandon their Federalist leaders, whom he privately considered as only "entitled to be protected & taken care of as other insane persons are."[10] He vowed "by the establishment of Republican principles" to "sink Federalism into an abyss from which there shall be no resurrection for it." Seeking "to render us again one people, acting as one nation," Jefferson sought to build a national consensus on his terms.[11]

To the dismay of more radical Republicans, Jefferson balked at purging all Federalists from federal office, cultivating instead a public image of moderation meant to lure soft Federalists into his growing majority. Regarding only the hardliners as "incurables," he sought "to keep their flock from returning to them."[12] He tended to displace more Federalists from the army, where he feared their dominance over the officer corps. During the late 1790s, Federalist army officers had deployed troops to terrify Republican critics in Pennsylvania, and their overall commander, Alexander Hamilton, had proposed invading Virginia to intimidate Jefferson's supporters. Fortunately President Adams had rejected that provocative advice. Always uneasy with a professional military as a threat to popular government, Jefferson especially sought reassurance after the close brush with civil war in early 1801. He replaced many Federalist officers and wooed moderates to embrace his new order in politics.

Jefferson also sacked those officials appointed by Adams in early 1801, after news of Jefferson's election but before his inauguration. Denouncing such "midnight appointments," Jefferson supplanted those who held office by the president's discretion, but he could not replace the life-term judicial appointees, including the new chief justice, John Marshall. To counteract the lingering Federalist predominance in the judiciary, Jefferson appointed new federal marshals and district attorneys "as a shield to the Republican part of our fellow citizens."[13]

Jefferson shrewdly deployed political symbols and public performance to woo popularity. To show his dependence on common voters, he eliminated the quasi-regal panoply of power favored by the Federalists. He abandoned the grand public receptions, known as "levees," held weekly by Washington and Adams. Jefferson sold the presidential coaches with their silver harnesses, and he refused to wear a sword on ceremonial occasions, breaking with Federalist precedents. Rather than exchange formal bows, as Federalist presidents did, Jefferson offered the familiarity of shaking hands to almost everyone he met. For exercise, he daily walked or rode through the muddy streets of Washington, unattended even by a servant. Shabby gentility became his fashion statement. A Federalist complained, "Jefferson is the supreme director of measures—he has no levee days—observes no ceremony—often sees company in an undress, sometimes with his slippers on—always accessible to, and very familiar with, the sovereign people."[14] A British diplomat complained that Jefferson pandered to "the low passions of a mere newspaper-taught rabble."[15] Ever since, Americans have accepted government by wealthy men so long as they pretend to have common manners.

More pessimistic about human nature and popular support, Federalists had sought a style meant to impress the common people with the majesty of their leaders. The more optimistic Jefferson cleverly understood that true power derived from the popularity that came from performing his subservience to the electorate. Even as he sought to weaken the federal government relative to the states, he meant to strengthen the executive within that government, for he understood his position as a tribune for the common people. While reserving domestic issues to the states, he jealously guarded federal supremacy, and particularly executive power, in foreign policy. "The conduct of foreign affairs is executive altogether," he had declared as secretary of state in the early 1790s.[16]

As president, Jefferson meant to guide his "official family," his small staff and the cabinet officers, rather than leave them alone to work with Congress, as his Federalist predecessors usually had done. By consulting them early and often, Jefferson cultivated collegiality and taught the department heads to adhere to the consensus that he elicited from their meetings. Jefferson also vetted all substantive communications from the department heads in order to master the information and intervene as needed. In managing his cabinet, Jefferson benefited from his close friendship with James Madison, who occupied the key position as secretary of state. Their close and harmonious relationship set a tone emulated by the other department heads. The administration was also fortunate to have Albert Gallatin of Pennsylvania as secretary of the treasury, for he nearly matched Hamilton's financial acumen while offering superior political wisdom.

Popularity gave Jefferson leverage with congressmen to push his agenda behind the scenes. Unlike the stiff and aloof Washington and Adams, Jefferson carefully cultivated congressional leaders through a stage-managed cycle of dinner parties at the White House. To promote equality and informality, he substituted round tables for the Executive Mansion's rectangular ones. Smaller gatherings of about a dozen highlighted Jefferson's seductive personal qualities for soothing disagreement and cultivating support. He had mastered a genial but polite affability that evaded contention while drawing on his immense intellectual versatility for clever conversation. He usually entertained Republicans and Federalists separately to avoid disagreement. And he served excellent food and wine. Jefferson also benefited from being the biggest fish in the small pond of Washington sociability—in marked contrast to President Washington's administration, which had to adapt to the high society of its more cosmopolitan temporary capitals, New York and Philadelphia.

Although Jefferson could charm congressmen, he could not command them. He later rued, "A forty years' experience of popular assemblies has taught me, that you must give them time for every step you take. If too hard pushed, they balk, and the machine retrogrades."[17] Jefferson and his cabinet took pains to show deference to Congress as the voice of the people. To get things done, Jefferson shrewdly gave credit to Congress for the success of his policies.

POPULAR POLICIES

While cultivating an aura of moderation, Jefferson pursued policies meant to bolster popular sovereignty by dismantling the elitism of his Federalist predecessors. Jefferson argued that federal officials should heed public opinion and tolerate public criticism. In 1798, the Federalists had imposed a Sedition Act to criminalize public criticism of federal office holders. They also adopted Alien Acts meant to discourage immigration, particularly from Ireland. On the eve of Jefferson's inauguration, Congress allowed the Sedition Act to expire, and he quickly pardoned those convicted under that law. To reward their immigrant supporters, Republicans in Congress reduced the period of naturalization to five years from the punitive fourteen years mandated by the Federalists in 1798.

The victorious Republicans halted the Federalist drive to build a powerful national government. Instead, they favored a decentralized union that entrusted to the states all responsibilities except foreign affairs, customs collection, a barebones military, and the postal service. Jefferson's inaugural address promised a "wise and frugal" government that would "restrain men from injuring one another" and then "leave them otherwise free to regulate their own pursuits."[18] Jefferson dreaded a peacetime military establishment because its great "expenses and the eternal wars in which it will implicate us, [will] grind us with public burthens, & sink us under them."[19] By cutting the army and navy, Republicans could abolish the unpopular excise and land taxes levied by the Federalists. Jefferson also tried to pay down the national debt that the great Federalist financier, Hamilton, had designed for perpetuity. During their twelve years in power, the Federalists had increased that debt from $76 million to $83 million; during his eight years as president, Jefferson reduced it to $57 million.

Jefferson had political debts to pay in the West, where he swept the electoral votes of Kentucky and Tennessee and Republicans secured every congressional seat. A frustrated Federalist, Roger Griswold, noted the symbolism in Jefferson's rearrangement of the Executive Mansion: "When Mr. Adams was President, the door of the president's House opened to the East. Mr. Jefferson has closed that door and opened a new door to the West."[20] Where Federalists had treated settlers as "white savages" who needed elite mentors, Republicans celebrated them as industrious farmers who redeemed a wilderness through hard work. Jefferson's administration promoted retail sales of federal land to common settlers by reducing the minimum tract to 160 acres, offering a credit of four years, and opening three new land offices in the West.

Jefferson promoted an "Empire of Liberty," which favored white men at the expense of Indians and blacks. A democratic but racially defined society would expand relentlessly westward, creating thousands of new farms to sustain relative equality among white men. Jefferson recognized that the strength of a diffuse nation lay in helping, rather than hindering, ambitious settlers. Jefferson's empire depended on consent from the majority, which he imagined as white men bearing an irresistible republican culture featuring the common law, juries, civil liberties, and elections. Affection rather than force would tether westerners to the union.

In 1804, voters rewarded Jefferson's moderate, public tone and his populist policies. He won reelection in a landslide, with George Clinton of New York as his running mate, replacing Burr. Jefferson and Clinton captured 162 of the 176 electoral votes and carried every state except Connecticut and Delaware. Republicans also secured super-majorities in the House, 116 Republicans to just 25 Federalists, and the Senate, 27 to 7. Never again would Federalists recover the presidency or a majority in either house of Congress. But the Republican hegemony bore some bitter fruit. No longer held together by fear of the Federalists, Republican congressmen could indulge in factional divisions over patronage and policies, weakening the cohesion that Jefferson had so painstakingly developed during his first term.

What lessons does Jefferson's first presidential year offer for future presidents more than two hundred years later? Thanks to his shrewd precedents, reinforced by the practice of his successors, new presidents will seek sustained popularity and carefully cultivate support in Congress through sociability. If truly deft, these presidents will cling to an aura of moderation while securing legislation to deliver on their political philosophy.

NOTES

1. Sara Dunn, *Jefferson's Second Revolution: The Election Crisis of 1800 and the Triumph of Republicanism* (Boston: Houghton Mifflin Harcourt, 2004), 200.

2. James Roger Sharp, *American Politics in the Early Republic: The New Nation in Crisis* (New Haven, Conn.: Yale University Press, 1993), 268.

3. Edward J. Larson, *A Magnificent Catastrophe: The Tumultuous Election of 1800, America's First Presidential Campaign* (New York: Free Press, 2007), 246.

4. Robert Goodloe Harper, *Papers of James A. Bayard, 1796–1815* (London: Bibliolife, 2013), 127.

5. Bruce A. Ackerman, *The Failure of the Founding Fathers: Jefferson, Marshall, and the Rise of Presidential Democracy* (Cambridge, Mass.: Harvard University Press, 2005), 204.

6. Dunn, *Jefferson's Second Revolution*, 223.

7. Thomas Jefferson, *The Writings of Thomas Jefferson*, ed. H. W. Washington (Cambridge: Cambridge University Press, 2011), 5:498.

8. Thomas Jefferson, *The Jefferson Cyclopedia*, ed. John P. Foley (New York: Funk and Wagnalls, 1900), 741.

9. Thomas Jefferson, "First Inaugural Address," Washington, D.C., March 4, 1801, https://jeffersonpapers.princeton.edu/selected-documents/first-inaugural-address-0.

10. Jon Meacham, *Thomas Jefferson: The Art of Power* (New York: Random House, 2012), 355.

11. Thomas Jefferson, *The Writings of Thomas Jefferson: 1801–1806*, ed. Paul Lancaster Ford (New York: G. P. Putnam's Sons, 1897), 78, 176.

12. Thomas Jefferson, *Memoirs, Correspondence, and Miscellanies from the Papers of Thomas Jefferson*, ed. Thomas Jefferson Randolph (Charlottesville, Va.: F. Carr, 1829), 405.

13. James Wilford Garner, Henry Cabot Lodge, and John Bach McMaster, *The United States* (New York: P. F. Collier and Sons, 1907), 1:390.

14. Kevin J. Hayes, ed., *Jefferson in His Own Time* (Iowa City: University of Iowa Press, 2012), xxv.

15. Robert Rutland, *The Democrats: From Jefferson to Clinton* (Columbia: University of Missouri Press, 1995), 18.

16. National Archives, "To George Washington from Thomas Jefferson, 24 April 1790," *Founders Online*, https://founders.archives.gov/documents/Washington/05-05-02-0225.

17. Thomas Jefferson, *The Jefferson Cyclopedia*, edited by John P. Foley (New York: Funk & Wagnalls Company, 1900), 900.

18. Joseph Nimmo, *Regulation of Commerce Among the States: The Governmental Policy of Thomas Jefferson* (Washington, DC: Rufus H. Darby Printing Company, 1906), 7.

19. Noble E. Cunningham, ed., *The Inaugural Addresses of President Thomas Jefferson, 1801 and 1805* (Columbia, MO: University of Missouri Press, 2001), 3.

20. Stephen H. Browne, *Jefferson's Call for Nationhood: The First Inaugural Address* (College Station, TX: Texas A&M University Press, 2003), 42.

ABRAHAM LINCOLN'S WORST FIRST YEAR

GARY W. GALLAGHER

Abraham Lincoln experienced a unique initial year in the presidency. No other incoming president has faced a comparable challenge. Yet there are broad parallels between his first year as president and the political situation prevailing in the early twenty-first century. In both instances, national party structures suffered internal fracturing, although it remains to be seen whether the experience of either current major party matches the Democratic Party's collapse in 1860–61.

A second parallel lies in the widespread unwillingness to engage in anything approximating bipartisanship, with people all along the political spectrum expecting the worst from their opponents, routinely accusing them of lying, and predicting dire consequences should an election go badly. Finally, the two eras underscore the need to bring different voices to bear on major national problems—in Lincoln's case, reaching out to Democrats and filling his cabinet with leading figures who held divergent opinions about issues such as emancipation but could be trusted to cooperate in the overriding task of saving the Union.

Lincoln's actions illuminate the importance of dealing with the most critical issue or problem and the difficulty of forging policy in the face of opponents loath to trust presidential motives or statements.

When Lincoln delivered his first inaugural address on March 4, 1861, seven states already had left the Union and established the Confederacy. The future of eight other slaveholding states remained uncertain, a dangerous situation at Fort Sumter in Charleston Harbor simmered, and political divisions within the loyal populace remained deep. Lincoln and members of his party often worked in concert, but sometimes their differences about how best to define the war's goals, especially pertaining to emancipation, placed them at odds. A large Democratic opposition criticized the president's use of executive power to suppress the rebellion and distrusted his disavowal of any intention to strike at slavery where it existed under the protection of the Constitution.

The key to understanding Lincoln's first year is his unwavering focus on restoring the Union. His single-minded pursuit of this goal raised a number of questions: Could Lincoln prevent more states from seceding? Could he unite Republicans and Democrats, including residents of loyal slaveholding states, in a military effort to bring the Deep South back into the national fold? Could he negotiate a course relating to emancipation that would satisfy both the radical and more conservative wings of the Republican Party, while at the same time not alienating Democrats and residents of the border states? And would success in all these arenas result in a restored Union?

Although the nineteenth-century meaning of "Union" has disappeared from our national historical memory, Lincoln knew that most of his fellow citizens cherished what they considered an exceptional government bequeathed by the founders—a democratic republic that featured a popular voice in political decisions and the chance to rise economically. Alone among the nations of the Western world, the United States—the Union—offered an almost universal white male franchise and allowed singular social and economic mobility. The new president, himself an example of how common men could rise in the American Union, identified what most people considered the twin pillars of American exceptionalism. What lay at stake in the war, he explained in December 1861, were "the first principle of popular government—the rights of the people," and the protection of a system that blocked "any such thing as a free man being fixed for life in the condition of a hired laborer."[1]

Lincoln's first inaugural address underscored the centrality of Union. It targeted different groups with varied appeals to their allegiance to the republic. "The Union of these States is perpetual," the president insisted, much older than the Constitution and made more perfect by the work of the Philadelphia convention of 1787. "Plainly, the central idea of secession, is the essence of anarchy," Lincoln proclaimed, a violation of the sovereignty of a free people in a nation dependent on acquiescence to majority rule. As a former Whig who remembered when that party had robust northern and southern wings, Lincoln mistakenly believed large numbers of white southerners possessed strong unionist sentiments. He reached out to this supposed pro-Union constituency, as well as to northern Democrats, promising that he had "no purpose, directly or indirectly, to interfere with the institution of slavery in the States where it exists" and affirming as well that he would uphold constitutional provisions regarding fugitive slaves—parts of his address that left abolitionists and some radicals within his own party deeply unhappy. Lincoln also sought to reassure northern unionists with a pledge "to hold, occupy, and possess the property, and places belonging to the government, and to collect the duties and imposts."[2]

Toward the end of his address, Lincoln emphasized slavery's role in the political fracturing of the nation, sought to separate secessionists from unionists in the South, and engaged listeners with an eloquent plea for Union. "One section of our country believes slavery is *right*, and ought to be extended," he observed, "while the other believes it is *wrong*, and ought not to be extended. This is the only substantial dispute." Culpability for destroying the Union and possibly bringing on armed conflict lay entirely with secessionists. "In *your* hands, my dissatisfied fellow-countrymen," stated the president clearly, "and not in *mine*, is the momentous issue of civil war. . . . You can have no conflict, without being yourselves the aggressors." Then he offered a lyrical tribute to Union that tugged at the people's shared memories of the revolutionary generation's sacrifice: "The mystic chords of memory, stretching from every battle-field, and patriot grave, to every living heart and hearthstone, all over this broad land, will yet swell the chorus of the Union, when again touched, as surely they will be, by the better angels of our nature."[3]

Lincoln continued to stress Union throughout his initial year in office. When efforts to manage the volatile standoff at Fort Sumter failed in mid-April, he used George Washington's precedent during the Whiskey Rebellion in 1794 to call forth 75,000 militiamen to crush the Confederate rebellion. "I appeal to all loyal citizens to favor, facilitate and aid this effort," he wrote, "to maintain the honor, the integrity, and the existence of our National Union, and the perpetuation of popular government."[4] Four states of the Upper South reacted to Lincoln's call for volunteers by joining the breakaway slaveholding republic, prompting the president to comment that in Virginia, Tennessee, North Carolina, and Arkansas, "the Union sentiment was nearly repressed, and silenced."[5] This evaluation overlooked the solid majorities in all these states that clearly supported secession rather than participation in a military effort to coerce the Deep South back into the Union.

With eleven states gone, Lincoln allocated a great deal of energy to keeping Kentucky, Maryland, and Missouri—three of the four remaining loyal slaveholding states—in the Union, as well as to framing mushrooming demands for men and materiel in such a way as to keep northern Democrats on board with the war effort. In both endeavors, he consistently highlighted the importance of Union, as well as the necessity of taking an array of sometimes controversial actions to save it.

On April 15, 1861, in the same message that called out the militia, Lincoln set July 4 as the date for the 37th Congress to meet in special session. The cumbersome election calendar occasioned this delay. Several states held congressional elections in the spring of odd-numbered years, which meant that all members would not be in place until June. Once the House and Senate convened, the president sent a message discussing his actions since taking office. He had instituted a naval blockade, commenced the enrollment of thousands of three-year federal volunteers, doubled the size of the regular army and navy, and authorized General in Chief Winfield Scott to suspend the writ of habeas corpus in parts of Maryland and elsewhere. All of these presidential decisions prompted complaints, principally from Democrats but to a lesser degree from conservative Republicans, about excessive executive authority. Lincoln defended his actions as necessary and legal. Creation of the Confederacy had placed "an imperative duty upon the incoming Executive, to prevent, if possible, the consummation of such an attempt to destroy the Federal Union." By firing on the federal garrison at Fort Sumter on April 12, averred the president, the rebels had "forced upon the country, the distinct issue: 'Immediate dissolution, or blood.'"[6]

Lincoln understood that Republicans could not restore the Union without help from the roughly 45 percent of the loyal citizenry who considered themselves

Democrats. He knew as well that only a war in the name of Union could galvanize Republicans and Democrats to fill the ranks of large national armies, pay an array of federal taxes, and accept other burdens related to the conflict. To promote a unified war effort, Lincoln walked a delicate line regarding emancipation. Most Democrats expressed vociferous opposition to the idea of fighting a war to end slavery, and a large majority of unionists in the four loyal slaveholding states especially balked at risking white lives to achieve black freedom. Within the Republican Party, some conservatives echoed Democrats while members of the radical wing pushed early and often to add emancipation to Union as a goal for the war effort. Tensions between the president and Democrats and between him and the radicals grew during 1861 and into the first three months of 1862.

Abolitionists and radicals saw the war as a political upheaval that could open the door to ending slavery. Many of them hoped to tie prospects for Union victory to emancipation, declaring the latter necessary to defeat the rebels. They would have preferred a grand moral crusade but understood how few white citizens would embrace such an idea. The longer and bloodier the conflict, they reasoned, the better the chances for emancipation. Radical senator Charles Sumner of Massachusetts made this point in a letter to abolitionist Wendell Phillips after the Union disaster on July 21, 1861, at First Bull Run. "The battle & defeat have done much for the slave," Sumner wrote on August 3, "I told the Presdt that our defeat was the worst event & the best event in our history; the worst, as it was the greatest present calamity & shame—the best, as it made the extinction of Slavery inevitable."[7]

Lincoln knew that such sentiments would outrage those who sought restoration of the Union as quickly and with as little bloodshed as possible. During his first year, almost 750,000 citizen-soldiers donned blue uniforms. News from battlefields such as Bull Run, Wilson's Creek, Ball's Bluff, and Forts Henry and Donelson buffeted Washington and the northern home front (all but the two forts marked Union defeats). Officers such as George B. McClellan, Henry W. Halleck, and Ulysses S. Grant rose in prominence. The attention of the people, and of the president, typically centered on operations conducted by Union forces.

Against that compelling military backdrop, Lincoln wrestled with the question of emancipation. As a private citizen, he would have joined Sumner and Phillips in cheering for slavery's earliest demise. But as president he had to balance competing political interests that came into play as the United States created and supplied armies on an unprecedented scale and dealt with the consequences of battles across a vast strategic landscape. On August 6, 1861, Lincoln reluctantly signed the First Confiscation Act, which freed slaves being directly used to support the Confederate military resistance, but three weeks later he instructed Major General John C. Frémont to rescind an order liberating all slaves belonging to pro-Confederate residents in Missouri. Frémont's action, counseled the president, "will alarm our Southern Union friends, and turn them against us—perhaps ruin our rather fair prospect for Kentucky." The general, Lincoln added, should bring his order into conformity with the more limited reach of the First Confiscation Act.[8]

In his first annual message to Congress on December 3, 1861, Lincoln again sought to reassure all friends of the Union. "The Union must be preserved," he stated, and all "indispensable means must be employed." But he set strict limits, arguing, with emancipation at least partly in mind, "We should not be in haste to determine that radical and extreme measures, which may reach the loyal as well as the disloyal, are indispensable." He did not want the conflict to "degenerate into a violent and remorseless revolutionary struggle," and "therefore, in every case, thought it proper to keep the integrity of the Union prominent as the primary object of the contest on our part, leaving all questions which are not of vital military importance to the more deliberate action of the legislature." If another congressional law relating to confiscating rebels' slaves were to be proposed, concluded Lincoln, "its propriety will be duly considered."[9] A flurry of congressional actions relating to slavery would reach Lincoln's desk during the next several months—ending slavery in the District of Columbia and the federal territories, vastly expanding the reach of the First Confiscation Act with a Second Confiscation Act, and addressing the status of black refugees who reached Union military lines—but none arrived before the first anniversary of his inauguration.

In line with his desire to court Democrats and border-state residents, Lincoln insisted that emancipation in loyal states must follow constitutional guidelines. He sought to persuade the border states to adopt individual plans that would yield gradual emancipation with compensation for owners. Newly liberated blacks, he thought, and perhaps those already free in the northern states, should be urged to colonize, as he put it in his December message to Congress, "at some [foreign] place or places in a climate congenial to them."[10] Lincoln urged Congress to vote money to help compensate owners who lost slaves and to defray the cost of colonization. His support for voluntary colonization, which continued late into the war (he never recommended forced emigration), likely stemmed from an honest belief that African Americans stood little chance of achieving anything approaching true equality in the mid-nineteenth-century United States. But it also represented an attempt to gain support from Democrats and others who detested the idea of integrating large numbers of free black laborers and their families into the nation's social and economic structures. Most black Americans, abolitionists, and many Radical Republicans stridently opposed Lincoln's thinking about colonization, while the border states rebuffed his recommendation that they draw up plans for emancipation.

Lincoln ended his first year in office as an executive who had taken bold actions to combat a vast rebel insurgency. He realized that only a war unequivocally waged to save the Union would inspire widespread support among the loyal citizenry of the United States. Assailed by Democrats on a range of issues, Lincoln also endured sustained criticism from Radical Republicans for his handling of emancipation. On March 6, 1862, two days after the first anniversary of his inauguration, he sent a message to Congress. If rebel intransigence continued, Lincoln remarked, "the war must also continue; and it is impossible to foresee all the incidents, which may attend and all the ruin which may follow."[11] Neither he nor anyone else could imagine what was to come. The massive bloodletting at Shiloh, just one month hence, would recalibrate the scale of military slaughter, after which three years of escalating political upheaval, profound swings in civilian morale, and a stark pivot toward more revolutionary outcomes more than once threatened a permanent sundering of the Union.

NOTES

1. Abraham Lincoln, "Annual Message to Congress," December 3, 1861, in *The Collected Works of Abraham Lincoln,* ed. Roy P. Basler, 9 vols. (New Brunswick, N.J.: Rutgers University Press, 1953–55), 5:51–52 (hereafter Lincoln, *Collected Works*).

2. Abraham Lincoln, "First Inaugural Address," March 4, 1861, in ibid., 4:264–65, 268, 263, 266.

3. Ibid., 4:268–69, 271.

4. Abraham Lincoln, "Proclamation Calling Militia and Convening Congress," April 15, 1861, in ibid., 4:332.

5. Abraham Lincoln, "Message to Congress in Special Session," July 4, 1861, in ibid., 4:427.

6. Ibid., 4:423, 426.

7. Charles Sumner, *The Selected Letters of Charles Sumner,* ed. Beverly Wilson Palmer, 2 vols. (Boston: Northeastern University Press, 1990), 2:74–75.

8. Abraham Lincoln to John C. Frémont. September 2, 1861, in Lincoln, *Collected Works,* 4:506.

9. Abraham Lincoln, "Annual Message to Congress," December 3, 1861, in ibid., 5:49.

10. Ibid., 5:48.

11. Abraham Lincoln, "Message to Congress," March 6, 1862, in ibid., 5:145–46.

WHY PRESIDENTS DON'T RUN THE GOVERNMENT— AND WHY THEY NEED TO

ELAINE C. KAMARCK

To head off failure that can affect not just their time in office but also their permanent legacies, new presidents need to become familiar in their first years with two critical aspects of the government they inherit: what it can and cannot do, and what it does and does not know.

This sounds elementary, but it is not standard procedure. The modern-day presidency is more preoccupied with communications, messaging, and politics, and less with the nuts and bolts of leading an enterprise that is as large and diverse as several Fortune 500 companies put together.

A behind-the-scenes look at the transition from one administration to the next illuminates both the scale of the executive branch—the bureaucracy—and how the political focus takes root. While the rest of the country is digesting election results and slowing down for the holidays, a team from the Government Services Administration is working overtime to make sure that photographs of the outgoing president and vice president are removed and official photographs of the incoming leaders are taken, reproduced, and placed in 8,603 government offices in the United States, approximately 250 embassies and consulates around the world, and every U.S. military installation.

On the morning after Inauguration Day, approximately 2.6 million civilians and 1.5 million military personnel report to their jobs serving the federal government. The claims adjuster at the Social Security office in Rochester, New York; the deputy chief of mission in Tirana, Albania; the forest ranger at Yellowstone National Park in Wyoming; the biologist at the Centers for Disease Control in Atlanta, Georgia; the soldier stationed in Stuttgart, Germany—all of them see the same thing when they arrive: a photograph of their new boss hung prominently on the wall.

Over at the White House, on the morning after the inaugural festivities, a tired president and vice president get to work. New employees surround them, most in military uniform. They open the doors, fly the helicopter, serve in the White House mess, and man the guns that sit on top of the building. The new leaders also receive their first daily visit from a Central Intelligence Agency employee with a briefcase handcuffed to his or her wrist. This contains the President's Daily Brief—a compilation of the most sensitive goings-on collected overtly and covertly from around the world by American spies.

Yet on the morning after the inauguration, the people most likely to talk to the new president are the same people who have been talking to him or her for the past two years: close campaign advisors. They are a tiny comfort zone for presidents coping with their overnight transformation into the boss of several million people they do not know.

A new president is aware, intellectually, that the government is out there, but few presidents actually walk the halls of the vast federal office buildings in Washington, or anywhere else. In fact, given the size and far-flung nature of the federal government, to do so would be almost impossible. Thus, unlike a CEO, the president cannot "walk the shop floor" and get a sense of his or her team. Firsthand experience is replaced with stereotypes. Republican presidents, beginning with Richard Nixon, have assumed that these federal workers did not vote for them and will try to undermine their goal of smaller government. Democratic presidents assume that these people are part of their coalition and will do what they want done. This may be true for the simple yes-no choice that is an election, but it is a gross exaggeration when it comes to the complexity of governing.

The newly elected president is, *ipso facto*, a master of campaigning. But the work of figuring out who all these people in the government really are, what they do, and how to get them to do what you want—that is overwhelming. And no one around a new president is telling him or her that this is important, possibly crucial, to the success of their first year and potentially of their entire legacy. Instead, as one campaign ends, the next one begins. In part that is because those closest to a new president are rock stars in politics and communications who assume that these skills can trump governing.

Ever since Franklin D. Roosevelt, considered the first media president because of radio and his mastery of it, we have tended to place a high value on what presidents say and how they make us feel. Communication is unquestionably a significant part of a president's ability to assemble the public and political support needed to lead. But communication is not a substitute for the hard work of learning about a massive bureaucracy and bending it to one's will.

To their dismay, presidents discover that they cannot talk themselves out of really big failures. In 1980, a military mission to rescue the hostages taken in Iran failed spectacularly. For President Jimmy Carter, there was no talking his way out. In 2005, a hurricane hit New Orleans and the government response was as disastrous as Katrina itself. For President George W. Bush, there was no talking his way out. Fast forward to 2013 when the rollout of the federal health insurance website crucial to President Barack Obama's signature accomplishment, the new Affordable Care Act, failed. There was no talking his way out of that one, either.

So what should future presidents do in their first year to guard against the big failures that no amount of talking will fix or paper over? The answer hinges on learning what the government can do and what it knows.

The first challenge involves understanding the organizational capacity of the vast entity that is the federal government. Carter's attempt to rescue the hostages in Iran was preceded by decades of warning signs that the military as then constituted might have a problem executing a special forces mission involving multiple branches acting jointly. In the case of Bush's failure to rescue New Orleans after Katrina, there had been many warning signs that the Federal Emergency Management Agency (FEMA) had been downgraded and become a dumping ground for political appointees.

When Obama handed implementation of his signature health care legislation to the Centers for Medicare and Medicaid Services (CMS), there were many who knew that CMS was having trouble implementing the enormous programs they already had and that a new mission was likely to stretch it past the breaking point.

The second challenge involves figuring out what the government knows and making sure the president hears all of it. During the George W. Bush administration, Vice President Dick Cheney created a system that blocked information and analysis from the intelligence establishment and State Department that might have made Bush think twice about invading Iraq. At other times, government officials fail to spot trouble until it is too late. This was the case when Obama discovered, to his dismay, that veterans were waiting so long for appointments at Veterans Administration (VA) facilities that some were dying before they were seen, and that some in the VA were keeping fake lists to cover up the wait times.

The history of the recent presidency tells us that perceived presidential failure is often a failure of the executive branch. But the public (and history for that matter) rarely differentiates between the two.

Clearly it is time to consider the benefits of a "managerial presidency." How can a new president begin to manage an undertaking of this size? The best kind of managerial presidency takes a large view, encompassing the likely effects of a policy and the trials it will encounter in the implementation process. Speaking about the challenges of the presidency, Bill Clinton told an audience at the Brookings Institution in Washington D.C., in 2014, "They hire you to look down the street and around the corner."[1]

The problematic neglect of management stems from the fact that modern presidents find the federal government distant and ungovernable. As a senior staffer in the Clinton administration, my job was to "reinvent" government. In my first meeting with Clinton and Vice President Al Gore, I wanted to impress upon them the dimensions of the entity they now headed. So I told them that at the time (early 1993), that there were more employees in the federal government than there were people in the state of Arkansas, and there was more land under federal control than the entire state of Tennessee.

Back in the middle of the twentieth century, the federal government was both smaller and simpler. It was composed mostly of clerks who recorded Social Security payments, veteran's benefits, and other transactions. But by the twenty-first century, those jobs were done by computers. The clerks were replaced by programmers, lawyers, doctors, molecular biologists, nuclear physicists, engineers, and other specialists. The federal government had grown so big, its functions so complex, that recent presidents have not seen it as something they could run and use to help them govern. Instead, they have viewed it as foreign, and they expect it to cause trouble. Once presidents stop assuming responsibility for the government they are leading, they are bound to fail.

Nothing illustrates this better than the changes that have taken place in the role of the president's cabinet. In Abraham Lincoln's day, being a member of the cabinet was a big deal. His cabinet, memorialized in Doris Kearns Goodwin's book *Team of Rivals,* helped Lincoln decide the major issues of the day—such as how to run the Civil War. However, by the time Robert Reich was appointed secretary of labor under Clinton, the importance of the cabinet had deteriorated. "From the view of the White House staff, cabinet officials are provincial governors presiding over alien, primitive territories," Reich wrote in a memoir of his time in the administration, *Locked in the Cabinet.* "Anything of any importance occurs in the national palace."[2]

Most presidents have tried to stay in touch with their cabinets through a high-level White House staff member with the designation "assistant to the president for cabinet affairs." But in recent years this has not been a very important job. At one point, Bush downgraded the role of cabinet affairs assistant to "a young woman with a phone in a closet," according to a White House correspondent who covered that administration. Obama's cabinet met only nineteen times in his first term, mostly for ceremonial or meaningless photo opportunities. And in one famous incident, Obama's first chief of staff, Rahm Emanuel, was heard banishing the secretary of the Department of Energy, a Nobel Prize winner, to the outer circles because he did not stick to the message of the day.

The president's distance from those "alien, primitive territories" run by cabinet secretaries is at the heart of many leadership failures. In order for new presidents to figure out the government and how to run it, they must think differently about how they organize the White House staff, how they use their cabinet, and how they spend their time.

Let us start with the White House. The Office of Cabinet Affairs needs to be bigger and have a broader mission. In recent years, in keeping with presidents' passion for communication, the White House has tended to use the cabinet to "magnify" the message. So cabinet secretaries are sent out "on the road" to help the White House communicate on the president's behalf. In the meantime, cabinet secretaries receive the clear message that the White House is only interested in hearing good news from them—and certainly not bad news. Surfacing management problems and bringing them to the attention of the White House are generally not part of a cabinet secretary's mandate.

Presidents would be well served if, in their first year, they called for a systematic performance assessment from their cabinet secretaries. What agencies are functioning well? What agencies are struggling? In other words, where is the organizational capacity strong and where is it lacking? All presidents need this information. Republicans like to assume that the whole thing is a mess and should be cut; Democrats like to assume that it all works just fine and should be expanded. In any group of organizations that collectively employ more than 4 million people, the law of averages guarantees that things are going very right in some places and very wrong in others. A new president would be well advised to seek out this information. The president who discovers a scandal at the Department of Veterans Affairs and fixes it, for example, is in a very different position than the president who does not seem to know what is going on in the government he or she is charged to run.

The next thing a new president should do is to construct an early warning system inside the White House. The management wing of the Office of Management and Budget (OMB) was established in 1970 and has since assumed many important missions within the government. But no one in the executive branch is charged with systematically looking for management weaknesses and problems. The adoption of performance metrics through the Government Performance and Results Act was a step in the right direction and has been incorporated into the budget process within the White House. The problem, however, is that when an organization is in trouble, people often lie or manipulate the metrics. Building "dashboards" and tracking data are certainly valuable tools in trying to understand the performance of large organizations—but they have not prevented government failure. Used incorrectly, they can build a false sense of security.

The problem with establishing an early warning capacity at OMB is that, to the rest of the government, OMB is where budgets are cut. Thus career people in the agencies are loath to share too much with OMB, lest it result in punishment in the budget process. A performance review process separate from OMB and perhaps located in the White House could help establish the early warning system that is so important in avoiding presidential failure.

What makes sense for the presidency also makes sense for Congress. Much has been written about how Congress has all but given up its oversight function except when there is an emergency. Like the White House, Congress does not really have a system for anticipating trouble—its members simply react. The Government Accountability Office (GAO) and the Congressional Research Service (CRS) do research work for Congress, and they often study management and organizational-capacity issues. However, both organizations work at the request of congressional committees, subcommittees, and individual lawmakers. Their mandate does not include the sort of horizon-scanning that would allow for leadership and the avoidance of failure.

The creation of units in the White House and Congress charged with evaluating governmental performance before there is a crisis fits with a new theory of governance offered by Leon Fuerth, former national security advisor to Al Gore. Fuerth calls this "anticipatory governance." He and co-author Evan Faber defined it in a 2013 *Futurist* article as "a systems-based approach for enabling governance to cope with accelerating, complex forms of change. . . . Anticipatory governance would register and track events that are just barely visible at the event horizon; it would self-organize to deal with the unanticipated and the discontinuous."[3]

Understanding the capacities and knowledge of the federal government should be a high priority for the first year of any presidency, and it should help a new president anticipate trouble and implement policy. But presidents need to make time to learn. Instead of the bifurcated and sometimes hostile relationship between the political team and the policy teams that surround the president, a chief executive needs to realize that bad government is bad politics. The long-term consequence of failure—the perception that the president does not control the government— creates a political problem that is not easily overcome by employing campaign-style techniques. Striking a better balance between politicking and governing will not guarantee success, but it will improve the odds.

NOTES

1. "President Bill Clinton Delivers the Inaugural Robert S. Brookings President's Lecture," Brookings Institution, May 15, 2014, https://www.brookings.edu/events/president-bill-clinton -delivers-the-inaugural-robert-s-brookings-presidents-lecture/.

2. Robert Reich, *Locked in the Cabinet* (New York: Vintage, 1998), 111.

3. Leon Fuerth and Evan Faber, "Anticipatory Governance: Winning the Future," *Futurist* 47 (2013): 43.

PROCESS WITH CAUTION
The Insufficiency of Early Executive Action

ANDREW RUDALEVIGE

First-year presidents seeking to make a quick mark on the nation have limited options. Legislative action in most cases is slow and requires compromise. New appointees help to signal change but require both Senate confirmation and time to become effective in their new organizational homes.

A tempting avenue, then, is unilateral executive action—holding out the promise of achieving both symbol and substance. The drama of bypassing American government's checks and balances—directly transforming presidential preferences into public policy in front of a bank of cameras—is hugely appealing. As Bill Clinton aide Paul Begala exulted, "Stroke of a pen, law of the land. Kind of cool!"[1] Cool enough, anyway, for every recent president to have begun his term with directives affecting everything from executive branch ethics to the disposition of foreign aid to the interrogation of detained suspects.

Such tactics remain a crucial part of setting the policy agenda and putting longer-term processes in motion. And in some cases, when crises ensue, unilateralism jumps to the top of the to-do list. Indeed, after the attacks of September 11, 2001, President George W. Bush effectively began his first year again, with new military and security orders drafted to fight the new war on terror. In foreign affairs, especially, presidents have a good deal of autonomy, either delegated by Congress or claimed by executive branch interpreters of vague statutory language.

Even so, for all their advantages, unilateral directives may prove a fragile foundation for a presidential policy legacy. They may not obtain lasting results—or any results at all. On his third day in office in January 2009, Barack Obama promised in an executive order to close the Guantanamo Bay prison in Cuba within one year. But when he left office eight years later, the facility was still open, the president's pledge overridden by congressional resistance. Executive orders can likewise be overturned by subsequent executive orders, and departmental guidance by subsequent departmental guidance. Thus, as Obama prepared to leave office in December 2016, he told an NPR interviewer: "My suggestion to the president-elect is, you know, going through the legislative process is always better, in part because it's harder to undo."[2]

EXECUTIVE ACTION: TAXONOMY AND SCOPE

What administrative tools are available to the president? It is common for journalists, politicians, and even scholars to call any sort of presidential directive an "executive order," but executive orders are only one mechanism presidents use to influence the executive branch. The family of unilateral presidential directives also includes proclamations, memoranda, findings and determinations, designations, administrative orders, policy guidance letters, signing statements, waivers, and a whole range of (usually secret) national security decision documents that take different names in different administrations. All told, more than two dozen kinds of documents can help shape the way in which the wider executive branch implements the law.[3] The president can also prod—or seek to prevent—regulations being promulgated by departments and agencies.

How much can presidents do on their own, using these tools? That varies, not least because executive actions must be grounded in authority granted to the president either by the Constitution or Congress. The clearer the claim to power, the less legal or political controversy is likely to ensue.

This means presidents tend to have more autonomy in foreign affairs. But even in the domestic arena presidents have a lot of possible delegations to choose from. As "chief executive," the president's power has expanded in concert with the executive branch, which itself has grown dramatically since the 1930s, thanks to Depression, wars (hot and cold), civil rights, and regulatory zeal.

Presidential authority thus aggregates as the U.S. Code, with its vagaries of statutory language, grows. Bill Clinton sought to prevent striking workers from being replaced using a 1949 contracting law. Franklin D. Roosevelt temporarily closed the nation's banks in 1933 under authority granted to Woodrow Wilson in World War I. A series of recent presidents have set aside millions of acres as national monuments, based on a 1906 statute. As Bush administration official John Graham noted in 2007, "Creative lawyers can find lots of lawful ways for a determined president to advance an agenda."[4]

Even congressional efforts to constrain executive authority sometimes legitimate it. For example, in 1977, Congress passed the International Emergency Economic Powers Act to limit the way presidents imposed sanctions on disfavored foreign regimes. But by providing a statutory process for declaring emergencies as a means of preventing those economic transactions, Congress legitimized a previously shadowy claim to executive power—and presidents have frequently invoked it.

It is worth keeping in mind that executive actions are just that—they are directed to, and govern actions by, people in the executive branch. Thus, they affect the broader public only indirectly except in rare and controversial cases, including, for instance, the military detention of Japanese Americans during World War II.

Still, indirect does not mean trivial. Barack Obama could not issue an order raising the federal minimum wage. He could, however, order that the contracts negotiated with private-sector companies doing business with the federal government include an increased minimum wage.[5] More generally, presidents have a good deal of sway over how the federal government purchases goods and services from the private sector. Since these purchases amount to 3–4 percent of gross domestic product—more than $400 billion annually—setting conditions on how those funds are spent can have an important effect on the wider economy.[6]

The president's directives can also shift the interpretation of ambiguous statutory language to favor or disfavor certain interests or individuals. Or they can reorder or reprioritize the government's "prosecutorial discretion," by directing that perpetually scarce resources be spent in one area rather than another. For example, the Obama administration skirted Congress's failure to pass criminal justice sentencing reform by seeking to avoid charging nonviolent offenders with crimes that would incur mandatory minimum sentences which the president considered unfair. It also declined to prosecute recreational marijuana users in states that had legalized that practice, even though such drug use was still illegal under federal law.

THE POWER OF PROCESS

Presidents cannot by themselves produce new regulations—that power is normally delegated to the heads of departments and agencies, not to the president, and is subject to the requirements of the Administrative Procedure Act. But they can prod agencies to consider drafting new rules or rescinding old ones. Presidents can also change administrative processes in ways they hope will lead to the bureaucratic outcomes they want.

For instance, in 1981, Ronald Reagan issued an executive order mandating that all proposed regulations be reviewed by the Office of Management and Budget (OMB) before being issued by a department or agency, and that such rules not be issued at all unless analysis showed that their benefits outweighed their costs. At the start of his second term, in 1985, he added a requirement that agencies produce a regulatory agenda to give the White House advance warning of what rulemaking processes were underway. These procedures have been affirmed by all subsequent presidents, who made tweaks of their own to reflect the regulatory direction they wanted their administrations to take.

The regulatory review process that Reagan put in place is a cousin of the central clearance long exercised by the president's staff of career civil servants in the OMB. Under a system first put in place by Franklin Roosevelt in the 1930s, executive orders (as well as proclamations and presidential memoranda) go first to the OMB, whose job it is to solicit comments from other interested parts of the government. After the OMB signs off, the order goes to the Department of Justice for consultation on its "form and legality."

The idea behind this practice is to take advantage of agencies' specialized knowledge; to make sure those who must implement the order are familiar with it; and, not least, to make sure that the president is not taken by surprise by the order's effects. Especially at the beginning of the term, presidents and their closest advisors may not know much about policy. It is "extremely important," the Clinton transition warned, "that the President take no action having legal consequences that has not received careful legal review by appropriate Transition, Department of Justice, White House and other agency personnel."[7] Smart use of career staff and agency expertise can be critical to avoiding directives having unintended consequences. It also helps the administration avoid not only judicial review—since executive orders frequently wind up being challenged in court—but bureaucratic resistance. The clean lines of textbook organization charts mask the president's real-world relationship to the federal bureaucracy, which often has its own authority and sometimes its own policy preferences.

GETTING STARTED

As presidents start their terms, the directives they issue tend to fall into three main categories.

The first comprises things that any president might want to do. This includes declarations about expectations of their appointees' behavior. George H. W. Bush's order creating a commission on ethics law reform in January 1989 was followed by early Bill Clinton, George W. Bush, and Barack Obama orders all seeking to establish high ethical standards for their administrations. Another common action has been to order a freeze on pending regulations that were promulgated late in the preceding president's term and are not yet in effect.

A second category is actions that any president of a given party does. The issuance of some orders has become almost a matter of partisan routine. A policy memorandum preventing foreign aid from going to nongovernmental organizations that provide abortion counseling or referrals (known as the "Mexico City Policy") was put in place by President Reagan, reversed by Bill Clinton, restored by George W. Bush, and removed again by Barack Obama. A similar sequence took place with regard to labor unions, when George H. W. Bush sought to decrease union sway among employees of federal contractors. Clinton reversed Bush's orders in 1993, and George W. Bush restored them in 2001, only to see Obama revoke them again in 2009.

Finally, presidents use early executive actions to make a new mark and signal a new direction. As the Clinton transition memo put it, directives proposed for the first days of the administration "should be of the utmost urgency and reflect a singular commitment by the President during the campaign to take immediate action upon coming into office."[8] For Clinton, that meant focusing on ethics (with his ethics order), economics (establishing the National Economic Council), and equality ("ending discrimination in the armed forces" against gays and lesbians, a measure so controversial that it resulted in the "don't ask, don't tell" policy). In all,

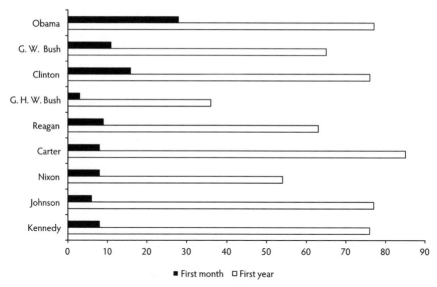

FIGURE 1. Executive orders and memoranda issued, first month and first year of elected term, 1961–2009. (*Source:* Kenneth Lowande and Thomas Gray, "Public Perception of the Presidential Toolkit," September 7, 2016, http://www.lowande.com/uploads/2/8/0/2/28027461/lowandegray-2016.pdf.)

Clinton issued a combined total of sixteen executive orders and presidential memoranda in his first month in office and seventy-six during his first year. This figure is comparable to those of all elected presidents in the past half-century, as figure 1 shows—although Clinton began a trend of doing more, earlier, that George W. Bush and especially Obama expanded upon.

The least active president with regard to orders and memoranda in either his first month, or first year, was George H. W. Bush. But Bush was also the only new president in this era to succeed a two-term incumbent of his own party. Presumably he had less need to substantively or symbolically separate himself from his popular predecessor. Indeed, incoming presidents routinely review their predecessors' executive achievements as a means of making their own mark. One group of George W. Bush aides, for instance, was tasked with reviewing all extant executive orders, memoranda, proclamations, and other administrative actions.[9] The "Mexico City Policy" was designated as something to restore on "1st day"; the aides also recommended that Clinton's executive order on federalism be rescinded so as to "reinstate Reagan E.O. [in] Week 1." But, they advised, a Clinton order dealing with disabilities in the workplace "would be politically difficult to revoke . . .—it would have been nice if President-elect Bush had the opportunity to issue this E.O., not President Clinton."

Another Clinton order extending specific protections against workplace discrimination to gay and lesbian federal workers also stayed in place. But Bush apparently took another, less visible administrative route to undoing it: federal workers' unions and LGBT interest groups soon charged that the order was no longer being enforced.

Of course, not all executive action happens at the very start of the first year. Strategic administrations will time the rollout of directives in coordination with a wider policy agenda, perhaps in concert with a broader legislative program. Further, as Bush aide Karl Rove put it, "history has a way of intruding on you."[10] The September 11 attacks activated a particularly large reservoir of unilateralism, not least through the broad delegation of the war powers granted to the president by Congress in its open-ended authorization of the use of military force. But less critical happenings—on Capitol Hill or around the world—can also prod presidential responses.

COMMANDING A SEPARATED SYSTEM

An aide to President John F. Kennedy once observed that "everybody believes in democracy—until they get to the White House."[11] In the American constitutional system of separated but intertwined institutions, policy change is slow, so executive action is appealing. With Congress by its nature a divided body run by collective choices, presidents have inherent advantages: even if they don't get the last say, they often get to make the first move. That shapes the landscape over which subsequent options range. Setting up new policy directives or new interpretations of old law or new administrative processes may embed new outcomes that are hard to overcome.

Yet executive action is no cure-all. It is inherently more fragile than legislative change because successive administrations can cross out a stroke of a previous president's pen with one of their own. And its temptations may lead to overreach— and thus to court or congressional backlash. Even within the not-so-unitary executive branch, presidents cannot assume automatic compliance, especially if they have not done the hard work of ensuring agency buy-in. Bill Clinton griped after leaving office of his "frustration" that, having issued "all these executive orders, . . . you can never be 100 percent sure that they were implemented."[12]

These complications of presidential management are one reason presidents need to issue directives in the first place. But they highlight, too, the benefits that may accrue from bargaining with the policymaking system instead of trying simply to command it.

NOTES

1. James Bennet, "True to Form, Clinton Shifts Energies Back to U.S. Focus," *New York Times*, July 5, 1998, http://www.nytimes.com/1998/07/05/us/true-to-form-clinton-shifts-energies-back-to-us-focus.html?mcubz=1.

2. "NPR's Exit Interview with President Obama," December 19, 2016, http://www.npr.org/2016/12/19/504998487/transcript-and-video-nprs-exit-interview-with-president-obama.

3. Harold C. Relyea, *Presidential Directives: Background and Overview,* Congressional Research Service report 98–611 GOV, November 26, 2008, https://fas.org/sgp/crs/misc/98-611.pdf.

4. Rebecca Adams, "Lame Duck or Leapfrog?" *CQ Weekly,* February 12, 2007, 450.

5. This order (EO 13658) was one of a series of Obama administration orders regarding government procurement, some of which were later blocked by judicial or legislative action.

6. Daniel P. Gitterman, *Calling the Shots: The President, Executive Orders, and Public Policy* (Washington, D.C.: Brookings, 2017).

7. Cynthia Lebow and Larry Simms, "Guidelines for Consideration of Potential Executive Orders to Be Signed by President Clinton on or Shortly after Inauguration Day," Leon E. Panetta Archive, box 21, file 33, Panetta Institute, Marina, Calif.

8. Ibid.

9. Quoted documents are from the Records of the OMB General Counsel, 2001–2009, "Review of Presidential Directives," Accession #051–11–0012, boxes 1–2, Washington National Records Center, Suitland, Md.

10. Dan Balz and Michael Fletcher, "Looking to Apply Lessons Learned," *Washington Post,* January 19, 2005, A1.

11. Thomas E. Cronin, "'Everybody Believes in Democracy until He Gets to the White House,'" *Law and Contemporary Problems* 35 (1970): 573–625.

12. From a September 2007 interview with ABC News, quoted in Andrew Rudalevige, "The Administrative Presidency and Bureaucratic Control," *Presidential Studies Quarterly* 39 (March 2009): 18.

MAXIMIZING CONTROL

First-Year Presidents and the Appointment and Agenda-Setting Powers

PATRICK O'BRIEN

First-year presidents who want to improve the economy or otherwise accomplish their goals should focus on two critically important and often ineffectively used powers: the appointment power and the agenda-setting power.

Not surprisingly, most presidential candidates routinely offer plans for improving economic mobility in particular and economic growth in general. Indeed, doing so has been an all but official requirement of the job since changes were made in the presidential nomination process during the 1970s that shifted control from party elites to regular party voters. Yet contemporary presidents have substantially less control over the economy than their counterparts before the 1970s. This is largely because of two major developments in the economic policy-making process.

First, although the Budget and Accounting Act of 1921 directed the president to transmit a budget to Congress each year, the Congressional Budget and Impoundment Control Act of 1974 layered a separate congressional budget process over the old, president-dominated process, thereby severely diminishing presidential control even during periods of unified party government. This was evident, for example, when the president and his advisors struggled to set a new course for the budget during the Carter administration. "At some point, the line must be drawn in the sand if we are ever to be taken seriously in the [congressional] budget process," explained Stuart Eizenstat, the head of the Domestic Policy Staff, to Jimmy Carter. "We are increasingly a minor player."[1]

At the same time, the 1974 law created the Congressional Budget Office, essentially the congressional counterpart to the Office of Management and Budget and the Council of Economic Advisers. The new institution was charged with "secur[ing] information, data, estimates, and statistics directly from the various departments, agencies, and establishments of the executive branch of Government." Moreover, this new congressional information base has further diminished presidential control due to the prevalence of economic forecasting and budget scoring in the post-1974 era of multiyear budgeting. In practice, not only do the president and Congress put forward their own budget proposals but a congressional agency plays a critical role in the consideration of both. This constraint became evident during the Carter administration as well. "When we developed our welfare reform proposal in 1977," Eizenstat explained,

> President Carter openly directed Secretary Califano and Secretary Marshall to assure that their proposal had not greater cost than the current welfare system. . . . Based on [the Department of Health, Education, and Welfare's] calculations using 1978 dollars, the program's additional cost was estimated in the President's message at around $7 billion annually. [The Congressional Budget Office] did its own estimate. I remember my shock and dismay at reading in the *Washington Post* that CBO, discounting the Administration's cost-savings in other programs and using 1982 dollars, calculated the price tag of this once "no additional cost" program at $17 billion a year! The program was dead as of that moment—and could never be resurrected after the CBO estimate. The President's figures, based on HEW estimates, were no more incorrect than CBO's. Both had legitimacy. But because the President's monopoly on cost estimates had been ended, he had lost significant power and control over his legislation.[2]

Second, and operating in conjunction with the new, layered, multiple-agency budget-making process, the decades-long growth in human resources spending has shackled fiscal policy, effectively diminishing its role as an economic stabilization instrument while increasing the importance of monetary policy. Consequently, the Federal Reserve's influence over the economy has increased substantially, even as the president's influence has decreased. This was increasingly evident by the end of the Reagan administration. "Fiscal policy in the United States remained frozen," Paul Volcker, the chairman of the Federal Reserve, later explained.[3] By the 1990s, the Fed's preeminent position was indisputable. "I vividly recall the day in Little Rock in January 1993," Alan Blinder, a top presidential advisor, said, "when I told President-elect Clinton that, where the economy was concerned, he had just been elected to the *second* most important position in the country—the first was already filled by [Fed Chairman] Alan Greenspan."[4]

In inheriting this highly decentralized policymaking environment, new presidents should look more to the appointment power than has been typical in order to achieve their goals. Even though the Constitution and various statutes grant every president the same power of appointment, the effectiveness of this power varies considerably from one chief executive to the next. Consider, for example, the Clinton and Reagan administrations.

When Bill Clinton came into office in 1993, he appointed Lloyd Bentsen as treasury secretary. Bentsen had been a senator for more than two decades and had served as chairman of the Senate Finance Committee during the latter part of the Reagan administration and the whole of the George H. W. Bush administration. Deeply experienced in the federal government, Bentsen generally supported established policies and procedures and therefore was often unsupportive of President Clinton's desire to propose and implement major changes. As Clinton himself put it, the administration's economic leaders—particularly the treasury secretary—were "incrementalists."[5]

In contrast to Clinton, when Ronald Reagan came into office in 1981, he appointed as treasury secretary Donald Regan, a banker with no previous experience in the federal government. Without any indoctrination in the established policies and procedures, Regan was more open to supporting the president's efforts to propose and implement major changes. The treasury secretary "operated on the 'echo' principle," David A. Stockman, the director of the Office of Management and Budget, later remarked. "Whatever the President insisted on, [Regan] would try to get—without regard to price."[6]

Although the appointment power is critical to the success of any modern president, especially those operating in the modern economic policymaking environment, variation in the use of the appointment power is by no means unique to the modern period. Consider, for example, the Jefferson and Jackson administrations as parallels to the Clinton and Reagan administrations, respectively.

After assuming office in 1801, Thomas Jefferson appointed Albert Gallatin as treasury secretary. Like Bentsen, Gallatin had substantial experience in the federal government. In particular, he had helped to create the Ways and Means Committee in the House of Representatives and had then served on it during the last years of the Washington administration and the whole of the Adams administration. Accordingly, Gallatin largely supported established policies and procedures after he became treasury secretary. Most notably, he was highly unsupportive of Jefferson's desire to destroy or weaken the Bank of the United States. It is "not proper to displease" the directors of the Bank "because they place our money where we may want it, from one end of the Union to the other," Gallatin explained to Jefferson after the president suggested that the administration should attempt to prevent the Bank from obtaining an "exclusive monopoly" of the government's deposits.[7]

In contrast to Jefferson, Andrew Jackson relied substantially on Roger Taney, a lawyer with no previous experience in the federal government. Lacking any indoctrination in the established policies and procedures, Taney, like Regan, supported the president's efforts to make major changes, particularly with regard to the Second Bank of the United States. He assisted Jackson in developing the argument for the Bank veto while serving as attorney general in 1832, and then, while serving as treasury secretary in 1833, he helped the president remove the government's deposits in order to destroy the institution once and for all. "I am fully prepared to go with you firmly through this business and to meet all of its consequences," Taney wrote to Jackson.[8]

To explain this variation in the use of the appointment power in more general terms, the first-year president can appoint either principals who have substantial experience in the federal government and are likely to support the established policies and procedures or principals who have little or no experience and are likely to be more responsive to a new president's desire to change those policies and procedures. Furthermore, most presidents don't realize that this variation exists, mistakenly assuming that the appointment power automatically ensures responsiveness. By the time they become aware that this isn't so, it is often too late.

As with the appointment power, the Constitution and various statutes grant every president the same agenda-setting power. Yet here, too, there is considerable variation in how effectively presidents use this power. Consider, for example, the Obama and Roosevelt administrations.

After assuming office in 2009—and following the appointment of several principals with substantial experience in the federal government, particularly during the Clinton administration—Barack Obama immediately addressed the issue of fiscal policy, putting forward a stimulus proposal to strengthen the rapidly declining economy. This "economic stabilization legislation," the president declared, referring to the American Recovery and Reinvestment Act, "will lower the cost of health care by billions and improve its quality. It will modernize thousands of classrooms and send more kids to college. And it will put billions of dollars in immediate tax relief into the pockets of working families."[9] Yet throughout his eight years in office, Obama said nothing about monetary policy, relying exclusively on his appointment power to fill vacancies at the Federal Reserve when they occurred. Moreover, his use of even this power was rather limited in practice, as demonstrated by his quick reappointment of his Republican predecessor's Fed chairman in 2009.

In contrast, Franklin D. Roosevelt came into office in 1933 and—with the assistance of several associates who had no previous experience in the federal government—took the lead in creating and implementing a new monetary policy during his first term. "The march toward 'managed currency' came quickly in legislation following Roosevelt's inauguration," the president's predecessor, Herbert Hoover, later lamented. Underscoring the significance of this development, Hoover added, "Congress . . . gave to the President legal authority over money as absolute as that of Tiberius Caesar or Henry VIII, Stalin or Hitler. It consummated the dreams and promises of every American tinkerer with the currency since the foundation of the Republic."[10] Roosevelt also oversaw the creation and implementation of a new fiscal policy during his second term. "In the early thirties . . . fiscal policy was exceedingly simple in theory and extraordinarily disastrous in practice," the president explained. Regarding the change in course, he added, "The experience of 1938–1939 should remove any doubt as to the effectiveness of a fiscal policy related to economic need."[11]

As with the appointment power, variation in use of the agenda-setting power is by no means unique to the modern period. Consider, once again, Jefferson and Jackson. Although Jefferson personally believed that the Bank of the United States was "one of the most deadly hostility existing against the principles [and] form of our constitution," he left matters of monetary policy to his experienced treasury secretary while addressing only some matters of fiscal policy himself.[12] In contrast, Jackson addressed both economic policy domains directly. "Under no circumstances and upon no conditions whatever" should the Bank of the United States be rechartered, the president wrote to his treasury secretary and other principals shortly before vetoing a bill to extend the life of the Second Bank.[13]

More generally, the first-year president can use the agenda-setting power to put forward either proposals that fall within or shift the accepted policy parameters and scope of presidential influence. Furthermore, as with the appointment power, most presidents—having limited historical knowledge and policy expertise—are unaware of the extent to which this variation exists; by the time they become aware, it is often too late. As Obama himself acknowledged in the final weeks of his presidency, "There is no doubt I'm a better president now than I was when I start[ed]."[14]

Using history as a guide, new presidents who want to change the existing trajectory of the economy in general or economic mobility in particular should put more resources into maximizing the effectiveness of the appointment power. At the same time—and relying on the assistance of advisors not indoctrinated in the established operations of the federal government—new presidents should work to shift the accepted policy parameters and scope of presidential influence.

To be sure, most of the focus after the election will be on how Congress is likely to respond to the administration's new legislative program. But one of the most important steps—if not *the* most important step—is for the president and economic team to determine the scope and components of that program in the first place. Or, as Martin Anderson, a top advisor to both Richard Nixon and Ronald Reagan, put it more generally, "The problem every winning campaign faces is how to ensure that those with more distinguished reputations who will be chosen for the cabinet posts do not betray the policies the campaign was fought on."[15]

NOTES

1. Iwan Morgan, *The Age of Deficits: Presidents and Unbalanced Budgets from Jimmy Carter to George W. Bush* (Lawrence: University Press of Kansas, 2009), 69.

2. W. Carl Biven, *Jimmy Carter's Economy: Policy in an Age of Limits* (Chapel Hill: University of North Carolina Press, 2002), 53.

3. Paul Volcker and Toyoo Gyohten, *Changing Fortunes: The World's Money and the Threat to American Leadership* (New York: Times Books, 1992), 260.

4. Alan Blinder, "Comments," in *American Economic Policy in the 1990s*, ed. Jeffrey A. Frankel and Peter R. Orszar (Cambridge, Mass.: MIT Press, 2002), 47.

5. Bob Woodward, *The Agenda: Inside the Clinton White House* (New York: Simon and Schuster, 1994), 197–98.

6. David A. Stockman, *The Triumph of Politics: Why the Reagan Revolution Failed* (New York: Harper and Row, 1986), 235.

7. Albert Gallatin to Thomas Jefferson, June 18, 1802, in *The Writings of Albert Gallatin*, ed. Henry Adams (Philadelphia: J. B. Lippincott, 1879), 80.

8. Bernard C. Steiner, *Life of Roger Brooke Taney: Chief Justice of the United States Supreme Court* (Baltimore: Williams and Wilkins, 1922), 130.

9. Barack Obama, "Statement on House of Representatives Passage of Economic Stabilization Legislation," January 28, 2009, American Presidency Project, http://www.presidency.ucsb.edu/ws/index.php?pid=85703.

10. Herbert Hoover, *The Memoirs of Herbert Hoover: The Great Depression, 1929–1941* (New York: Macmillan, 1952), 393, 395.

11. Franklin D. Roosevelt, "Annual Budget Message," January 3, 1940, American Presidency Project, http://www.presidency.ucsb.edu/ws/?pid=15922.

12. Thomas Jefferson to Albert Gallatin, December 13, 1803, in *The Works of Thomas Jefferson*, ed. Paul L. Ford (New York: G. P. Putnam's Sons, 1905), 59.

13. Robert V. Remini, *Andrew Jackson: The Course of American Democracy, 1833–1845* (Baltimore: Johns Hopkins University Press, 1998), 54.

14. "'This Week' Transcript: President Barack Obama," January 8, 2017, ABC News, http://abcnews.go.com/Politics/week-transcript-president-barack-obama/story?id=44630949.

15. Martin Anderson, *Revolution* (New York: Harcourt Brace Jovanovich, 1988), 197.

THE POTUS AS CEO-TUS

Lessons That CEOs Can Teach New Presidents

CAROLYN DEWAR, TOM DOHRMANN,
ANDREW ERDMANN, RYAN HARPER,
AND KUNAL MODI

Although not all lessons from the private sector are transferrable to the public sector, there are nevertheless some for the transition period of incoming presidential administrations that CEOs can offer.

The following are a dozen such lessons, in three broad groupings, drawn from McKinsey and Company's work with public- and private-sector leaders globally and discussions with current and former CEOs of iconic companies who have undergone similar transitions. These lessons are broadly applicable to leaders transitioning into senior roles in the government, regardless of professional background.

1. Establish an agenda—an overarching aspiration and a limited set of priorities.

► *Get a clear view of the lay of the land.* Understanding an organization's context is vital, particularly in government institutions in which so much of the staff is nonpolitical. The president should learn what important constituencies expect and what experiences various institutions or departments have recently been through. Even incoming leaders who are "insiders" and have past experience in the organization or possess deep expertise in an issue area benefit from assessing anew the operational landscape. In doing so, deliberately challenging any biases that the new leaders may have inherited—such as who might be allies or adversaries—is important. Time and again, government leaders have stumbled because they did not take the time to reflect on and understand their institutions' issues and stakeholders. In sum, understanding the past is often the best way to diagnose the present to ensure future success.

► *Start with a vision.* Decide what should be accomplished for the American people and what themes to emphasize before setting an agenda. The transition period is the time for a president to refine the goals set during the campaign and then ruthlessly prioritize those that will define his or her tenure. The former CEO of Juniper Networks Kevin Johnson remarked that this approach does not require that "you translate your point of view into a new strategy on day one" but rather that one should develop and prioritize a basic list of long-term goals fairly quickly.[1] A recent survey of executives found that they considered the most important transition activity to be creating a shared vision and aligning their organization with this strategic direction.

▸ *Focus on all four years, not just the first hundred days—or even the first year.* From the start, striking a balance between the near and long term is important. The media will argue that success is determined in a sprint over the first hundred days. Inevitably, one hears invocations of Franklin D. Roosevelt's "First 100 Days," when he pushed through much of the legislative agenda that defined the New Deal. As Andrea Ayers, CEO of Convergys Corporation, notes, it is important to stay focused on what matters and for "your early wins [to] tie back to your major goals. The former has to be connected to the latter." Although a cabinet secretary's tenure is shorter, on average, than a CEO's (three years versus five), the president needs to prepare for more than just the first hundred days or the first year.[2] Indeed, trying to do too much right away will not allow the organization sufficient time to achieve buy-in.

▸ *Act not prematurely but boldly.* CEOs who make four or more strategic moves in their first two years tend to outperform similar organizations and stay longer than their more hesitant counterparts. Despite the constraints of government, successful leaders must take risks and act as boldly as the operating environment allows.

▸ *Communicate, communicate, communicate.* Effective CEOs understand their unique strategic role as communicators. Leonard Schaeffer, the founding chairman and CEO of WellPoint, who also has diverse public-sector experience at the state and federal levels, emphasizes that "a government leader or CEO's job is to explain the organization to the world, and to explain the world to the organization."[3] Given this need, it is important for a president to be trusted as a communicator by being as transparent as possible with both internal staff and external stakeholders. New CEOs are routinely asked what their long-term strategy is for the company within the first few days. CEOs we interviewed said that the best answers tended to recognize and acknowledge major constituencies, project confidence in the company's prospects, and have clear ideas about where progress is possible.[4]

2. Build a team that will support and challenge you—and help you deliver.

▸ *Build a top team with "trusted hands" and new faces.* Although new leaders understandably want (and often need) to bring in people they know and trust, many leaders fail because they are too insular and resistant to including outsiders in decision-making processes. A new president needs to retain and rely on career staff in many positions. It is essential to gain buy-in early and build a joint leadership team consisting of career professionals, political appointees, and outside experts. As former secretary of defense Robert Gates put it: "If [career staff] don't like what you're doing, they can just outlast you. They were there before you got there. They'll be there after you leave. And all they have to do is wait you out."[5] Although there will inevitably be tensions between incoming and outgoing teams—even when a transition is between administrations of the same political party—it is important for an incoming president to ask predecessors for their perspectives on the strengths and weaknesses of the career staff.

▶ *Surround yourself with diversity.* Research from McKinsey and Company shows that companies in the top quartile for gender or racial and ethnic diversity are more likely to see superior performance as measured by average financial returns. Among other factors, more diverse leadership teams tend to improve problem solving and decision making. Sheryl Sandberg, Facebook's chief operating officer and author of *Lean In,* reminds us that "endless data show that diverse teams make better decisions. We are building products that people with very diverse backgrounds use, and I think we all want our company makeup to reflect the makeup of the people who use our products."[6] In an increasingly diverse and multicultural America, that aspiration is even more important in government.

▶ *Welcome thoughtful internal critics.* In any organization, but particularly in government, there is a natural tendency to rely on a trusted inner circle. Sometimes this is by necessity, as with national security challenges in which only those with a "need to know" can be included. But often the circle of discussion reflects the emotional and psychological pressures of the senior-level jobs themselves. Being a senior executive in either the private or public sector is lonely, which often fosters a desire for reassurance. Many senior government leaders, for instance, ask their staffs to convene groups of outside experts with different viewpoints for meetings or informal discussions over meals to ensure that critical voices and creative ideas are shared. A president needs to manage dissent, not avoid it.

▶ *Make tough decisions on personnel as early as possible.* Although there is little flexibility in removing civil service staff from government agencies, cabinet secretaries and agency leaders retain the power to adjust who is charged with what responsibilities. The president should use this power as soon as the need arises, particularly for important initiatives. In a recent McKinsey and Company survey on executive transitions, respondents noted, with hindsight, that they wished they had acted more rapidly on personnel decisions.[7]

▶ *Recruit "doers" as well as policy experts.* The temptation in government is to hire a team of the best thinkers and policy experts rather than those focused on internal management or the implementation of policy. A good management and operating team is also essential. Likewise, our research underscores that leaders need a team of managers who can both deliver performance immediately and foster the organizational health that enables their institution to sustain that performance.

3. Define a personal operating model to manage the demands of the job over the long haul.

▶ *Manage energy.* A new president is on call 24/7, experiencing the acute time pressure to deliver rapidly. Yet delivering is complex, demanding, and at times depleting—physically and psychologically. As CEO experience attests, the president should decide early what his or her cadence will be, establish the culture for the leadership team, and then ensure that the right people are in place to execute. There are times when even cabinet secretaries must support the president directly in a staff-like capacity, thereby placing extra demands on the president's time and schedule. For example, in the national security domain, the secretary of defense is in charge of leading and managing the largest organization in the country, with millions of employees, but also has to devote significant time to preparing and then advising the president when he or she is making major national security decisions.

▶ *Set ground rules.* The president should ensure that any action could appear on the front page of a major newspaper or be widely shared through social media without embarrassment. Warren Buffett, CEO of Berkshire Hathaway, once warned, "It takes 20 years to build a reputation and five minutes to ruin it."[8]

The peaceful transition of power from one administration to the next reaffirms a great hallmark of American democracy. It is a unique opportunity to chart a new course for the country—and the right kind of planning and preparation can greatly improve a new administration's ability to succeed. The twelve foregoing suggestions, based on diverse leadership experience and spanning many different types of organizations, should help any new president and senior leadership team define their path forward.

NOTES

1. Endre Holen and Allen Webb, "My Transition Story," *McKinsey Quarterly,* June 2010, http://www.mckinsey.com/global-themes/leadership/my-transition-story.

2. Phillip Bump, "Eric Holder and a Brief History of Cabinet Tenures," *Washington Post,* September 25, 2014, https://www.washingtonpost.com/news/the-fix/wp/2014/09/25/eric-holder-and-a-brief-history-of-cabinet-tenures/; Jeffrey Sonnenfeld, "CEO Exit Schedules: A Season to Stay, a Season to Go," Fortune, May 6, 2015, http://fortune.com/2015/05/06/ceo-tenure-cisco/.

3. Michael Birshan, Thomas Meakin, and Kurt Strovink, "How New CEOs Can Boost Their Odds of Success," *McKinsey Quarterly,* May 2016, http://www.mckinsey.com/global-themes/leadership/how-new-ceos-can-boost-their-odds-of-success.

4. Rajiv Chandran, Hortense De La Boutetiere, and Carolyn Dewar, "Ascending to the C-Suite," McKinsey and Company, April 2015, http://www.mckinsey.com/global-themes/leadership/ascending-to-the-c-suite.

5. "The Management Style of Robert Gates," interview by Adi Ignatius, *Harvard Business Review,* January 13, 2015, https://hbr.org/ideacast/2014/01/the-management-style-of-robert.html.

6. Jessica Guynn, "Facebook's Sheryl Sandberg on tech's diversity gap," *USA Today,* August 12, 2014, https://www.usatoday.com/story/tech/2014/08/12/facebook-sheryl-sandberg-diversity-gap/13787731/.

7. Birshan, Meakin, and Strovink, "How New CEOs Can Boost Their Odds of Success."

8. Brad Tuttle, "Warren Buffet's Boring, Brilliant Wisdom," *Time,* March 1, 2010, http://business.time.com/2010/03/01/warren-buffetts-boring-brilliant-wisdom/.

GOING LOCAL TO BREAK GRIDLOCK

BRUCE KATZ

During the past several decades, partisan divisions and ideological polarization at the federal and state level have crippled the American political system. Although our broken politics have been difficult to watch, there has been a silver lining to the dysfunction: it has helped spark a burst of positive, pragmatic energy in the nation's cities and metropolitan areas.

Cities and metropolitan areas have been forging ambitious, bottom-up solutions in nearly every area of national importance: the skilling of workers, the education of children, the mitigation of climate change, the financing of infrastructure, the development of affordable housing, and the creation of high-quality places for our young and elderly populations.

This surge of innovative local action, combined with the paralysis at higher levels of government, has created a new dynamic in national problem-solving. Cities have become the primary engines of social and economic progress by planning, designing, and executing strategies to overcome their problems with limited or no help from Washington or their states. This has amounted to the emergence of a New American Localism.

Several times during the past century, presidents have entered office focused on remaking our nation's federal compact, devoting enormous political capital to shifting the balance of power between the federal government and the states. Lyndon B. Johnson, Richard Nixon, and Ronald Reagan all saw remaking federalism as an essential component of achieving their governing vision.

Johnson's "Great Society" legislation was an expansion of federal power rivaled in scale only by the New Deal, and his time in office was marked by an unprecedented increase in the number and size of federal grants to states and localities.[1] This vaulted the federal government's influence over state and local governments to previously unseen heights.

Nixon's "New Federalism" sought to "rationalize" government. He wanted to rein in the power the federal government had acquired under Johnson and reduce the prescriptiveness of federal aid to states and localities, which he saw as intrusive and ineffective. The centerpiece of this component of his agenda was General Revenue Sharing, a program that provided no-strings-attached block grants to state and local governments. But Nixon also saw the need to centralize a number of government functions, particularly in the regulatory realm. This was most clearly manifested in his support for the creation of the Environmental Protection Agency in 1970 and the Occupational Safety and Health Administration in 1971.

Where Nixon sought to "rationalize" government, Reagan sought to reduce it at all levels. Riding into office on a historic wave of antitax, antigovernment sentiment, he slashed federal aid to states and localities, ended sixty-two federal grant programs completely (one-tenth of them), and consolidated fifty-seven programs into nine new or revamped block grants, which included the Low-Income Home Energy Assistance Program, the Social Services Block Grant, the Community Services Block Grant, and the Community Development Block Grant.[2]

Current challenges would be better approached with a different strategy—one that goes beyond the bounds of traditional federalism, focusing less on the relationship between the federal government and the states and more on the dynamic between the federal government and cities. States are often a critical middleman between cities and the federal government, and state policy often has much greater bearing on what cities are able to do than federal rules and regulations. Leadership in state capitals varies dramatically—some state governments have been critical partners in helping their cities succeed, while others have been near-constant antagonists to bottom-up metropolitan efforts.

Regardless, in a great number of areas the federal government can either bypass states and work directly with cities or encourage states to collaborate closely with cities on issues of mutual concern. The imperative must be to strengthen the new localist dynamic that has taken root in the country.

THE NEW AMERICAN LOCALISM AT WORK

The emergence of a new era of localism can be seen throughout the country as cities, for example, reduce income inequality by raising the minimum wage; use locally generated revenues to build new infrastructure; enhance competitiveness by bolstering advanced manufacturing, exports, and foreign direct investment; and create innovation districts to advance the commercialization of research and the start and scale-up of entrepreneurial firms.

To further energize cities, a future president must understand how the New American Localism is different from past approaches to problem-solving.

First, rather than relying on public-sector solutions alone, cities are harnessing the power generated when government, business, civic, philanthropic, university, and community institutions and leaders work collaboratively. The focus of the New American Localism on unlocking the latent capacity of public, private, and civic networks differs markedly from federalism's traditional emphasis on relationships between levels of government, particularly the federal government and the states.

Second, cities and metropolitan areas are forging responses that are holistic, multidisciplinary, and guided by local priorities. This is a sharp contrast from the federal penchant for one-size-fits-all, hyper-specific programs administered by slow-moving, siloed federal agencies. Tailoring solutions to the circumstances of local challenges and enabling cross-sector initiatives creates the opportunity to solve problems more efficiently and effectively than traditional federal approaches.

Finally, cities and metropolitan areas are deploying capital from an array of public, private, and civic sources at the local, national, and even global levels. Rethinking financing from the bottom up is imperative. With mandatory federal spending for older Americans rising, discretionary spending on infrastructure, education, and other competitive levers probably will not keep pace with demand and population growth. Financing for critical investments, therefore, will increasingly come from collaboration among the public, private, and civic sectors at all levels and require experimentation around new forms of innovative finance.

A FIRST-YEAR AGENDA

Invigorating localism by remaking the relationship between the federal government and cities would be an historic accomplishment for a first-year president.

A new president's top priority, of course, must be retaining strong federal support for activities that cities cannot undertake, like investing in the safety net, defense, and research and development at national labs and advanced research universities.

There are a number of ways that the president can strengthen the New American Localism that do not require major expansions of executive power. One way is to provide cities with more transparency with regard to federal and private investments, more flexibility in how cities use public resources, and a more comprehensive set of tools to leverage private and civic capital for transformative projects.

TRANSPARENCY FOR CITIES

The federal government is the largest single investor in cities through a variety of taxing, spending, and credit-enhancing vehicles, but the way it invests is unacceptably opaque. Incredibly, we know more about where banks lend (thanks to the Home Mortgage Disclosure Act) than where the federal government spends. A central mission for a first-year president should be to make federal resource flows more transparent. If cities had a clear sense of the full scope of federal investments coming into their communities, they would be able to leverage that information for more effective local public action and greater private and civic investment. Here are some ideas for federal action:

- ▸ Issue an Annual Metropolitan Investment Statement to disclose the level and geographical distribution of all federal tax and spending resources for each city, urban county, and metropolis.

▸ Pioneer a City Children's Budget, showing how scores of unconnected federal program resources come (or do not come) together to support, for example, disadvantaged children or neighborhoods in each city.

▸ Take a Public Asset Inventory, enabling select cities to gauge the value of government-owned assets like land, buildings, and infrastructure, thereby providing additional revenue sources for core urban priorities.

As described above, cities and metropolitan areas use financing in many forms and from a variety of sources to shape their economies and equip their workers with the skills they need to compete. Like federal investment flows, the stock of public, civic, and private capital that can be aggregated and deployed through new means of "metropolitan finance" has not been captured by traditional measurement tools. Therefore, the federal government could:

▸ Create a new Office of Metropolitan Finance in the Treasury Department to complement the existing Office of State and Local Finance.

▸ Explore options for unveiling and sizing the public, private, and civic capital in cities that can be unlocked for investment purposes.

FLEXIBILITY FOR CITIES

Once a president helps provide a clearer look at metropolitan finance streams, he or she should give cities the flexibility to adapt federal investments in transportation, housing, workforce development, education, and other domestic areas to their specific needs and local priorities. The resources the federal government provides are often heavily prescriptive and compartmentalized, making it extremely difficult for cities to create coherent local strategies to address their toughest problems. For example, in its efforts to create better outcomes for disconnected youth, New Orleans must navigate eight separate grant-funding streams for workforce development, six for education, eight for human services, and six for justice, housing, and other services. Ten of these grants are worth less than $2 million, and several are so miniscule that they can hardly be cost-effective to administer. This approach is completely out of sync with the networked and integrated way that cities solve problems today. Federal resources should be provided with fewer prescriptions, and cities should have the ability to adapt federal investments to local conditions in exchange for greater accountability.

The president should consider emulating the "City Deals" and devolution agreement process underway in the United Kingdom, which has created a vehicle for British cities to gain greater flexibility and discretion in how central government funds are used locally.[3] Cities, counties, or metropolitan areas could apply for the ability to allocate federal resources to drive specific social, economic, or environmental outcomes rather than attempt to braid together many small federal grants with rigid determinations into a coherent local strategy. A process along these lines would better align federal resources with local priorities and fully unleash the creative problem-solving potential of local public, private, and civic actors. Regardless of the specifics from place to place, City Deals would be a badly needed corrective to the notion that the dizzying array of small federal grant programs provided to American communities can somehow match the varying needs and conditions on the ground.

A BIPARTISAN COMPACT ON DEVOLUTION?

Since 2009, a period of extreme partisan gridlock, Congress has managed to reauthorize major federal education, transportation, and workforce investment programs in ways that provide cities, metropolitan areas, and states with greater flexibility in the deployment of federal resources.[4]

These legislative successes could point to new possibilities for bipartisan collaboration in what is likely to be recurring divided government. Local control has been a longstanding tenet of Republican conservatism. To a large extent, pushing for greater devolution of power and responsibilities would return the Republican Party to the conservative federal visions espoused by Presidents Nixon, Reagan, and George H. W. Bush. It could also bring coherence to the version of conservativism articulated by intellectuals like Yuval Levin, the editor of *National Affairs*. As Levin argues, a diverse, dynamic society requires conservatives to empower local problem-solvers "to mix resources, advice, experience, and more leadership in a continuing process of bottom-up experimentation."[5]

For their part, Democrats, long seen as the party supporting central government power and uniform national solutions, could pursue a more realistic path that aligns with their control of many central cities and urban counties. The Obama administration made a number of small but promising moves to empower local areas with initiatives like the Partnership for Sustainable Communities, the Performance Partnerships for Disconnected Youth, the National Network for Manufacturing Innovation, and the Upward Mobility Project.[6]

It is time for the federal government to recognize that responsibility for solving problems is shifting downward to cities. It must adjust the way it interacts with cities by becoming more of a partner and less of a decider, more of an enabler and less of a dictator. Strengthening American localism will be the most effective and politically savvy way for future administrations to navigate our broken political system and energize progress on issues of grave concern to millions of Americans.

NOTES

1. Vertonique De Rugy, *Federal Grant Aid to State and Local Governments*, George Mason University Mercatus Center, http://mercatus.org/sites/default/files/Federal-grant-aid-state -and-local-chart-analysis-pdf.pdf.

2. Margy Waller, "BlockGrants: Flexibility vs. Stability in Social Services," Center on Children and Families, no. 34, Brookings Institution Policy Brief, 2005.

3. https://www.local.gov.uk/topics/devolution/devolution-deals.

4. Sarah Binder, "Polarized We Govern," Brookings Institution, May 27, 2014, https://www
.brookings.edu/research/polarized-we-govern/.

5. Yuval Levin, "The Next Conservative Movement," *Wall Street Journal,* April 15, 2016,
http://www.wsj.com/articles/the-next-conservative-movement-1460741085.

6. Ross Tilchin and Bruce Katz, "The New Localism: An Obama Legacy?" Brookings
Institution, February 26, 2016, https://www.brookings.edu/blog/metropolitan-revolution/
2016/02/26/the-new-localism-an-obama-legacy/.

VII ★ PRESIDENTIAL COMMUNICATIONS

THE HUNDRED DAYS MYTH

DAVID GREENBERG

Since the landmark opening session of Franklin D. Roosevelt's first term, presidents and the news media have touted the first hundred days of a new administration as a precious window during which ambitious goals may be achieved or forsaken.[1] That early record is even said to foretell the overall fortunes of an entire presidency. It is easy to see why. A rookie president, entering office with as much goodwill as he or she is ever likely to enjoy, has room to maneuver and opportunities to act that seldom last long. At least since Roosevelt, presidents have intently followed the media's short-term judgments about success and failure—leading to overweening attention to favorability ratings, the tenor of insider opinion, and whether the president had "a good week." Moved by such concerns, presidents and their staffs have bought into the hundred days mythology, working hard to ensure positive headlines when the deadline arrives.

But presidents and their staffs would be wise to pay a bit less attention to the hype about the first hundred days. Historically, that arbitrary benchmark has rarely correlated with the subsequent success or failure of a president's time in office. All modern presidents go through ups and downs, periods of positive and negative coverage, none of which matters much in the long run. Above all, it is a myth that presidents can succeed through good public relations. On the contrary, those presidents whom we recall as skilled communicators are typically remembered that way only because they actually accomplished things. A reputation for facility with communication follows from a record of achievement, not the other way around.

Given all this, it's time for presidents and their aides to stop trying to amass a list of accomplishments that can be rolled out for the news media at the start of May. Instead, they should prioritize substantial issues. In particular, successful presidencies—even those with rocky launches—have begun with the passage of a major economic plan that can both set the ideological tenor for the administration and, if it spurs recovery and growth, create space politically and fiscally to achieve other goals in subsequent years.

To be sure, the hundred days mythology dies hard. The term has a long history. It originally came not from Roosevelt's time but from Napoleon's (*les cent jours*). In 1815, the exiled conqueror escaped from his redoubt on the island of Elba, rallied the French Army, and briefly restored his rule until his defeat at Waterloo.

Technically, all of this took 111 days to unfold, but the period came to be called the Hundred Days: a period of dramatic accomplishment and transformation.[2]

It was after 1933 that the term entered into widespread American usage and became a benchmark for presidential achievement. That year, Roosevelt took office amid unprecedented economic crisis. Not only had Herbert Hoover's laissez-faire ideology failed to pull the nation out of the Depression, but in the winter of 1932–33, banks were failing at an alarming rate. With his first-ever fireside chat, an executive fiat declaring a bank holiday, and the quick passage of banking reform, FDR ended and reversed the run on the banks that was threatening to make a dire economic situation worse.[3]

The prevailing sense of urgency muted serious political opposition, creating a situation that was practically unprecedented in presidential politics. When Roosevelt called Congress into session five days after his inauguration to pass his banking legislation, House Republican leader Bertrand Snell urged his party to vote yes—despite not having read the bill. "There is only one answer to this question, and that is to give the president what he demands," he said.[4] The bill sailed through the House unchallenged; no vote was recorded. The Senate passed it seventy-three to seven.

The banking legislation was just one of dozens of achievements of Roosevelt's first hundred days. From the Civilian Conservation Corps to the National Industrial Recovery Act, from new public-works programs to emergency relief, fifteen major bills were signed into law. That itself was a staggering feat, but FDR did still more: the historic departure from the gold standard, the creation of federal bodies like the Tennessee Valley Authority and the Federal Deposit Insurance Corporation, and a dynamic new leadership style expressed most famously through his fireside chats.

A quickie book published in early July 1933 dubbed this period "The World's Greatest Ninety-Nine Days." But in a fireside chat on July 24, the president replaced that label with his own. He spoke of "the crowding events of the hundred days which had been devoted to the starting of the wheels of the New Deal."[5] The phrase appeared in headlines the next day and caught on.

It's essential to realize that the conditions that enabled Roosevelt's flurry of achievement were so rare as to make his record unreproducible. Subsequent presidents and the journalists who covered them have seldom highlighted the uniqueness of that historical moment. Instead, reporters have inflated the importance of the hundred-day marker and presidents have angled for short-term publicity victories, however uncertain their long-range importance.

Thus, in the weeks before Dwight D. Eisenhower's inauguration in 1953, Washington bristled with chatter about what his first hundred days might achieve. Pundits noted that he enjoyed not only Republican majorities in both chambers of Congress but also vast trans-ideological support among the electorate. He entered office, the *Washington Post* commented, with "more favorable legislative auspices" and "a deeper reservoir of bipartisan goodwill" than any president since

1932. When the fateful date rolled around, the reviews were disappointing. Arthur Krock of the *New York Times* cited the president's "slow start," marked by "miscalculations of timing and interpretation." In the long run, however—indeed, even by 1956, when he ran for and won reelection—evaluations of Eisenhower's presidency completely ignored his halting beginning.[6]

By 1961, the start of John F. Kennedy's presidency, talk about the first hundred days had become, in the judgment of historian and Kennedy aide Arthur Schlesinger, a "trap." Kennedy griped about the pressure to work magic in those early weeks. "I'm sick and tired of reading how we're planning another 'hundred days' of miracles," he said to his chief aide, Ted Sorensen, as they drafted the inaugural address. "Let's put in that this won't all be finished in a hundred days or a thousand."[7] The result might well be engraved on an Oval Office wall: "All this will not be finished in the first one hundred days. Nor will it be finished in the first one thousand days, nor in the life of this Administration, nor even perhaps in our lifetime on this planet. But let us begin."[8] Kennedy's effort to lessen expectations failed. Approaching the hundred day mark, Sorensen was enlisted to draft a memo showing how the president's early accomplishments stacked up favorably against those of Harry S. Truman and Eisenhower.

The pressure did not abate. In 1965, Lyndon B. Johnson enjoined his congressional liaison Larry O'Brien to "jerk out every damn little bill you can and get them down here by the 12th." Then, the president said, "you'll have the best hundred days. Better than he did! . . . If you'll just put out that propaganda . . . that they've done more than they did in Roosevelt's hundred days."[9] Richard Nixon thought similarly. A clutch of his advisors formed a "Hundred Days Group" to sell the idea that his administration was a hive of activity, while trying, as he said, to get him "off the hook on quantity of legislation being the first measure of success of the first hundred days."[10] No president since has been indifferent to such concerns.

Presidents ought to realize that getting caught up in the hundred days deadline sets them up for failure. Like Joe DiMaggio's fifty-six-game hitting streak, Roosevelt's burst of accomplishment—made possible not just by his distinctive political gifts but also by the exigencies of the Depression—is unlikely to be equaled. Presidents ought to bear in mind as well that early accomplishments are not always the enduring aspects of their legacy. Some of the most highly touted policies of FDR's Hundred Days fizzled. The National Industrial Recovery Act was invalidated by the Supreme Court, and his intended course of fiscal austerity was repudiated. In contrast, it was later in his presidency that Roosevelt signed into law such historic measures as Social Security, unemployment insurance, the right to collective bargaining, and the federal minimum wage.

Certainly, presidents need to plan carefully to take advantage of the brief honeymoon that typically follows their inauguration. Sometimes that period can present a chance to pass legislation that will prove elusive once the opposition finds its footing. But the focus should be on policies and legislation that can lay the groundwork for a propitious environment and long-term gains.

Two examples may suffice: Ronald Reagan and Bill Clinton. Although possessed of diametrically opposed ideological orientations, they were comparably eager to set the nation on a new direction, based on a fundamental reconception of how the government collected and spent its funds. Both men ran for president amid economic hard times, touting new visions of economic renewal in their campaigns; both engaged in serious pre-inauguration planning in order to launch their economic programs early; and both weathered short-term bouts of unpopularity to see their plans pay off with economic recovery and, in time, reelection and sustained popularity.

Reagan famously ran on what came to be called Reaganomics: deep reductions in domestic spending along with supply-side tax cuts that he believed would stimulate the economy following the stagflation of the Jimmy Carter years. Significantly, his team began planning how to implement his agenda while the campaign was still in full swing. Reagan's campaign manager, the pollster Richard Wirthlin, deputized his aides David Gergen and Richard Beale to study how presidents from Roosevelt onward had fared in their opening days, hoping to discern lessons for the incoming administration. Carter, for example, had capitulated to the media's expectation of a headline-filled hundred days, but that goal was short-sighted. As Gergen told Reagan biographer Lou Cannon: "The main theme that came through was that Carter had engaged in a flurry of activity. There had been a blizzard of proposals that had gone to the Hill, but there was no clear theme to his presidency." Focus, Beale and Gergen concluded, was indispensable.[11]

Dubbed the "Initial Actions Project," the Beale-Gergen undertaking yielded a fifty-five-page report of recommendations on how the White House should expend its energies. In December, aides laid out the key findings for the president-elect at Blair House. "We ought to have three goals," summarized James A. Baker, who would wind up as chief of staff, "and all three of them are economic recovery." This tight focus disappointed the social and religious conservatives who had helped give Reagan his victory, but the decision generated little dissent internally.[12] Unblinking attention to overhauling the budget was necessary to secure its passage, but it was not sufficient. In fact, Reaganomics might well have died in Congress had not the deranged gunman John Hinckley critically wounded the president outside the Washington Hilton in March. The ensuing flood of sympathy buoyed Reagan's approval ratings. The next day, Treasury Secretary Donald Regan went on TV, where, borrowing a famous Reagan movie line, he urged Congress to "win one for the Gipper" by passing the budget bill. At a subsequent Blair House strategy meeting, Gergen proposed that Reagan stage his triumphant return from the hospital by calling for his plan's passage before a joint session of Congress. Reagan did just that, delivering a speech that caused even Democrats to marvel and brought much of the opposition around. The radical tax-cutting measure, once deemed a long shot, passed easily into law.

The bill was historic for multiple reasons. Most immediately, its reductions in many tax brackets, including the top tiers, ratified and encouraged the rising antitax sentiment across the country. As a matter of public policy, the tax cuts remain controversial, credited by supporters with boosting economic growth but blamed by critics for exploding the budget deficit and crowding out investment opportunities. Perhaps most important, the bill defined not only the Reagan presidency but contemporary conservatism for a generation afterward.

Like Reagan, Bill Clinton won election against a politically weak incumbent. Running during economic hard times, he offered a recovery plan that, like Reagan's, was not just a list of policies but a full-fledged economic vision. Clinton's vision was the polar opposite of Reagan's: restoring progressive taxation (instead of curtailing it) and investing in infrastructure and research and development (instead of paring it) to meet the new challenges of an emerging global economy. During the campaign, Clinton promised to "focus like a laser beam on this economy," and before his inauguration he convened an economic summit to survey the particular challenges, hearing testimony from a wide range of experts.

A series of controversies early in Clinton's term diverted the news media's focus from economics and required White House attention. These controversies ranged from difficulties with cabinet appointments to sideshows like the debate about whether to let gays serve in the military to pseudo-scandals such as the replacement of personnel in the White House travel office. At the time, these episodes loomed large and seemed to betoken a troubled presidency. But the White House, despite considerable dysfunction, forged ahead and adapted Clinton's campaign promises into a budget bill, reckoning that the budget deficits that had been mounting through the presidencies of Reagan and George H. W. Bush had become even more dire than projected.

At the hundred days mark, Clinton's prospects did not look bright. Yet just a few months later, he secured his plan's passage, by one vote in the House and, with Vice President Al Gore's tiebreaker, one vote in the Senate. The bill was perhaps the most important of Clinton's presidency. It began the process of retiring the deficit, and by his final years in office the nation was running budget surpluses for the first time since 1969. The bill also restored a measure of fairness to the tax code, raising the top bracket and expanding the Earned Income Tax Credit for those of low income. And it began a multiyear pattern in which the White House wrought major change not through banner new laws but through quiet but consistent victories in the budgeting process. Just as Reagan's economic vision lasted into the presidencies of both George Bushes, so Clinton's was emulated by Barack Obama.

Although Clinton and Reagan promulgated very different economic visions, both succeeded on their own terms. Whatever lip service their administrations paid to the hundred days marker, they recognized that it was infinitely more important to develop and pass budget bills that would not just promote recovery but also set new ideological directions for the country. They understood that the work that goes on in the White House communications office toting up laws passed and orders issued is in the end far less important than the work that goes on in forging the economic direction of the country, influencing what writers will say not in one hundred days, nor even one thousand, but over the lifetime of the administration and afterward.

NOTES

1. Kenneth T. Walsh, "The First 100 Days: Franklin Roosevelt Pioneered the 100," *US News,* February 12, 2009, http://www.usnews.com/news/history/articles/2009/02/12/the-first-100-days-franklin-roosevelt-pioneered-the-100-day-concept.

2. Claire Suddath, "The 100-Day Benchmark: It All Started with Napoleon," *Time,* April 29, 2009, http://content.time.com/time/nation/article/0,8599,1894531,00.html.

3. Ibid.

4. Thomas E. Woods, Jr., "The Great Gold Robbery of 1933," *Mises Daily Articles,* August 13, 2008, https://mises.org/library/great-gold-robbery-1933.

5. Franklin Roosevelt, "On the Purposes and Foundations of the Recovery Program—July 24, 1933," http://docs.fdrlibrary.marist.edu/042433.html.

6. David Greenberg, "The First Hundred Days Myth: It's The Long Run That Matters," *Bloomberg Government,* October 24, 2016, https://about.bgov.com/blog/the-first-hundred-days/.

7. David Greenberg, "The Folly of the 'Hundred Days,'" *Wall Street Journal,* March 21, 2009, https://www.wsj.com/articles/SB123759302359600669.

8. John F. Kennedy, "Inaugural Address of President John F. Kennedy," Washington, D.C., January 20, 1961, https://www.jfklibrary.org/Research/Research-Aids/Ready-Reference/JFK-Quotations/Inaugural-Address.aspx.

9. Lyndon Baines Johnson, *Reaching for Glory: Lyndon Johnson's Secret White House Tapes, 1964–1965* (New York: Simon and Schuster, 2002), 277.

10. Richard Ellis, *The Development of the American Presidency* (New York: Routledge, 2012), 188.

11. Lawrence Nesbitt, *What Reagan Couldn't Tell Us* (Bloomington, Ind.: iUniverse, 2011), 146.

12. Ibid.

THE NOT SO BULLY PULPIT

JEFF SHESOL

If a president gave an Oval Office address and the networks refused to air it, would it make a sound? This is not, most likely, a question that occupies philosophers, but it does cause White House communications staffers to wake up in the middle of the night in a cold sweat. It certainly did during my time as a speechwriter for President Bill Clinton.

In May 2000, as Congress prepared to settle a consequential question—whether to normalize trade relations with China on a permanent basis—I helped prepare an Oval Office address urging a "yes" vote. The national security advisor, national economic advisor, and White House chief of staff all signed off on the draft after much discussion.

And then, with just twenty-four hours to go before the Sunday night address, two of the major television networks begged off. The issue, they said, was not newsworthy enough to justify preempting prime-time programming. Briefly, the White House considered going forward with the speech, but this was too humiliating a prospect; we knew that reports of the networks' indifference to a presidential address would trump the speech itself as the news of the day.

The diminishing draw of the bully pulpit is a reality of the contemporary presidency. Barack Obama gave fewer Oval Office addresses than any president since Gerald Ford—in part, his aides say, because he viewed the format as stilted and anachronistic but also because the networks are less and less interested in offering air time to presidents. "You can only play this card every once in a while," Dan Pfeiffer, a former Obama advisor, told Politico in 2015.[1]

The networks are not saying no out of spite; they see it as a sort of self-protection. Mainstream media—not just the broadcast networks but cable news channels too—are losing ground to the countless other choices on other screens, large and small, and presidential speeches do not promise a ratings boost. The average number of viewers for President Obama's State of the Union addresses, according to Nielsen, was 38.8 million; for George W. Bush, the average was 45.3 million, and for Clinton, 45.6 million. Some viewers, to be sure, have shifted to streaming the speech on their laptops or phones—activity that Nielsen cannot track—but there is no question that it is getting harder to induce Americans to tune in to a presidential speech outside a moment of crisis. Attention deficit disorder is a national affliction—and possibly a permanent condition.

At the same time, new platforms present new opportunities. Obama took that tired and outmoded institution, the weekly presidential radio address, and turned it into a weekly video address, which he posted on YouTube and the White House website. It may not have drawn an audience on par with "Carpool Karaoke" or the man who climbed inside a giant water balloon, but online video services create, in effect, a permanent library of presidential speeches, instantly accessible and uninterrupted by cable news commentators. The reach of this distribution system is one that pre-digital presidents might have envied; it is possible to imagine Franklin D. Roosevelt or Ronald Reagan putting it to effective use. But the onus is on presidents to build and hold an audience—by giving speeches worth streaming.

The fundamentals of effective communication are not much different today than they were in Roosevelt's time. (Or Aristotle's, for that matter.) At the most basic level, leaders should speak in a clear, honest, and compelling way about the challenges they see and the actions they advocate to meet those challenges. In a democracy—no matter who may or may not be tuning in—that is a president's obligation. Rhetorical leadership, however, is not a science but (at its best) an art, and understandings must evolve to keep pace with new realities.

In the first year of an administration, a new president and his or her team can put a little more bully back in the pulpit by applying three basic principles to presidential communications. First, the president should, for the most part, forgo high rhetoric and formal oratory in favor of a more conversational style and greater candor. Second, the president should shake free from the dead hand of tired traditions, especially the State of the Union address as it has too long been conceived. And third, because speechwriting is an essential, inextricable part of the policy-making process, the president should fully empower the speechwriting staff.

1. Talk like a real person.

This is harder than it seems. The presidential podium—the bullet-proof "Blue Goose"—is, by design, an imposing structure, less a lectern than a national monument. It is useful for making pronouncements because it gives a kind of grandeur to even mundane moments. But at other times, it can be like addressing a family dinner with a bullhorn: It does not tend to promote an easy rapport. Lyndon B. Johnson, who was powerfully effective one-on-one or in a small room, rarely sounded like himself from behind the Blue Goose; straining for stature, he appeared overbearing. The problem is not the podium but the presidency—an office so far removed from the lives of real Americans that it takes hard and consistent work to narrow the distance. In 1914, Woodrow Wilson admitted to the Washington press corps that he yearned to give the public "a wink, as much as to say, 'It is only me that is inside this thing.'"[2]

In the modern era, Ronald Reagan set the standard. He was a master of what Kathleen Hall Jamieson has called the "conversational style." Reagan's rejection of the familiar, formal tropes of presidential rhetoric—in favor of (seemingly) ad-libbed asides, transitions like "well . . . ," and sentences that sometimes trailed off—led many Americans, as Jamieson observed in 1987, to "conclude that we know and like him" and that his presidency was "based in common sense." Bill Clinton, too, insisted on sounding like an actual person. "No, no," he often complained to his staff, "this is a speech—I just want to talk to people." Clinton didn't mean that he didn't want to give a speech; he wanted to give a speech that didn't sound like a speech.[3]

The challenge is even greater today than it was in the 1980s or 1990s. The toxicity of the political climate—a cause and a symptom of the stalemate in Washington and so many attendant national problems—has heightened Americans' distaste not only for politicians but for the language that they use. All those careful, guileful phrases—crafted by committees of consultants—sound, in the worst epithet of our age, "inauthentic." We have seen the powerful appeal of candidates who speak sloppily, circuitously, even incoherently, in the way that real people sometimes do. In *Enough Said,* a book about the state of our public language, Mark John Thompson—the president and CEO of the New York Times Company—worries about the growing resort to racist and dishonest statements, but he does see one "lesson to learn from the anti-politicians. . . . They look and sound like human beings . . . they're not automata." The arguments—what the Greeks called *logos*—of angry populists are weak and dishonest but they make effective use of *ethos,* an expression of personal character, as well as *pathos,* the ability to match the mood of the audience.[4]

For presidents to succeed, they have to be strong in all three areas. It is possible to combine *logos, ethos,* and *pathos* by grounding a policy argument in real evidence while also reflecting something of actual human experience. It is also possible to express authenticity in a scripted speech, so long as the script says something resonant and true. This is the daily work of rhetorical leadership. It should also be leavened, when possible, by genuinely unscripted, unmediated moments—direct engagement with the public. Political risk attends every such encounter. But the people's trust, like their votes, has to be earned.

2. Break foolish traditions.

On July 2, 1932, Franklin Roosevelt boarded a Ford trimotor airplane in Albany and flew to his party's national convention in Chicago, where he accepted its nomination in person, rather than maintain the practice of awaiting the news at home in feigned ignorance. "Let it be from now on the task of our party to break foolish traditions," Roosevelt told the delegates.[5]

The presidency is a more than two-century-old institution. Some of its traditions provide continuity with the past and a source of stability, however symbolic, in times of change. The White House residence, home to every president since John Adams, is one of those. But other traditions have become a kind of dead weight, a burden that the past, however unwittingly, imposes on the present. The greatest presidential communicators—both Roosevelts, of course, among them—have been innovators, willing to alter or abandon old, tired rhetorical customs.

Woodrow Wilson, in 1913, became the first president in more than a century to present his report on the State of the Union as a spoken address rather than a written statement; he hoped to convey, as he told members of Congress in a different speech, that "the president of the United States is a person, not a mere department of the government hailing Congress from some isolated island of jealous power, sending messages, not speaking naturally and with his own voice. . . . He is a human being trying to cooperate with other human beings in a common service."[6] FDR, twenty years later, delivered the first presidential "fireside chat" on the radio. These relaxed, informal, occasional speeches, broadcast to 60 or 70 million "friends" (as he called them) across America, "bound them to him in affection," as his secretary of labor, Frances Perkins, later recalled.[7] President Obama, embracing Roosevelt's spirit of "bold, persistent experimentation," created a White House Office of Digital Strategy, live-streamed the State of the Union address on the White House website, and "enhanced" the speech with interactive slides posted in real time.

We have today more traditions worth breaking. The State of the Union address would be a good place to start. Within the White House, it is widely acknowledged that the State of the Union is a joyless, and largely pointless, exercise. In an era of bitter, partisan polarization, the speech has lost much of its ability to set the legislative agenda for the year ahead. You would not know this from listening to it, however. It is almost invariably overlong, loaded with wish lists of disconnected policies, and punctuated by artificial applause lines telegraphed with cues like "Make no mistake." Every year, it confirms Newton's law of inertia, which states, in part, that an object in motion stays in motion with the same speed and in the same direction unless acted on by an unbalanced force. This is a speech in need of an unbalanced force. It is a ritual in search of a rationale—beyond the inconvenient fact that article II, section 3, of the Constitution requires the president to report to Congress "from time to time" on the state of the union.

The framers, in their wisdom, left the precise form of that report up to the president. Almost every year, recent presidents have promised that this time, the speech won't be a laundry list and might actually have a theme, but none seems to have had the courage of his convictions. In 2016, Obama gave a State of the Union address—the last of his presidency—that proposed few new policies and made an extended, if somewhat unfocused, argument for greater civility in our national life. Future presidents will have an opportunity to improve further on the form, giving a shorter, crisper, and more purposeful speech. Although the audience may be smaller than it once was, it is still likely to be tens of millions strong, and many of those Americans would relish a reason to applaud with enthusiasm. Richard Goodwin, who wrote speeches for Lyndon Johnson and both John and Robert Kennedy, has said that the purpose of political speech is to "move men to action and alliance."[8] That is a fine goal going forward for this policy address.

3. Treat speech writing as policymaking.

When Ted Sorensen, who worked with President John F. Kennedy on his inaugural address and nearly all of his major speeches, published a memoir in 2008, he gave it the title "Counselor," not "Speechwriter." Sorensen—and, indeed, Kennedy—understood his role as one that transcended writing, because the shaping of presidential speeches is the shaping of presidential policy. That status was not unique to Sorensen: Sam Rosenman was Franklin Roosevelt's chief speechwriter and one of his closest advisors, and Harry McPherson, as special counsel to President Johnson, wrote and edited many of his most memorable addresses while advising LBJ on strategies to deescalate the war in Vietnam and repair race relations in a time of violent unrest.

It was Richard Nixon who formalized the speech-writing process, creating a Writing and Research Department. At the same time, he disempowered the writers, who lacked guidance and access; they dealt with the president mostly through his chief of staff. Reagan, too, established a firewall between speech writing and policy, leaving his writers to intuit his thinking on crucial questions and leaving his speeches frequently riddled with holes and stuffed with rhetorical filler. "If you think he sounds stale," his speechwriter Peggy Noonan complained to a colleague, "it's because the speechwriters haven't met with him in over a year."[9] Bill Clinton mostly repaired the breach, working closely with his writers and giving them a seat at the table for all important discussions of policy and strategy. Bush and Obama followed suit, and gave more effective speeches as a result.

But the Johnson-McPherson partnership half a century ago was the last of its kind. Since then, nearly every White House function has been specialized and subspecialized, and the pace and volume of work in the modern White House may well make it impossible for anyone to inhabit the dual role that McPherson, Sorensen, and Rosenman did. Still, the start of a new presidency is the right time to reaffirm that speech writing is policymaking, and to ensure that the president's writers are empowered with all the information and access they need in order to advance, and help shape, the president's agenda.

NOTES

1. Sarah Wheaton, "Oval Office Address, RIP?" Politico, December 7, 2015, http://www.politico.com/story/2015/12/oval-office-address-rip-216509.

2. John Milton Cooper, *Woodrow Wilson: A Biography* (New York: Knopf, 2009), 255.

3. Kathleen Hall Jamieson, *Eloquence in an Electronic Age: The Transformation of Political Speechmaking* (New York: Oxford University Press, 1988).

4. Mark John Thompson, *Enough Said: What's Gone Wrong with the Language of Politics?* (New York: Macmillan, 2016).

5. Franklin D. Roosevelt, "Address Accepting the Presidential Nomination at the Democratic National Convention in Chicago," Chicago, July 2, 1932, http://www.presidency.ucsb.edu/ws/?pid=75174.

6. Woodrow Wilson, "Message Regarding Tariff Duties," speech, Washington, D.C., April 8, 1913, http://millercenter.org/president/wilson/speeches/message-regarding-tariff-duties.

7. Frances Perkins, *The Roosevelt I Knew* (New York: Viking Press, 1946).

8. Olivia Zhu, "The Politics of Poetry," *Harvard Political Review,* September 3, 2012, http://harvardpolitics.com/literary-supplement-1/the-politics-of-poetry/.

9. Peggy Noonan, *What I Saw at the Revolution: A Political Life in the Reagan Era* (New York: Random House, 1990), 65.

REACHING AMERICANS
WHERE THEY LIVE—
ON THEIR SMARTPHONES

MARY KATE CARY

The digital world is changing quickly, and the way people consume information digitally is too. As of 2016, nearly three-quarters of all Americans own a smartphone, and two-thirds prefer to use that device rather than a computer to access the internet. According to Google, we check our phones about 150 times a day, spending a daily average of 177 minutes—which means that most of us check our phones for only about a minute at a time but repeat that habit dozens of times a day.[1]

Google calls these "micro-moments"—defining them as "I want-to-know moments, I want-to-go moments, I want-to-do moments, and I want-to-buy moments"—and they have transformed everything from corporate marketing and nonprofit fundraising to traditional news delivery.[2] Micro-moments occur when people grab their smartphones to answer a question, learn a fact, watch a video, or make a purchase.

Those micro-moments are affecting political decision making and voter behavior more than ever before, rapidly transforming the nature of political communications strategy.[3] Any new president must master these trends from the start in order to build trust and support among voters. If not, a new administration risks being left behind by the increasingly media-savvy American electorate.

Let's start with the number of Americans who increasingly access political news on social media through a mobile device.

- According to Pew Research, in January 2016, 44 percent of American adults reported having learned about the presidential election from social media in the previous week. Pew also reported that the share of registered voters who follow political figures on social media had doubled since 2010.[4]
- The Brookings Institution reports that social media has become a key platform for debate among voters. Although President Barack Obama was the first to use social media successfully, employing Twitter, Facebook, and Reddit to communicate with hard-to-reach audiences, the use of social media by

campaigns has continued to grow even more interactive. During the election of 2016, Donald Trump's "activity network"—meaning the number of times voters interacted with his Facebook page in the form of likes, shares, and comments—was three times the size of Hillary Clinton's.[5]

▸ Many of those voters are also watching videos. According to Google, since April 2015 Americans have watched more than 110 million hours of political content (either candidate- or issues-related) on YouTube. That is a hundred times longer than it would take to watch all content ever aired on CNN, C-SPAN, MSNBC, and Fox News combined. In fact, searches for election-related content on YouTube have grown nearly fourfold in the same time period. And it is not just young people: nearly six in ten voters under thirty-five are turning to YouTube to learn more about the candidates, but so are one in four who are over forty-five.[6]

▸ Twenty-one percent of Americans age twelve and older listened to a podcast in the last month; that is the same percentage who use Twitter.[7] Nearly two-thirds of all podcasts are accessed on a mobile device. Podcastchart's top two hundred podcasts worldwide lists the New York Times's 2016 election coverage, called The Run Up, as the fourth most popular podcast that year.[8] Monthly podcast listenership surged by a whopping 75 percent since the previous presidential election.[9]

In the not-too-distant past, many of us got our political news either from the print copy of a local newspaper on our doorstep at daybreak or from the broadcast networks' nightly news programs. There was not a whole lot of choice. These days, we curate our own content.

"We watch what we want, when we want it, on whatever platform we want, on whatever device we want," explains Celie O'Neil-Hart of YouTube, referring to voters as "video neutral." As a result, she says, "They don't care whether they're watching video online or on television. They care that it's in front of them right now."[10] In addition, much of our content comes to us through news feeds, referred to us by our social streams and our filtered preferences, and is the product of algorithms, browsers, and even personal relationships.

This changing media landscape calls on new presidents to adopt a two-step strategy. First, the White House should still focus on influencing traditional news outlets in its first year, since they are the original source of much of the news that people consume, even though many are not encountering those reports by visiting nytimes.com or watching CBS Evening News. Instead, they are finding them through social media on a variety of devices and platforms.

Margaret Brennan, CBS's White House correspondent, emphasizes the need for nuanced, analytical coverage of policies and initiatives—something traditional news sources can deliver, but Twitter and YouTube cannot. "YouTube and Snapchat can be good at generating interest, but not deep analysis," Brennan says. "You need traditional media for that."[11]

If a new president wants to win over the public on a variety of issues, the smart move would be to start by increasing, not decreasing, the number of presidential press conferences, as well as expanding press access to top White House officials. This may help drown out some of the less-than-credible news outlets that make it into some voters' news feeds.

The White House also needs to go a step further to meet citizens in that micro-moment when they break out of the bubble of their newsfeed to search for information. To do that, administration officials ought to provide content that matches the medium, so that it is not only easy to find but trustworthy.

1. Draw citizens to engaging content that can be opened on any mobile device.

Citizens are hungry for issues-oriented news and information. The twenty-first-century equivalent of what used to be known as a white paper—the PDF file—takes time to download, cannot be cut and pasted to share with friends, and often cannot be found by search engines unless the user knows its title and author. It is no wonder that one-third of all the PDFs published by the World Bank between 2008 and 2012 were not opened by a single person.[12]

Instead, the next White House should consider creating card stacks the way the news and opinion website Vox does. These convey long-form content through a series of cards that readers can click through and then easily share.

Video also needs to be adapted to the new mobile environment. Live-streaming of political rallies and speeches on Facebook Live gained popularity during the 2016 election campaign and gave voters what they wanted without the filter of the "mainstream media." One live-streaming app, Twitter's Periscope, allowed Democrats to broadcast their sit-in on the House floor in 2016, giving them a new political tool when the television networks' attention strayed elsewhere.

Rather than uploading forty-five-minute videos of speeches and panel discussions, the White House should take a page from TED Talks, which publishes videos with crowd-sourced transcripts in both English and Spanish, along with time marks alongside the text. That way shorter clips can be shared easily, embedded in other media, or combined into a highlights reel.

Another example: In November 2016, the congressional commission studying the feasibility of establishing an American Museum of Women's History issued the first-ever digital report to Congress. Instead of sending a dusty, phonebook-sized document to the Hill and White House, the commissioners designed a microsite complete with computer animation, short video clips, and drop-down menus for readers to drill down for more information. It was all optimized for mobile devices and intended for interested citizens to share with friends to help build momentum for the proposed museum.

Media Theory's James Kimer, the creative force behind that congressional report, emphasized the importance of continuing to adapt to the latest platforms.

"Citizens used to get their information from newspapers and television, then moved toward websites, and are now in a very dynamic social space," he said. "The next move will probably be to messaging apps, which are growing explosively, like WhatsApp and its interactive news chatbots. But it's one thing for agencies to use social media for customer service; it's another to try to raise awareness of public policy issues and build an audience. That's a tough nut to crack."[13]

The worlds of business and media figured out a long time ago how to expand audiences and gain loyal customers through social media. Public policymakers can do the same if they are willing to change the way they connect with citizens.

2. Remember that authenticity is crucial.

Spontaneity, unscripted moments, behind-the-curtain views—anything other than administration talking points delivered on a teleprompter or as a PDF file—are wildly popular. For example, one of the most popular podcast series in 2016 was *Keeping It 1600,* an informal, behind-the-scenes political chat between former Obama staffers Jon Favreau and Dan Pfeiffer. Sidewire, a mobile app, hosted regular on-the-record, unscripted, 250-character text-based conversations between political newsmakers.[14] Snapchat Discover allowed sponsors (CNN and BuzzFeed, for example) to post video-with-text stories that have a very behind-the-scenes feel.

The most successful podcasts, Snapchat stories, YouTube videos, BuzzFeed lists, Vox card stacks, and LinkedIn posts match the message to the medium, which adds to the feeling of authenticity. For example, a five-hundred-word take on the top trends in health care works well on LinkedIn—and could even be sliced into an embeddable card stack—but would not be so great read out loud on a YouTube video. The best podcasts are either conversations between two people (think of NPR's *Fresh Air*) or informal TED-style monologues—and the less slickly produced, the better. Matching the culture and tone of each social media platform adds to the sense of trustworthiness and authenticity and increases the chances that content will go viral—all of which are vital if the goal is better coalition building and community organizing.

3. Engage communities by anticipating what they're looking for and meeting them there.

To build a governing majority in its first year, the White House needs to make it easy for existing communities to share its content with people who align with its policy priorities, even if they are not typical supporters. To do that, internet pioneer Tim O'Reilly has argued that "the right way to energize social media isn't to try to find people to tout your products. It's to find people who care about the same things you do, and to tell a story that amplifies their voice because it helps people who haven't yet heard the word also come to know and care." In fact, O'Reilly writes, "real engagement with the people who care about the issues that the administration is trying to advance is far more effective than broadcasting administration messages and talking points, and hoping they get repeated."[15]

The idea is to break out of the echo chamber of one's own supporters and engage with new constituencies in order to build broader coalitions when the right moment comes. Policymakers can anticipate when voters will be looking for information on specific issues by keeping up with Google Trends and its sister page, Trending on YouTube. The White House should have persuasive content ready to go based on upcoming "firsts," whether those are the administration's first budget, first Supreme Court nominee, or even first state dinner.

One platform for thought leadership might be LinkedIn Pulse, a mobile app that is fast becoming a vehicle for policy analysis and think pieces from experts looking to influence others. LinkedIn offers a huge platform of more than 450 million members, split almost evenly between Republicans, Democrats, and independents, and in 2016 it was used by 92 percent of congressional staff, 87 percent of White House staff, 82 percent of cabinet agency staff, and 76 percent of state legislators. Not surprisingly, LinkedIn is the one social medium that has more members who are older than fifty than under twenty-five. Andrew Phillips, the head of LinkedIn's outreach to center-right groups, campaigns, and coalitions, points out that LinkedIn is fast becoming the top social media destination for policy and news content on the internet. The White House, as well as the House and Senate leadership, would be smart to get on board to maximize the ability to convey long-form content to millions of citizens.

With trust in government so low, connecting with reliable assets such as LinkedIn contributors or popular podcasters could be a way to reach the many Americans who do not visit whitehouse.gov and probably never will.

Clearly, legacy media outlets are suffering from declining readership and waning trust. Even so, the White House press corps must remain part of first-year communications strategies, since those outlets create much of the content on voters' news feeds.

What is changing in Washington is the burgeoning amount of political news that is passed on through social media links on a phone—triple the amount shared on a phone since the 2012 election—especially in those I-want-to-know micro-moments. Any new administration would be smart to provide its best arguments in easily accessible, findable, and shareable formats. If it does, policymakers will be able to disseminate content targeted for different ages and demographics, tailored to different mobile platforms, to voters who may or may not be looking for White House–branded content but will grab it when they need it.

In many ways, it is old-fashioned public outreach and coalition building, but in the palms of citizens' hands.

NOTES

1. Sridhar Ramaswamy, "The Next $50 Billion," speech, IAB Annual Leadership Meeting, Palm Desert, Calif., January 25, 2016, https://doubleclick-publishers.googleblog.com/2016/01/a-better-mobile-experience.html.

2. Ibid.

3. Sridhar Ramaswamy, "How Micro-Moments Are Changing the Rules," Think with Google, April 2015, https://www.thinkwithgoogle.com/articles/how-micromoments-are-changing-rules.html.

4. Jeffrey Gottfried et al., "The 2016 Presidential Campaign—A News Event That's Hard to Miss," Pew Research Center, February 4, 2016, http://www.journalism.org/2016/02/04/the-2016-presidential-campaign-a-news-event-thats-hard-to-miss/.

5. Kevin C. Desouza et al., "Tracking Presidential Campaigns on Facebook," Brookings Institution, April 13, 2016, https://www.brookings.edu/blog/techtank/2016/04/13/tracking-presidential-campaigns-on-facebook/.

6. "How Political Ads and Video Content Influence Voter Opinion," Think with Google, March 2016, https://www.thinkwithgoogle.com/articles/political-ads-video-content-influence-voter-opinion.html.

7. Nancy Vogt, "Podcasting: Fact Sheet. State of the News Media 2016," Pew Research Center, June 15, 2016, http://www.journalism.org/2016/06/15/podcasting-fact-sheet/.

8. "Top 200 Podcasts," Podcast Chart, https://www.podcastchart.com/categories/top-200-podcasts.

9. Vogt, "Podcasting: Fact Sheet."

10. Interview with the author, August 2016.

11. Interview with the author, August 2016.

12. Doerte Doemeland and James Trevino, "Which World Bank Reports Are Widely Read? Policy Research Working Paper 6851," World Bank, May 2014, http://documents.worldbank.org/curated/en/387501468322733597/pdf/WPS6851.pdf.

13. Interview with the author, August 2016.

14. Christine Magee, "Sidewire Is Your Hotline to Political Insight," Techcrunch, September 16, 2015, https://techcrunch.com/2015/09/16/sidewire-is-your-hotline-to-political-insight/.

15. Tim O'Reilly, "#SocialCivics and the Architecture of Participation," Radar, March 31, 2015, http://radar.oreilly.com/2015/03/socialcivics-and-the-architecture-of-participation.html.

MANAGING THE PRESIDENT'S PUBLIC PERSONA

SUSAN J. DOUGLAS

What must future presidents do in the first year to manage the overheated, ubiquitous, yet fragmented media environment?

Facebook. Instagram. Snapchat. Twitter. Multiple 24/7 cable channels and continually updated online news sites. All of these media platforms offer opportunities and create perils. The president can connect more directly and quickly with the electorate than ever before, but also is placed under more intense and relentless scrutiny.

Today's media are not primarily controlled by top-down, one-to-many modes of communication. Anyone with a cell phone can record and circulate what a president or presidential candidate says. The face a president wants to present to the public—the frontstage persona—can be exposed as fraudulent when comments or images from unguarded moments—the backstage persona—contradict a carefully crafted public image. E-mail, Twitter feeds, and websites can be hacked to reveal such backstage moments. And the multiplication of media platforms has allowed for the rise of avowedly partisan cable channels and websites, stoking political animus in the country that amplifies both praise for and criticism of the president.

Future presidents will face an unprecedented challenge in navigating—and trying to harness—the multiple media outlets available. It can seem as if there are no lessons from the past that can help a new president manage this unruly media environment. Yet since the late nineteenth century, most presidents upon taking office have found themselves in new, seemingly unpredictable media environments that had the potential to enhance their ability to advance their policies and bolster their public approval or, alternatively, to thwart their efforts. Thus, presidents and their staffs have had to have a keen appreciation of what academics call the particular "affordances" of new media platforms and communications technologies—that is, their inherent properties that favor or even require certain kinds of communication strategies and public performances.[1]

Affordances are the possible uses we can and cannot make of a particular medium. For example, radio did not offer pictures to its audience and thus words, music, and sound effects had to carry all the weight of enabling listeners to "see" with the mind's eye. This was what Franklin D. Roosevelt had to come to terms with when he assumed office. For John F. Kennedy, it was the visuality of television. For George H. W. Bush and Bill Clinton, it was the rise of cable news and the overheated 24/7 news cycle. And for Barack Obama and Donald Trump, it was the speed, immediacy, and many-to-many networks of the internet and social media and their interplay with traditional media outlets.[2]

What have been the effects of all this on the presidency? Each of these technologies has reduced the distance between the president and everyday Americans. This increased access has allowed people to judge presidents on a much more personal level. Does he seem sincere? Does she convey authority and knowledge? Is he telling the truth? By hearing the president's voice on the radio and, later, seeing him on television, many Americans develop "para-social relations" with him: responding to his media performances as if he were a personal acquaintance who was with them in a face-to-face social relationship.

Presidents have had to come to terms with this heightened intimacy, evolving their news management strategies and approaches, and crafting a public persona that appears authoritative, genuine, and relatable. The characteristics Americans have responded to most positively are a blend of policy expertise and personal authenticity. This requires increased discipline and an acceptance of increased transparency. Given the enormous public distrust of government, a sense of transparency and a genuine concern for all Americans as conveyed through the media will be absolutely crucial to any new president's success. Despite the digital revolution, media fragmentation, and rapid-fire news cycle, the past still offers valuable communications lessons for the president's first year.

1. Know the tools.

Presidents must understand the various media at their disposal, the advantages of each, and the differences among them. They need to be disciplined and prepared in using these media.

Franklin Roosevelt, unlike his predecessor, Herbert Hoover, understood what radio afforded him—the intimacy of his voice penetrating each American home and seeming to speak, simultaneously, to every individual. Indeed, you can't say Roosevelt's name without immediately thinking "fireside chats," so effective was his command of the relatively new technology. He deliberately imagined his audience as a few people sitting around his fireplace with him; he did not use the stentorian political oratory of the stump but rather the intimate "I-you" mode of address. He opened the chats with "My friends" and was careful to use simple, direct, informal language. The chats sounded relaxed and unrehearsed, yet each was the result of extensive preparation and multiple drafts. Having discovered that a separation between his two front lower teeth produced a slight whistle on the air, Roosevelt had a removable bridge made that eliminated the sound. That is called paying attention to the advantages and requirements of a particular medium!

Dwight D. Eisenhower was the first president to have televised "fireside chats" and introduced the recorded televised news conference in 1955. But it was Kennedy and, later, Ronald Reagan who truly mastered the visual (and increasingly live) possibilities of the medium. Both men understood the importance of visual symbolism and a commanding stage presence. Kennedy's use of the live press conference, often peppered with witticisms and helped by his handsome and youthful appearance, made him seem authoritative and spontaneous—someone genuine. Reagan, the seasoned actor, also appreciated the importance of off-the-cuff humor on live TV, the symbolism of his cowboy hat, and how to use visual props—for example, thick sheaves of the government regulations he was replacing with just a few pages of new ones—to sell his programs.

By 2000, a new medium was in its nascent stage: the internet. By the time Obama ran for president in 2008, 68 million Americans had broadband connections. With the explosion in the internet's reach, and the new possibilities offered by social media like Facebook, YouTube, and texting, presidents and presidential candidates once again confronted an emerging, transitioning media environment while also having to master traditional media, especially television. Trump employed Twitter to an unprecedented degree to reach voters directly.

Campaigns and presidents can now communicate to the electorate with no filter, circumventing traditional gatekeepers. But increasing numbers of people are using Facebook, Twitter, and Instagram to post their own political information, both factual and false, over which presidents have no control. Social media, and especially Twitter in 2016, received mainstream media attention, often driving the news cycle. And Twitter, with its 140-character limit and, for some, anonymity, promotes short, simple, dramatic posts that have led to linguistic bombast and even aggression, especially against women. The pitfall for a president is to overuse Twitter, email, and Facebook, leading to overexposure and a possible loss of credibility. With the ubiquity and ceaseless introduction of new apps, a new president will need both young people (the so-called digital natives) and seasoned pros to work together to grasp the benefits of each platform and navigate this treacherous and fragmented terrain.

2. Watch the front—and the back.

With the 24/7 news cycle and the ongoing surveillance of presidents through traditional and social media, presidents must cultivate their frontstage and protect their backstage while still seeming relatable. The explosive growth of celebrity journalism in the twenty-first century and its "they're just like us" paparazzi shots has increased the public's appetite for seemingly unguarded, candid moments of famous people to gauge their authenticity. John Kennedy's carefully staged shots of his children playing in the Oval Office, and the multiple photos and videos of Barack Obama joyfully engaging with children, conveyed tenderheartedness, a sense of fun, and a genuine human connection. But the media, traditional and digital, relish discovering unguarded moments—Gerald Ford tripping, Jimmy Carter collapsing while jogging—so protecting one's backstage, while providing some access to it, is an increasingly tricky proposition. And in this age of hacking and cyberattacks, presidents need to secure their communications to and from others in the administration.

3. Traditional media still matter.

The president needs to accommodate the journalistic needs, routines, and practices of the major news organizations. Despite everything, the "old media" still matter.

Beginning with George Washington, many presidents have hated the press, and public trust in the news media today is low. But an informed public is crucial to democracy, and the truth is that those who accommodate journalists' needs get better coverage. Ronald Reagan's team tended to the "care and feeding" of the press, providing them with the president's daily schedule and press releases, giving them summaries or full copies of his speeches in advance, and adhering to the "message of the day." Thus, the White House staff did much of the journalists' work for them, making their jobs easier. Understanding that sound bites on news programs were getting ever shorter and that imagery mattered, Reagan's team planned photo opportunities so the optics would be positive and reinforce the message. It also used carefully orchestrated leaks to shape foreign policy and its coverage.

Bill Clinton and his staff, by contrast, infuriated many reporters. One of the administration's first blunders was to challenge the geography and traditions of the White House pressroom. This room is cramped, with reporters jammed in cheek by jowl, and it is connected by a narrow hallway to the press briefing room. Before or after briefings, reporters could also go to the "upper press office" where the press secretary was located. George Stephanopoulos, Clinton's first press secretary, cut off this access, producing an outcry. Reporters complained that briefings were late, often by hours; that some interviews were cancelled; and that Clinton's team failed to return phone calls. Thus, despite Clinton's considerable personal skills as a communicator, his administration's unskilled media apparatus gave him one of the shortest presidential honeymoons in recent history.

Because the news media gets wise to news management strategies, especially if they become obvious, too much stagecraft is a mistake. But with a few exceptions, news outlets today have been defunded and operate with fewer resources. To the dismay of many journalists themselves, conflict, sensationalism, and the superficial are valued more than substance. A president and a staff who work with this state of affairs by presenting policy proposals in simple, telegraphic terms, and thereby provide the news media with the tools and information to do their jobs, will fare much better than an administration that does not.

4. Beware mixed messages.

Presidents should never use the media to stage events or promote positions that are at odds with actual policy. No gaps should appear between presidential pronouncements and the reality of what's occurring.

The most infamous recent example of this mistake was George W. Bush's "top gun" landing on the U.S.S. *Abraham Lincoln* in May 2003 to announce the end of major combat operations in Iraq. Every aspect of the event was choreographed, especially the "Mission Accomplished" banner strung across the ship. Bush himself arrived wearing an olive-green flight suit with a helmet tucked under his arm, having allegedly copiloted a navy jet onto the ship's deck. But after the initial dazzle, journalists noted that the mission had not been accomplished at all; American troops were still in Iraq and would remain there for years. Also revealed was that there had been no need for Bush to fly in on a jet. You could see San Diego from the *Abraham Lincoln;* he could have come out on a motorboat or helicopter.

"News management" is both a dirty word and suspect practice, but it is central to presidential success. With distrust of so many institutions at historic highs, Americans need a president with policy expertise who also conveys authenticity and is not defensive. All of this is more daunting in the current media environment.

NOTES

1. I. Hutchby, "Technologies, Texts and Affordances," *Sociology: The Journal of the British Sociological Association* 35, no. 2 (May 2001): 441–56.

2. Jenning Brown, "All The Presidents' Media," *Vocativ,* September 16, 2015, http://www.vocativ.com/227899/all-the-presidents-media/.

COMMUNICATING WHILE GOVERNING

ANITA DUNN

When President Barack Obama took office, there was no White House chief digital officer and very little in the way of a digital office. One could not access Facebook from White House computers. The White House had never sent a tweet. Millions of Americans were just then buying their first smartphones.

There is a romanticized view of the White House communications and press office that *The West Wing* viewers embrace when contemplating the suite of offices across from the Roosevelt Room. There is also a cynical view held by the press and some in the public of the operation as an information-control, state media–propaganda machine—the so-called permanent campaign.[1] And in some quarters, there is still nostalgia for the days of legendary communications greats like Mike Deaver and the beautiful visual images of the Reagan White House.

As those of us who were part of the incoming Obama administration in 2009 came to know, the reality was different from all of these views. The lessons that we learned at the White House are particularly relevant for a future president's team during the crucial first year. Do not be afraid to change as the media environment evolves. Be an early adopter of new technologies. Go where the audience is and do not expect them to come to you. Engage allies. Allocate resources appropriately.

The team of communications professionals coming into the White House in the future will have lived the newer reality of multiplying platforms, continued consolidation of legacy media, and the competition for clickbait, a reality in which the challenge of attracting the nation's increasingly short attention span for longer than a moment appears more daunting every day. And now for the even tougher reality: communication when governing takes more time and effort than communication on a campaign.

The hardest lesson for us to accept in 2009 was that the bully pulpit—the ability to command the nation's attention using the office of the presidency—does not exist, except at times when the country wants to hear from the president. Those times are rare, mostly involving national crises or moments of triumph. The ability to hold the nation's attention when you want, how you want, and on the issues you want is no longer part of what you get when you become president. There is no magic associated with winning the White House that changes the new communications realities, and accepting this fact will help an administration design a communications operation that meets the needs of the new president.

To that end, the White House communications operation should be seen as part of a system that delivers vital information to the American people—how they want it, when they want it, and on the platforms where they want it. People receive the news in full or in chunks, interactively or in six-second Vines, on tablets or phones or television, on YouTube or network news, and everything in between. A huge part of this task is figuring out who is following what news through which mediums or platforms, then effectively using that knowledge to deliver the news people are looking for where they expect to receive it. And that is a resource-intensive process.

Here is why it is important: the ability to communicate effectively is central to the ability to govern effectively. Communications is often lumped in with the political functions of the White House and thus seen as concerned with enhancing the president's image, poll ratings, and reelection prospects. The reality is that communications is much more of a governing function—educating the public and working to build consensus around policies. This means that White House communications must take proportionately more presidential time, staff, and resources than campaign communications, in which one could draw on millions of dollars for television and digital advertising, states-based press operations, and a significant digital team to get a message out. In a polarized nation whose news sources are fragmented, the amount of time the president, vice president, and cabinet officers need to communicate basic policy choices and information is much more than senior staff members will want to give. It is not a question of "taking care of the press corps" or "Comms wants some time to do some things around the speech." It is critical to the education and consensus-building function of government.

In addition to using a multiplicity of platforms in interesting and engaging ways to communicate with the public, the White House website is an important tool for original content. The White House as a content provider is not a new concept—after all, what is a press release or a speech if not original content? During the 2016 campaign, the candidates communicated directly with the American people in numerous ways—print, television, and radio interviews; op-eds; tweets; Facebook videos; podcasts—some of which were through the news media and many through their campaign websites. Using whitehouse.gov to continue that direct engagement is a critical way to communicate with the public. This is not in competition with the role the news media play; as with everything in communications, it is additive.

As Facebook becomes America's largest media company, and the redefinition of media continues with breaking news covered by civilians on Periscope and Facebook Live, the White House's relationship with the press corps and its use of press briefings and press conferences should be revisited as well. Whatever tensions exist during a campaign, winning the election provides a great moment to push "reset." The White House press corps plays an invaluable role in our democracy, and some of the best journalists in America are in that press room every day. It would be a great service to modernize the White House briefing process, which is labor-intensive and often not as productive for the reporters participating in it as both sides would like. A president should consider taking the briefing online once or twice a week, to encourage greater participation, as well as doing more issue-specific briefings to go deep on policies that the administration is pursuing.

Another use of the briefings is to provide access to senior White House officials on a regular basis, in addition to the press secretary, so that reporters have the opportunity to speak with decision makers and policymakers directly. Decades of media consolidation, buyouts, and tight newsroom budgets have resulted in less expertise and specialization in the press, and fewer beat reporters who truly understand issues in detail. Momentum and horse-race coverage of legislative priorities is not as important as combating the misinformation and lies that become attached to issues. If not vigorously disputed, an inaccuracy or untruth becomes a bad fact, and then an accepted fact, for large numbers of people.

The White House communications operation has been adapting since 2009 as the media environment has evolved. Both the structure and infrastructure of the office need to reflect these continuing changes, which means presidents need to review what they have in relation to what they need on an ongoing basis. In a dynamic media world, the White House cannot be static. It must be an early adopter of new technologies and fight for resources for the cabinet agencies' communications operations as well. The White House can only communicate so much. Cabinet agencies and officials can do a great deal to help the overall effort, but not if they are working from an old model.

On February 9, 2009, in his first White House press conference, President Obama "crossed a Rubicon of sorts" in the words of *Time* magazine by becoming the first president to call on a reporter from a web-only site (the Huffington Post) at a White House press conference.[2] By Obama's final year in office, it was no longer news that the president was using nontraditional forums such as *Between Two Ferns* to promote enrollment in the Affordable Care Act; the Players' Tribune and a video interview with Derek Jeter to promote "My Brother's Keeper"; a discussion about technology in emerging markets with Mark Zuckerberg on Facebook Live; or individual interviews with a broad range of reporters, columnists, bloggers, radio hosts, local television anchors, and entertainment personalities to reach audiences beyond traditional White House news outlets.[3]

What works during a campaign in terms of communication is even more important when applied to governing. Every day the president needs to allocate limited resources—presidential time, senior staff time, communications staff bandwidth—to build support for the administration's agenda and make sure the American people feel that the White House is communicating with them. One thing is certain: the communications operation will look very different at the end of four or eight years than it did when taking office, and any new president will be using platforms that may not exist at the outset to communicate with the public.

NOTES

1. Elisabeth Bumiller, "In Ex-Spokesman's Book, Harsh Words for Bush," *New York Times,* May 28, 2008, http://www.nytimes.com/2008/05/28/washington/28mcclellan.html? mcubz=1.

2. Belinda Luscombe, "The HuffPo Gets to Question Obama—Making History," *Time,* February 10, 2009, http://content.time.com/time/nation/article/0,8599,1878625,00.html.

3. The Players' Tribune: My Conversation with President Obama," Players' Tribune, June 22, 2016, https://www.theplayerstribune.com/2016-6-22-video-derek-jeter-president-obama -conversation/; "Facebook Live with Mark Zuckerberg and President Obama," Facebook, June 24, 2016, https://www.facebook.com/zuck/videos/10102920321354391/; "Between Two Ferns with Zach Galifainakis: President Barack Obama," Funny or Die, March 11, 2014, http://www .funnyordie.com/president_barack_obama.

CONTRIBUTORS

DOUGLAS A. BLACKMON is the Pulitzer Prize–winning author of *Slavery by Another Name: The Re-Enslavement of Black Americans from the Civil War to World War II* and a Senior Fellow at the University of Virginia's Miller Center.

HAL BRANDS is Henry A. Kissinger Distinguished Professor of Global Affairs at Johns Hopkins University. His books include *What Good Is Grand Strategy? Power and Purpose in American Statecraft from Harry S. Truman to George W. Bush.*

H. W. BRANDS teaches at the University of Texas at Austin, where he holds the Jack S. Blanton Sr. Chair in History. His books include *Traitor to His Class,* which was a finalist for the Pulitzer Prize.

ROBERT F. BRUNER is University Professor, Distinguished Professor of Business Administration, and Dean Emeritus at the Darden School of Business, University of Virginia.

MARY KATE CARY is a former White House speechwriter for President George H. W. Bush. She writes a digital column on politics for *U.S. News and World Report.*

JEFFREY L. CHIDESTER is Director of External Affairs at the University of Virginia's Frank Batten School of Leadership and Public Policy and co-author (with Stephen F. Knott) of *The Reagan Years* and *At Reagan's Side: Insiders' Recollections from Sacramento to the White House.*

CAROLYN DEWAR leads McKinsey & Company's Organization Practice's senior executive transitions service line and is a partner in McKinsey's San Francisco office, where KUNAL MODI is a consultant. TOM DOHRMANN, a senior partner, and ANDREW ERDMANN, a partner, are leaders in McKinsey's Public Sector Practice and are based in McKinsey's Washington, D.C., office, where RYAN HARPER is a consultant.

SUSAN J. DOUGLAS is the Catherine Neafie Kellogg Professor and Arthur F. Thurnau Professor of Communication Studies at the University of Michigan. She is the author of *Listening In: Radio and the American Imagination,* which won the Hacker Prize.

ANITA DUNN is Managing Director of SKDKnickerbocker. She served as White House Communications Director and Senior Advisor to President Barack Obama's presidential campaigns.

MICHAEL ERIC DYSON, a Professor of Sociology at Georgetown University, is an academic, author, and radio host. His most recent book is *Tears We Cannot Stop: A Sermon to White America.*

JEFFREY A. ENGEL is the Founding Director of the Center for Presidential History at Southern Methodist University. His most recent book is *The Four Freedoms: Franklin D. Roosevelt and the Evolution of an American Idea.*

MICHÈLE A. FLOURNOY is Co-Founder and Chief Executive Officer of the Center for a New American Security. She served as the Undersecretary of Defense for Policy from 2009 to 2012.

JEFFRY FRIEDEN is a Professor of Government at Harvard University. His most recent book is *Currency Politics: The Political Economy of Exchange Rate Policy.*

GARY W. GALLAGHER is the John L. Nau III Professor in the History of the American Civil War at the University of Virginia. His books on the Civil War have won several awards, including the Tom Watson Brown Book Prize, the Lincoln Prize, and the Laney Prize.

WILLIAM A. GALSTON holds the Ezra K. Zilkha Chair in the Brookings Institution's Governance Studies Program. He served from 1993 to 1995 as Deputy Assistant for Domestic Policy to President Bill Clinton.

DANIEL J. GALVIN is Associate Professor of Political Science and Faculty Fellow at the Institute for Policy Research at Northwestern University. He is the author of *Presidential Party Building: Dwight D. Eisenhower to George W. Bush.*

STEFANIE GEORGAKIS ABBOTT is the Assistant Director of Presidential Studies at the University of Virginia's Miller Center and is co-editor (with Yannis Stivachtis) of *Addressing Integration and Exclusion: Democracy, Human Rights, and Humanitarian Intervention.*

DAVID GREENBERG is a Professor of History at Rutgers University. His most recent book is *Republic of Spin: An Inside History of the American Presidency.*

WILLIS JENKINS is an Associate Professor of Religious Studies at the University of Virginia. He is the author of *The Future of Ethics,* which won an American Academy of Religion Award for Excellence in the Study of Religion.

ELAINE C. KAMARCK, the Director of the Management and Leadership Initiative at the Brookings Institution, served on the Clinton White House staff. Her books include *Primary Politics: Everything You Need to Know about How America Nominates Its Presidential Candidates* and *Why Presidents Fail: And How They Can Succeed Again.*

BRUCE KATZ is the Centennial Scholar at the Brookings Institution and co-author of *The Metropolitan Revolution: How Cities and Metros Are Fixing Our Broken Politics and Fragile Economy.*

MELVYN P. LEFFLER is Edward Stettinius Professor of American History at the University of Virginia and a Faculty Associate at the Miller Center. He is the author of *A Preponderance of Power: National Security, the Truman Administration, and the Cold War*, which won the Bancroft, Hoover, and Ferrell Prizes.

GUIAN MCKEE is an Associate Professor at the University of Virginia's Miller Center. He is the author of *The Problem of Jobs: Liberalism, Race, and Deindustrialization in Philadelphia*.

SIDNEY M. MILKIS is the White Burkett Miller Professor of Politics and a Faculty Associate at the Miller Center of Public Affairs at the University of Virginia. His books include *The President and the Parties: The Transformation of the American Party System since the New Deal*.

MICHAEL NELSON is the Fulmer Professor of Political Science at Rhodes College. He has published multiple books, the most recent of which is *Resilient America: Electing Nixon, Channeling Dissent, and Dividing Government*, which won the American Political Science Association's Richard E. Neustadt Award for best book on the presidency published in 2014.

PETER NORTON is an Associate Professor of History in the Department of Engineering and Society at the University of Virginia's School of Engineering and Applied Science. He is the author of *Fighting Traffic: The Dawn of the Motor Age in the American City*.

PATRICK O'BRIEN is a Ph.D. candidate in the Department of Political Science at Yale University.

MARGARET O'MARA is an Associate Professor at the University of Washington and a historian of the modern United States. Her most recent book is *Pivotal Tuesdays: Four Elections That Shaped the Twentieth Century*. During the Clinton administration she worked in the White House and at the Department of Health and Human Services.

ORLANDO PATTERSON is the John Cowles Professor of Sociology at Harvard University. His most recent book is *The Cultural Matrix: Understanding Black Youth*.

BARBARA A. PERRY is White Burkett Miller Center Professor of Ethics and Institutions and Director of Presidential Studies at the University of Virginia's Miller Center. She is the author of *The Priestly Tribe: The Supreme Court's Image in the American Mind*.

ANDREW RUDALEVIGE is Thomas Brackett Reed Professor of Government at Bowdoin College. He is a regular contributor to the *Washington Post*'s Monkey Cage blog.

MARC SELVERSTONE is Chair of the Presidential Recordings Program and Associate Professor of Presidential Studies at the University of Virginia. He is the author of *Constructing the Monolith: The United States, Great Britain, and International Communism, 1945–1950*, which won the Stuart L. Bernath Book Prize from the Society for Historians of American Foreign Relations in 2010.

JEFF SHESOL is a Founding Partner of West Wing Writers, a strategic communications firm. He was deputy chief speechwriter to President Bill Clinton and is the author of *Supreme Power: Franklin Roosevelt vs. the Supreme Court.*

STEPHEN SKOWRONEK is the Pelatiah Perit Professor of Political and Social Science at Yale University. His books include *The Politics Presidents Make: Leadership from John Adams to Bill Clinton.*

JEREMI SURI holds the Mack Brown Distinguished Chair for Leadership in Global Affairs at the University of Texas at Austin, where he is also a Professor in the Department of History and the Lyndon B. Johnson School of Public Affairs. His most recent book is *The Impossible Presidency: The Rise and Fall of America's Highest Office.*

ALAN TAYLOR is the Thomas Jefferson Memorial Foundation Professor of History at the University of Virginia. His book *The Internal Enemy: Slavery and War in Virginia, 1772–1832* won the Pulitzer Prize for history in 2014.

DANIEL TICHENOR is the Philip H. Knight Professor of Political Science at the University of Oregon. His books include *Dividing Lines: The Politics of Immigration Control,* which won the American Political Science Association's Gladys Kammerer Award for the best book on U.S. public policy.

PETER WEHNER is a Senior Fellow at the Ethics and Public Policy Center. He is a contributing opinion writer for the *New York Times* and headed the Office of Strategic Initiatives for President George W. Bush.

MASON B. WILLIAMS is an Assistant Professor of History at Albright College. He is the author of *City of Ambition: FDR, La Guardia, and the Making of Modern New York.*

PHILIP ZELIKOW is the White Burkett Miller Professor of History at the University of Virginia. He has held various posts in the White House, State Department, and Pentagon. He also directed the 9/11 Commission.

INDEX

Abdullah II (king of Jordan), 36
abolitionists, 234, 235
abortion, 26, 27, 77, 78, 246, 247
Abraham, Henry J., 78
Abraham Lincoln (ship), 291
Abramowitz, Alan, 60
"accidental presidents," 62, 63
Adams, John, 2, 85, 90, 223–28, 252, 277
administration, appointments, and confirmations, ix, xii, 3; appointment power, 7, 250–54; CEO transitions, lessons from, 257–58; chief of staff's understanding of Washington, 68; diversity on presidential team, importance of, 258; executive appointment power, 7, 250–54; foreign policy development and, 137–38; importance of, 94–96; national security team, 130–31; presidential experience and, 62–63; Supreme Court appointments, ix, 4, 27–28, 74–79. *See also* cabinet; *specific presidents*
Administrative Procedures Act, 26, 245
Affordable Care Act (ACA): Bill Clinton's health care reform efforts and, 167; Medicaid expansion under, 30; Obama and, 1, 12, 31–32, 58, 60, 81, 238, 239, 294; Trump's efforts to repeal and replace, ix, 26, 31–33; website rollout, 238, 239
affordances, 287–88
Afghanistan: George W. Bush administration and, 126; Soviet invasion of, 65, 108; Taliban, 127; U.S. war in, 36, 127
African Americans. *See* race and racism
Agency for International Development, 103
agenda-setting power, 7, 250, 253–54
AIDS epidemic, 6, 96, 162–63
air traffic controllers' strike under Reagan, 94
Alien Acts, 227–28
Allen, Richard, 107, 110, 111
Alliance for Progress, 103
al-Qaeda, 125, 126
Altman, Roger, 69, 70
Amash, Justin, 40

"America First," 35, 37
American Enterprise Institute, 193
American Medical Association (AMA), 155–60
American Museum of Women's History, 283
American Recovery and Reinvestment Act (2009), 88, 176, 253
Americans with Disabilities Act (ADA), 6, 163–65
Anderson, Martin, 254
Anthous, William, xi
Anthropocene Epoch, environmental issues in, 6, 178–83
Anti-Ballistic Missile Treaty (1972), 125
appointment power, 7, 250–54
appointments. *See* administration, appointments, and confirmations
Apprentice, The (TV show), 33
apprenticeship programs, 25
approval ratings, 20, 25
Aristotle, 276
Armitage, Richard, 123, 125
Aronson, Bernard, 137
Asiatic Barred Zone, 203
al-Assad, Hafez, 119
Australia, immigration policy in, 191
authenticity in communication, 276–77, 284
Ayers, Andrea, 257

Baker, James A., 63, 68, 72, 95, 115, 136–37, 272
balancing the budget: under Carter, 250–51; under Bill Clinton, 72–73, 273; deficits under Reagan and George H. W. Bush, 273; foreign policy implementation and, 139–40; Medicare and Medicaid, fiscal consequences of, 158–59; multiple-agency process, 250–51; national debt, 17, 19, 152, 158, 223, 224, 228; FDR and, 64, 91
Balkans, unrest in, 2, 117, 119, 120
Bank for International Settlements, 144
Bank of the United States, 223, 252
Bannon, Steve, 22, 23, 24, 37